William Empson (1906–84) was one of the twentieth century's most distinctive critical voices, and left (perhaps unwittingly) a profound mark upon Anglo-American literary culture. This book is the first full study of Empson's literary criticism in its various aspects, taking account of recent developments in critical theory and of Empson's complex – at times deeply antagonistic – attitude towards those developments. In their diversity of viewpoint and critical approach the essays reflect this sturdy resistance to the fashionable trends of 'Eng. Lit.' opinion. Topics include Empson's speculative treatment of language and the sublime in *Seven Types of Ambiguity* (1930); his brilliant redefinition of the pastoral genre; the logico-semantic theory of multiple meaning developed in *The Structure of Complex Words* (1951); his critique of 'neo-Christian' values and assumptions in *Milton's God* (1961) and the essays of his last two decades; and the relation between Empson's and Derrida's approaches to the issue of textual 'undecidability'. There are also chapters on his highly individual methods of teaching and postgraduate supervision, as well as his prominent (if unwilling) role in the shaping of English as an academic discourse.

The nine essays by experts on twentieth-century criticism and theory follow on from Christopher Norris's introductory piece which charts the ground and offers a major revaluation of Empson's place in the broader theoretical tradition. Altogether, the book presents Empson as by far the most intelligent, inventive, humane, and sheerly *readable* of critics in the modern 'analytical' school.

WILLIAM EMPSON

WILLIAM EMPSON: THE CRITICAL ACHIEVEMENT

EDITED BY

CHRISTOPHER NORRIS

Professor of English, University of Wales, Cardiff

and

NIGEL MAPP

Sir James Knott Fellow in English Literature
University of Newcastle upon Tyne

CAMBRIDGE
UNIVERSITY PRESS

Published by the Press Syndicate of the University of Cambridge
The Pitt Building, Trumpington Street, Cambridge CB2 1RP
40 West 20th Street, New York, NY 10011–4211, USA
10 Stamford Road, Oakleigh, Victoria 3166, Australia

First published 1993

Printed in Great Britain at the University Press, Cambridge

A catalogue record for this book is available from the British Library

Library of Congress cataloguing in publication data

William Empson: the critical achievement / edited by
Christopher Norris and Nigel Mapp.
p. cm.
Includes index.
ISBN 0 521 35386 6
1. Empson, William. 1906–84 – Knowledge – Literature.
2. Literature – History and criticism – Theory, etc.
3. Criticism – England – History – 20th century.
I. Norris, Christopher. II. Mapp, Nigel.
PR6009.M7789 1993
801′.95′092 – dc20 92–8736 CIP

ISBN 0 521 35386 6 hardback

CE

Contents

Contributors

William E. Cain is Professor of English at Wellesley College. He is the author of *The Crisis in Criticism* (1984), *F. O. Matthiessen and the Politics of Criticism* (1988) and a study of modern American literary criticism, 1900–45 (forthcoming).

Alan Durant was Director of the Programme in Literary Linguistics at the University of Strathclyde before taking up his current appointment as Professor of English at Goldsmiths' College, University of London. He has published *Ezra Pound: Identity in Crisis* (1981), *Conditions of Music* (1984) and, with Nigel Fabb, *Literary Studies in Action* (1989). He also co-edited *The Linguistics of Writing: Arguments between Language and Literature* (1987).

Paul Fry is Director of Graduate Studies in English at the Whitney Humanities Center, Yale University. His books include *The Poet's Calling in the English Ode* (1980), *The Reach of Criticism* (1984) and *William Empson: Prophet against Sacrifice* (1991); also a collection of interpretive and theoretical essays entitled *The Moment of Evocation* (forthcoming).

Neil Hertz teaches in the Humanities Center at Johns Hopkins University. He is the author of *The End of the Line: Essays on Psychoanalysis and the Sublime* (1985) and co-editor of Paul de Man, *Wartime Journalism* and *Responses: on Paul de Man's Wartime Journalism* (1989).

Philip Hobsbaum is Professor of English Literature at the University of Glasgow. He worked as a research student under Empson's supervision at Sheffield, completing a Ph.D. thesis which was later published as *A Theory of Communication* (1970). Other critical works include *Tradition and Experiment in English Poetry* (1979), *Essentials of Literary Criticism* (1983), and readers' guides to Charles Dickens, D. H. Lawrence and Robert Lowell. He has also published four volumes of poems.

Jean-Jacques Lecercle is Professor of English at the University of Nanterre, Paris. He is author of *Philosophy Through the Looking-Glass* (1985), *Frankenstein: mythe et philosophie* (1988) and *The Violence of Language* (1990). He is currently working on a philosophical study of literary unreason.

Colin MacCabe is Professor of English at the University of Pittsburgh. During the 1970s he was a Fellow of King's College, Cambridge, after which he was appointed to a Chair in English at the University of Strathclyde. Among his books are *James Joyce and the 'Revolution of the Word'* (1978), *Godard: Images, Sounds, Politics* (1980), and *Theoretical Essays: Film, Linguistics, Literature* (1985). He is also the editor of *High Theory/Low Culture* (1986).

Pamela McCallum is Professor of English at the University of Calgary. She is the author of *Literature and Method: Towards a Critique of I. A. Richards, T. S. Eliot and F. R. Leavis*, and is co-editor of a forthcoming volume of essays on *The Construction of Gender and Modes of Social Division*. She is currently writing a book on French Revolution narratives.

Nigel Mapp is Sir James Knott Fellow in English Literature at the University of Newcastle upon Tyne. He has published on various topics in philosophy and literary theory, and is currently completing a doctoral thesis on the work of Paul de Man.

Christopher Norris is Professor of English at the University of Wales in Cardiff. His publications include *William Empson* (1978) and various works of philosophy and literary theory, among them *Derrida* (1987), *Paul de Man* (1988), *Deconstruction and the Interests of Theory* (1988), *What's Wrong with Postmodernism?* (1990) and *Spinoza and the Origins of Modern Critical Theory* (1991).

William Righter is Reader in English and Comparative Literary Studies at the University of Warwick. He has written widely on aspects of literature, criticism and literary theory, including two books: *Logic and Criticism* and a forthcoming volume entitled *The Myth of Theory*.

Gary Wihl is Professor of English at McGill University. He is the author of *Ruskin and the Rhetoric of Infallibility* (1985) and has recently completed *Critical Agency and the Language of Theory*. His previous writings on Empson include articles in *The British Journal of Aesthetics* and *Literature and Ethics*.

Foreword

Editing this book has been an enjoyable task for various reasons, not least the unfailing helpfulness and generosity of my contributors, the encouragement received at every stage from Kevin Taylor and Josie Dixon of Cambridge University Press, and the welcome opportunity to reread Empson in the company of colleagues and students, some of them encountering his work for the first time. As the essays came in I often asked myself how Empson might have responded had he lived to offer comments on their many and varied lines of approach. In 1978 I sent him the proofs of my own early book (*William Empson and the Philosophy of Literary Criticism*) and invited him to write a short postscript addressing any points of interest or passages where he thought I had got him wrong. The result was a mild but firm rebuke in the familiar late-Empson manner, remarking that the book had caused him to wonder 'whether my work deserved such devoted scrutiny, or at least to wish I had not written so confusedly that it was needed'. Moreover, Norris's kind intentions turned out to have sharp limits; 'anything I had printed for the last quarter of a century was irrelevant nonsense, to be dismissed briefly with a sigh'. So yes, he would write the postscript as requested, but wanted to make it clear that – *pace* Norris – 'I have not been entertaining myself with frippery in my old age; . . . I have continued to try to handle the most important work that came to hand'.

I thought then – and still do – that Empson's response was oddly out of key with what I had written about his later work. All the same I can see why he found it so irksome to be taken up as a kind of honorary precursor by a whole new school of 'bother-headed' theoretical critics whose enterprise – as Empson understood it – had nothing in common with his own outlook of sturdy common-sense rationalism, his principle that 'theory' was only of use in so far as it helped to clear away the sources of confusion (or the downright corruptions of moral and intellectual judgement) brought about by the current neo-Christian revival in orthodox Eng. Lit. circles. 'Surely', he concluded, 'when things have got as loony as that, it becomes a duty to speak up; even if it feels less momentous than propounding a theory of Ambiguity.' Anyway – to cut short this brooding reminiscence – it strikes me that Empson would probably have had mixed feelings about the present volume of essays. They are by no means all given over to 'theory', in Empson's disapproving sense of that term, although some (Hertz, Norris, McCallum, Durant and MacCabe among them) make large claims for Empson's importance as a theorist *malgré lui*, one whose work – especially *The Structure of Complex Words* – may be said not only to 'anticipate' recent developments but also to go far beyond them in certain crucial respects. Certainly there is no attempt to annex his criticism to any one prevailing theoretical trend, whether post-structuralist, New Historicist, deconstructionist or whatever. On the contrary, one could take it as a hopeful sign that 'theory' is coming of age when it manages to find room for a strong but problematical figure like Empson, a critic whose thinking goes so markedly against some of its basic precepts and principles. Besides, the book offers what Empson might have thought a decent leavening of non-theoretical pieces, or – more accurately – essays which bear out his point from the closing chapter of *Seven Types of Ambiguity*: that 'normal sensibility is a tissue of what has been conscious theory made habitual and returned to the pre-conscious', so that 'conscious theory may make an addition to sensibility' even where the critic shows little interest in addressing such matters. Here, as so often, his remark is worth bearing in mind when confronted with the warring claims and counter-claims of present-day critical debate.

The editors would like to thank Kathy Kerr and Peter Sedgwick for various pieces of help and advice during the preparation of this volume; Sumie Okada, an authority on Empson's pre-war years in Japan; John Haffenden for his interest in the project (and also for his splendid editorial work on the posthumous collection *Argufying*, a scholarly labour of love if ever there was one); Terence Hawkes for his many good ideas about Empson over the past decade; Lady Hetta Empson for kind permission to reproduce material featured in Philip Hobsbaum's essay; and our friends in Cardiff for their constant supply of good humour and intellectual stimulus.

CHRISTOPHER NORRIS
Cardiff

Note: Neil Hertz's essay – or a version thereof – has appeared in *diacritics* 20:3 (Fall 1990), 2–27, having first been commissioned by the editors for a special number on Paul de Man. Paul Fry's essay is based on a chapter of his book *William Empson: Prophet against Sacrifice* (London: Routledge, 1991), a volume in the series Critics of the Twentieth Century.

CHAPTER 1

Introduction: Empson as literary theorist: from Ambiguity to Complex Words and beyond

Christopher Norris

William Empson didn't read much in the way of recent (post-1970) literary theory, but made it very clear that he disliked – even hated – those few books and articles that latterly came in for review, or that well-meaning commentators (myself included) sent along in the hope of provoking some lively response. His aversion to 'theory' has been found rather puzzling by many of Empson's younger admirers since he was, after all, by widespread assent the most theoretically minded and intellectually resourceful of twentieth-century English critics, as well as having written – in *The Structure of Complex Words* – a book which explored philosophical issues with a fine disregard for the standard academic division of intellectual labour. But the whole point of *Complex Words* was to rescue literature from the vagaries of subjective or emotive response by providing some more or less adequate bits of theoretical 'machinery' – the equations, or various forms of logico-semantic entailment – by which to make sense of multiple meaning without falling back on the catch-all notion of poetic 'ambiguity', or (even worse) the irrationalist rhetoric of 'paradox' raised into a quasi-theological absolute by the adepts of American New Criticism. The only use for theory in literary studies was to clear away non-existent problems and sources of bafflement – doctrines like emotivism and the so-called 'Intentional Fallacy' – and show the way back to a decent respect for authorial meaning, historical context and literature's capacity to communicate truths of human experience despite all the difficulties dreamed up by theorists in the grip of some modish sceptical dogma. Like Empson in his own later essays, one could then go on in a sturdily untheoretical way and set about rescuing those various authors whose work had been

For more detailed information on sources and matters of publication history, see Frank Day, *Sir William Empson: an Annotated Bibliography* (New York: Garland, 1984).

'kidnapped' – or grievously misread – by the zealots of this latest bother-headed critical orthodoxy.

For the prevailing anti-cognitivist bias went along with what Empson saw as a 'cult of unnaturalism', a perverse desire to cut literature off from any wider background of ethical or socio-political debate (see Empson, 1987a, pp. 563–5; 627–31). This cult had its origins in the 1890s and was carried across into the academic study of literature by critics who adopted the aestheticist posture as a part of their crusade against scientism, rationalism and other such bugbears of the modern literary imagination. Hence the various efforts – from Arnold, through Eliot to Richards, Leavis and the New Critics – to devise some alternative account of poetic 'truth', one that would have no truck with the truth-claims of scientific reason. For his part, Empson regarded all this as an absurd misunderstanding of what 'science' was about, coupled with a narrowly professionalized ethos which disguised its own failure of intellectual nerve with various kinds of obscurantist jargon designed to keep readers from questioning the sacrosanct values handed down by the high priests and commissars of latter-day Eng. Lit. fashion. The rot had set in by 1951, when he came back to teach at Sheffield after the years in China and Japan. Empson was made to feel, as he wrote at the time, like a wild old man who had now lost touch and couldn't catch up with the newly invented rules of the game. What made the situation still more irksome was the fact that those rules had been derived in large part from the kind of close-reading 'analytical' approach that Empson himself had done much to popularize. By the early 1950s *Seven Types of Ambiguity* had taken its place as a set-piece classic of modern critical method, the single most sustained and impressive example of what T. S. Eliot was soon to label the 'lemon-squeezer school of criticism' (1933). Eliot himself was in no strong position to complain, since his own early essays on seventeenth-century poetry and drama had helped to establish the idea that criticism is best, most rewardingly engaged in the business of detailed verbal exegesis with a minimal reliance on 'background' history and a marked aversion to those heterodox strains of thought that were liable to emerge if one took poets to be seriously *arguing a case*, rather than just playing with ingenious 'conceits' or inventing elaborate rhetorical structures devoid of any truth-claims or real argumentative force. Meticulous attention to the 'words on the page' – or analytical close-reading in the early Empson style – could thus be turned into a pretext for ignoring everything that gave those words their significance and saved poetry from becoming just a plaything in the hands of this or that revisionist school.

Eliot had now put such interests behind him, regarding merely 'technical' (or verbal) criticism as a species of frivolous distraction, and declaring that the act of interpretive judgement had to be 'completed' by a disciplined awareness of larger (ethical and ultimately religious) values. But this was just a smokescreen, Empson thought, since those same techniques of verbal exegesis had helped to give rise to an academic movement of decidedly orthodox neo-Christian persuasion. Moreover, *Seven Types* had itself played a role in promoting this dismal trend. For ambiguity was soon transformed – mainly at the hands of the American New Critics – from a loose (even casually inclusive) term for any kind of multiple meaning into a full-dress critical orthodoxy where 'paradox' and 'irony' were treated as the measures of true poetic worth, and where any hint of heterodox or dissenting ideas – as for instance in poets like Donne, Milton or Coleridge – could be kept out of sight by strict application of the relevant critical ground-rules (Wimsatt, 1954). In short, it had become a form of surrogate or ersatz theology, along with all the attendant baggage of canonical dogmas and heresies. The connection was visible in Eliot's praise for that form of devotional technique epitomised by Lancelot Andrewes: 'dividing the word of God', or seeking out layers of associative meaning to drive home the doctrinal point (Eliot, 1928). There were clear links between the new style of secularized close-reading and a long tradition of scriptural hermeneutics in the service of dogmatic or revealed religious truth. *Seven Types* had indeed found some of its most striking examples in poets like Donne and Herbert, engaged (as Empson reads them) in a desperate struggle of conscience between 'decent human feelings' and the cruel exactions of orthodox Christian belief. Thus the book reaches a climax with Herbert's 'The Sacrifice', where this conflict engenders a violent series of unresolved verbal clashes and tensions. But in other hands the method could be put to very different uses, including the standard neo-Christian ploy of ignoring the rational *resistance* to paradox and praising the poet for his 'deep' perception of religious truths beyond reach of mere analytic reason. Close-reading thus became a sure route of access to regions of the soul untouched by the spirit of latter-day secular critique.

For Empson, returning to discover this orthodoxy now firmly in place, it seemed that he had somehow lived on into a twilight era, depressingly remote from his Cambridge years when the 'two cultures' were still closely in touch, and when a poet like Empson could confidently emulate a poet like Donne, since both were alive to the full range of moral and imaginative possibilities opened up by a knowledge of new scientific ideas. But this was just impossible, according to the current wisdom, since now critics were required to accept (1) that poetry had nothing to do with arguments, truth-claims or rational debate; (2) that a poet's intentions were in any case unknowable; and (3) that one would surely fall into error – the so-called 'heresy of paraphrase' – if one took Empson's line of figuring out the sense of some complex passage and then treating it as properly subject to the usual kinds of reasoned assessment on logical, ethical, social or political grounds. To Empson this seemed nothing more than a species of abject irrationalist doctrine backed up by an appeal to the worst elements of instituted Christian belief. He was quick to see what the New Critics were at when – objecting to the vagueness of 'ambiguity' as a handle for critical analysis – they replaced it with other, more clear-cut notions like 'paradox', 'irony', 'tension' or 'plurisignification'. This wasn't just a matter of terminological tidiness, or even of improved interpretive grasp. What these concepts served to underwrite was a notion of the poem as 'verbal icon', a structure of inwrought rhetorical figures whose meaning was henceforth declared unavailable to mere prose summary or rational critique.

Hence the various New Critical 'heresies' declaimed against those (Empson included) who so far mistook the name and nature of poetry as to talk about the poet's intentions, ideas or anything that might be rendered by way of plain-prose commentary. Worst of all, from this point of view, was Empson's habit of reading poetry always in light of his own decidedly liberal, secular-humanist values. Rather than respect poetic language for its peculiar, uniquely 'paradoxical' character, Empson insisted on trying to make sense of it in terms continuous with those of our everyday – and often no less complicated – choices, motives, problems and decisions. The result, in John Crowe Ransom's words, was to 'suggest a reading of the poet's mind by some later, freer and more self-conscious mind' (1938–9, p. 333). The New Critics were unable to accept this, first because it broke down the privileged autonomy of the poem as 'verbal icon', and second because it opened the way to all manner of subversive speculation on the psycho-pathology of Christian belief. Empson's commentary on Herbert's 'The Sacrifice' makes a point of *not* letting the poem settle down into some region of profound theological 'truth' where reason finds itself ultimately played off the field. To take it on faith – as the New Critics did – that poetry just *is* paradoxical through and through is to miss the whole point of what Empson describes as the tortured and nerve-racking style of Herbert's poem, its refusal (at whatever 'unconscious' level) to acquiesce in the grim doctrine of Atonement forced upon the poet by his official creed. In short, Empson turns back the charge brought against him by mystery-mongering critics like Ransom by assuming that any 'muddles' (or irrational beliefs) in the poet's mind go along with a measure of resistance encountered in the process of working these confusions out into some kind of decently intelligible poetic and narrative form. On the other hand he could hardly deny that *Seven Types* had lent itself all too readily to the purposes of a critical movement squarely opposed to any such rational-humanist outlook.

The main result of this realization on Empson's part was the work in theoretical semantics and philosophy of language that went toward *The Structure of Complex Words* (1951). Even so, he makes it clear that the chapters of 'theory' are intended primarily as a ground-clearing exercise, an attempt to see beyond the cramping orthodoxy of currently fashionable 'Eng. Lit'. ideas, and must therefore be judged successful only in so far as they offer support – or show themselves intuitively adequate – when put to work in the 'practical' essays on Shakespeare, Milton, Pope, Wordsworth and others. 'The idea that the theorist is not part of the world he examines is one of the deepest sources of error, and crops up all over the place' (1951, p. 445). This applies just as much to ethics and linguistics – on both of which topics Empson has a good deal to say – as to matters of interpretive judgement where thinking can go very badly wrong if it gets out of touch with the everyday business of trying to understand what people mean. And in literary criticism especially there is no point having 'theories' – Empson believes – if they don't feed back into a better, more accountable or humane practice of readerly response. If the academic study of literature could defend its specialized domain only by erecting such counter-intuitive principles as the 'Wimsatt Law' (or the Intentionalist Fallacy), then in Empson's opinion it had failed the first test of any such communal sense-making enterprise, and its pretensions needed showing up along with their morally and intellectually harmful effects. 'Theory' would have to play a part in this therapeutic effort, since one major source of the prevailing obscurantist ethos was a widespread revolt against science, reason and truth-values in criticism, resulting – as he thought – from an absurdly simplified view of what science (and philosophy of science) had been up to since the early years of this century. Thus trying to figure out an author's intentions 'is much better than pretending you can't know anything (imitating a Logical Positivist in a different field of study)' (Empson, 1987a, p. 125). More specifically: theory could provide at least the working basis for a critical hermeneutics alert to the varieties of 'compacted doctrine' (or logico-semantic entailment) contained within the different orders of complex word. By so doing, it could put an argued case against the various strains of obscurantist doctrine promoted by critics who sought – for whatever reason – to insulate poetry from the interests and values of enlightened communicative grasp. But in this case theorists had better accept that theirs was a mainly corrective endeavour, one whose only practical use was to clear away unnecessary sources of confusion or bewilderment, and thus put criticism back in touch with those ordinary, everyday modes of understanding involved in all forms of linguistic transaction. However, Empson saw little evidence of this in the various 'bother-headed' theoretical books that turned up for review during the heyday of New Criticism and its various successor movements on the US academic scene. On the contrary: these theorists only seemed happy when raising bafflement – to adapt a phrase from one of Empson's poems – into a boast they could take as some kind of doctrinal or professional guard.

In *Complex Words* Empson puts the case for a broadly rationalist approach to all kinds of language, poetry among them, and sees no need to suspend this principle when dealing with particularly complex, resistant or paradoxical forms of expression. Other theorists – notably Chomsky – have likewise argued that language reflects the very grammar of human rationality, its 'deep' logical structure as opposed to its surface relativities from culture to culture (see Chomsky, 1957). But for Chomsky these linguistic universals are derived by starting out from the level of syntax and applying a series of increasingly abstract rules and transformational procedures. In its early form at least, the theory made no allowance for the ways in which meaning (the province of semantics) might have to be included in any such generalized picture. Subsequent versions went so far as to build in a structural-semantic system of rules, such that meaning could be given its place in a more refined and adequate theory of language (Chomsky, 1966). But syntax has remained the chief interest and methodological focus of this whole 'transformational-generative' approach in linguistics, philosophy of mind and cognitive psychology. For Empson, conversely, semantics is the main route of access to whatever truths about human rationality language has to show. It is in the structures of semantic implication contained in certain 'complex words' that Empson locates the most significant (and humanly revealing) facts about language. And so it becomes a matter of unpacking those words, not merely to pile up multiple meanings (like the conjuror producing rabbits from a hat), but in order to show how their senses relate through a 'grammar' of semantic entailment which in turn points back to the normative structures of human understanding in general. Thus 'the term Ambiguity . . . implying that the reader is left in doubt between two readings, is more or less superseded by the idea of a double meaning which is intended to be fitted into a definite structure' (Empson, 1951, p. 103n).

In short, the 'grammar' of Empsonian semantics is best regarded as a working system of rational assumptions about language, meaning and interpretive competence which are mostly taken for granted in our everyday linguistic dealings, but which may on occasion need stating explicitly in face of some perverse new theory or other. As so often with such arguments, 'there is a sense in which it [i.e. the 'machinery' or grammar of reader-response] does not need to be expounded; if it is true, we are already acting on it all the time' (Empson, 1987a, p. 107). But this didn't prevent theorists like Wimsatt from inventing all manner of elaborate theories to back up their absurdly counter-intuitive doctrine that poetic 'intentions' were inherently unknowable, or that any attempt to paraphrase the meaning of a poem (as for instance by teasing out its logico-semantic 'grammar') must always involve a kind of ontological violence, a failure to recognize the qualitative difference between poetry and other sorts of language. Sometimes Empson responded with a bluff, common-sensical line of argument, suggesting that 'theory' was altogether useless if it tended to promote such patent falsehoods as the anti-intentionalist dogma. 'Estimating other people's intentions is one of the things we do all the time without knowing how we are doing it, just as we don't play catch by the Theory of Dynamics . . . Only in the criticism of imaginative literature, a thing delicately concerned with human intimacy, are we told that we must give up all idea of knowing his [the author's] intention' (Empson, 1987a, pp. 124–5). And again, from the same article (his 1950 review of Wimsatt's *The Verbal Icon*): 'in the teasing work of scholarship, a man must all the time be trying to imagine another man's mind; as soon as that stops, he is off the rails. One cannot have a sheer theory to *keep* him off them' (p. 125).

What is more, such doctrines had a harmfully narrowing effect on the critic's range of moral and imaginative sympathy, since they seemed to imply – like some currently fashionable forms of neo-pragmatist thinking (see Fish, 1989; Rorty, 1982) – that one could never get outside the goldfish bowl of one's own cultural presuppositions. Thus Empson is startled by Wimsatt's apparently taking it for granted that 'there is only one right code of morals, a thing already known to himself'. But there is a sense in which this follows inexorably from the anti-intentionalist case, since the logic of that position makes it hard to conceive how anyone could experience the reading of literature as anything other than a comforting reflection of their own preexistent values and beliefs. 'The idea that a piece of writing which excited moral resistance might be a discovery in morals, a means of learning what was wrong with the existing system, somehow cannot enter his [Wimsatt's] mind' (p. 126). In which case, as Empson rightly remarks, there wouldn't be much point in reading literature at all, let alone subjecting it to the kind of close analytical scrutiny that critics like Wimsatt had raised to such a high point of method and principle.

So it is hardly surprising that Empson's antipathy to 'theory' became all the stronger with each new manifestation of what he saw as a rampant professionalist ethos allied to a stubborn narrowness of moral judgement and a total disregard for authorial intentions where these went against the current consensus of 'informed' Eng. Lit. opinion. In his later work Empson goes various ways around to combat this rising tide of anti-humanist or downright irrationalist prejudice. One response – as we have seen – was to adopt a line of sturdy common-sense wisdom, pointing out the sheer absurdity of trying to read poems on a theory so remote from our shared experience as language-using creatures. Thus 'to say that you won't be bothered with anything but the words on the page (and that you are within your rights, because the author didn't *intend* you to have any more) strikes me as petulant, like saying "of course I won't visit him unless he has first-class plumbing". If you cared enough you would' (1987a, p. 125). Then again, there were the essays of his later years – most of them collected in the posthumous volume *Using Biography* – where Empson mounted a sustained polemical assault on the doctrine (also put about by the New Critics) that one couldn't, or shouldn't, interpret texts in the light of 'extraneous' biographical information (Empson, 1984). Of course he has no time for this purist attitude, regarding it as just another aspect of the prevailing guild mentality, designed to keep professional critics in business by ruling the amateurs strictly off bounds. Furthermore, he suspects that it is often used to smuggle in meanings of an orthodox, conservative or neo-Christian cast that happen to suit the current interpretive trend. The essays bring up all kinds of biographical material, some of it the product of painstaking archival research, though on occasion Empson gives free rein to a highly speculative (not to say fanciful) mode of treatment which allows him to fit the available facts into a satisfying narrative shape.

What comes across most strongly is his deep-laid humanist conviction that the best – indeed the only – way to make sense of complex or problematic novels and poems is to read them with a mind unburdened by the self-denying ordinances of modern critical dogma, and willing to entertain the widest possible range of human experiences, motives and desires. Like R. G. Collingwood (1936, 1939) – whose work he read while preparing to write the 'theoretical' chapters of *Complex Words* – Empson thinks it an important truth about criticism, historiography and the human sciences in general that one cannot make a start in really understanding a text – as opposed to just decoding its sign structure – except by way of such imaginative insights arrived at through a mode of rational reconstruction based on an adequate working knowledge of the author's motivating interests. And this means paying close attention to the story, whether fictive or biographical, since it is here that one finds the best possible evidence of those interests working themselves out through a sequence of humanly intelligible choices and decisions. In fact Empson regularly explodes against critics who show themselves incapable of following a narrative line (or noticing salient details of the plot) while claiming to uncover extraordinary subtleties of style, structure or imagery (1987a, pp. 147–66; 167–73). Hence his impatience with the modern fashion for 'symbolist' readings which ignored this essential narrative dimension in their quest for some timeless, transcendent order of meaning and truth indifferent to details of plot, circumstance or background history. Thus on Yeats's 'Byzantium' poems he admits (rather grudgingly) that a 'deep' interpretation seems called for at various points, but maintains none the less that an interest in the story will improve matters (1984, pp. 163–86). With Eliot likewise, he refuses to go along with high-toned symbolist readings of *The Waste Land*, since the poem – as Empson sees it – is a brave if tortuous attempt to work out some kind of narrative frame (or decently intelligible story-line) for episodes that can make little sense unless interpreted in light of Eliot's neurotic conflicts, especially those brought about by his adherence to the Christian religion at its most repellently orthodox. All the same, Empson concedes that the poem remains a 'mystery', one of Symbolism's few successes (1987a, pp. 189–200). But he then goes on to adduce such a mass of significant or suggestive 'background' information that his essay effectively retracts this concession and turns into a full-scale polemical assault on the Symbolist 'programme' and its various offshoots in present-day Lit. Crit. fashion.

In fact one can see the same principle at work in some of Empson's earliest writings, long before he came to associate depth-hermeneutical techniques with the strain of neo-Christian obscurantism which Eliot had done so much to promote. Most often he preferred to coax the meaning up, so to speak, from the twilight zone of preconscious or irrational motives to the level of 'open public debate' where those motives achieved articulate form, as for instance by being reworked into narrative shape or through the kind of 'multi-consciousness' – the appeal to a broad range of human sympathies and impulses – typically encountered in a good theatrical production. This attitude comes across clearly in a review of Auden's 'Paid on Both Sides' which Empson wrote for the Cambridge magazine *Granta* in 1931 (1987a, pp. 369–71). The charade involved a 'sort of surrealist technique' which Auden had used most effectively to communicate the protagonist's divided feelings, his near-schizophrenic confusions of will and desire. 'They could only, I think, have been conveyed in this way, and only when you have accepted them can the play be recognized as a sensible and properly motivated tragedy' (p. 369). The surrealist connections are interesting enough, but not so much for their 'deep' psychological import as for their usefulness as a consciousness-raising device, a means of convincing the audience (or the reader) that such complications are best handled with the intellectual faculties fully in play. Thus one reason why the Auden piece so impresses Empson is that it situates in a 'rational tragic form' the 'irrationalist' proclivities of modern thought, psychoanalysis and surrealism included (p. 371). It is much the same attitude in *Milton's God* that readily admits the fascination – the psychological interest – of Milton's 'appalling' theology, while insisting that we can only make decent moral sense of the poem by attending to the story as closely as possible, and giving due credit for the complicated motives that emerge both in Milton's narrative treatment of the theme and in his characters' agonized facing-about between various impossible choices and temptations. For otherwise, so Empson argues, we will fail to appreciate the poet's generosity and breadth of sympathetic judgement, or the extent to which his feelings were 'crying out' against the tenets of orthodox Christian belief.

So one can see why Empson was somewhat dismayed to find his own techniques of verbal analysis being put to work in the service of a depth-psychological approach with small regard for the interests of improved communicative grasp or enlightened human understanding. In fact he had always been troubled by the notion of a deep (Freudian or Jungian) unconscious to which critics could appeal without fear of rational rejoinder. His earliest reflections on this topic occur in a 1928 review of George Rylands's book *Words and Poetry*, a piece that clearly glances at his own work-in-progress towards *Seven Types*, and which also implicitly acknowledges his debt to the Graves–Riding *Survey of Modernist Poetry* published just three years previously. Such criticism is only impressive, Empson writes,

> when the analysis it employs becomes so elaborate as to score a rhetorical triumph; when each word in the line is given four or five meanings, four or five reasons for sounding right and suggesting the right things. Dazzled by the difficulty of holding it in your mind at once, you feel this at any rate is complicated enough, as many factors as these could make up a result apparently magical and incalculable. (1987a, p. 69)

And he then goes on to fault Rylands for 'seldom bringing off the trick with sufficient concentration', or for simply offering a range of associative meanings without any sense of real argumentative *point*, so that the reader is left – very much in the Symbolist manner – with a vague intimation of truths beyond reach of the rational, analytic mind. In *Seven Types* (especially the last two chapters) this produces a constant tension between Empson's pursuit of ever more complex and 'deeply rooted' psychological conflicts and his belief that any adequate response to poetry must engage the intellect at full stretch and not seek refuge in some last-ditch appeal to the realm of unconscious motives and meanings. But as it turned out, and despite all his warnings to the contrary, this latter was the message most often extracted by admiring and hostile commentators alike.

Hence – as I have said – the very marked change of tack in Empson's later criticism, a change that registered his growing unease with the professionalized uses and abuses of textual close-reading. In one direction this led him to the kind of flat no-nonsense attitude which treated topics like the Intentional Fallacy as mere academic foibles, notions that could easily be brushed aside by appealing to the plain facts of human experience. In another, it produced a whole series of essays – like those collected in *Using Biography* – where Empson argues for a humanist ethics of criticism based on the broadly Benthamite principle that judgements of value must always come down to the question of what satisfies the greatest range of human desires, satisfactions, communicative impulses and so forth. From this it follows that good literature will tend to display such qualities through the appeal to a broad-minded tolerant acceptance of different moral codes and the sheer variety of motivating values and belief-systems. In fact one can trace this principle back to the much-quoted sentence from *Seven Types* where Empson reflects that 'the object of life, after all, is not to understand things, but to maintain one's defences and equilibrium and live as well as one can; it is not only maiden aunts who are placed like this' (1953, p. 247). But as critical fashion showed every sign of hardening into a new orthodoxy with marked theological overtones, so Empson decided that the case needed stating more strongly, or that the Benthamite position deserved a more explicit defence against high-toned detractors like F. R. Leavis (see Leavis, 1972). In *Milton's God* it is a main plank in his argument that the neo-Christian zealots have got Milton wrong by allowing their judgements to be warped or corrupted by a straightforward endorsement of the poet's 'official' creed. That is to say, they have gone along with the orthodox view of Milton as an apologist for doctrines like original sin, predestination and (worst of all) the idea of Christ's 'atonement' as a way of buying off God the Father by 'satisfying' his desire for sadistic torture inflicted on an innocent scapegoat figure by way of vicarious 'redemption' for some small number of elect human souls. The best way to counter such readings, Empson thinks, is to point out the sheer barbarity of Christian theology when set against the standard Benthamite measure of enlightened self-interest coupled with a decent degree of altruistic or other-regarding sentiment.

It should thus be possible to 'rescue' Milton from the two main camps of orthodox opinion: on the one hand those pious admirers who celebrate the poem for all the wrong reasons, and on the other those sternly dissenting critics (like C. S. Lewis (1942)) who acknowledge the problematic nature of Milton's theology but put this down to various flaws or heresies in the poet's handling of biblical themes, so that readers had better blame Milton – not Christianity – for any muddles or enormities that result. On the contrary, says Empson: the poem is so good because it takes on the grim burden of Christian dogma at its most orthodox and morally appalling, while also giving scope for those 'decent human feelings' which Milton's theology could not wholly repress, since they emerge (for any reader properly attentive to details of plot, character and motive) *despite and against* the poet's proclamations of a Christian-orthodox intent. In short, the Benthamite ethic goes along with a principled willingness to give Milton credit for not having completely yielded up his moral conscience to the tenets of a false and repugnant theology. And it also connects with Empson's belief – as expressed in his sharp rejoinder to Wimsatt – that critics who claim privileged access to truths known only to themselves (or to partisans of the same religious or doctrinal persuasion) are thereby revealing a hopeless narrowness of moral and intellectual judgement. Thus 'the main purpose of reading imaginative literature is to grasp a wide variety of experience, imagining people with codes and customs very unlike our own; and it cannot be done except in a Benthamite manner, that is, by thinking "how would such a code or custom work out?"' (Empson, 1987a, p. 218). And in Milton's case this means trying to understand *both* how a doctrine like the Christian Atonement could implant itself so firmly in the Western cultural tradition, *and* how various thinkers within that tradition struggled to avoid its worst, most sadistic implications by telling the story over again while refusing – at whatever 'unconscious' level – to endorse the official creed. In short, Empson believed that academic Eng. Lit. had taken a disastrous wrong turn when it followed the fashion set by Eliot and Leavis, and hitched its 'values' to a downright rejection of the Benthamite ethic, that is to say, the basic principle that 'the satisfaction of any impulse is in itself an elementary good, and that the practical ethical question is merely how to satisfy the greatest number' (Empson, 1965, p. 259). For without some such rational machinery of judgement it would always be possible for high-minded zealots to sanction any amount of cruelty and wickedness in the name of religious truth.

Of course literary critics were not well placed to adopt more drastic measures of doctrinal enforcement. But this was no cause for complacency, Empson thought, since a widespread retreat from enlightened secular values in the cultural sphere could always give rise to other, more dangerous forms of revivalist sentiment. Thus 'at any time, especially in parts of the world where an endemic tolerance has not been acquired, allowing a traditional influence from a rational ethic, worthy Christians may again feel it their evident duty to plunge headlong into great wickedness' (1965, pp. 258–9). Commentators on Empson have mostly treated such passages either as a wild aberration that developed out of earlier 'eccentric' leanings, or – more tactfully – as a quirkish sideline which shouldn't detract from his other, more significant and truly representative achievements. Predictably the greatest hostility has come from critics of an overtly religious persuasion, among them the Catholic Hugh Kenner (1958) who treats Empson with pitying fondness as a washed-up relic of the 'old' nineteenth-century rationalist or liberal-humanist outlook. The New Critics, as we have seen, had problems of their own in coping with the secularist impulse in Empson's early work, while preferring not to tackle such questions head-on but to meet them obliquely on the surrogate ground of interpretive method and theory. It is only in recent years that a few commentators – among them Jonathan Culler and Paul Fry – have risen to the challenge on Empson's side and taken full measure of his case against Christianity, regarding it not as an unfortunate foible but as deeply bound up with his entire critical output, from the reading of Herbert in *Seven Types* to the rationalist semantics of *Complex Words* and the polemical engagement of his late essays (Culler, 1988, pp. 69–82; 85–95; Fry, 1991). One reason is no doubt the current upsurge of neofundamentalist passions, as witnessed not only by the controversy surrounding Salman Rushdie's novel *The Satanic Verses*, but also by various threatening signs of a right-wing Christian revivalist crusade. Certainly Empson would have viewed these developments as a gloomy confirmation of his own deepest fears with regard to the potency of irrationalist doctrines and the prospect of a large-scale relapse into forms of paranoid scapegoat-hunting.

At any rate there is now less excuse for treating this as a tedious obsession on Empson's part, or for arguing – as many commentators have – that his remarks on the topic were in bad taste, since clearly Christianity had left such things far behind on the path to its present-day civilized stance. It is hard to resist quoting one of those passages from *Milton's God* which critics have found so baffling on account of their knife-edge balance between joky informality and deadly serious cautionary intent. 'When the Church had sufficient power', Empson writes,

> it would regularly happen that a man was promoted to high place in it through a widespread recognition that he was genuinely imitating Jesus Christ; and then he would say to himself 'Come now; a man with my responsibilities has a duty not to go on imitating Jesus Christ; it is time to imitate God the Father'; and immediately he would start behaving with monstrous cruelty, apparently without any psychic shock. The other side of his nature had long been growing underneath; he had been reconstructing himself in the image of the Trinity. (1965, p. 244)

This passage is interesting partly for the fact that it leads straight on to a brief discussion of the mechanism of 'false identity', the verbal trick that manages to conflate two meanings ('A = B') without suggesting any logical 'machinery' – or grammar of rational implication – by which to make sense of the thought-processes involved. Thus it brings out very clearly the link between Empson's more specialized researches in *Complex Words* and those later writings where he appears to abandon this whole line of interest in favour of an overtly moralizing stance, a rhetoric of bluff 'common-sense' values, and a refusal to allow mere questions of 'theory' to distract him from the much more urgent business of attacking the Christian revivalist ethos and its manifold corrupting effects. For this was not so much a break or a new direction as a tactical shift of priorities forced upon Empson by his growing awareness of just how widespread and harmful those effects had become. *Complex Words* had concerned itself mainly with providing the theoretical groundwork for a rational hermeneutics aimed squarely against these manifestations of latter-day militant unreason. Now it remained to put the theory into practice through a direct engagement with those moral, religious and socio-political issues that were raised most explicitly by critics like Kenner, those who made a wholesale programme of trashing the secular-humanist enlightenment and all its works. In short, the theoretical 'machinery' of *Complex Words* is still very much there in the background, offering what amounts to a generalized rational assurance, a set of largely tacit enabling assumptions that allow Empson to get on with the business of 'rescuing' Milton, Donne, Coleridge, Joyce and others from their wrongheaded neo-Christian exegetes. Thus 'our minds have a wonderful readiness to satisfy themselves with admittedly false identities, but any orderly schooling needs to drive the process into the background of its area of practical work' (1965, p. 244).

Seven Types had come up with some striking examples of the kind, especially in the passage on Herbert's 'The Sacrifice', a reading that pushed 'false identity' to the point where the poem seemed based on a whole series of mind-wrenching paradoxes and flat contradictions, viewed as giving access to regions of deep psychological conflict where analysis finally came up against the limits of rational-discursive thought. But this approach was positively harmful, as Empson came to feel, since it lent itself all too easily to the purposes of a neo-orthodox obscurantist creed backed up by the appeal to precisely such kinds of 'profound' paradoxical wisdom, or to truths known only through the inward revelation vouchsafed to those readers, fit though few, whose minds were untouched by the spirit of latter-day enlightened secular reason. Empson is quite clear that 'false identity' is a deeply rooted habit of the human intellect, a process that we could never be induced to give up simply by having our attention drawn to its logically fallacious character or its tendency to generate false beliefs, some of them (like the doctrine of the Trinity, or the slogans of Orwellian Newspeak) capable of inflicting great moral harm. On the contrary: 'I tried in my book *Complex Words* to show how very fundamental it is; the baby could not learn without it, and the learned man still needs to fall back upon it whenever he gets an obscure feeling that his work has been missing some essential point' (1965, pp. 244–5). But there is a crucial difference – as Empson sees it – between the normal machinery of human judgement that uses false identity as a handy conceptual resource, a stage on the way to more adequate understanding, and those other exploitative uses of the same fundamental device that contrive to insinuate all manner of dogmatic irrational beliefs. Unless we could learn to recognize and act upon this basic distinction then there seemed little hope of saving humanity from the recurrent bouts of intolerance, sectarian hatred and renewed religious persecution that were caused in the main by a failure to perceive the 'active false logic' of identity-thinking when divorced from any kind of common-sense judgement or process of rational critique.

The following passage from *Milton's God* puts the case in terms that leave no doubt as to the close relation, in Empson's later work, between questions of 'theory' (that is to say, issues of a broadly hermeneutic, epistemological or logico-semantic character) and questions that go directly to the heart of his case against Christian and other such forms of irrationalist mystery-mongering. 'Regarded simply as a bit of our mental equipment', he writes,

> it [false identity] carries within itself a kind of recognition that the matter would bear looking into, or an impulse to do that later, though enough is settled for the immediate decision. The most staggering misuse of [this process] is the Doctrine of the Trinity. One can hardly discuss whether a man believes this doctrine, because it is merely a thing which his mind can be induced to do ... because the mind so easily falls back on the primitive assurance that the Father and the Son both are and are not identical. The machine is best described in the terrible book *1984*, where it produces a number of horror-slogans such as 'War is Peace'. I have thus to conclude that the Doctrine of the Trinity is a means of deceiving good men into accepting evil; it is the double-talk by which Christians hide from themselves the insane wickedness of their God. (1965, p. 245)

So far as Empson could see, the whole enterprise of 'advanced' literary thinking since Eliot had been premised on a downright refusal to acknowledge the harmful effects of such irrationalist doctrine, and a corresponding drive to dissociate critical judgement from the values of enlightened secular reason or (more straightforwardly) 'decent human feelings'. It had done so by offering various sophisticated theories in support of the view that literature just wasn't in the business of arguing, advancing truth-claims, criticizing false beliefs or giving access to an author's genuine intentions as communicated in good faith to readers in possession of the relevant 'background' knowledge. This orthodoxy ran all the way from I. A. Richards, via the New Critics to theorists of fiction like

Wayne Booth, interpreters whose hyper-articulated talk of narrative 'viewpoint' or the 'implied author' enabled them to avoid anything so vulgar or reductive as the appeal to what somebody *actually meant to say* about this or that real-life or imaginary situation (see Booth, 1974; Empson 1987a, pp. 178–83). In short, criticism had fallen prey to a wholesale anti-cognitivist fashion whose effect was to cut literature off from any dealing with matters of urgent practical and moral concern. So it was scarcely surprising that the neo-Christian adepts could exploit this situation to their own advantage, as, for instance, by quarrying poems for their structures of 'deep' paradoxical import, or by reading plays and novels in determined pursuit of some obscure allegorical or 'symbolist' meaning totally at odds with the manifest story-line or the author's professed intent.

II

Hence the large number of late-Empson essays devoted to the 'dreary but necessary' task of countering this confidently orthodox trend by reasserting the claims of a rational-humanist ethic based in equal measure on Benthamite principles and a sturdy rejection of 'bother-headed' theories like the anti-intentionalist doctrine. The chapter on Fielding in *Using Biography* is perhaps the best example of how Empson brings these two lines of argument together (1984, pp. 129–57). It is not enough, he suggests, to demonstrate the tricks of 'double irony' by which Fielding manages simultaneously to implicate the reader and maintain his good-humoured tolerant stance as against any kind of narrow, dogmatic or self-exculpating moral code. Certainly this is a major resource of Fielding's narrative technique, and helps to explain why his novels gave offence to those (like Dr Johnson) whose religious sensibilities were rattled by the hint of a humanist latitude on matters like Original Sin. But talk of 'double irony', though useful up to a point, can still be actively misleading – Empson thinks – in so far as it attempts to pin the novel down to a typecast rhetorical structure, a standard device which the expert critic can expound at leisure without any need to elaborate on matters of so-called 'background' interest. It thus falls in with other notions like the 'implied author', the Intentionalist Fallacy, the irrelevance of biography and so forth, all of which help to perpetuate the formalist (or latterly the post-structuralist) idea of criticism as essentially a code-breaking exercise, a technique of geared-up rhetorical exegesis brought to bear upon texts that somehow exist in a realm cut off from all the puzzles and perplexities of everyday human experience. For Empson, such ideas are just a handy escape route from the critics' most difficult (but also most rewarding) task: that is to say, the necessity of reading poems or novels with a mind fully open to the range of likely motives, value-commitments and circumstantial factors that enable one to reach an informed judgement in matters of authorial intent. Concepts like 'double irony' can indeed be a help in explaining what is distinctive about a novelist's tone or ethical standpoint, just so long as they don't then become a substitute for this larger, more humanly demanding activity of reader response. Otherwise the notions of 'author' and 'reader' get emptied of all experiential or real-life content, so that narrative theorists can then come up with a pair of neatly symmetrical abstract entities (the 'implied author' and 'implied reader') whose relationship is conceived in purely circular terms, with the one becoming simply a mirror-image or ideal counterpart of the other.

In short, such criticism manages to exclude everything that Empson considers most important in the reading of imaginative literature. It allows no room for biographical interests, for genuine puzzling over an author's intentions, or for any kind of reading that puts up *resistance* – ethical or principled resistance – to what the text has to say on its own behalf in matters of evaluative judgement. Thus when Fielding addresses his various remarks to the reader of *Tom Jones*, they convey a lot more in the way of complex reciprocal ironies and shrewdly self-implicating ploys than could ever be cashed out in terms of the 'implied author' and his clone-like accomplice, the 'implied reader'. For if there is one significant fact about Fielding that justifies the critic in 'using biography', it is the knowledge we possess of his record as a magistrate, a man well practised in weighing up cases on their merits and making due allowance for the sheer variety of human motives and intentions. So when trying to figure out the ethical stance behind Fielding's tricks of double irony, we had best envisage 'a person fit to sit on the bench as a magistrate, [one who] needs to know all about the people he is to judge; indeed, the unusual thing about Fielding as a novelist is that he is always ready to consider what he would do if one of his characters came before him when he was on the bench' (1984, p. 157). And this principle extends to the reader also, since Fielding's irony is regularly deployed against those – whether fictional characters or *hypocrites lecteurs* – whose readiness to take the worst possible view (or to judge from some God-like stance of superior virtue) always lays them open to a firm moral put-down when the real situation transpires. Thus it is the reader (or the critic) who is here on trial, since the whole effect of Fielding's 'double irony' is to appeal outside the self-insulating discourse of academic criticism – its habit of invoking surrogate concepts like the 'implied author' – and show up the kinds of self-ignorance, hypocrisy and sheer bad faith that can often be produced by such strategies of evasion.

It is the same basic point that Empson makes when he reproves various critics for adopting too high-toned or censorious a view of fictive characters whose behaviour exhibits a complexity of motive irreducible to their own tidy notions of moral virtue. Thus he reacts indignantly to Dover Wilson's claim that Falstaff is not so much a 'character' as a stock figure taken straight from the old (medieval or pre-Renaissance) morality play tradition, a personified treatment of the typecast vices which Prince Hal must overcome on his path to maturity and a rightful claim to the throne (Empson, 1986). On the contrary, says Empson: if we are to think of Shakespeare's handling of the Falstaff theme as a process of 'calculated degradation', then 'I do not know what we expect our own old age to be like' (1986, p. 68). And again: the question what one makes of a character like Hamlet is always within reach of the larger question 'whether you can put up with yourself and the race of man' (1986, p. 118). What comes across here is Empson's belief that criticism is a two-way or mutually revealing affair, an activity that requires not only specialized knowledge or techniques on the critic's part, but also a willingness to ask these kinds of frankly self-implicating question. The most memorable instance is the passage in *Milton's God* where Empson reflects that 'my life has turned out pretty easy so far, but, if some bully said he would burn me alive unless I pretended to believe he had created me, I hope I would have enough honour to tell him that the evidence did not seem to me decisive. I dare not despise Satan for making this answer' (1965, p. 89). That commentators have thought such remarks irrelevant, embarrassing or wildly off the point would thus go to confirm what Empson diagnosed as the main fault of modern academic Eng. Lit.: that is to say, its habit of inventing ever more ingenious (and sophistical) pretexts for avoiding any genuine engagement with literature beyond the safe confines of professionalized method and technique. For the result of these confidently orthodox procedures was to make it almost impossible that critics should once in a while encounter a shock to their moral systems, a reading experience that didn't fit in with their stock responses or routine habits of judgement. And yet surely, as Empson says, 'it is unsafe to explain discovery in terms of a man's intellectual preconceptions, because the act of discovery is precisely that of stepping outside preconceptions' (1987a, p. 531).

One can only speculate on how Empson might have responded had he lived to witness the current fashion for neo-pragmatist theories (like that of Stanley Fish) which make a wholesale programme of denying the idea that we could ever 'step outside' our existing language-games, in-place conventions, cultural 'forms of life' etc., and discover some truth hitherto obscured by precisely those ruling assumptions (see Fish 1980, 1989). But it is clear that he would have thought it just another piece of artificial paradox-mongering, symptomatic of the fondness among literary critics for irrationalist doctrines that ignored all the evidence of real progress in the scientific disciplines, as well as the commonplace human experience of finding one's beliefs called into question by some alternative, more cogent or convincing set of principles. 'The distinguishing feature of a primitive explanation', Empson once wrote, 'is that it does not even start to explain; the mind realises that some explanation is needed but it can be fobbed off, as a hungry baby can with a soother' (1987a, p. 169). The Fish line of argument would no doubt have struck him as a 'primitive explanation' in exactly this vein, albeit decked out – like so many instances of present-day academic theorizing – with a vast apparatus of scholarly cross-reference and a high-gloss professional rhetoric. He might also have observed that Fish can bring off his regular trick of demolishing truth-claims of every kind – whether in science, philosophy, jurisprudence, ethics, psychoanalysis, literary criticism or whatever – only in so far as those disciplines have tied themselves down to a narrowly positivist or formalist idea of what counts as an adequate theoretical argument. For it is then quite easy for a skilful debunker like Fish to show that such claims simply *cannot make sense*, given their dependence on a whole informing context of values, beliefs and presuppositions which the theorist either tacitly endorses (thus falling into a version of the well-known 'hermeneutic circle'), or deludedly pretends to break with altogether (in which case his or her argument would lack any semblance of 'rational' or persuasive force). From which Fish concludes (1) that theory is an utterly useless enterprise; (2) that 'theory-talk' is just a rhetorical ploy, or at most a psychological confidence-boosting exercise; (3) that the meaning of literary or other sorts of text is always a product of consensus interests which mistake themselves for features objectively 'there' in the work; and (4) that critics – even critical theorists – would be wrong to fret unduly about this, since they can carry on talking and arguing exactly as before just so long as they accept this scaled-down version of what their activities really amount to. For there is nothing they could offer by way of persuasive counter-argument that wouldn't necessarily appeal to some existing (i.e. consensus-based or professionally sanctioned) set of ideas and values. In which case they might as well drop all the talk of truth-values, principles, method, theory etc. and learn to live happily with the unsurprising fact that theirs is a communal or culturally warranted activity with no kinds of ultimate or transcendental guarantee.

Irony is a crucial test case here, since on the one hand critics often claim to have 'discovered' some hitherto unnoticed subtle irony at work in a text, while on the other it is plain that such 'discoveries' have always had to wait until there existed a climate of opinion – or as Fish would say, an 'interpretive community' – ready to abandon the old-fashioned 'straight' interpretation and endorse the new one (the ironic reading) as somehow self-evidently better, more adequate or truer to the author's original intentions as supposedly manifest in the words on the page (Fish, 1989, pp. 180–96). For both critics (Fish and Empson) there is something deeply suspect about such claims to have pinned down irony to some clear-cut structure, some regular device or rhetorical function whose workings could then be laid out to view in a decently systematic fashion. Moreover, they both take Wayne Booth's book *A Rhetoric of Irony* as an instance of this approach pushed to the limit, and thus a useful pointer to the problems involved. But here the resemblances have an end, since Fish – unlike Empson – goes on to extract his usual neo-pragmatist moral, that is, that interpretation goes 'all the way down', and that irony is wholly a product of those readerly expectations which are created, sustained and inevitably reconfirmed by each new encounter with a literary text. 'For Booth', Fish writes, the great question is, How can you know without doubt whether a work is ironic? My answer is that you always know, but that what you know, because it rests on a structure of assumptions and beliefs (which produce both literal and ironic meanings), is subject to challenge and revision, as a result of which you will still always know, even though what you know will be different. (1989, p. 196)

In short, there is always room for change – even drastic change – in the currency-values of critical belief, like the shift that ushered in a fashion for ironic interpretations in place of older (straightforward or literal) readings. But we should be wrong to imagine that these come about – as Booth wants to show, at least in cases of 'stable' irony – through a closer attention to the 'words on the page', or a better, more adequate structural grasp of the relevant cues and clues. For the signs of ironic intent are only there to be read if we approach the text with a mind predisposed to seek out precisely such confirmatory evidence. And we shall do so, Fish argues, only in so far as we belong to a present-day 'interpretive community' which places a premium value (or a seal of professional approval) on readings that can plausibly claim to have 'discovered' some irony missed by previous critics.

When Empson reads Booth – in his 1975 review of *A Rhetoric of Irony* – he thinks the book admirable in most respects, especially for its effort to clarify the various meanings of a term which 'gets applied much too loosely, so that it had become almost useless' (1987a, p. 178). But he then goes on to find Booth often missing the point – or producing some plainly wrong interpretation – through this very attempt to tidy things up and persuade himself that the really problematical cases belong to a borderline category (that of 'unstable irony') which somehow breaks the rules of the game and is therefore a Bad Thing. Typically, Empson backs up his argument with a range of practical examples, taken not only from novels and poems but also from incidents in his own life history, including an encounter with Japanese officialdom in Korea at the time of the Manchurian takeover, an episode that involved a highly complex interplay of knowledge, ignorance and covert double irony, but whose 'structure' could hardly be spelled out in anything like the clear-cut fashion seemingly demanded by Booth. All the same, Empson thinks, there is a 'basic situation' which usually includes three people, and whose logic (or tacit background of assumptions) can be described roughly as follows:

> There is a speaker, 'A', an understanding hearer, 'B', and a censor who can be outwitted, a stupid tyrant, 'C'. A successful use of the pure form is not very frequent, because people aren't such fools as you think. However, it is even more satisfactory when 'C', though he knows what is going on, dare not complain – because the effect would be a ridiculous confession, or because the only available penalty would appear so excessive as to make him unpopular ... Or the ironist may be taking a balanced view, trying to be friends with both sides; but even so one of them can be picked out as holding the more official or straight-faced belief, and the literal meaning will support that one. If this condition did not hold, there would be no impulse to use the form. (1987a, p. 178)

The point about this passage – the nearest Empson gets to a 'structural' definition of irony – is that almost every phrase in it carries an appeal to some wider situation or interpretive context, in the absence of which one couldn't make a start in explaining how the irony worked, or how far the analyst might have to go in accounting for the sheer range of motives, interests and circumstantial factors that made up the relevant background. From which it follows that the iniquitous 'Wimsatt Law' – the orthodox veto on talk about biography, authorial intentions and so forth – is just a species of perverse self-denying ordinance, a principle which, if acted upon consistently (and even Wimsatt fails to do so, as Empson notes with satisfaction) would render literary criticism a wholly pointless and self-defeating enterprise.

Thus the trouble with Booth's tidy-minded approach is that it tries to narrow down the range of admissible 'structures' while cutting out too many aspects of the 'total situation' that enables us to interpret more complex instances as and when they arise. Again, it is Fielding who provides an interesting test case, since there are passages in *Tom Jones* – like Allworthy's 'whimsical' hope of reunion with his lately dead wife in Heaven, as related in the novel's Introduction – for which the term 'irony' seems unavoidable but somehow crassly inappropriate. As Empson reads it:

> If you grasp his feeling here, you are prepared for the deep cases of 'double irony' later in the book, as when Tom brings consternation upon Allworthy by forgiving Black George; Fielding is simply not sure himself how far a practical magistrate could allow himself to obey the precepts of Jesus. For most of the book he is confident, especially when he uses irony; but he is aware of extreme cases where he would feel doubtful. (1987a, p. 182)

So an adequate response will involve far more than could ever be provided by a 'rhetoric' of irony – no matter how elaborate – which respected the basic formalist principle that the text is all that critics have to work with, so that any imputation of authorial meaning will need to stake its case on structural features demonstrably 'there' in the work. It is this notion that underwrites Booth's strong preference for instances of 'stable' irony, that is to say, manifestations of a governing intent that the interpreter can then decode in the confident knowledge that his or her reading corresponds point-for-point to the relevant textual cues. And it is also what enables Fish to perform a merry dance around Booth's objectivist rhetoric, showing that the signs can always be read in very different ways, either 'straight' (as by literal-minded earnest dupes) or – more in line with current fashion – as leading to the endless *mise-en-abîme* of self-reflexive signification opened up by the theorists of Romantic Irony and its deconstructive avatars. For in both cases – so Fish argues – criticism will seek out just the kinds of 'evidence' required to make tolerable sense of the text on terms laid down by some existing 'interpretive community', some background consensus of scholarly ideas, values or beliefs that define the very nature of 'informed' debate within this or that socio-cultural context.

In short, interpretation goes 'all the way down', since there is nothing objectively *there* in the text – no ultimate ground of appeal, whether to authorial viewpoint, manifest structures of meaning, tokens of ironic self-distancing intent or whatever – that would settle the issue once and for all by establishing the marked superiority of one such reading over another. Most deluded of all are those critical theorists, 'positive' or 'negative', who adopt a whole range of conflicting positions on the matter of interpretive method or truth. For it is simply the case that we *do* impute intentions whenever we read a text and consent (as we must) to treat it as more than just a mass of unintelligible marks on a page (see Mitchell, 1987, Norris, 1990, pp. 77–133). No amount of anti-intentionalist argument in the Wimsatt/Beardsley mode can alter the fact that reading – like everyday conversation – is a matter of trying to figure out what an utterance means according to various contextual cues, speech-act implicatures, cultural presuppositions and so forth. But this is not to say that 'positive' theorists are right when they bring up all manner of heavyweight arguments from philology, hermeneutics, philosophical semantics, speech-act theory or whatever by way of *proving* that authorial intentions somehow live on in the 'words on the page' and must therefore be respected by any interpreter who seeks to understand the work or passage in question, as opposed to just using it as a handy pretext for some geared-up display of their own brilliance at the work's (or the author's) expense. For Fish's main purpose is precisely to show (1) that theory *has no consequences*, positive or negative; (2) that the activity of construing utterances in light of some (real or imagined) speaker's intention is simply what we mean by 'interpreting' language, quite aside from all the spurious 'theoretical' problems involved; and (3) that in fact what governs our operative ideas of intention, of right reading or fidelity to the text is a complex of present-day interpretive conventions – like the premium on 'irony' as an index of literary worth – that will always have decided the issue in advance for any critic sufficiently in touch with the latest professional rules of the game. 'Respecting intentions' is simply not an option, for on the one hand we are always implicitly doing so, like it or not, while on the other there is nothing – no hermeneutic theory, no appeal to what the text actually says, no quasi-objectivist 'rhetoric of irony' in the Wayne Booth mode – that could ever achieve the required degree of self-confident access to authorial intent.

This whole debate strikes Fish as a massive irrelevance, a tedious distraction from the critic's proper business of just getting on with the task in hand, by which he means – quite simply – playing the professional game for all it's worth and scoring points off those other more flat-footed types who still think that 'theory' is something more than a rhetorical buzz-word, a means of gaining attention or prestige at a time when such talk is regarded (absurdly) as a token of intellectual depth or grasp. The best way of demolishing these solemn pretensions is to look at the history of variant readings for any canonical text which critics have reinterpreted over and again in accordance with their likewise changing ideas of what constitutes a good (i.e. an adequately detailed, truthful or rhetorically sophisticated) approach. For it then becomes obvious that debates about the much-vaunted 'problem' of intentions – along with other vexed topics like irony, authorial viewpoint, the status of fictional truth-claims and so forth – are in fact just a kind of pseudo-theoretical spin-off, a series of high-sounding alibis or pretexts for the straightforward fact that critics differ in their interpretation of literary texts. Any position adopted in theory (or in principle) on these or other such topics will always turn out to support some set of in-place interpretive codes and conventions which carry weight only in the context of this or that language-game, social institution or cultural 'form of life'. Having a *theory* about the matter can make no difference, whether the theorist sets out (like E. D. Hirsch (1967)) to uphold the 'principle' of a decent respect for authorial intention, or whether – as more often of late – he or she prefers to celebrate the 'death of the author', the inscrutability of original meaning or a deconstructive licence to read against the grain where rhetorical complexities render such a reading possible. In the latter case critics are prone to imagine that they have *discovered* something there in the text – maybe some 'structural interference' between meaning and intent, grammar and rhetoric, constative and performative levels of sense (see de Man, 1979) – that would demonstrate their own superior powers as close-readers as against other, more naïve or deluded schools of interpretive thought. Moreover, they often make far-reaching claims for the radically transformative effects of such reading, its power to subvert all our conventional ideas about truth, language, representation, history, politics and so forth. But these claims cannot possibly hold up, Fish argues, since the only way that they could gain credence – or even make sense for the theorists who propound them – is by appealing to *some* kind of tacit consensus on what counts as an adequate piece of critical argument, no matter how marginal the interest-group involved or how far it seeks to trade on a dissident rhetoric opposed to the currency of orthodox opinion. Critics cannot fail to find what they are looking for, since the text has no meaning in and of itself, but only when read – as invariably happens – with certain interpretive ends in view or in keeping with the predisposed values and assumptions of this or that communal enterprise.

Thus deconstructionists are 'always already' convinced that a text will show signs of a disjunct relation between grammar and rhetoric, literal and figural meaning, etc., so long as one reads it with an eye sharply trained for the problematic details overlooked by more conventional exegetes. And the same applies to those other (e.g. Freudian or Marxist) variants of 'negative theory' which claim to reveal some ulterior meaning, some repressed or dissimulated motive in the text whose presence can be brought to light by a reading alert to such symptomatic evidence. Here again, the interpreter takes it for granted that there must be something demonstrably *there* in the text by which to validate the truth – or at any rate the superior diagnostic insight – of his or her reading when set against other, naïve or mystified, accounts. But in fact such claims are nothing more than a species of *post hoc* rationalization, a means of warding off the uncomfortable knowledge that interpretive conventions are all we have, that textual meaning is wholly a product of the expectations we bring to it, and therefore that critics are sadly deluded when they think to have 'discovered' some complicating feature of the work in hand, whether a subtle irony unnoticed by previous interpreters or a conflict between manifest and latent sense. For Fish, that is to say, criticism is a purely circular activity where standards of relevance, truth or right reading are always set in advance, and where interpretive foreknowledge (or presupposition) is the last – and only – court of appeal. To imagine otherwise is to fall, like Booth, into the patently self-deceiving belief that one might come up with some ironcast theory or method, some generalized 'rhetoric' of irony, which enabled one to break clean out of the hermeneutic circle by establishing a basic rule of recognition by which to judge in disputed cases. On the contrary, says Fish: such a rule could only take effect through its suasive or rhetorical force, its appeal to a certain community of readers (the aspirant rule-giver among them) who already agreed pretty much on what should count as 'evidence' of ironic intent.

In short, Booth is attempting the impossible by offering his stipulative definition of irony – or the good, 'stable' kind of irony – as that which can be grasped by rhetorical explication while also putting an end to the vagaries of 'mere' rhetoric. His argument self-deconstructs at the point where this objectivist approach breaks down and where his readings are forced to acknowledge – albeit unwittingly – the lack of any clear or tenable distinction between the two senses of the term. Thus:

> The whole of Booth's theory rests on the possibility and the undoubted fact of agreement; but he seems to think that there are two kinds of agreement, a good kind, to which persons are compelled by facts that are unassailable, and a bad kind, to which persons are forced by the illegitimate power of a discourse which rests on nothing. But unassailable facts are unassailable only because an act of persuasion has been so successful that it is no longer regarded as one, and instead has the status of a simple assertion about the world. In short, there are no facts that are not the product of persuasion, and therefore no facts that stand to the side of its operations; all agreements are the result of the process for which Booth seeks an independent ground, and therefore no agreement, however securely based it may seem for the moment, is invulnerable to challenge. (Fish, 1989, p. 194)

Of course – and Fish readily concedes the point – critics may have good *psychological and professional* reasons for ignoring this fact, or for working to persuade themselves and others that right reading is indeed possible, that interpretation is *not* just a product of vested communal interests, and therefore that criticism (their own especially) is aimed towards a demonstrable truth of the text which in turn offers an index of scholarly acumen or genuine critical insight. Such beliefs may indeed be almost indispensable in so far as they provide literary critics with a measure of professional self-esteem, a conviction that theirs is a 'real' discipline with shared standards of truth, accountability or intellectual good faith. But this leads on to yet another of Fish's favourite paradoxical twists: namely, his argument that 'anti-professionalism' (or the appeal to values that somehow transcend the dictates of careerist self-interest or academic advancement) is in fact the most thoroughly professional of attitudes, a stance that has long enjoyed great prestige among the arbiters of intellectual worth in the humanistic disciplines. And so it comes about, as Fish writes, that

> [p]rofessionalism cannot do without anti-professionalism; it is the chief support and maintenance of the professional ideology; its presence is a continual assertion and sign of the purity of the profession's intentions. In short, the ideology of anti-professionalism – of essential and independent values chosen freely by an independent self – is nothing more or less than the ideology of professionalism taking itself seriously. (1989, p. 245)

Thus the case is much the same as with 'positive' theorists who likewise adopt a high-toned rhetoric of truth, respect for authorial intentions, disinterested scholarly enquiry or whatever. For that is just what it is, a rhetorical strategy designed to gain credit (or get oneself 'taken seriously') by members of the relevant cultural community or professional interest group. And if readers respond – as Fish knows they will – by calling this a piece of low-minded cynical opportunism, then of course he will come back with the standard riposte: that those readers are invoking a rhetoric of authenticity whose persuasiveness derives entirely from the fact of its supporting their own self-image as bearers of a high cultural vocation. So professionalism, like rhetoric, goes 'all the way down', whatever one's views on the merits (or otherwise) of Fish's debunking neo-pragmatist stance. And besides, this predicament is no cause for concern since critics can (and will) carry on talking about principles, theories, values, methods, interpretive truth-claims and so forth, no matter how frequent the reminders that their talk amounts to nothing more than a species of rhetorical special pleading. For if indeed it is the case (as Fish urges) that theorizing *makes no difference* – that it merely offers suasive support for beliefs that could just as well be affirmed or upheld without benefit of theory – then equally it is true that coming out 'against theory' will have not the slightest practical effect on the conduct of these and similar debates. Things will go on pretty much as before, except that some few canny individuals – those persuaded by Fish's line of argument – will know that it is all just a matter of 'theory-talk' and that nothing really crucial is at stake in these arguments for and against theory in the strong, consequentialist sense.

It seems to me that Empson anticipated this turn in recent 'post-theoretical' debate when he held out against the formalist drive to reduce ambiguity, irony and other such tropes to a generalized poetics or a method of rhetorical close-reading indifferent to matters of biography or authorial intent. After all, it is precisely this tendency in Booth that Fish can exploit to such mischievous effect by showing how irony eludes the grasp of any self-assured methodical account, any attempt to pin it down to a clear-cut 'rhetoric' of stabilized meaning and intent. There is a standard sequence of argument in all Fish's essays, repeated in much the same form whether he is writing about theory (positive or negative), about 'principles' in literary or legal interpretation, or again, about the ethos of anti-professionalism as an instance of self-promoting professional rhetoric. The trick is to select his opponent with care, home in on some extreme or untenable statement of the theory, principle or method involved, and then – in time-honoured sophistical fashion – declare that such claims are *always* self-defeating since in this case they mustered so little resistance to Fish's well-practised line of knock-down riposte. What Empson disliked about the growing professionalization of literary studies was the fact that they could so easily be swung into just this kind of passive compliance with the dictates of an orthodox consensus view. And the formalist approach was especially vulnerable since it renounced any dealing with matters of authorial intention, biography etc., and instead took refuge in a range of quasi-objective substitute terms – from Wimsatt's idea of the poem as 'verbal icon' to Booth's 'implied author' and its various structural correlates – which offered little more than a standard pretext for various geared-up strategies of evasion.

Empson didn't live to witness the current neo-pragmatist turn with its reduction of every issue in criticism and theory to a question of what happens to be 'good in the way of belief' for some well-entrenched interpretive community defined entirely in terms of professional self-interest. But he would have seen clearly enough how this fashion came about, that is to say, how it emerged as the cynical upshot of a revolt 'against theory' whose origins lay in the failure of successive formalist (or structuralist) movements to make good their claims for a critical method that perversely denied itself any kind of access to an author's life-history or intentions. In short, the whole drift of professional Eng. Lit. since the later 1940s struck him as a sad example of the way things could go if critics allowed their minds to be captured by a false idea of special expertise – or professional method – that did nothing more than erect unnecessary obstacles to the better understanding of literary works.

Hence the note of growing impatience that marks so many of his book reviews during this period, especially those where Empson comes across some instance of New Critical precept carried into practice and (as he sees it) producing yet more evidence of the doctrine's harmful effects. In face of such 'bother-headed' theories he felt it as nothing less than a plain moral duty to insist on the fact that making sense of intentions was a basic human need, in literature as in life, and that one couldn't make adequate sense of them unless one took a waking interest in biographical matters. A letter to Philip Hobsbaum contained what is perhaps Empson's strongest statement on the topic.

> I must not make extravagant claims for a process which all persons not insane are using in all their social experience; I have only to say that the effect of renouncing it (in the unique case of the most delicate and intimate formulations of intention) produces dirty nonsense all the time, with a sort of tireless unconscious inventiveness for new kinds of nonsense.[1]

His main point, here and elsewhere, is that even the best critics will go seriously wrong if they pin their faith to a formalist method, a 'rhetoric of irony' or other such delusive system that substitutes its own kind of special expertise for the much more difficult (but rewarding) business of grasping what authors actually 'wanted to mean'. Such is Empson's quarrel with Booth's *A Rhetoric of Irony*, a

[1] Empson, letter to Philip Hobsbaum, dated 2 August 1969; cited by John Haffenden in his Introduction to *Argufying* (1987a, p. 21).

book which he admires in many respects but whose limits come out in its self-imposed restriction to an immanent or structural account of authorial intent, a refusal to entertain sources of knowledge and insight beyond those provided by the 'words on the page'.

Once again, *Tom Jones* is the test case here, since Fielding quite explicitly demands of the reader that he or she take an informed general interest in matters of real-life moral concern. Thus Booth, as Empson says,

> includes practically nothing about biography, although there is a natural connection [i.e., between our knowledge of relevant biographical details and our capacity to pick up the signs and markers of ironic intent]. When an author is admitting the source of his interest in a subject, and thereby asking the reader to share it with him, he will often want to keep the surface of his argument unbroken; perhaps to reassure one type of reader without disturbing another type. This leads to irony at once, and it is practically the only means for an author to break the Wimsatt Law, to tell some of his readers what he is not telling. Of course they may all know, with an enjoyable connivance, that he is only pretending to keep it from some of them ... A student of literature ought to be trying all the time to empathize with the author (and of course the assumptions and conventions by which the author felt himself bound); to tell him that he cannot even partially succeed is about the most harmful thing you could do. (1984, pp. vii–viii)

Of course, as Empson readily admits, there are problems about claiming to 'know' an author's intentions, not least the kind of difficulty that commentators raised with regard to his own more inventive or extravagant performances in *Seven Types*. Even so, he thought, critics like Wimsatt were missing the point, since one could always appeal (whether on Freudian or Romantic-inspirational grounds) to the idea that an author 'may be *hardly* answerable for his intentions', or that poets may unconsciously *mean* a lot more than they could possibly have realized – or explained to themselves – at the time of composition. Of course there is room for a good deal of face-saving argument in this vein, made possible partly by the semantic looseness of the English verb 'to mean', as contrasted (say) with the two different German verbs *meinen* and *bedeuten*. But Empson clearly came to feel that such defences were a bit too shuffling and evasive. Hence the very marked shift of interest in his later work, abandoning the style of verbal exegesis which had made *Seven Types* such an influential source-text for the American New Criticism, and adopting an approach that construed the vexed issue of authorial intention in a far more direct and unqualified sense of the term.

III

One can roughly distinguish three main lines of argument by which Empson sought to turn back this tide of anti-intentionalist doctrine, serving as it did – and he was quick to perceive the connection – as a prop for religious (anti-humanist) beliefs which could pass themselves off under cover of a professional concern with matters of interpretive method and technique. The first was his brisk, no-nonsense dealing with proponents of the thesis in its full-blown doctrinal form, those (like Wimsatt) who advanced it as a matter of *de jure* principle that we couldn't – or shouldn't – display the least interest in questions of authorial intent. On the contrary, says Empson:

> any speaker, when a baby, wanted to understand what people meant, why mum was cross for example, and had enough partial success to go on trying; the effort is usually carried on into adult life, though not always into old age. Success, it may be argued, is never complete. But it is nearer completeness in a successful piece of literature than in any other use of language. (1987a, p. 124)

His second line of argument we have seen already in Empson's way of opening up the intentionalist issue so as to take account of motives, biographical details and circumstantial factors that prevent it from becoming just a 'problem' in the abstract, a talking-point for puzzle-headed literary theorists. And this involves not only a view of literature as language raised to its highest power of communicative subtlety and range, but also an *ethics* of interpretation with its own, distinctively humanist sense of what constitutes an adequate response. Empson's later essays – especially those collected in *Using Biography* – all make this appeal to a standard of judgement which cannot be defined (as Booth would have it) in immanent, structural or formalist terms, but which serves none the less as a fair indication that interpreters haven't gone wide of the mark in pursuit of some orthodox or modish idea of what the text ought to mean by their own current lights. Thus Fielding's 'double irony' only achieves its full (intended) effect if one allows for meanings that could never be explained by any 'rhetoric' (or skilled hermeneutical technique) compliant with the dictates of formalist method. It involves the realization

> that any man who puts forward a general ethical theory implies a claim to have very wide ethical experience, therefore should be ready to laugh at his own pretensions; but also he isn't likely to mean nothing when he jeers at you for failing to see his point. Actually, the modern critic does know what kind of thing the secret is; but he has been badgered by neo-classicism and neo-Christianity and what not, whereas the secret is humanist, liberal, materialist, recommending happiness on earth and so forth, so he assumes it is dull, or the worldly advice of a flippant libertine. (1984, p. 134)

And if the tone of this passage seems wildly remote from what we are used to in present-day academic criticism, then so much the worse for us, Empson would say. For it struck him that the whole endeavour of post-war professionalized literary scholarship – especially in its more theoretical manifestations – had been invented in order to conceal that 'secret' and promulgate a different set of values, a neo-Christian ethic whose chief purpose was to raise criticism into a kind of high-priestly expert discourse and thus prevent readers (students in particular) from challenging its sacrosanct truths. The best hope of reversing this gloomy trend was to stick up for authorial intentions wherever possible and show how the professional disdain for such talk was just the product of an orthodox (proto-theological) cult with its own very definite value-agenda and design on the reader's powers of imaginative grasp.

So Empson's first two lines of counter-argument involved a resistance to theory, or at least the kind of theory that was currently so much in vogue. But there was also a need, as Empson saw it, to provide some *alternative* theoretical approach, some sufficiently generalized account of how criticism could (1) respect the claims of authorial intentions, (2) demonstrate the basic rationality of language, as against the New Critical cult of 'paradox' and other such bywords of poetic unreason and (3) bring out the essential relation between a secularist hermeneutics of this sort and an ethics based upon the same principles of enlightened mutual understanding and regard for the varieties of human experience, values, belief-systems etc. Such was his aim in *The Structure of Complex Words*, a book of extraordinary range and argumentative force whose neglect can only be explained by the fact of its standing so utterly opposed to the currents of orthodox critical opinion. Indeed, one could hardly find a better counter-example to Fish's claim that interpretive conventions go 'all the way down', so that any theorist who hopes to make sense *even on his or her own terms of argument* must always appeal to some established consensus of in-place values and beliefs. For it is not simply a matter of Empson's advancing a theory that places him way outside that 'interpretive community' whose foregone assumptions – according to Fish – make up the very conditions of intelligibility for any such project. More specifically, his argument in *Complex Words* is aimed squarely against all versions of the consensualist or neo-pragmatist doctrine that 'truth' is nothing more than what is (presently and contingently) 'good in the way of belief'.[2] The book sets out to defend a rational-humanist position that encompasses not only issues in the province of literary criticism but also some of the most fundamental questions in linguistics, anthropology, philosophy of mind, ethics and historiography. And it does so, moreover, from the standpoint of a critic who is by no means given to premature absolutes or strong universalist truth-claims, and whose experience of other cultures – notably through his periods of teaching in China and Japan – left him with a keen nose for any form of smug ethnocentric prejudice.

But Empson was also quick to perceive how relativism could become yet another kind of cramping orthodoxy, one that gave interpreters a ready excuse for ignoring (or adapting to their own revisionist purposes) whatever fell outside the charmed circle of received Eng. Lit. opinion. For the relativist argument can easily lean over from an attitude of easy-going tolerant pluralism to an attitude which says: since *all* beliefs are a product of some localized cultural consensus, 'interpretive community' etc., and since *nobody* can get outside the value-judgements or informing presuppositions that characterize their own time and place, *therefore* (QED) it is simply impossible to estimate other people's motives, meanings or intentions except in terms of what locally counts as an adequate or relevant mode of understanding. This is, of course, the familiar rhetorical device by which Fish contrives to 'prove' the self-refuting character of all claims to criticize consensus values or beliefs from some alternative ground of judgement. Recent analytical philosophers (Hilary Putnam among them) have seen very well how it leads

[2] See especially the two appendices to *Complex Words* (pp. 414–43) where Empson anticipates likely objections to his theory from a range of philosophical, linguistic and socio-methodological standpoints, most of them having some affinity with the current neo-pragmatist line of thought.

to an equally familiar relativist impasse, a position where its claims turn out to undermine their own argumentative force. And Putnam has also shown, in a vigorous rejoinder, that such liberal-sounding talk may often have a hidden (and none too liberal) agenda to promote, one that makes it easier for first-world philosophers, anthropologists, political theorists and the rest to promote their world-view under cover of the notion that they *have no choice* but to interpret other cultures as seen from this particular – admittedly self-interested – standpoint (Putnam, 1981; 1983). Thus the upshot of Fish's neo-pragmatist argument writ large, so to speak, in an age of US global hegemony would be to justify any amount of ethnocentric bias by invoking the ultimate relativity of values and the strictly incommensurable character of different ideologies, belief-systems, cultural 'forms of life' and so forth. In which case the appeal to what is 'good in the way of belief' can only come down to the somewhat less edifying question of which power-bloc (or 'interpretive community') has the greater measure of world-wide economic and socio-cultural clout. For this conclusion seems impossible to avoid if one follows out the logic of the relativist argument along with its usual adjunct or corollary, the incommensurability thesis. So there is good reason to accept Putnam's claim that relativism is a double-edged doctrine, and that its pluralist credentials need looking at more closely in light of this deep-laid ambivalence.

A review written in 1949 finds Empson taking a fairly relaxed approach on suchlike philosophical problems. Thus it is, he remarks, 'a familiar paradox; any serious attempt at establishing a relativity turns out to establish an absolute; in the case of Einstein the velocity of light, and I understand a good deal more by this time' (1987a, p. 212). The error comes in when relativists assert that theirs is the only reputable game in town, or the only outlook capable of providing a defence against authoritarian truth-claims or forms of unwarranted doctrinal imposition. Thus:

> It seems to me that twenty years ago we were too frightened of absolutes, because of a confusion with politics which even the most abstract mind can hardly escape. To believe in an absolute beauty or goodness does no political harm, so long as you don't believe that you yourself have got a secret ticket into its bedroom that you can put up for sale. As soon as a body of priests or commissars or what not is organised (as has been done so often) on the specific basis of claiming that each such official has been issued with the secret key – there you have got something to worry about. (pp. 212–13)

But over the next few years Empson's attitude changes, partly (I would guess) as a result of his exposure to the new growth-industry of academic criticism that combined an ultra-relativist disregard for the virtues of plain-prose reason with the commitment to a full-blown aesthetic ideology, a creed with its own kinds of absolute value grounded in the proto-theological tenets of formalist precept and practice. His review of Wimsatt's *The Verbal Icon* (1955) marks the point at which Empson came up against this movement in its most doctrinaire and – to him – most repellently orthodox guise. Thus 'I became rather startled when I realised that he [Wimsatt] takes it for granted there is only one right code of morals, a thing already known to himself' (1987a, p. 126).

What Empson found so disturbing in this new school of thought was the way that it managed to extrapolate rigid dogmas (like the veto on talk about authors' intentions, the 'heresy' of paraphrase etc.) from a flat denial that poetry made sense according to the normal rational-deductive processes of human linguistic grasp. Hence his aversion to the cult of 'paradox' that took such a hold among the American New Critics, and which gave them scope (as Empson saw it) for all kinds of irrational mystery-mongering and covert religious propaganda. This technique derived from the 'discontinuity principle' announced by earlier theorists like Eliot and T. E. Hulme; namely, the idea that poetry belonged to a realm quite apart from the interests and values of straightforward prose communication, and that critics were falling into some kind of godless, humanistic 'heresy' if they ignored this basic (ontological) difference. Worst of all was the effect that such notions had when put to work in the service of a full-scale professional enterprise – the New Criticism – whose partisans were fortified in their own dogmatic beliefs by claiming what amounted to a doctrine of infallibility, a privileged exemption from the usual requirements of moral, intellectual and political debate. Thus in Wimsatt's case 'the idea that a piece of writing which excited moral resistance might be a discovery in morals, a means of learning what was wrong with the existing system, somehow cannot enter his mind; and yet surely this has often happened and provides the only interesting question for his article' (1987a, p. 126). Empson's main point here – developed most fully in the essays that went toward *Complex Words* – was that reading could only generate such 'resistance' (and thus give rise to genuine moral 'discoveries') so long as the reader was not prevented from exercising his or her powers of rational judgement by some misconceived doctrine, like the 'fallacy' of paraphrase, which made it unthinkable that poems should effectively *argue a case*, and should thereby provoke an active critical response, whether hostile or sympathetic. The attack on such ideas seemed to him nothing less than a collapse of enlightened principles and values, a reversion to habits of unquestioning doctrinal adherence which could always be used to insinuate beliefs of a thoroughly irrationalist (and morally harmful) character. Hence what Empson sets out to provide in the various chapters – 'theoretical' and 'practical' – that make *Complex Words* such a sturdy defence of the rational-humanist position. For it is his central claim in that book that poetry is *not* a 'special' kind of language, cut off from the normal modes and procedures of open-minded critical debate. On the contrary, he argues: good poems always work by engaging the mind at full self-critical stretch, and any dogma that gets in the way of this process can only produce bad readings (or excessive admiration for poetry that doesn't so work).

Hence also Empson's quarrel with I. A. Richards, who had argued that poetic meaning required an 'emotive' (as opposed to a cognitive) approach to questions of meaning and value (see Richards, 1926a, p. 6). Empson, by contrast, claims that when a word has alternative interpretations, it will be a 'cognitive one' which has 'the important effects on sentiment and character' (1951, p. 10). And *Complex Words* goes on to develop this argument through chapters that range all the way from 'technical' issues in the realm of logico-semantic analysis to readings of Shakespeare, Milton, Pope, Wordsworth, Keats and others where this interpretive 'machinery' is tested against varying odds of paradox, seemingly 'emotive' rhetoric, or mystifying commentary on the part of those critics who take an opposing (anti-cognitivist) line. In my view the book is remarkably successful in its crusade against these far from obsolete items of belief. Above all, Empson seeks to vindicate the claim that 'theory' need not follow the path marked out by the zealots of New Critical doctrine, but that it can – and should – put interpreters back in touch with the relevance (and general accessibility) of authorial intentions, the basic rationality of language and the prospects of achieving a workable synthesis of textual close-reading and a broad-based historical approach. Thus, as Empson argues, 'it is because the historical background is so rich and still so much alive ... that one can fairly do what seems absurdly unhistorical, make a set of equations from first principles' (1951, p. 213). And, furthermore, this attentiveness to the sometimes discrepant relation between the logic, the semantic grammar and the rhetoric of literary works is what enables Empson to resist the kind of orthodox reading – the purely circular 'logic' of foregone interpretive assumptions – which prevents critics like Wimsatt from perceiving any challenge to their routine habits of thought. For there was, he came to think, no hope of refuting this widespread anti-humanist and irrationalist trend unless one could demonstrate the plain *inadequacy* – the failure in matters of basic intellectual grasp – of any critical doctrine that pinned its faith to a rhetoric of 'paradox' completely divorced from the 'tradition of fair public debate'.

If *Complex Words* is Empson's great theoretical *summa*, leading him into regions that at times seem remote from the interests of 'practical criticism', one can find many passages in his other writings that make the same point in a somewhat more direct and (often) polemical style. One such piece is his 1963 essay 'Argufying in Poetry', where Empson extends his case against New Criticism and its damaging moral effects to the French Symbolist movement whose influence (*via* Eliot) he thinks largely to blame for this current fashionable *trahison des clercs*. 'Argufying', he writes,

> is perhaps a tiresomely playful word, but it makes my thesis more moderate; I do not deny that thoroughly conscientious uses of logic could become a distraction from poetry. Argufying is the kind of arguing we do in ordinary life, usually to get our own way; I do not mean nagging by it, but just a not specially dignified kind of arguing. This has always been one of the things people enjoy in poems; and it can be found in every period of English literature; but the effect of the Symbolist movement is that you are forbidden to do it, with no reason given; except that the anti-intellectual movement, which has been one of the causes of Symbolism, tells you that thinking is sordid or low-class. What I want to say amounts to a revolt against Symbolism. (1987a, p. 167)

This 'revolt' had to do with Empson's life-long admiration for argumentative poets like Donne, his growing distaste for the 'Eliotic' manner of high-toned pious obscurantism, and also – most importantly – his sense that critics were now being led into all kinds of false and morally corrupting belief by their refusal to read with a 'waking interest' in what the poet actually had to say. Of course, as he admits, 'good poems have been written which appear to carry out the Symbolist rules'; indeed, 'the best poems written in English during this century are Symbolist, and they are very good' (p. 167). Clearly Empson is thinking of *The Waste Land* here, a poem he admired early and late, although his 1970 essay on Eliot goes every way around – biographical, historical, psychological, family-anecdotal – in order to undermine its Symbolist pretensions and tease out the sense at a basically narrative level (1984, pp. 187–200).

Such treatment is justified, in Empson's view, because the fashion has 'gone on long enough; poets are now finding the rules an obstacle, all the more so because literary theorists talk as if no other kind of poetry is possible' (1987a, p. 167). In fact, his own poems of the Cambridge years had been an odd mixture of 'conceited' intellectual argument in the Donne manner and hints of a different, more obscurely analogical style for which Eliot (and indeed the French Symbolists) were one likely source of inspiration. Thus it may be no coincidence that Empson officially 'gave up' writing poetry at a time when he was starting work on *Complex Words*, when the claims of reason (or 'fair public debate') were a matter of increasingly urgent concern and when his interests had veered sharply away from anything resembling Eliot's idea of the modern (post-Symbolist) line of poetic descent. Be that as it may, there is no doubt that he regarded the French influence on Anglo-American literary theory as a lamentable series of episodes which the odd few Symbolist 'successes' (like *The Waste Land*) did little to redeem or offset. For it seemed to Empson that things had got steadily worse with the passage from an 'old' New Criticism whose ideas about poetry, though false and misleading, at least had the merit of focusing attention on real complexities demonstrably there in the text, to a school of thought (post-structuralist or deconstructive) where theory became an end in itself, an excuse for leaving literature behind altogether and delighting in the prospects thus opened up for an endless display of free-wheeling interpretive licence. At any rate, such was Empson's regular response when confronted with evidence that British critics had been picking up ideas from the French. It all tended to confirm his suspicion – going back over several decades – that literary theorists were exceptionally prone to chase after any new idea that gratified their sense of professional self-esteem.

His feelings were summed up in a letter of 1971, addressed to the present author and explaining what he thought was so wrong with the current state of 'advanced' literary opinion. For the record, I had sent him Derrida's essay 'Structure, Sign and Play in the

Discourse of the Human Sciences', Paul de Man's 'Literary History and Literary Modernity' and some pieces by Barthes including (as I recall) 'The Discourse of History' and various items from *Mythologies*. 'I feel very bad', Empson wrote,

> not to have answered you for so long, and not to have read those horrible Frenchmen you posted to me. I did go through the first one, Jacques Nerrida [*sic*], and nosed about in several others, but they seem to me so very disgusting, in a simple moral or social way, that I cannot stomach them. Nerrida does express the idea that, just as people were talking grammar before grammarians arose, so there are other unnoticed regularities in human language and probably in other human systems. This is what I meant by the book title *The Structure of Complex Words*, and it was not an out-of-the-way idea, indeed I may have got it from someone else, but of course it is no use unless you try to present an actual grammar, an actual grammar of the means by which a speaker makes his choice while using the language correctly. This I attempted to supply, and I do not notice that the French ever even try ... They use enormously fussy language, always pretending to be plumbing the very depths, and never putting your toe into the water. Please tell me I am wrong. (Cited in 1987a, pp. 52–3)

I follow John Haffenden in printing this passage exactly as it appeared in Empson's letter, since the sheer exasperation comes across most effectively in the mix-up over Derrida's name and the unlikelihood that anyone – let alone Empson – could so misread 'Structure, Sign and Play' as to think it a muddled attempt to do what grammarians had always been doing, at least when not distracted from their proper business by the siren-call of speculative thought. Of course it would be wrong to mount some generalized case about Empson's 'resistance to theory' on the basis of such comments fired off in haste and manifesting a resolute incomprehension of Derrida's meticulous (though, to Empson, perverse and 'bother-headed') arguments. All the same the passage does find numerous parallels in the essays and reviews of Empson's later years, among them his markedly hostile pieces on Raymond Williams's *Keywords* and Frank Kermode's *The Genesis of Secrecy* (1987a, pp. 516–21; 184–9).

In short, he came to feel that 'theory' had been kidnapped by a conspiracy of geared-up professional types whose devotion to unreal problems in the realm of language, meaning and representation was a cover for their shameful lack of concern with the human (social and ethical) issues that alone made the study of literature a worthwhile occupation. Of his own earlier work – *Seven Types of Ambiguity* in particular – Empson ruefully acknowledged that it had to take some of the blame for that nit-picking style of verbal exegesis, coupled with a cavalier disregard for questions of biography and authorial intent, whose upshot was this latest appalling phase of high mandarin 'textualist' mystification. What he says about Kermode (see Kermode, 1979) is a fairly mild example of the bluff no-nonsense tone which Empson tended to adopt whenever such books came in for review. 'We know that Oscar Wilde is much revered on the mainland' Empson writes, 'and it looks as if Kermode has merely been getting the aesthetic nineties echoed back at him' (1987a, p. 516). His main objection to the new French criticism was that it worked out in practice as a means of excluding all truth-claims, values or argumentative viewpoints that didn't subscribe to its own fixed agenda. That is to say, it offered yet another, more extravagant instance of the way that these seductive ultra-relativist doctrines could be used to promote a mystifying rhetoric which seemingly opened up the text to all manner of divergent interpretive views, but which in fact placed authority firmly in the hands of a specialized interest group – a 'hermeneutic mafia' – skilled in debating such matters. Here, as with the 'old' New Critics, an anti-cognitivist drive to block the appeal to any truth 'outside' the play of textual representations very easily becomes a doctrinaire claim that only certain interpreters have the 'secret key', the ticket that gives them privileged access to whatever dark meanings the text may reluctantly reveal.

Empson was quick to discern the hints of a quasi-theological dimension to this latest line of high-powered theoretical talk. Thus he singles out Kermode's treatment of the episode from the gospel of Mark where the disciples ask Jesus why he chooses to speak in such riddling parables, and Jesus replies: 'That seeing they may see, and not perceive, and hearing they may hear, and not understand, and it should be forgiven them.' Of this passage Kermode remarks that Jesus must be 'telling stories in order to ensure that they will miss the point'. But this strikes Empson as just the sort of text that shouldn't be taken on trust as an instance of divine wisdom, human fallibility or the profoundly paradoxical nature of religious understanding. The disciples go on to question Jesus about the parable of the sower, at which point he responds simply, 'The sower soweth the word' and offers nothing more by way of explanation. But come now, says Empson: 'this is an unusually pointless allegory. Does it mean that the seeds which fell on stony ground are doomed to eternal torture? It suggests that God is a casual and wasteful type of farmer: not an intolerable view, but then he ought not to put the blame on us' (1987a, p. 518).

The tone and gist of this passage are very like those of *Milton's God*: a forthright appeal to common-sense values and 'decent human feelings', coupled with a sturdy rejection of theological paradox-mongering and an insistence that we attend to the story-line (or the logic of motive and narrative situation), rather than making the episode a pretext for 'deep' allegorical rumblings on the critic's part. And this is what most offends Empson about Kermode's approach to questions of interpretive method and truth, whether in the context of biblical criticism or in his dealing with the topic of narrative 'secrets' in novelists like Joyce and Henry Green. His book seems to argue 'that no history or biography can be believed, but must be regarded as a kind of novel', and moreover that 'any narrative is necessarily incomplete, and the details left out may for some readers be the important ones – what is taken for granted may become the crucial question' (1987a, p. 516). Such ideas are fairly harmless, Empson thinks, so long as one doesn't take the next (post-structuralist) step of denying all commerce between word and world, or declaring what amounts to a rigid embargo on any attempt to understand texts in light of their socio-historical background and the author's likely motives in writing as he or she did. For the result of this attitude is to set the interpreter up as a privileged dispenser of the only kind of 'truth' that counts, that is to say, the message that no truths exist, that textuality (or narrative convention) goes all the way down, and therefore that meaning can only be divined through expert procedures whose operative rules are known to just a handful of skilled exegetes.

So one can see why Empson expressed such deep misgivings about a style of commentary – backed up by a range of 'advanced' theoretical ideas – which allowed critics to divine all manner of narrative secrets, typological significance, intertextual allusions and so forth, while claiming exemption from the basic need to make sense of what they read in straightforward moral and historical terms. What this amounted to (he thought) was a thoroughly regressive habit of mind, a revival of Christian exegetical techniques for which perhaps T. S. Eliot had opened the way with his admiring comments on the sermons of Lancelot Andrewes and their devotional method of extracting multiple layers of allegorical sense, or 'dividing the word of God' (Eliot, 1928). It thus ignored the whole history of brave endeavour on the part of those secularizing critics and commentators who had striven against massive odds of entrenched theological and institutional power to establish that the gospels contained such a mass of anachronisms, errors of fact, contradictions and downright historical absurdities that they could not any longer be treated as a source of revealed truth vouchsafed to some elite group of knowing insiders. Kermode strikes a more ambivalent stance, renouncing any claim to belong to this privileged community – since he writes expressly from a position of 'clerkly scepticism' that acknowledges the modern 'hermeneutics of suspicion' produced by a long history of secular thought – but also seizing every possible pretext for the display of a specialized interpretive insight unavailable to other, more literal-minded exegetes. And it is just this aspect of Kermode's book that Empson singles out as a gloomy indication of the current theoretical trend. In short, 'there is no problem about whether we may read St Mark as a novel, but there really is a problem about whether Kermode and the rest of his school are allowed to read a novel properly' (1987a, p. 521). His review typically closes on a conciliatory note, remarking that '[Kermode's] last chapter about the mystery of the Gospel, its incessant glimmering of the unapprehensible, is a fine piece. This is the way Whistler contrived to look across the Thames' (p. 521). But the compliment may appear more double-edged if one recalls Empson's previous remark on the damaging effect of such aestheticist notions when applied in conjunction with a hermeneutic theory that denies any appeal to truth-claims or evidence outside the charmed circle of interpretive foreknowledge. Thus Kermode, in Empson's words, 'looks at a landscape with half-closed eyes through a mist, or in a Claude-glass, or upside down from between his legs; and this is not a good way to read a novel, which is usually better read as if it were a history' (p. 516).

It seems to me that Empson had good reason for thinking that these new forms of textual criticism were headed toward an orthodox consensus with distinctly theological overtones. The trend is most visible – oddly enough – in thinkers of a firmly post-structuralist or neo-pragmatist persuasion, those for whom 'truth' is entirely a product of cultural conventions, interpretive communities, Foucauldian 'discourses', signifying practices, 'final vocabularies' (in the phrase of Richard Rorty) or modes of textual representation which supposedly prevent any access to a knowledge that wouldn't be 'always already' a figment of rhetorical or narrative contrivance (see Norris 1990; 1991). What such arguments very often produce is a strain of dogmatic relativism – or a flat refusal to entertain alternative viewpoints – which sits (to say the least) somewhat uneasily with their liberal-pluralist claim to respect the variety of human cultures, values and belief-systems. It is a version of the paradox noted by Empson and philosophers like Hilary Putnam: namely, the fact that relativist doctrines have a habit of turning into ready-made pretexts for sticking to one's cultural world-view since that, after all, provides the only interpretive framework within which one could possibly understand *anything*, including the beliefs of other people or communities that differed radically (but how could one know?) from the ideas and attitudes current in one's own (Norris 1985; Putnam, 1981). And from this point it is a short distance to those forms of high-textualist theory which outdo even the 'old' New Criticism in their stern contempt for any kind of reading that appeals to factual or historical truth-claims – or, God forbid, to reconstructions of likely authorial intention – beyond what is given to rhetorical analysis in the current post-structuralist mode.

Empson finds a useful test case in Kermode's treatment of the 'legend' of Sir Philip Sidney, telling how, when 'lying wounded on a battlefield, the aristocratic young officer was brought a cup of water, but handed it on to a wounded trooper, saying: "Thy need is greater than mine."' Kermode sees this as a story quite removed from questions of historical authenticity, since it was first set down by Sidney's friend and admirer, Fulke Greville, some twenty-five years after the incident (supposedly) occurred, and his biography then had to wait yet another forty years before being published, so that the time lapse would have made it impossible to check out the details on a reliable first-hand basis. Besides, Kermode comments, 'we know from what he says of Sidney's own writings that Greville approved of characters in books only when their conduct might serve as an example to the reader'. And again: 'there were no surviving eyewitnesses to his dying act, for which we have only Greville's word, and it has been pointed out that Greville seems to have been remembering a passage in Plutarch's *Life of Alexander*' (cited in 1987a, pp. 516–17). All of which Empson finds highly unconvincing, not least for its failure to consider the obvious possibility that Sidney also knew the passage from Plutarch and was behaving in exactly the manner prescribed. The idea that this episode could only have been concocted as a fictive *exemplum* long after the event – at any rate, for all that we can know – strikes Empson as a piece of textualist fabrication that simply falls apart as soon as one switches to a rational appraisal of the story and its background situation. But, of course, this involves a flouting of the rules by which literary theorists of this 'puzzle-headed' tendency insist on treating everything as an imaginary construct out of their own theoretical predilections. Thus 'Kermode feels that the man making a document at a desk, by copying bits from previous documents – he is real, but any man on a battlefield is a kind of puppet. Even Sidney, though a writer himself, could not have done any copying on a battlefield, when he was a puppet' (1987a, p. 517). In short, the main effect of this latest critical trend is to stop interpreters from doing what they always need to do when confronted with such a case: that is to say, making the best possible sense of it with reference to the known background of events, the circumstantial logic and the likeliest reasons why the characters involved should have acted in this way or that. By denying themselves access to any such knowledge – by treating the text (or 'intertext') as all that criticism has to work with – interpreters not only create all manner of unnecessary puzzles and paradoxes, but also contrive to suggest that since *everything* is a fiction, and since historical occurrences have no 'reality' outside the text, therefore we should think of their own activity as a paradigm instance of human understanding in general. Clearly there are large disciplinary claims being advanced under cover of this modish textualist creed, and Empson thinks it a matter of some importance that the claims should not go unchallenged.

It is worth citing some more from his comments on the Sidney/Greville episode since they bring out both the logic of Empson's counter-argument and the extent of his quarrel with the current post-structuralist wisdom. In fact, I shall need to quote at length in order to make the point.

I do not mind the evident craving of Kermode to assault the story, only his conception of evidence. *When* were there no surviving eye-witnesses, pray? The man who brought the cup must have been one, at the time ... 'The story was first told' twenty-five years later – how on earth can Kermode claim to know this? Greville was a clumsy writer, prone to the labours of the file, but he was the same age as Sidney and a close friend, and had been in the Low Countries, taking notes, just around the time when Sidney died there. Kermode would be credible if he said: 'The story was first written down . . .'. But even this is very unlikely. Greville would write notes as soon as he got reports, and write them up at his leisure for a formal memoir. And what can we make of the phrase 'characters in books', implying that Sidney became a mere figment in a novel as soon as he stopped writing his novel? (1987a, p. 517)

Of course this is all exceedingly remote from the methods, assumptions and preferred idiom of present-day literary theory. For one thing, it totally ignores the standard veto on talk of historical background, documentary evidence, authorial motives or other such items of (so-called) 'extraneous' interest. Moreover, it assumes that the best way to understand *any* kind of text – historical, biographical or fictive – is to ask the sort of question that would occur to an investigator keen to work out what actually happened in some given case, and ready to undertake a rational reconstruction of the events and motivating factors involved. For otherwise there is nothing to prevent the interpreter from devising all sorts of ingenious ploy – like the appeal to narrative 'secrets' divined through the play of intertextual or typological allusion – which can then claim exemption from commonplace standards of critical accountability.

Thus Empson's approach is much the same whether he is writing about Sidney's (presumably) real-life experience or offering some plausible series of conjectures by which to make sense of puzzling episodes in a poem like *Paradise Lost* or a novel like *Tom Jones*. In both cases there is a need to supply some measure of informed guesswork, some appeal to that larger context of humanly intelligible actions and motives which may not be demonstrably 'there' in the text, but which none the less constitutes the precondition for any kind of adequate response. However, this is definitely *not* to say – in keeping with the current post-structuralist wisdom – that there is no difference between factual and fictive modes of narrative discourse, since both display the same varied forms of emplotment, modalities of viewpoint, rhetorical structures or whatever (see White 1973; 1978). The difference is simply that we read one, and not the other, with a knowledge that it claims veridical status and should therefore be assessed more directly in terms of those various operative truth-conditions – causal, circumstantial, chronological, socio-historical etc. – that properly apply when we attempt to make sense of some particular real-world sequence of events. It is the same kind of knowledge that we bring to bear when interpreting works of fiction, except that in this case the reader is aware that the world in question is *to some extent* an imaginary construct, one that no doubt involves the suspension of certain (e.g. factual or historical) truth-claims, but which still makes reference to a whole vast range of background information whose primary source is our knowledge and experience of other (non-literary) modes of understanding (see Pavel, 1987; Norris, 1991).

Clearly the balance will shift a good deal from one type of novel to another, so that (for instance) a *nouveau roman* or a typical piece of postmodernist fiction would hardly make sense on the terms established by works in the high realist tradition, or by a text like *War and Peace* which makes explicit reference to real-life historical characters and events. But it is equally clear that any attempt to devise a comparative ontology of fictional worlds – on a scale that would run, roughly speaking, from George Eliot, Zola or Tolstoy at the one extreme to Sterne, Borges or Italo Calvino at the other – must eventually come up against the sheer impossibility of making such distinctions stick. For it would soon become evident (1) that even the most committed works of postmodernist, experimental or anti-mimetic fiction involve some appeal to a shared background of truths and realities 'outside' the text; (2) that, conversely, 'realism' in literature is always shot through with fictive elements that prevent (or complicate) any direct passage from text to world; and (3) that one could only address the topic of 'truth in fiction' by working on a sentence-by-sentence basis and showing that (e.g.) *War and Peace* or a novel like Vonnegut's *Slaughterhouse Five* alternate constantly between the two types of discourse. In which case it might be thought that post-structuralism must inevitably have the last word, since in principle there is no good reason why this argument should not be extended beyond the province of narrative fiction to encompass *all* kinds of narrative, including works of historical scholarship or factual-documentary research. At any rate, such is the standpoint adopted by many partisans of current critical theory in its 'advanced' (i.e., post-structuralist or pan-textualist) form. And it is precisely this tendency that Empson deplores, on account of its leaving the interpreter free to attribute any kind of modish significance to the text under cover of a neo-orthodox creed with its own obscurantist ends in view.

Of course, it is not only post-structuralist critics who have made heavy weather of this 'problem' of explaining how truth can play any role in fictional texts. Analytic philosophers have also been much exercised by the topic, coming up with various more-or-less technical answers, from Russell's 'theory of descriptions' to the argument – as canvassed by speech-act theorists – that fiction involves a lifting of the usual requirements (or types of 'illocutionary force') that pertain to utterances offered in the mode of straightforward truth-telling discourse (see Pavel, 1987). But one cannot help feeling that there is less to this debate than meets the eye of well-trained critics and philosophers. For, as Empson remarks, this is one of those issues that only crop up when reading has become a highly specialized activity, attached to certain guild-values or professional interests that place a high premium on difficulties of exactly this kind. Otherwise it should be fairly evident that the reading of novels involves nothing more mysterious than a capacity to pick out the bits that have to do with matters of real-world knowledge, and a readiness to treat what remains as a product of fictive contrivance or imaginary projection. And this is not just an issue in the routine shop-talk of 'puzzle-headed' literary theorists, since the ability to distinguish truth from falsehood – and to see how fiction forms (so to speak) an intermediate zone between the two – is closely tied up with that history of secularizing thought whose greatest achievement is the freedom to challenge the truth-claims of revealed or dogmatic religion, and whose legacy Empson thinks threatened by this latest form of fashionable Lit. Crit. parlance.

In a recent book I have argued the case for Spinoza as the first modern thinker who addressed this topic of truth in fiction, and who thus laid the groundwork for a critical hermeneutics that would draw upon textual scholarship, comparative philology, historical research, political theory and narrative analysis in order to break the monopoly of those who would restrict the practice of scriptural exegesis to a narrow interest group of like-minded orthodox interpreters (Norris, 1991). What this involved, first and foremost, was a principled refusal to treat the sacred text as a vehicle of truths known only to readers with the proper, self-authorizing warrant to pronounce on matters of ultimate concern. For such a doctrine could produce all manner of harmful effects, from the imposition of a hard-line monolithic creed (with punitive sanctions attached) to the growth of rival 'interpretive communities', each claiming its own unique access to Truth as revealed through some privileged insight or specialized hermeneutical procedure, and thus giving rise to the history of civil discord that had continued more or less uninterrupted from the origins of Judaeo-Christian religion down to Spinoza's own time. The only way of avoiding these conflicts – or resisting the appeal of charismatic figures whose authority derived from suchlike textualist ploys – was to open the Scriptures up to a process of rational critique and socio-historical commentary which would lay bare their manifold factual errors, discrepancies of detail, chronological enormities etc., and thus make it plain to any competent reader that they *were not and could not be* the word of God vouchsafed to some elect minority of knowing exegetes. And this entailed another crucial line of argument, first developed by Spinoza and then taken up by various demythologizing commentators, from the nineteenth-century Higher Criticism to present-day theorists of fiction like Pierre Macherey (1978). Briefly stated, it is the argument that narrative fictions are neither 'true' nor 'false' in any straightforward, unproblematical sense of those terms, but that they offer a knowledge – a true understanding – of the falsehoods, errors or misrecognitions by which texts contrive to accommodate or reconcile the conflict between their avowed (manifest) and their latent ('unconscious' or ideologically determined) structures of meaning.

Such is Macherey's Marxist understanding of Spinoza's three-fold distinction between truth, untruth and fiction, an approach that derives very largely from the work of Althusser and Balibar, themselves much indebted to Spinozist ideas, as can be seen from numerous passages in *Reading Capital* (Althusser and Balibar, 1970). Most importantly, it shows how narrative fictions are a hybrid or multiplex genre of discourse, on the one hand performing the work of imaginary (ideological) recruitment, while on the other providing all the materials for a diagnostic reading in the Marxist-structuralist mode that can bring out the extent of this deep-laid rift between *what the text says* about its own project and *what the text reveals* about its own material and socio-historical conditions of production. All of which goes to affirm Spinoza's great importance as the first thinker to have decisively broken with that 'religious myth of reading' (Macherey's phrase) which conceived interpretation as the questing-back for some divinely authorized meaning or truth that invested certain texts – and certain well-placed exegetes – with an insight beyond reach of critical scrutiny or reasoned counter-argument.

It is the same basic issue that Empson raises with regard to Kermode's super-subtle treatment of narrative 'secrets' in biblical and secular narrative. More generally, it helps to explain his attitude of sturdy rationalist dissent when faced with the various schools and movements of present-day literary theory. What these interpreters are letting us in for, he thinks, is a wholesale regression to forms of textual exegesis which appear to offer plenty of scope for the exercise of free-ranging critical response, but which in fact stake their own authority – and their vested institutional power – on a mystified appeal to occult truths available only through expert divinatory techniques. Having first discerned this tendency in Wimsatt, Cleanth Brooks and the 'old' New Criticism, Empson was dismayed to find it resurgent – and assuming a yet more sophisticated form – in the latest wave of French-influenced literary theory. For the effect of such ideas was precisely to reverse that process of enlightened or secularizing thought which had liberated commentary from its erstwhile deference to the truth-claims of scriptural revelation.

Not that Kermode counts himself a member of any such *de facto* privileged community or hermeneutical elite. On the contrary, he writes expressly from the standpoint of a latter-day secular critic, dedicating his book 'to those outside' (albeit printing the epigraph in Greek as well as English, which somewhat qualifies the inclusiveness of this democratic gesture – noted in Arac (1987)), and addressing himself to readers who likewise cannot share the sense of belonging to an elect inner circle of true-born Christian believers. All the same, he proposes that the best way to understand issues in present-day literary theory – questions of canon-formation, orthodox as opposed to heterodox readings, the dynamics of 'interpretive communities' and so forth – is to treat them as analogous to the forms of institutional control and the process of selective transmission by which the Church has maintained its authority to decide on matters of interpretive truth (see also Kermode, 1983). Thus the issue of what counts as a competent or good-faith reading – whether in the religious or secular sphere – can only be determined by reference to the rules, conventions or hermeneutic procedures that currently define the permissible limits of deviant or 'strong revisionist' practice. To this extent he adopts much the same position as Fish, making 'truth' – or right reading – a product of consensus interests which set the agenda for informed debate between those inside the current orthodox fold and those (like Kermode) who stand self-consciously outside it, but never so far 'outside' that their alternative conjectures, deviant readings, detection of hitherto unnoticed narrative 'secrets' etc. would fail to make sense on the terms established by that same scholarly community.

In short, Kermode contrives to have it both ways, speaking on behalf of a secular readership that would lay claim to interpretive freedoms far beyond those envisaged by an orthodox doctrinal approach, but also – in his more 'hermeneutic' or divinatory vein – appealing to the warrant of specialized procedures (allegorical, typological, intertextual or whatever) whose authority depends precisely on their access to an 'inside' knowledge unavailable to readers lacking the required expertise. Hence the feeling of unease – sometimes mounting to outright moral revulsion – that surfaces in Empson's review of *The Genesis of Secrecy*. It struck him, like so much of the 'advanced' critical work produced during the 1960s and 1970s, as a cautionary instance of the way things could go if interpreters adopted this seductive line of out-and-out 'textualist' talk, and allowed it to prevent them – on principled grounds – from entertaining any truth-claims save those smuggled in by some arcane technique of rhetorical close-reading with distinct theological overtones. Typically, Empson contrasts this latest mode of high-priestly 'hermeneutic' mystification with his memories of an earlier period, that of the late 1920s, when religious belief was very much on the retreat – at least among most intellectuals – and literary criticism had not yet succumbed to the 'Eliotic' fashion for pious neo-orthodox readings of poets like Donne, Coleridge or (indeed) Eliot himself.

One book that clearly left its mark at the time was Bertrand Russell's *Why I am not a Christian*, since Empson cites it in the course of his Kermode review as a salutary reminder of just how odd – not to say perverse – this latest fashion must look to anyone whose thinking has not been 'kidnapped' by the current high-mandarin style. Thus Russell: 'In the Gospels, Christ said: "Ye serpents, ye generation of vipers, how can ye escape the damnation of hell?" That was said to a people who did not like his preaching. It is not really to my mind quite the best tone' (Russell, 1957). To which Empson adds the following, decidedly counter-canonical gloss:

Surely it must be agreed that Jesus miscalculated: it would be torture for him to have to watch what has been done in his name since his death. But if you grant that he was presenting himself as a Messiah, of a special kind but fulfilling the Scriptures, it was part of his programme to recall the prophets; and scolding had been their regular custom. You may feel that Jesus was all too human here, but not, like Kermode, that he is unintelligible. (1987a, p. 519).

'Like Kermode' is a grammatical Ambiguity of the Second Type, suggesting on the one hand that Kermode's approach is 'unintelligible' in and of itself, and on the other – what amounts to much the same charge – that it renders the words of Jesus incomprehensible by putting up multiple barriers of textualist mystification. Empson's argument seeks to remove these unnecessary obstacles by treating Christ's intemperate outburst *not* as an isolated utterance taken out of context, *nor* as an obscure typological reference to this or that specific Old Testament passage, which would thus provide an intertextual gloss on the words in question, but rather as a perfectly understandable *human* response, given both the background of Old Testament prophetic 'scolding' and the current highly charged situation in which Jesus found himself. Here as always, Empson resists any tendency to complicate matters of interpretation by raising 'the text' – or, for that matter, the poem as 'verbal icon' – into a kind of shibboleth, a 'keep out' notice for readers not possessing the requisite hermeneutic skills, the 'secret key' that would unlock the sacred mysteries vouchsafed to some elite group of knowing exegetes. And the best way to demolish such pretensions, he thinks, is to read with a 'waking interest' in the story, to use whatever historical or biographical details come to hand, and then to ask just the sorts of everyday, common-sense question that are ruled out of court by adepts of the textualist approach.

Above all, this entails the (surely reasonable) assumption that when someone – be it Jesus or Sir Philip Sidney – responds to some particularly trying situation by alluding to an earlier source-text, then the allusion is almost sure to be *intentional* on their part, and not just a product of the endless, free-floating 'intertextuality' so much in vogue among present-day literary theorists (see Worton and Still, 1990). In which case the only adequate response to such passages is to treat them in much the same way that one would treat similar episodes in a novel, attempting to figure out causes, reasons and motives with a due regard for the background situation and the likeliest explanatory theory. Empson thoroughly approves of this method, as applied not only in Russell's anti-Christian polemic but also in Robert Graves's book *The Nazarene Gospel Restored*, which seeks not so much to discredit the Christian articles of faith as to demythologize the biblical account by reconstructing the narrative in broadly novelistic terms with more in the way of credible character-psychology (Graves and Podro, 1953). Empson picks out his treatment of Christ's final words (at least as reported in Mark and Matthew): 'My God, why hast thou forsaken me?' And he proceeds to elaborate the Graves version by supplying his own distinctly humanist and counter-theological reading of the passage in question:

> Jesus might have said it to let off steam without any risk of betraying his cause, even if he did fall into doubt at the end. After saying it, he gave a loud cry and died; he had been under torture for several hours. It may seem improbable that anyone would make a literary quotation at such a moment, but it is believable in so strange a case, whereas the Gospel-writers were very unlikely to invent it, as two of them [Luke and John] found it embarrassing. Robert Graves thinks he felt a quite practical despair, having been sure that this procedure would force God to take immediate action, and after his recovery felt intensely guilty, realising that one must never force the hand of God: that was why he appeared seldom and briefly. If you compare him with Graves, Kermode shows a remarkable inability to appreciate the literary effect of these literary quotations. (1987a, pp. 519–20)

One is struck by the immense difference between this treatment of the episode and the reading of Herbert's 'The Sacrifice', which Empson had presented, some fifty years earlier, as his crowning example of seventh-type Ambiguity. And the change had come about for two main reasons, both having to do with his growing conviction that academic 'Eng. Lit.' was far advanced along the road to a revival of orthodox religious beliefs which had done great harm to critics' powers of intellectual and moral judgement. For it now seemed to Empson – having witnessed the rise of New Criticism and later developments – that this unfortunate trend was very largely a result of the turn toward rhetorical or 'textualist' modes of close-reading, techniques which all too readily fell in with a taste for paradox, narrative 'secrets', and other such forms of proto-theological mystification. Hence his firm insistence on reading for the story, for the 'human situation' or the background of motivating reasons and interests, rather than chasing after 'deep' (allegorical or symbolist) meanings that could only be grasped by a reader with access to truths beyond reach of mere unaided human intellect.

What this fashion amounted to – in Empson's view – was a wholesale abandonment of critical reason and a collapse of those secular-enlightenment principles which had (until recently) gone a long way toward securing basic freedoms of moral conscience and belief, and had thus helped to make something 'tolerably civilized' of the Christian religion. For one major sign of progress in this direction had been the demythologizing impulse which, on the one hand, challenged the presumptive self-evidence, the revealed Truth of scriptural narrative, while on the other it encouraged a reading more responsive to those different kinds of truth-claim – historical, sociological, psychological etc. – which placed such questions squarely in the public domain and removed them from the keeping of a priestly elect. Imaginative literature – the novel especially – had played a large role in this process, since it offered valuable scope for the exercise of just such humanly responsive capacities and skills. But the new breed of super-subtle exegetes seemed bent upon putting history into reverse by once again treating texts – whether sacred or secular – as objects of a reverently secretive approach that blocked off any route of access not authorized by the current theoretical wisdom. So far from bringing the Scriptures down to earth by reading them in light of novelistic (i.e. common-sense-realist) assumptions, they sought to read all kinds of text – novels included – as if they aspired to the condition of a Symbolist poem with marked theological overtones (see Empson, 1984, pp. 231–43; 1987a, pp. 632–7). And most often the result of this procedure was that critics completely lost interest in the story and devoted their efforts to devising some far-fetched intertextual or allegorical account which bore no relation to anything outside their own ultra-specialized scholarly interests.

IV

Empson's earliest response in this vein seems to have come in a letter of 1957, addressed to Graham Hough and commenting on his book *The Dark Sun: A Study of D. H. Lawrence* (Hough, 1956b). Characteristically the letter goes out of its way to offer an appreciative response, though Empson is obliged to say also that the book's best insights seem to be arrived at despite and against its methodological premises:

[your book] is a fine flower of the wilful refusal to attend to biography; it sticks to the text only till that process feels like Simon Stylites or the man who always faints after running a mile in four minutes ... However, looking over the pages I have dog-eared again, I think you do manage to get in a great deal of comment from a basis of human experience while maintaining the technical status of a judge who has only access to the text. It makes the book too impressive to be ignored. (Cited in 1987a, p. 466)

In fact Hough's criticism became something of a test case for Empson over the years, balanced as it was between an interest in the various new currents of 'advanced' (mostly Continental) theory and a principled resistance – very much in Empson's manner – when those ideas went against the common-sense grain, or offered a pretext for needless displays of geared-up critical ingenuity. Both attitudes are clearly visible in the essay on Empson – 'An Ambiguity of the Eighth Type' – that Hough contributed to Roma Gill's 1974 *Festschrift* (Gill, 1974, pp. 76–97). And one can follow his engagement with many of the same issues that provoked Empson's polemical response, from the false claims (as they both strongly argued) given currency by the Imagist and Symbolist movements, to the kinds of extreme anti-realist doctrine propounded by adepts of the 'textual revolution'. On the other hand, Hough was more willing than Empson to allow that these ideas, though actively misleading when applied in a doctrinaire fashion, might yet have something useful to offer if approached with a decent measure of sceptical reserve and a desire to make the best possible sense of obscure or recalcitrant passages. Thus in Hough's book *An Essay on Criticism* (Hough, 1956a):

the chapter on Interpretation starts by telling us that there are two conceptions of it: (a) revealing the intention of the author, and (b) expounding the latent sense of his work, which he need not consciously have intended; indeed, to think of it may have been impossible for anyone in his time. (Cited in 1987a, p. 174)

But this strikes Empson as a needless and unfortunate concession on Hough's part, a readiness to go along with fashionable doctrines of textual indeterminacy, 'strong revisionist' reading and so forth, whose usual effect is to license all manner of misunderstandings and downright failures to grasp what the author had in mind. 'Quotations are then given', Empson writes, to recall that critics of type (b) have always existed. But what was done to the *Song of Solomon* is not being achieved or even attempted by any critic of our time, and the only effect of the extra clause of Professor Hough's generalisation is to insinuate that some one *is* doing it. On the contrary, scholars are always telling us, often while expressing motives of piety, that the dullest meaning of an old text is the only permitted one. (p. 174)

In short, Hough has taken much too generous a view of these latest 'hermeneutical' fads, allowing them to work great mischief with his otherwise quite sensible approach to questions of right reading and respect for authorial intent. This harmful influence hasn't yet reached the point – as it will, on Empson's reckoning, some twelve years later, with Kermode as a leading representative voice – of denying all access to truths outside the realm of 'intertextual' echoes and allusions. But it has already gone far enough, he thinks, when a good critic's powers of sympathetic judgement can be regularly sidetracked or held in abeyance by the dutiful regard for a perverse new creed that raises anti-realist (or anti-intentionalist) prejudice into a high point of philosophic principle.

Clearly there is an element of implied self-criticism here, since Empson's readings in *Seven Types* – especially his virtuoso treatment of Herbert's 'The Sacrifice' – had long been a target of scholarly attack on the grounds that he had ignored all the proper constraints of generic or historical method, and had thus used the poem as a handy platform for his own free-wheeling exhibitionist performance. Empson never fully conceded the force of these arguments, continuing to hold – as against scholarly opponents like Rosemond Tuve (Tuve, 1950) – that he *had* in fact wanted to respect Herbert's 'intentions', even if the operative sense of that term needed extending to take in various levels of 'deep', unconscious motivation. Thus he rejects any notion of accepting Tuve's less-than-magnanimous offer that the critic (as opposed to the genuine scholar) 'may properly create an entirely new poem out of an old one by reinterpreting it'. On the contrary, any interpreter has to concentrate on 'how the poem was meant to take effect by its author and did take effect on its first readers'. But this need not be taken to settle the issue in Tuve's favour since 'the formula ... includes the way in which it took effect on them without their knowing it, and that opens an Aladdin's Cave of a positively limestone extent and complexity' (1987a, p. 254). In which case Empson's treatment of 'The Sacrifice' could still claim some degree of 'intentionalist' warrant. But he later came to feel that such pretexts were best avoided, since they could be used to justify any sort of perverse, tendentious, or plainly anachronistic reading. And this happened most often when the argument was joined to an attitude of orthodox 'neo-Christian' contempt for understandings arrived at through the exercise of our normal (i.e. common-sense, humanly responsive, rational-deductive) habits of thought. For otherwise, critics could always have resort to some geared-up technique of rhetorical exegesis – or depth-hermeneutical approach – which simply redefined 'intention' (in so far as it had any use for such a term) according to its own interpretive aims and priorities.

Hence what Empson reads as the tug of opposed loyalties in Hough's book, on the one hand evincing a healthy scepticism with regard to all forms of obscurantist 'textual' doctrine, while on the other giving rein to a certain – albeit qualified and speculative – interest in the way that such ideas might help to broaden the horizons of academic Eng. Lit. Empson's response is worth quoting at length since it brings out not only the depth of his hostility to this whole French-influenced (i.e. Symbolist to post-structuralist) episode in recent intellectual fashion, but also his attachment to the countervailing values of a liberal, secular, rational-humanist mode of critical address. 'Plainly', he writes,

> [Hough's book] represents a welcome development, with its numbered paragraphs, as of Spinoza, surveying the foundations of the subject. Cambridge needs this kind of thing, and Professor Hough has the grasp, the breadth of sympathy and of actual reading, the generous acceptance combined with astringent judgement, to be able to do it. I have rested great hopes in him ever since he remarked in print that he never set out to explain *The Waste Land* to his pupils without reflecting 'What a rude way to write it is!'. But the insight was not recognised as a source of further wisdom, and in this book he seems to me entangled among his different virtues; indeed, it works out as practically a capitulation, though rightly a grudging one, to the literary mystagoguery of France and the United States. But the mind of Professor Hough will go on developing, and the book, owing to its majestic structure, is eminently capable of being revised. (1987a, p. 174)

We should misread this passage if we took it as simply a piece of conventional politeness on Empson's part, a magnanimous gesture or a well-meaning effort to offset his other, more negative remarks. Still less can it be read as a series of ironic or double-edged compliments, 'praising with faint damns', so to speak. For the whole point of Empson's scrupulously balanced sentences is to offer something like a working model of the way that criticism – good criticism – manages to handle such complicated problems of method and address, while at the same time preserving the needful generosity of spirit, the readiness (as described in his essay on Fielding) to 'stretch one's mind around any situation' and appreciate the difficulties from another possible viewpoint. *The Waste Land* figures – as so often in Empson's later essays – as a warning instance of how Symbolist doctrine could be used to insulate literary discourse from this wider context of humanly accountable reasons, motives and interests. One great virtue of Hough's book, he thinks, is to hold out firmly against the erection of similar ideas into a full-scale critical orthodoxy.

What is more, Empson sees a good use for 'theory' in so far as it seeks (in Spinozist fashion) to clarify the logical and conceptual structure of our talk about literary works, and thus provide a decently intelligible basis for argument on these and other questions. I wouldn't want to make too much of Empson's passing reference to that style of reasoning *more geometrico* for which Wittgenstein's *Tractatus* is perhaps just as likely a source (see Norris, 1991). But it is worth recalling that Spinoza figures importantly (if briefly) in *Milton's God* as one of those courageous heretical thinkers who strove to reinterpret Judaeo-Christian belief so as to rid the religion of its worst doctrinal aspects, in particular the notion of an all-powerful executive deity who could somehow be 'satisfied' by the torture and death of an innocent scapegoat figure, a figure who was yet – in some mysterious way – identical with God the Father, in which role he would share the executive privilege of consigning nine-tenths of mankind to eternal damnation, despite having laid down his life on behalf of those same unregenerate creatures (see 1987a, pp. 622–6). It is this mind-wrenching doctrine of the Trinity that Empson finds both morally repugnant and logically absurd, and whose effect on those writers schooled to accept it – Herbert, Coleridge and Eliot among them – he considers harmful in the utmost degree, whatever its undoubted creative or imaginative yield (Empson, 1987a, pp. 256–9; 297–319; 1984, pp. 187–200). But with Milton the argument takes a different turn, since in this case the poet is struggling to devise some 'decent' (humanly intelligible) version of the biblical narrative, some means of conserving the basic doctrines – centrally that of the Christian Atonement – while avoiding their deep-laid sadistic implications. And it is here that Milton's heterodox theology takes on a distinctly Spinozist cast, suggesting (as Empson memorably puts it) that God plans to 'abdicate' his sovereign powers, or give up his role as tormenting tormentor, and become something more like the pantheist 'ground of all being' (*deus sive natura*) conceived by other, more civilized forms of religious belief. In short, we had best regard Milton's God as 'like King Lear and Prospero, turbulent and masterful characters who are struggling to become able to renounce their power and enter peace; the story makes him behave much worse than they do, but the author allows him the same purifying aspiration' (1965, p. 135). And again, with more markedly Spinozist overtones: '[t]he Father, I submit, has to turn into the God of the Cambridge Platonists and suchlike mystical characters; at present he is still the very disagreeable God of the Old Testament, but eventually he will dissolve into the landscape and become immanent only' (pp. 132–3).

To Empson, this achievement seems all the more impressive for the fact that Milton confronts the root paradoxes of Christian belief – including some of its worst, most rebarbative aspects – and yet manages to produce at least the outline of a humanly intelligible ethic. Thus 'Milton's poetical formula for God is not simply to copy Zeus in Homer but, much more dramatically, to cut out everything between the two ends of the large body of Western thought about God, and stick to Moses except at the high points which anticipate Spinoza' (p. 145). And indeed, looking back over Empson's criticism from *Seven Types* on, one can see how often his thinking reverted to those two possible kinds of belief-system, or those two ways of coping with the problems thrown up by any religion that stakes its claim to truth on the existence of a God-figure commonly invested with human (anthropomorphic) attributes. Such ideas could all too easily produce the kinds of wrenching paradox – the irrationalist contortions of moral and intellectual conscience – that Empson first explored in his brilliant pages on Herbert's 'The Sacrifice', and which were then taken up (albeit in a somewhat sanitized and routine form) by the proponents of New Criticism. Later on, having become more aware of this untoward trend, Empson set out to counter its influence by treating that passage as a piece of youthful extravagance, an example of how the close-reading method could be pushed too far into regions of advanced logical disorder or religious psychopathology. Thus:

> I put 'The Sacrifice' last of the examples in my book, to stand for the most extreme kind of ambiguity, because it presents Jesus as at the same time

forgiving his torturers and condemning them to eternal torture. It strikes me now that my attitude was what I have come to call 'neo-Christian'; happy to find such an extravagant specimen, I slapped the author on the back and egged him on to be even nastier. (1987a, p. 257)

But already in *Seven Types* – especially the reading of Wordsworth's *Tintern Abbey* – there are signs of an interest in that other, more humane tradition of religious thought, a pantheist tradition that seeks to avoid (or at any rate to soften) the harsh paradoxes of orthodox belief by treating 'God' as more or less synonymous with 'nature', and therefore as effectively relinquishing his role of all-powerful judge and torturer on the one hand, and all-suffering scapegoat figure on the other. Wordsworth thus offers a possible escape route from the conflicts engendered by the Christian doctrine of Atonement, a doctrine which Empson would later describe (in *Milton's God*) as 'the wickedest thing yet invented by the black heart of man' (1965, p. 251).

In *Seven Types* the alternative (pantheist) version doesn't yet strike him as a promising candidate for any such morally redemptive role. At this stage Empson is largely unconvinced by what he calls Wordsworth's 'shuffling and evasive' style, the way that the poem exploits certain local confusions of logic, grammar and rhetoric in order to communicate its vague sense of ecumenical uplift. Indeed – as I have argued at length elsewhere (Norris, 1985b) – this passage is the nearest that Empson ever comes to the kind of relentlessly negative critique, the undoing of mystified truth-claims or forms of premature aesthetic idealization, that would later achieve such prominence in the work of deconstructionist critics like Paul de Man (see de Man, 1984, 1986). Certainly he shows little willingness to let Wordsworth off the argumentative hook, or to give him (so to speak) the benefit of the doubt in matters of doctrinal and logico-semantic detail. After all, 'Wordsworth seems to have believed in his own doctrines', and it is therefore only reasonable that one should 'try to extract from this passage definite opinions on the relations of God, man, and nature, and on the means by which such relations can be known' (1953, p. 152). And he then proceeds to unpack the implications of Wordsworth's fuzzy rhetoric – its numerous aporias, logical *non sequiturs*, short-circuitings of grammatical sense etc. – with the purpose (as it seems) of utterly demolishing pantheism as a credible or self-respecting system of belief. What comes across most forcefully in these pages from *Seven Types* is the rationalist conviction, so strong in early Empson, that poetry cannot (or should not) enjoy any special dispensation from the sense-making standards that normally apply in our everyday, responsible dealing with matters of moral and intellectual conscience. And if Wordsworth's poetry fails to meet these standards, then Empson thinks it important to say so and not give way to some mood of rhetorically induced mystical rapture which would rule out any kind of reasoned argumentative response (1987a, pp. 232–8).

The lines from *Tintern Abbey* will, I hope, be familiar to most readers, so Empson's commentary is enough to make the point without citing the passage in question. 'It is not certain', he writes,

> what is more *deeply interfused* than what. It is not certain whether the *music of humanity* is the same as the *presence*; they are separated by the word *and* and a full stop. We may notice, too, that the word *in* seems to distinguish, though but faintly, the *mind of man* from the *light*, the *ocean*, the *air*, and the *sky*; this tends to separate the *motion* and the *spirit* from the *presence* and the *something*; but they may, again, all be identical with the *music*. Wordsworth may then have *felt* a *something far more deeply interfused* than the *presence* that *disturbed* him; we seem here to have God revealing himself in particular to the mystic, but being in a more fundamental sense immanent to his whole creation. Or the *something* may be in apposition to the *presence* (the *sense* equal to the *joy*); so that both are 'more' *deeply interfused* than the *music of humanity*, but apparently in the same way. This version only conceives God as immanent in his creation, and as affecting the poet in the same way as he affects everything else; or as only imagined by the poet as immanent in creation, in the same way as the *music of humanity* is imagined as immanent. Thus, the first version is Christian, the second, in part pantheistic, in part agnostic. Again, the *something* may possibly dwell only in the natural objects mentioned, ending at *sky*; the *motion* and the *spirit* are then not thought of at all as *interfused* into nature, like the *something*; they are things active *in the mind of man*. At the same time they are similar to the *something*; thus Wordsworth either *feels* them or *feels a sense* of them. With this reading the voice would rise in some triumph at the words *mind of man*; man has a spirit immanent in nature in the same way as is the spirit of God, and is decently independent from him. Or the *something* may also *dwell in the mind of man*, and have the *motion* and the *spirit* in apposition to it; under this less fortunate arrangement a God who is himself nature subjects us at once to determinism and predestination. (1953, pp. 152–3)

It is an extraordinary passage in many ways, not least for its dogged analytical pursuit of those puzzling features of Wordsworth's language that most interpreters – certainly the New Critics – would treat as so many striking instances of poetic 'paradox', and hence as confirming their own belief that poetry inhabits a special realm of discourse, a realm of *sui generis* imaginative truth where everyday standards of logical accountability simply don't apply (see Brooks, 1947). Empson is like de Man to this extent at least: that he refuses the easy escape route of 'aesthetic ideology', or a critical approach that suspends questions of truth and falsehood in favour of a mystified rhetoric of meaning and form whose upshot is to seal literature off from any kind of counter-canonical reading or critique. But he is unlike de Man in his steady conviction – running all the way from *Seven Types* to the writings of his last two decades – that the critic's main task is to *make good sense* of literary works, to attempt as far as possible to construe them in 'decently intelligible' terms, and only then – where the method comes up against its limits with some really intractable passage like the Wordsworth – to acknowledge not so much the 'aporetic' character of *all* literary language but the failure of *this particular passage* to communicate its meaning effectively.

Least of all could Empson ever be brought to concede the major premise of de Man's late work: that 'textuality' (or rhetoric) was the bottom line of critical appeal, the 'truth' of literature that relegated all other truth-claims (logical, cognitive, historical, ethical etc.) to the status of so many 'undecidable' propositions, shown up as such by the aberrant workings of language in its literary – that is, self-consciously rhetorical – aspect (see de Man, 1986; Norris, 1988). For such ideas would have struck him as just another version of the drive to insulate literature – and criticism – in a realm of ultra-specialized 'textualist' debate unaccountable to the interests of reason, truth and morality alike. And it was just this manoeuvre that Empson resisted in his reading of the lines from *Tintern Abbey*, a reading that refused to give rhetoric (or 'paradox') the upper hand over logic and grammar, and which insisted – on the contrary – that any 'confusions' in Wordsworth's language should be put down to his problems in handling the pantheist doctrine of God-as-Nature, and not to some uniquely paradoxical wisdom vested in poetic language. This remained a constant principle with Empson, as can be seen from the chapter on Wordsworth in *Complex Words*, where he allows that the poet's use of Type IV equations (i.e. those that 'jump over' some crucial stage in the structure of logico-semantic implication) often 'makes very good poetry, and probably suggests important truths', but none the less amounts to a kind of rhetorical cheating, an over-reliance on emotive – as opposed to rational-discursive – modes of persuasion. Thus 'the whole poetical and philosophical effect comes from a violent junction of sense-data to the divine imagination given by love, and the middle term is cut out' (1951, p. 296). And again: 'what is jumped over is "good sense"; when Wordsworth has got his singing robes on he will not allow any mediating process to have occurred' (p. 304).

All the same Empson now shows a much greater readiness to accept the variety of human beliefs and the fact that some kind of nature-mysticism or pantheist creed – as conveyed by Wordsworth's performance with the key-word 'sense' – may help to ward off the worst implications of orthodox Christian theology. Undoubtedly this change of attitude resulted in part from his pre-war periods of teaching in China and Japan, an experience which left Empson firmly convinced that Christianity was by far the least civilized of the great world religions, since it alone – unlike the Buddhist, Hindu or Confucian creeds – had clung to the neolithic craving for blood sacrifice, albeit symbolically reworked into the doctrine of Atonement.[3] What chiefly impressed him about those other cultures was the absence of that persecuting zeal brought about by belief in an omnipotent God-figure, a deity whose nature (or whose odd ideas of justice) could only be 'satisfied' by the infliction of eternal suffering on the vast majority of mankind, or only 'bought off' by the ritual sacrifice of an innocent scapegoat-redeemer. The wickedness of this doctrine was Empson's great theme in *Milton's God* and much of the work that occupied his later years. His arguments were intended partly as a downright moral rebuke to Christian-orthodox critics and readers, partly as a rational-humanist appeal to those secular (basically Benthamite) values that Empson himself espoused, but also partly by way of a reminder that there existed other, far preferable forms of religious belief, traditions – like Buddhism – that found no room for such odious doctrines as Original Sin, predestination, eternal punishment or vicarious Atonement. And he clearly came to feel that these alternatives offered an important (even necessary) means of escape from the hideous implications of Christian Trinitarian teaching, or the equally hideous

[3] See the various essays and reviews which Haffenden brings together under the heading 'Cultural Perspectives: Ethics and Aesthetics, East and West' (1987a, pp. 523–637). Haffenden's forthcoming biography of Empson will no doubt provide a great deal more in the way of valuable background information.

contortions of moral judgement which that teaching brought about in theologians, poets or critics trained up in such ways of thought.

Not that Empson ever 'converted' to Buddhism, as some readers were led to believe by his using the text of 'The Fire Sermon' as an epigraph to the 1955 edition of *Collected Poems* (1987a, pp. 599–600). His attitude was rather that Buddhism represented one possible way that the human mind could go, one expression – in this case harmless, even beneficent – of that religious impulse which seems to have existed (however protean its forms) in all cultures to date. And its greatest virtue, in Empson's opinion, was that Buddhism firmly rejected the belief in an anthropomorphic or all-too-human deity whose sovereign whims the theologians could then exploit as a pretext for their own preferred forms of doctrinal imposition, along with the various techniques adopted to enforce those beliefs where necessary. On the contrary, the highest stage of Buddhist enlightenment was the condition arrived at by renouncing all merely personal desires, among them the tendency – so clearly marked in the history of Christian theological dispute – to set God up as a distorted mirror-image of the will-to-power involved in these various (often lethal) wranglings. Thus 'the basic position', as Empson describes it,

> is that Buddhists believe in abandoning selfhood, sometimes interpreted as merging oneself into the Absolute or the impersonal Godhead. If you are good but rather a busybody you are liable to be reborn as a god yourself, which may hold up getting to Nirvana indefinitely; just as over here a too virtuous scholar is liable to be made to do administration. (1987a, p. 600)

One should not be deceived by the joky tone into thinking that Empson's thoughts on this topic are the product of casual interest or a sketchy acquaintance with Buddhist religion and culture. Indeed, one of his projects while teaching in the Far East was to write a comparative study of Buddha faces, a plan which involved much travelling to sites in China, Japan and Korea, and which produced not only a number of essays (now reprinted in *Argufying*), but also a book-length study of which the sole typescript copy was apparently lost in the post.

Of the surviving fragments there is one piece in particular ('The Faces of the Buddha', 1936) which shows the complexity of Empson's response to these artworks and his sense that they afforded a wisdom somehow forgotten or repressed through the centuries of Christian-dominated Western culture (1987a, pp. 573–6). 'The point about the archaic fixed smile', he suggests, is that it would be made by a pull on the main zygomatic, the muscle most under conscious control, leaving the others at rest; thus it is an easy way to make a statue look socially conscious, wilful, alert ... But you have only to sink the ends into the cheeks to give it an ironical or complacent character, and my example from Yun-kang, almost winking as it is, gets, I think, with these simple means, an extraordinary effect both of secure hold on strength and peace and of the humorous goodwill of complete understanding. (1987a, p. 575)

As John Haffenden has remarked, there are many points of contact between Empson's reading of the Buddha faces and his work-in-progress toward *Some Versions of Pastoral*, most of which was written on the hop, so to speak, during those hectic but formative years of Far Eastern travel, and whose expansive definition of the pastoral *genre* – 'putting the complex into the simple' – finds an obvious echo in the above passage and others of a similar reflective cast. But what really impressed Empson about the Buddhist attitude to matters of life and death was its sturdy resistance to anything like the Christian cult of blood-sacrifice, or the idea of a personal-executive deity whose character demanded such obscene ritual observances, whatever their 'symbolic' or sublimated form as manifest in current religious practice. Thus the main effect of Buddhist teaching 'is to remove *all* doctrinal props about immortality and still claim that death is somehow of the highest value. This rationalising escape from the fear of death is carried so far that there is much less sense of tragedy and of the fascination of a sacrificial death than in Christianity with its certainly immortal individuals' (1987a, p. 536). And in Empson's view this could only be a good thing, morally and socially, since it took away the standard Christian excuse for inflicting all manner of earthly torment *either* because God willed it, *or* because this was the only way to save the infidel's soul, *or* because one's own salvation depended on behaving in this brutal way. So one can see why Empson, though rejecting the idea that he had embraced Buddhist belief, nevertheless made a regular point of holding it up as a better, more humane or civilized alternative to the pieties of mainstream Christian thought.

This is also, I think, why he came to adopt a more tolerant view of Wordsworth's pantheist sentiments, despite continuing to fault the poetry – or at any rate resist its suasive appeal – on argued logico-semantic grounds. For it now seemed to Empson that some such doctrine, though sure to involve certain basic philosophical confusions, might still provide a hedge against the kinds of vicious paradox-mongering that resulted from accepting the Christian Trinitarian creed in its full-blown orthodox form. And there was always the example of Spinoza, regarded by many as a nature-mystic – an idea put about by Romantic poet-philosophers like Coleridge and Novalis, the latter having famously described him as a 'God-intoxicated soul' – but much more a figure in the rationalist-enlightenment line of descent, one who firmly rejected all notions of a personal or anthropomorphic deity, and whose key phrase (*deus sive natura*) was a coded argument for abandoning God-talk and adopting a thoroughly materialist philosophy of mind and nature. Certainly Wordsworth gives every appearance of having believed in his pantheist doctrines, unlike Spinoza, whose attempt to placate orthodox (Christian and Jewish) opinion by resorting to such double-edged language was indeed so unsuccessful that he suffered excommunication from the Amsterdam synagogue, after which 'Spinozist' and 'atheist' became near-synonymous terms of abuse among right-thinking persons of both creeds (see Norris, 1991). My point in all this is that Empson stands squarely in the same line of heterodox dissent, an allegiance that accounts for the two main aspects of his work, on the one hand its attachment to a secular hermeneutics, a rationalist theory of 'compacted doctrines' (or truth-conditional structures of semantic entailment) as developed in *Complex Words*, and on the other its readiness to entertain beliefs – like Buddhism or Wordsworth's pantheist sentiments – that may not meet these exacting standards of logic, consistency or truth, but which none the less offer a decent alternative to the doctrines inflicted by orthodox Christian faith. For they both involve that basic, indispensable appeal to the standards of rational intelligence and 'decent human feelings' which provide the only possible line of defence against a full-scale religious revivalist movement.

Hence Empson's praise for the approach of Graham Hough in his ground-clearing *Essay on Criticism*, 'with its numbered paragraphs, as of Spinoza, surveying the foundations of the subject' (1987a, p. 174). Such an approach was urgently needed, Empson felt, if literary critics were to break with that ethos of pious conformist zeal – or unresisting doctrinal adherence – which exerted a regular distorting influence on their powers of intellectual and moral judgement. With *Complex Words* he pushed this case to its logical conclusion, arguing for a truth-conditional semantics that applied not only to the discourse of literary theory but also to the language of literature itself, conceived as making sense in ways quite accountable to our normal (rational-deductive) modes of understanding. Thus 'the term Ambiguity, which I used in a book title and as a kind of slogan, implying that the reader is left in doubt between two readings, is more or less superseded by the idea of a double meaning which is intended to be fitted into a definite structure' (1951, p. 102). One reason for this change was undoubtedly Empson's suspicion – borne out by what he had seen of the American New Criticism – that talk of 'ambiguity' too easily leaned over into a wholesale doctrine of poetic 'paradox', a rhetoric with its own (whether overt or hidden) theological agenda. Thus *Complex Words* sets out to argue the case for a rationalist and secular-humanist approach to questions of interpretive theory and practice, an approach that carries on the demythologizing project – the critique of revelation or dogmatic theology – which Spinoza was among the first to articulate. All the same there are chapters where the method doesn't work, or where it comes up against deviant structures of rhetorical implication – like Wordsworth's short-circuiting of the senses of 'sense' – which in the end turn out to resist such treatment. Thus 'it does not seem unfair to suggest that he [Wordsworth] induced people to believe he had expounded a consistent philosophy through the firmness and assurance with which he used equations of Type IV; equations whose claim was false, because they did not really erect a third concept as they pretended to' (1951, p. 305). And yet, as Empson promptly (if ruefully) concedes, 'the result makes very good poetry, and probably suggests important truths'.

This will only look like an outright admission of defeat on Empson's part if we forget that other dimension of his criticism – most prominent in the essays published after *Complex Words* – which led away from those more specialized kinds of logico-semantic research. For there was also the appeal to a wider context of humanly intelligible motives, values and beliefs, a context that Empson had never ignored when engaged with theoretical issues or the close-reading of particular works, but which now seemed all the more important as a means of counteracting the narrowly 'textualist' bias of recent academic criticism. Such is the main purpose of the essays collected in *Using Biography*, especially the piece on Fielding's 'double irony', where – as we have seen – Empson finds no use for a purely rhetorical or formalist approach that would raise the exclusion of biographical 'background' or authorial intentions to a high point of critical dogma. And it is also what he means by that otherwise rather baffling passage in *Milton's God* which claims that we can best do justice to the poetry – that is to say, best respect its heroic efforts to make something tolerably decent of the Christian religion – by allowing for the sheer audacity of Milton's enterprise, his determination (as Empson puts it) 'to cut out everything between the two ends of the large body of Western thought about God, and stick to Moses except at the high points which anticipate Spinoza' (1965, p. 145). His argument here is that dissident thinkers – Milton and Spinoza among them – have often had to cope with extreme forms of doctrinal or ideological pressure, conditions under which it was plainly impossible to come straight out with some ringing indictment of the established belief-system. In Milton's case the pressures were somewhat relaxed, at least during that brief period of the early interregnum when the turmoil of conflicting religious and political interests created an extraordinary upsurge of radical thought (see Hill, 1977), along with an unprecedented liberty for the voicing of heterodox views. And Spinoza, as a free-thinking Jewish intellectual, was likewise fortunate in living at a time – and in a country, the loose-knit Dutch federal republic – which afforded at least some measure of protection, despite the notoriety that soon attached to his name. But it is clear that any too-overt attack on the basic articles of faith would have laid them both open to a prompt withdrawal of those same hard-won freedoms. Hence their resort – as Empson reads it – to a more indirect but none the less effective mode of critical engagement, an approach that involved the reworking of scriptural truth-claims into a pantheist (or immanent) conception of the deity lacking those personal-executive powers which had so far produced such a woeful history of dogmatism, intolerance and religious persecution.

In short, Christianity could only be knocked into a more civilized shape by abandoning its orthodox (Trinitarian) doctrine and adopting something like the Buddhist idea of an impersonal 'ground of all being'. This idea found its closest equivalent in Western thought with the Spinozist conception of *deus sive natura*, a God whose attributes were coextensive (or synonymous) with those of the natural order, including our own place within that order as creatures whose needs, desires, ethical values and motivating interests could only be accounted for in naturalistic terms. Of course there was a different reading of Spinoza, one that took hold among German and English poet-philosophers of the Romantic period – figures like Novalis and Coleridge – who tended to play down his rationalist critique of revealed religion in whatever form, and treat him as a pantheist or nature-mystic in line with their own predilections. It is this version of the Spinozist legacy that Empson encountered twice over in his reading of Wordsworth, first in *Seven Types* (where the lines from 'Tintern Abbey' produced those pages of hard-pressed and frankly rather baffled logico-grammatical analysis), and then in the chapter 'Sense in *The Prelude*' from *Complex Words*, where he still finds problems in construing the poet's deviant semantic 'equations', but none the less concedes that the poetry possesses great emotional power and most likely 'suggests important truths'. In fact, Empson has a note in the second [1953] edition of *Seven Types* where he recalls that some critics had 'disliked the meanness and fussiness of this passage', and admits to harbouring a wish 'that I had something wise and reconciling to say after all these years'. One could, he goes on, 'give a much more sympathetic account of the philosophical background of Wordsworth, and no doubt if I. A. Richards's *Coleridge on Imagination* had been already published I would have written differently' (1953, p. 153n).

All the same he feels obliged not to let the issue go without repeating his original point, established as it was through a close (even 'niggling') attention to the detail of Wordsworth's language, those points at which the logic, grammar and rhetoric failed to cohere or produce an intelligible sequence of argument. The footnote continues:

> Miss M. C. Bradbrook wrote that the nouns after the full stop are all obviously in apposition, because the theme is the transcendence of the subject–object relationship. It is, I suppose, almost certain that Wordsworth meant the grammar to run like this. But surely, even if clauses are in apposition, they must be supposed to be somehow distinguishable, or why do they have to be said one after another? ... [T]he more seriously one takes the doctrine, it seems to me, the more this expression of it seems loose rhetoric. (p. 153n)

These remarks were set down some ten years after Empson wrote the chapter on Wordsworth that subsequently appeared in *Complex Words*, so clearly there can be no question of his having altogether abandoned the working criteria – the standards of logico-grammatical intelligibility – that first gave rise to his doubts concerning the poet's 'shuffling and evasive' verbal strategies. In fact, those original pages on 'Tintern Abbey' were the closest that Empson ever came to the kind of deconstructive analysis – the symptomatic reading alert to any sign of conflict or unresolved tension between logic, grammar and rhetoric – that Paul de Man would later pursue with such rigorous zeal (de Man, 1979). What he shares with de Man is a deep resistance to the idea that language could possibly 'transcend' the subject–object antinomy, or attain to a condition of hypostatic union, an access to revealed truths above and beyond the prosaic requirements of sense-making logical grasp. Thus, as Empson puts it, 'whether or not a great deal of wisdom is enshrined in these lines, lines just as muddled, superficially speaking, may convey a mode of using their antinomies, and so act as creeds' (pp. 153–4). And in de Man's view also, it was wrong to treat poetry as somehow exempt from the standards or validity conditions of plain-prose argument, since history provided all too many examples – especially in the post-Romantic period – of aesthetic doctrines that were carried across into the realm of socio-political theory and practice, often with disastrous results.

Such were the high claims vested in Romantic metaphor and symbol not only by poet-philosophers like Coleridge and Goethe, but also by present-day mainstream critics of Romanticism, interpreters like M. H. Abrams who took it more or less for granted that the poets had actually *achieved* this ideal, creating a language of 'organic' fusion between subject and object, mind and nature, signifier and signified, or the order of phenomenal sense-presentation and the order of ultimate (noumenal) truth to which poetry aspired in its finest moments of mystic-inspirational or visionary insight (Abrams, 1953). For de Man, these ideas amounted to a species of false (though none the less potent) 'aesthetic ideology', a belief that ran deep in the discourse of post-Romantic criticism and theory, and whose untoward effects – including their extension into the realm of history and politics – could only be resisted through a vigilant practice of deconstructive reading, one that held out against the seductive claims of high Romantic argument (de Man, 1983, pp. 187–22). For otherwise this strain of mystified organicist thinking could easily produce the kind of national-aestheticist doctrine of which Heidegger was the prime (and cautionary) modern instance; a doctrine, that is to say, which set up some *particular* language or culture as the source of uniquely 'authentic' insights unattainable by those outside its privileged sphere. And even if the claims were not pressed that far they could still give rise to a dangerous habit of confusing the aesthetic and the political, or conceiving society on the model of an 'organic' artwork in which the various component parts (read: subjects or citizens) were thought of as fulfilling the roles assigned them by some ultimate – transcendent or supra-historical – vision of order vouchsafed to the bearers of this high cultural vocation. Hence de Man's remark (referring specifically to Schiller's idea of 'aesthetic education'): that 'the "state" which is here being advocated is not just a state of mind or of soul, but a principle of political value and authority that has its own claims on the shape and the limits of our freedom' (1984, p. 264).

Of course, I am not suggesting that Empson has any such dire prospects in view when he comments on the puzzling discrepancies between logic, grammar and rhetoric in Wordsworth's 'Tintern Abbey'. But he does make the point – as against Bradbrook – that this poetry has definite designs on the reader, that it offers at least a semblance of 'deep' philosophical truth, and therefore requires that we take a waking interest in the means by which its effects are achieved. Thus 'the reason why one grudges Wordsworth this source of strength is that he talks as if he owned a creed by which his half-statements might be reconciled, whereas, in so far as his creed was definite, he found these half-statements necessary to keep it at bay' (1953, p. 154). Hence Empson's objection to the standard New Critical line, the idea that poetry just *was* paradoxical, that paradox was in some sense the touchstone or hallmark of genuine poetic worth, so that any attempt to explicate its meaning in rational-argumentative terms was sure to miss the point in some fundamental way. It was the same attitude – or a version of the same aestheticizing impulse – that led many critics of Wordsworth to adopt what amounted to a fideist approach, an interpretive line of least resistance, or a willingness to ignore those anomalous details (like the disjunct relationship between logic and grammar) which would otherwise impede their enjoyment of the poetry. There is no sign in Empson's later work that he ever gave up this basic principle: that literature ought to make sense according to the best, most accountable standards of validity and truth, and that any deviation from those standards – any appeal to 'paradox' or rhetorical figures claiming to transcend such prosaic requirements – should at least give the critic pause before lending credence to its (often seductive) claims. For otherwise the way was clearly open to all manner of linguistic pseudo-profundities masquerading as revealed truths, from the paradoxes of Orwellian Newspeak (see 1987a, pp. 601–4) to the values smuggled in by neo-Christian exegetes with their own strong revisionist agenda.

The point is made firmly in the following passage from 'Sense in *The Prelude*', a passage that once again locates certain problems with the logic and the grammar of Wordsworth's poetry, and which signals Empson's continuing refusal simply to go along with the rhetorical drift where the argument (or structure of semantic equations) resists the best efforts of elucidating prose commentary. 'A conceivable meaning for *the sense*', Empson writes,

> is the archaic 'common sense', that which correlates the messages of the different external senses. It is 'the senses regarded as unified', and that is already a kind of rudimentary power of interpreting them ... On the other hand, the passage as a whole [*Prelude*, Book 1, lines 544–66] obviously means 'My imagination was already stirring', but which of the words means his imagination, if *the sense* does not? This may be an unreasonable process of thought, but it seems to describe the way we are driven to give the term an obscure but splendid claim. It must be remembered that, here as so often in the poem, the language is in any case extremely loose; the theoretical turns of phrase in the first paragraph lead us to expect 'the bond of union' to be between the child and the external world – an epistemology is being given – but the peroration sweeps this aside to contemplate only 'life and joy'. No doubt the reason why this seems fine is that one accepts *life* as the child and *joy* as inherent in Mother Nature, but such extreme optimism is made plausible only by being left vague. In the same way *the sense* feels inherently vague; but this is no reason why we should not try to account for its behaviour. (1951, p. 299)

Again – as in the passage from *Seven Types* – Empson thinks it important not to let Wordsworth off too lightly by suspending our normal logico-semantic 'machinery' of rational judgement, enjoying what the poem has to offer by way of uplifting pantheist sentiment, and thus falling in with a suasive rhetoric capable of other (less innocent or high-minded) uses. Like de Man, he is aware that such poetry makes large claims not only on the reader's imaginative credence but also on his or her powers of intellectual, cognitive and ethical judgement. That is to say, it raises crucial issues in the discourse of modern (post-Kantian) philosophy of mind, issues that were often sidestepped or elided in that subsequent history of mystified thinking – what de Man terms 'aesthetic ideology' – which began with Schiller's widely influential misreading of Kant, and was then taken up into the mainstream tradition of 'high Romantic argument' represented by contemporary scholar-critics such as M. H. Abrams. Most importantly, it led to certain deep-laid confusions – or category mistakes – whose upshot was to elevate aesthetic experience (conceived as the unifying faculty of all human knowledge) to a status above all those Kantian antinomies of subject and object, mind and nature, concepts and intuitions, free will and determinism, speculative reason *versus* theoretical understanding etc. And in doing so it tended to treat epistemological or ethical questions as if these could finally be subsumed or transcended through the appeal to some notional aesthetic ideal – some model of the faculties working harmoniously together in the 'free play' of understanding, practical reason and imagination – that would thus put an end to the vexatious boundary disputes that form the main topic of Kant's three *Critiques*. In de Man's words: 'the aesthetic is, by definition, a seductive notion that appeals to the pleasure principle, a eudaimonic judgment that can conceal and displace values of truth and falsehood likely to be more resilient to desire than values of pleasure and pain' (1986, p. 64).

It seems to me that Empson is raising both issues – the epistemological and the ethical – when he holds out against the aestheticizing drift of Wordsworth's pantheist rhetoric, and asks that we read with a critical eye to the various confusions, logical and grammatical, that prevent the poetry from ever quite meaning what it says or saying what it means. For these problems with language have a wider significance, as comes out most clearly in the passage from *Seven Types*, where the question whether Wordsworth can really make good his claim to have 'transcended' the subject/object dualism is inseparable from the question whether God can be conceived as *both* immanent in nature *and* as somehow dwelling 'in the mind of man', a doctrine which – as soon as one examines it more closely – turns out to involve the monistic idea of a deity 'who is himself nature [and] subjects us at once to determinism and predestination' (1953, p. 153). It is therefore a matter of some urgency that we should not, in de Man's terms, allow the seductions of aesthetic ideology (or the 'eudaimonic' appeal of a reading indifferent to values of truth and falsehood) to distract us from those other, more important questions that such poetry raises when read with a view to its epistemological truth-claims on the one hand, and its claims upon our moral and political freedom on the other. And in this case we will be much better equipped to resist the more sinister forms of manipulative rhetoric, those that likewise achieve their effect by inducing an attitude of uncritical acquiescence in all manner of paradoxical truth-claims or 'profound' pseudo-wisdom.

V

Empson addresses this issue more directly in the chapter of *Complex Words* entitled 'A Is B', an essay that deals with identity statements of the type 'Might is Right', 'God is Love', 'Beauty is Truth', 'Mind is Matter' and so forth (1951, pp. 350–74). In general, he thinks that we are pretty good at sorting out the semantic 'grammar' of such expressions, so that (for instance) when confronted with a seeming tautology we redefine the terms so as to make the statement carry some meaningful or informative content. And in the opposite sort of case – where the statement involves a paradox or what looks like a flatly contradictory set of semantic entailments – then we try to make sense of it by casting around for some alternative meaning of one or the other term that will give the equation 'A = B' at least a semblance of valid propositional form. After all, such sentences cover the whole range from scientific truth-claims ('light is a vibration in the ether') to political maxims ('Might is Right'), ethical injunctions ('Right is Might'), religious slogans ('God is Love'), aesthetic or poetical creeds ('Beauty is Truth'), and items of vaguely common-sense wisdom (like 'the style is the man') which perhaps won't bear too much in the way of close logical inspection. What particularly interests Empson is the extent to which, in any given case, one can switch the terms around and still extract some kind of doctrine or intelligible meaning from the sentence thus produced.

'God is Love' is the obvious test-case here since it evokes the whole complex of vaguely pantheist ideas which he had grappled with in the chapter on Wordsworth. 'The reason why "Love is God" feels puzzling is that we are not sure which definite idea to take about love, how much sex to put into it for instance, nor yet how we are to generalize or diffuse the idea of God; the slogan is likely to mean some kind of pantheism, but we cannot tell what till we hear more' (1951, p. 354). And this ambivalence extends to other, more political versions of the same device, slogans which exploit the interchangeable order of subject and predicate so as to leave one uncertain of the speaker's standpoint on issues of ethical priority or social conscience:

> A state which receives worship, or a people with a 'destiny', are in the same position as God because they are expected partly to create the standard of rightness by which they are to be judged. This idea, I think, was clearly present in 'Might is Right', and though 'Right is Might' is a less reckless piece of self-justification there does seem to be an assumption in it that virtue gets plenty of reward. (p. 362)

All the same, Empson argues, we do have resources – a range of logico-semantic 'machinery' or techniques for handling such problem cases – which come into play, at whatever 'preconscious' level, when we are faced with some puzzling instance of the kind. These include the various sorts of implicit qualifying clause which enable us to construe the identity-statement ('A = B') in terms that make sense without producing either a vacuous tautology or a piece of mind-wrenching paradox. Thus 'the copula ... can be interpreted as "entails" or "is part of" or "is like" or "is typical of"', or perhaps as an instance of what Empson calls 'mutual metaphor', requiring that we treat both terms to a process of reciprocal redefinition. In this way it is usually possible to assign a meaning – or a set of relevant equations – which would explain why the slogan carried weight for some particular speaker, interest-group or political faction, even if it failed to make sense in more strictly propositional or logico-semantic terms.

Of course there are extreme cases (and here he cites a passage from Mary Baker Eddy, the advocate of Christian Science) where the doctrine involves such a mass of redundant, pleonastic, paradoxical or downright nonsensical 'equations' that it has to be regarded as belonging more to the psychopathology of belief than to language as a medium of rational-communicative exchange. Thus Mrs Eddy: 'God is all in all. God is good, good is mind. Good spirit being all in all, nothing is matter.' And her 'argument' went on (as Empson reports it) to claim that 'these sentences give the same message when read backwards, which proves mathematically that they are true' (1951, p. 352). On the contrary, he argues: 'what it proves ... is that she pairs off either two of the good words or two of the bad words, and they are all simple names either of the good or the bad Thing'. The passage reduces to nonsense – or mere verbiage – in so far as it empties the words of all determinate meaning, collapses any sense of the logic (or the 'grammar' of semantic entailment) that would otherwise give a handle for sorting out their various implications, and thus offers nothing more than a string of emotive pseudo-statements. But Empson's point is that such cases are highly untypical and can best be reckoned with by looking to the motives – the confused promptings of religious or political sentiment – that account for their suasive appeal among true believers. They have to be distinguished from those other (superficially similar) instances where there is likewise a suggestion of transcendent truths – or a knowledge beyond reach of commonplace human experience – but where the doctrine is carried by verbal equations that have the definite virtue, as Empson sees it, of allowing for some fairly complex strategies of contextual redefinition. So

> a philosopher who said 'matter is mind', though no doubt leaving his position very obscure, would at least imply that he was an idealist. We let the word *mind* include all sorts of ideas about mind, and at the same time are ready to give him a good deal of choice about its defining property; whereas we expect that *matter*, being the subject, will keep to its ordinary Range even if not its ordinary definition ... On the other hand, if we suppose him to mean 'matter is typical of mind', or the norm in terms of which mind must be interpreted, we have made him a materialist; clearly this is not what would be expected from the sentence, but in speaking we would expect a stress on *mind*. To say it with a stress on *matter* would be more baffling, perhaps because that makes the 'typical' idea more possible, but even so it would not be clearly in play. (1951, pp. 352–3)

What this passage brings out to striking effect is the shift that had occurred in Empson's thinking about a range of interconnected topics, among them the mind/nature dualism, the truth-claims of idealist (or pantheist) doctrine, the relation between cognitive and emotive uses of language, and the extent to which we can or should make sense of utterances conveying some 'deep' truth beyond reach of clear-cut linguistic expression. Compared with the 'niggling' pages on Wordsworth in *Seven Types* it is obviously prepared to treat such claims with a much greater measure of tolerance, a willingness to take them as probably implying some structure of semantic equations (or subtly qualified entailment clauses) which doesn't just exploit the mechanism of 'false identity', but which gives the interpreter a fair chance to make decent – humanly accountable – sense of the thought processes involved. Not that Empson is any better disposed toward massively 'deviant' examples of the kind, as in the downright vacuous pronouncements of Mary Baker Eddy. But he does make the point throughout this chapter – and likewise in 'Sense in *The Prelude*' – that we possess a whole range of interpretive strategies, or techniques for redefining the senses carried by subject and predicate in any given case, which mostly provide some intelligible meaning for the doctrine or truth-claim concerned.

Thus, for instance, 'you can take a wide sense for "B", and colour all this field with the feelings due to a normal use of it ... and meanwhile you take a narrow sense for "A", the "essential" one, so as to include only such cases as the epigram wants to deal with' (1951, p. 352). His case in point here is the philosopher who says 'matter is mind', thus inviting us to cast around for construals of the statement that give it a fair claim to be taken seriously, at least as an outlook that falls within the range of conceivable (or humanly imaginable) 'solutions' to the mind/nature antinomy. And the chapter comes up with various examples from Christian, Buddhist, Hindu and other sources, all of which involve some kind of nature-mysticism or some appeal beyond the limits of common-sense rational thought, but which Empson now treats – with the benefit of his new analytical 'machinery' – as often having something of importance to say about the modes and varieties of religious belief. The typical form here is the identity statement whose terms are reversible ('A is B' or 'B is A') and where the order of priority is established – if at all – only by the appeal to some background context or communal belief-system. Such ideas can still do great harm, he thinks, if attached to a strain of political propaganda (or national-aestheticist ideology) which allows them to take on a mobilizing force in the service of this or that Absolute value equated with the manifest destiny of some particular language, culture or dominant interest group. Even so, the device has its more benign uses, as Empson suggests in the following passage of acute socio-political commentary:

> The practice of making deep philosophical assertions in the form 'A is B', obviously prominent among the Germans, seems to have come in with the first translations of the Hindu sacred texts. The 'That art Thou' of Hindu mysticism ('with the accent on the Thou') may well have a historical connection with 'Might is Right', though nationalism is about the last idea it was originally intended to convey. The idea that everything is One seems to have been particularly welcome, not merely where the intellectuals were moving away from Christianity, but where a lack of national unity made them feel insecure. Boston was taking a special interest in transcendentalism during the thirty years or so up to the American Civil War; and

perhaps one could claim the line from Vico to Croce as showing the same movement in Italy, the third striking case of a country trying to become One. The relations of Marxism to Hegel are a more baffling topic, but the One might be taken to imply either that the whole world should become communist or that no activity can be independent of the class struggle. (1951, p. 362)

There are, I think, some crucial points to be made about Empson's approach to these far-reaching questions in the realm of language, politics, ideology and representation. The first is that he clearly appreciates the dangers of a creed – like the German or Italian autonomist movements – which may start out with the expression of genuine progressive or emancipatory ideals, but which can then be exploited to produce a rhetoric of mystified organicist values, a language whose undoubted suasive appeal derives from its treating the nation-state as a kind of natural entity, subject to 'laws' of growth and evolution that readily translate into the fascist doctrine of manifest national destiny. Heidegger would, of course, be the prime example of a thinker who had taken this path, staking his entire philosophical project – his quest for an 'authentic' language with access to primordial sources of Being and truth – on the notion that such access was vouchsafed only to the bearers of a privileged national culture, one that had received the 'question of Being' bequeathed by the ancient Greeks, and whose destiny it was to redeem that promise in the moment of its imminent self-realization as the voice and conscience of world-historical Spirit (see Heidegger, 1958; 1971). But the same tendency is visible, as Empson remarks, across a wide range of cultures and socio-linguistic contexts where the background situation involves some appeal to a transcendent unifying principle, whether God, Nature or Truth as embodied in the sovereign nation-state. In such cases one finds that expressions of the form 'A = B' take on a particular prominence, most often in conjunction with a deviant structure of equations *within the two terms* which makes it difficult or impossible to assign a clear-cut order of logico-semantic priority. For at this point language gets so far out of touch with our usual 'machinery' for interpreting complex words – that is to say, the normal range of predicative functions or forms of 'compacted statement' – that it operates almost entirely by means of emotive or rhetorical effect, and can thus be used to insinuate all manner of false (but none the less potent) irrational belief.

Other commentators – Paul de Man among them (de Man, 1983,

pp. 246–66) – have pointed to the deep-laid affinity that exists between Heidegger's appalling political 'misjudgement' and his mystified ontology of language, Being, and truth (see also Norris, 1990, pp. 222–83). There is no mention of Heidegger anywhere in Empson's work, but his reference to Croce in the above passage gives a hold for similar reflections. For it is here that one finds the closest convergence between Empson's and de Man's otherwise very disparate (indeed antagonistic) modes of approach. What is it about language, they both want to know, that encourages this drive toward monistic or holist philosophies of mind, nature and history, doctrines whose import carries across – at least under certain socio-historical conditions – from the realm of arcane metaphysics ('Matter is Mind', 'God is All in All' etc.) to the realm of national-populist sentiment and downright political propaganda? For de Man, the answer is to be sought in that potent (but none the less delusory) strain of 'aesthetic ideology' that collapses the distinction between phenomenal experience, intuitive knowledge or sensuous perceptions on the one hand, and language, textuality or structures of figural representation on the other. One can thus – so he argues – trace a line of descent, or a history of deepening mystification, that runs all the way from Schiller's seminal misreading of Kant to the various schools of present-day linguistic, philosophical and literary thought, movements whose seemingly diverse character conceals their common point of origin in the error (the phenomenalist or organicist delusion) that assimilates language to the naturalized order of 'common-sense' perceptual grasp.

Hence de Man's well-known (and knowingly provocative) statement in his essay 'The Resistance to Theory': that

> [w]hat we call ideology is precisely the confusion of linguistic with natural reality, of reference with phenomenalism. [From which] it follows that, more than any other mode of inquiry, the linguistics of literariness is a powerful and indispensable tool in the unmasking of ideological aberrations, as well as a determining factor in accounting for their occurrence. (1986, p. 11)

In which case one can see why he attaches such importance to the rhetorical close-reading of those various influential texts – from Kant, Hegel and Schiller to Heidegger, the American New Critics and exponents of mainstream Romantic scholarship – where the question is raised of how aesthetic judgement stands in relation to the other (cognitive or ethical) dimensions of human self-knowledge. 'Mere reading' can accomplish this critical task, according to de Man, since 'very often in spite of itself [that is to say, whatever its foregone doctrinal commitments] it cannot fail to respond to structures of language which it is the more or less secret aim of literary teaching to keep hidden' (p. 24). What typically occurs in the discourse of 'aesthetic ideology' is a blurring of ontological distinctions, a will to elevate certain kinds of language (especially metaphor and symbol) to the point where they assume a transcendent or quasi-mystical status, a capacity to reconcile mind and nature – along with all the other Kantian antinomies – in a moment of achieved visionary insight somehow giving access, as Wordsworth believed, to 'the one life, within us and abroad'. But we had better beware this deep-laid aestheticizing impulse – this desire for a language surpassing the limits of commonplace thought and perception – if it can always give rise to those other, more insidious 'claims on our freedom' that emerge in the post-Romantic discourse on art, culture and the nation-state as principles of revealed truth.

This is why de Man pitches the claims so high when recommending a 'return to philology', or a renewed attentiveness to aspects of language (especially its figural aspect) that tend to disrupt or resist the smooth passage from word to world. And one (if not the only) means of such resistance is the practice of a vigilant deconstructive reading alert to the various symptomatic blind-spots – in particular, the discrepancies between logic, grammar and rhetoric – that occur most often when critics or philosophers fall into this mystified habit of thought. 'For it is', de Man writes, 'as a political force that the aesthetic still concerns us as one of the most powerful ideological drives to act upon the reality of history' (1984, p. 264). Again, Heidegger is the preeminent case of a thinker who raised this 'overcoming' of Western metaphysics into a wholesale national-aestheticist creed where the German language and its privileged exemplars – poets like Hölderlin and Rilke chief among them – were treated as the oracles of a revealed truth, a fulfilment of the destiny that also took shape (or which found its most 'authentic' political expression) in the advent of Hitler and the rise-to-power of a populist movement founded on the same principles. It is for this reason that de Man's late pronouncements on aesthetic ideology adopt such an urgent, even minatory tone, as when he asks us to note 'the potentially violent streak' in Schiller's philosophy of art and culture, or when he comments – again with reference to Schiller

– that '[i]f the aesthetic model is itself flawed or, worse, if it covers up this lesion by a self-serving idealization, then the classical concept of aesthetic education is open to suspicion' (p. 280). And we should be wrong to underestimate the real-world consequences of an issue that might appear as just a matter of specialized concern among a few literary theorists or philosophers of language. For there is, so he argues, a fateful seductiveness about such notions – an appeal to values deeply enshrined within the discourse of modern (post-Kantian) speculative thought – which very easily persuades us to take them on board without attending *either* to their strategies of argument, epistemological truth-claims, modes of textual articulation etc., *or* to their possible effects when translated into a full-blown nationalist mystique of origins and destiny, a creed backed up by the rhetorical will-to-power vested in 'totalizing' figures like metaphor, synecdoche and symbol. Thus '[a]esthetic education by no means fails; it succeeds all too well, to the point of hiding the violence that makes it possible' (p. 289).

This 'violence' can take effect in manifold ways, from the textual-hermeneutic – as with Heidegger's 'blind and violent' appropriative reading of Hölderlin's poetry – to those forms of political mass indoctrination that likewise depend upon the suasive power of a language whose rhetoric brooks no resistance, since it claims to transcend or to have finally 'overcome' the antinomies of enlightened critical reason. This is why it became such an urgent question for de Man 'whether aesthetic values can be compatible with the linguistic structures that make up the entities from which these values are derived' (1986, p. 25). For it was only in so far as rhetorical exegesis could go against the grain of aesthetic ideology – that is to say, provide cogent argumentative *proof* of the errors, confusions, textual misprisions, interpretive blind-spots etc. brought about by compliant or complicitous readings – that criticism might hope to expose the workings of that same ideology and counter its more harmful effects. 'What gives the aesthetic its power and hence its practical, political impact is its intimate link with knowledge, the epistemological implications that are always in play when the aesthetic appears over the horizon of discourse' (1984, p. 265). And again, more specifically: 'what is called, in conscious reference to Kant and to the questionable version of Kant that is found in Schiller, the *aesthetic*, is not a separate category but a principle of articulation between various faculties, activities, and modes of cognition' (p. 265). De Man's argument – pursued with great subtlety and rigour in the essays of his last decade – is that the course of aesthetic speculation after Kant was in most respects a retrograde movement, a series of failures (or blind refusals) to acknowledge the significant problems which arise whenever Kant appeals to that category as a mediating term between sensuous cognitions and concepts of understanding (as in the first *Critique*), or again, between judgements of taste and issues in the realm of ethics or practical reason. Where these commentators mostly go wrong – taking a lead from Schiller, Goethe, Coleridge and other such proponents of symbol or metaphor as figures of transcendent imaginative truth – is in supposing that the aesthetic can actually *achieve* what it sets out to do, that is, offer a means of ultimate reconciliation between these various modes or faculties of knowledge. Hence the idea of the poem as a 'verbal icon' or (in more Hegelian parlance) as a 'concrete universal', a structure of inwrought rhetorical figures – metaphor, irony, paradox etc. – which somehow gives access to a realm of jointly sensuous, intellectual and spiritual understanding beyond all the vexing antinomies of plain-prose reason (Wimsatt, 1954; 1976).

Small wonder, as de Man very pointedly remarks, that this 'aesthetic ideology' should then give rise not only to a certain idealizing bent among post-Romantic critics and philosopher-poets, but also to 'a principle of political value and authority that has its own claims on the shape and the limits of our freedom' (1984, p. 264). For the effect of such large-scale investments in the aesthetic – especially when linked to the organicist idea of language as providing a direct link between concepts and the realm of natural or phenomenal experience – is to bring *all* the faculties under the rule of that implacably determinist logic that, for Kant, applied only to epistemological questions, and not to matters of reflective self-knowledge, practical reason or ethico-political judgement. One can therefore understand why de Man laid such stress on the need for a thoroughgoing critical re-assessment of the texts that had played a major role in promoting this mystified aesthetic ontology. It would involve, first and foremost, a continuing engagement with the kinds of rhetorical close-reading which the American New Critics had brought to a high point of sophisticated method and technique, an achievement that de Man – unlike some of his more fashion-conscious acolytes – never sought to dismiss as just a relic of old (i.e., pre-deconstructive) times. For it remained the great merit of this approach that it focused attention squarely on the text, on local complexities of logic, grammar and rhetoric, and thus enabled students to register anomalous or discrepant details that might always be passed over by a reading whose primary aim – as in Heidegger's exegeses of Hölderlin – was to discover some 'deep' ontological import, some meaning or moment of revealed truth beyond the mere 'words on the page'. Thus

> [students] were asked ... to begin by reading texts closely as texts and not to move at once into the general context of human experience or history. Much more humbly or modestly, they were to start out from the bafflement that such singular turns of tone, phrase, and figure were bound to produce in readers attentive enough to notice them and honest enough not to hide their non-understanding behind the screen of ideas that often passes, in literary instruction, for humanistic knowledge. (de Man, 1986, p. 23)

In this respect, at any rate, the 'old' New Criticism still had much to commend it. But its limits showed up – so de Man thought – at the point where rhetorical close-reading gave way to yet another form of mystified 'aesthetic ideology', in this case a doctrine of the poem as 'verbal icon', as an instance of language transcending the limits of everyday communicative discourse through a specialized rhetoric of irony, paradox and other such New Critical master-tropes. For there could then be no question of resisting their suasive ontological appeal by reading with an eye to those moments of potential *disruption* in the text – moments of unresolved tension between logic and grammar, grammar and rhetoric or the constative and performative aspects of language – which alone gave a hold for the kind of deconstructive *Ideologiekritik* that de Man sought to practise in his late writings. 'To empty rhetoric of its epistemological function is only possible', he argues,

> because its tropological, figural functions are being bypassed. It is as if, to return for a moment to the model of the *trivium*, rhetoric could be isolated from the generality that grammar and logic have in common and considered as a mere correlative of an illocutionary power. (1986, pp. 18–19)

That is to say, the New Critical version of 'rhetoric' is one that can easily be put to such mystifying uses, since on the one hand it invests certain rhetorical figures (irony, paradox etc.) with a truth-telling power beyond reach of critique or counter-argument, while on the other it proposes a wholesale ontology of poetic meaning, value and form on the basis of this same seductive appeal to that which inherently transcends the grasp of rational-discursive thought. Thus aesthetic ideology always lays claim to a 'wisdom that lies somewhat beyond cognition and self-knowledge, yet that can only be reached by ways [*sic*] of the process it is said to overcome' (1984, p. 265).

Hence de Man's insistence that the study of rhetoric cannot be divorced from the 'epistemology of tropes', or the critical dimension that opens up as soon as one allows that language may contain disruptive, problematic or anomalous functions that resist this powerful aestheticizing drive. For '[d]ifficulties occur', as he puts it most succinctly, 'only when it is no longer possible to ignore the epistemological thrust of the rhetorical dimension of discourse' (1986, p. 14). And Nietzsche provides the best source of guidance here, since on de Man's reading it is Nietzsche's 'final insight' – achieved through a strenuous labour of deconstructive analysis – that

> what is called 'rhetoric' is precisely the gap that becomes apparent in the pedagogical and philosophical history of the term. Considered as persuasion, rhetoric is performative but when considered as a system of tropes, it deconstructs its own performance. (de Man, 1979, p. 131)

It should be obvious by now how mistaken is that widespread view of de Man's criticism – or of 'deconstruction' more generally – as a mere technique for making trouble, a species of out-and-out 'textualist' licence for flouting all the rules of interpretive fidelity and truth, provided the result goes against some received (canonical or common-sense) view. On the contrary: it is de Man's claim that rhetorical close-reading in the deconstructive mode is more truthful, more attentive to the letter of the text, and above all more resistant to those various kinds of deep-laid motivating prejudice – like the complex of notions summed up in his phrase 'aesthetic ideology' – which induce critics to ignore what is demonstrably there on the page and substitute their own preferred reading of the passage in question. Thus de Man (in his 'Foreword' to Jacobs (1978)):

> Understanding is not a version of one single and universal Truth that would exist as an essence, a hypostasis. The truth of a text is a much more literal and empirical event. What makes a reading more or less true is simply the predictability, the necessity of its occurrence, regardless of the reader's or of the author's wishes ... It depends, in other words, on the rigour of the reading as an argument. Reading is an argument ... because it has to go against the grain of what one would want to happen in the name of what has to happen. (p. ix)

In short, de Man's project has nothing in common with those other, more flamboyantly 'textualist' versions of the deconstructive enterprise that renounce all concern with matters of validity or truth, since surely we *know* by now (after Nietzsche and Derrida) that such values are rhetorical through and through, that truth-claims are merely the expression of an epistemic will-to-power, that concepts are just a species of sublimated metaphor, philosophy just one more 'kind of writing', etc.[4] If this were the case then de Man would clearly be deluded in advancing such high claims for the effectiveness of deconstruction as a means of countering aesthetic ideology and its various harmful extrapolations into the realm of history and politics. For those claims depend entirely on the *truth* of his readings, their capacity not only to persuade us through the exercise of superior rhetorical skills, but to bring out the errors, misprisions, aberrations and moments of symptomatic 'blindness' that result when interpreters fail to respect the imperatives of textual close-reading.

This is why it is so important, in de Man's view, to distinguish the two chief senses of 'rhetoric', or the tension that has always inhabited that term: on the one hand its suasive or performative aspect (as appealed to by neo-pragmatist adepts like Rorty and Fish), and on the other its 'epistemological impact' as a study of the tropes and rhetorical figures that cannot be straightforwardly assimilated to the model of language as suasive utterance. This is why, as he puts it, 'speech-act oriented techniques of reading read only to the extent that they prepare the ground for the rhetorical reading they avoid' (1986, p. 17). For the upshot of any such exclusively performative approach – as exemplified by Fish's repeated debunkings of 'theory' in any whatever shape or form – is to make it strictly inconceivable that reading could ever go against the grain of some existing consensus, 'interpretive community' or set of in-place cultural values and beliefs. For de Man, on the contrary, this move to narrow down the working definition of 'rhetoric' – to empty the term of its critical or epistemological function – must be seen as a strategy of evasion, a refusal to engage with texts at precisely the point where language generates maximal resistance to

[4] For the most influential statement of this view, see 'Philosophy as a Kind of Writing' (Rorty, 1982, pp. 89–109); also Norris, 'Philosophy as *Not* just a "Kind of Writing": Derrida and the Claim of Reason' (in R. W. Dasenbrock, 1989, pp. 189–203); and Rorty, 'Two Meanings of "Logocentrism": a Reply to Norris' (in Dasenbrock, 1989, pp. 204–16).

naïve or phenomenalist readings. And it is a move, moreover, that only becomes possible 'because its [i.e. the text's] tropological, figural functions are being bypassed', thus allowing a critic like Fish to argue – often, be it said, with a great show of plausibility – that meaning is entirely a product of readerly conventions, that suasive rhetoric goes 'all the way down', and that any such talk of textual 'resistance' (or of readings that go 'against the grain' of our normal expectations) must therefore be utterly deluded.

So the stakes are indeed pretty high in this debate, and never more so than when de Man makes out his case for aesthetic ideology as the major (and continuing) source of those confusions whose 'impact' in the realm of history and politics we ignore at our peril. 'Mere reading, it turns out, prior to any theory, is able to transform critical discourse in a manner that would appear deeply subversive to those who think of the teaching of literature as a substitute for the teaching of theology, ethics, psychology, or intellectual history' (1986, p. 23). But it can only make good these far-reaching claims – only function, that is to say, as an effective form of *Ideologiekritik* – in so far as 'mere reading' is also, simultaneously, an *argument* that challenges received interpretive views, that takes full account of discrepant or resistant details in the text, and which engages such issues at a jointly rhetorical and epistemological level. Otherwise one could hardly make sense of de Man's seemingly exorbitant claim that 'more than any other mode of inquiry ... the linguistics of literariness is a powerful and indispensable tool in the unmasking of ideological aberrations, as well as a determining factor in accounting for their occurrence'. And again, with likewise provocative (but none the less serious) intent:

> [t]hose who reproach literary theory for being oblivious to social or historical (that is to say, ideological) reality are merely stating their fear at having their own ideological mystifications exposed by the tool they are trying to discredit. They are, in short, very poor readers of Marx's *German Ideology*. (1986, p. 11)

These and other passages from de Man's late essays should at least give pause to any reader who comes to them persuaded (as Fish would have it: *irresistibly* persuaded) that deconstruction is a rhetorical licence for making what one will of texts, or treating them with a blithe disregard for all the forms and protocols of right reading. For it is de Man's chief aim to give demonstrative *proof* that some readings are better – more truthful, cogent, or adequately argued – than others and, furthermore, that such issues can only be settled on the basis of a scrupulous regard for the text and a principled resistance to foregone ideas of what the text should or must mean according to some current consensus-belief. And nowhere is this argument more powerfully deployed than in de Man's reading of those poets, critics and philosophers – from Schiller to the present – whose work has been instrumental in promoting or contesting the claims of aesthetic ideology.

VI

I have taken this lengthy detour via de Man because his thinking converges with Empson's up to a point, and then – in ways that are equally instructive – pursues a quite different course. What unites them, as I have argued already, is a deep mistrust of those irrational doctrines – or those appeals to a higher, 'paradoxical' truth beyond the limits of everyday thought or cognition – which literary critics seem all too willing to endorse, even when the text (if examined more closely) turns out to controvert such claims, or to generate resistance through marked discrepancies of logic, grammar and rhetoric. To this extent Empson and de Man can be seen as engaged in kindred projects of critical deconstruction, a term that would apply to (say) the pages on Wordsworth in *Seven Types*, or the subsequent chapter in *Complex Words*, without losing its specific sense and becoming just a catch-all label of convenience. Again, they are both committed to the kind of analytic close-reading that refuses the blandishments – the rhetorical seductions – of a mystified aestheticist creed, and which holds to the principle of sometimes interpreting texts quite explicitly 'against the grain', rather than assenting to the suasive appeal of a language whose rhetoric (as distinct from its logic or grammar) would tend to encourage more compliant, unresisting or acquiescent habits of response. And for Empson, like de Man, it is important to keep up one's critical defences against such forms of readerly collusion, since poetry is *not* – as the New Critics would have it – an autonomous domain of inwrought ambiguities, ironies, paradoxes, structures of metaphorical meaning or whatever, a domain where issues of truth or falsehood are completely beside the point, and where value is defined exclusively in terms of *sui generis* 'aesthetic' criteria. On the contrary: any adequate reading of a poem will involve not only a meticulous attention to its formal and rhetorical structures, but also a proper waking interest in the *arguments* – the truth-claims, logico-semantic entailments, propositional attitudes, 'compacted doctrines' etc. – which cannot be simply ruled out of court by the interpreter in quest of some profound wisdom unbeholden to the standards of rational-discursive thought.

For poetry can and does 'make things happen', despite W. H. Auden's well-known statement of the contrary case,[5] and despite the numerous disclaimers to similar effect issued by critics from antiquity to the present. Moreover, its power to exert such an influence on thoughts, actions and events cannot be accounted for unless one acknowledges the truth-claims (that is to say, the cognitive, referential and socio-historical interests) that are always bound up with our reading of literary texts. After all, it was Auden – the late, 'apolitical' Auden – who effectively abandoned his own high-formalist stance by insisting on a poet's right (indeed, his moral duty) to suppress whole poems or particular passages that now struck him, in the wisdom of retrospect, as lending support to some dubious creed. 'This does not mean', as de Man puts it, 'that there can be a true reading; only that no reading is conceivable in which the question of its truth or falsehood is not primarily involved' (in Jacobs, 1978, p. xii). And any criticism that denies this relation between literature and truth-values – or which seeks (like so many present-day schools) to 'empty rhetoric of its epistemological impact' – will thereby demonstrate a plain incapacity for coping with the ethical issues involved.

Up to this point Empson and de Man appear embarked upon a similar task: that of undoing the specious truth-claims of aesthetic ideology and defending those other, less grandiose truths that emerge from the close-reading of literary texts. But then, as I have suggested, their paths diverge sharply, with the result that Empson came to regard the whole enterprise of recent (post-1970) critical theory as a massive and deplorable swing of fashion, a movement whose influence on critics like Kermode and Raymond Williams he found great cause for regret. What finally separates Empson from de Man is his downright rejection of the 'textualist' imperative, the idea – pushed to such extraordinary lengths in de Man's late essays – that the 'ethics of reading' can only be a matter of attending

5 'For poetry makes nothing happen: it survives / In the valley of its saying where executives / Would never want to tamper.' W. H. Auden, 'In Memory of W. B. Yeats' (1979, p. 82).

sedulously to the words on the page, excluding all reference to history, biography or other such 'extraneous' matters, and taking as one's law the absolute priority of language (or rhetoric) in the moment of encounter with this or that particular text. The point is driven home with such singular – not to say obsessive – regularity in de Man's writing that it scarcely needs documenting here. Its most extreme (and therefore best-known) formulations would include those passages from *Allegories of Reading*, especially in the chapters on Rousseau and Proust, where the question is raised 'whether a literary text is *about* that which it describes, represents, or states', and where the answer comes back – in this case concerning the episode of Marion and the purloined ribbon in Rousseau's *Confessions* – that 'the entire construction of drives, substitutions, repressions, and representations is the aberrant, metaphorical correlative of the absolute randomness of language, prior to any figuration or meaning' (1979, pp. 57 and 299). Then again, there is his essay on the *Social Contract*, tracking the various points of disjunction between rhetoric and grammar (or the performative and constative aspects of language), and commenting – in a passage that has predictably scandalized the Marxists and New Historicists – that 'textual allegories on this level of complexity generate history' (1979, p. 277).

But perhaps the most provocative of de Man's statements in this mode are those that concern the 'ethics of reading', the claim (taken up by J. Hillis Miller in his book of that title (Miller, 1987)) that deconstruction – or the kind of rhetorical exegesis practised in de Man's late essays – is the only way that criticism can do justice to the ethical demands placed upon it by the encounter with literary, philosophical or other types of text. Thus there is, Miller writes, 'a necessarily ethical moment in [the] act of reading itself, a moment neither cognitive, nor political, nor social, nor interpersonal, but properly and independently ethical' (p. 3). And this 'moment' can occur only on condition that the reader suspend his or her concern with those other kinds of notionally 'real-world' interest – social, historical, political etc. – that incessantly clamour for attention, and concentrate his or her efforts *solely and exclusively* on the text or the passage in hand. Those rival approaches are always to some extent 'vague and speculative', since they involve the importation of truth-claims, values, motivating interests etc. which derive from 'outside' the text, and which therefore offer a series of alibis – or readily available excuses – for *not* reading with sufficient attentiveness to the actual words on the page. And it is the great virtue of deconstruction, of the 'ethics of reading' as conceived by de Man and Miller, that it focuses directly on 'the real situation of a man or woman reading a book, teaching a class, writing a critical essay' (Miller, 1987, p. 4).

Clearly Miller is fighting what he takes to be a crucial campaign in the current faculty war between deconstruction and those in the other – mainly Marxist or New-Historicist – camp who have denounced it as a mere strategy of evasion, a set of geared-up rhetorical techniques for avoiding any talk of history, politics or gender issues. After all, what is left of the 'real situation' in which readers (men and women) currently find themselves if the act of reading is prescriptively defined as excluding all appeals to a context beyond the pure, self-isolating, apodictic 'moment' of encounter between reader and text? 'No doubt', as Miller somewhat grudgingly concedes, 'that "situation" spreads out to involve institutional, historical, economic, or political "contexts", but it begins with and returns to the man or woman face to face with the words on the page' (p. 4). And his book follows de Man with extreme – at times near-verbatim – fidelity in arguing that ethical questions always come down to a certain 'linguistic predicament'; that they involve moments of unresolvable conflict between different (e.g. performative and constative) 'codes' in the text; that these conflicts can only be addressed through the kind of rhetorical close-reading which de Man advocates; and finally, that any appeal to 'contexts' beyond this moment of first-hand encounter is sure to indicate a symptomatic failure of grasp, not only at the textual-interpretive level but also as regards the 'ethical' imperative to read what is given and close one's ears to the siren-calls of history, politics, social 'relevance' etc. Furthermore, we should see that this was always the case, even with philosophers – notably Kant – who sought to provide an absolute grounding for ethics (or practical reason) in the dictates of a sovereign faculty of judgement transcending all merely short-term, contingent or self-interested motives and values. For in Kant also, as Miller reads him, 'it is never possible to be sure that duty is not a fiction in the bad sense of an ungrounded act of self-sustaining language, that is, precisely a vain delusion and chimerical concept, a kind of ghost generated by a sad linguistic necessity' (p. 24).

Such is the upshot of Miller's argument – again following de Man – that there is and can be no moral law that would not turn out, in the last instance, to constitute a primary 'law of the text', an ethical injunction that we read with an eye to those fictive, allegorical or figural moments where the discourse of Kantian morality reveals its inescapably 'literary' (or rhetorical) character. Miller makes the point through an intertextual reading that couples some shrewdly chosen passages of Kant with Kafka's parable 'Before the Law', an episode from his novel *The Trial*. What de Man enables us to see in this conjuncture, Miller writes, is the fact that

> ethical obligations, demands, and judgments work in the same way as the court system in *The Trial* works ... that is, as one perpetually unverifiable referential dimension of an irresistible law, in de Man's case, a law of language ... The failure to read or the impossibility of reading is a universal necessity, one moment of which is that potentially aberrant form of language called ethical judgment or prescription. (p. 51)

In other words, 'ethics' is a name we give to that all-pervasive linguistic 'predicament' which requires nothing less than the suspension – the principled *ethical* suspension as Miller would have it – of every other claim upon our moral, social and political consciences. This is why, in Miller's view, an 'ethics of reading' is the nearest we can come to a genuine respect for those values of disinterested judgement, self-abnegating principle, detachment from self-seeking personal motives, etc., which have more or less defined the discourse of moral philosophy in its modern (post-Kantian) form. It is able to assume this exemplary role because, as de Man repeatedly argues, there is a 'law of the text' that compels readers – or at any rate those readers with sufficient powers of sustained analytic grasp – to take account of certain discrepant or unexpected details, aspects of the text that generate *resistance* precisely in so far as they thwart, baffle or frustrate one's desire for the pleasures of assured understanding. To read in this way is thus to meet up with the ultimate test of ethical good faith, that is to say, one's readiness to abandon such easy-going modes of personal fulfilment in compliance with a law that may always dictate a reading quite opposed to conventional habits of interpretive belief, aesthetic value-judgement or 'competent' reader-response.

Hence Miller's assertion, echoing de Man, that any serious engagement with ethical questions 'begins with and returns to ... the words on the page'. For it is only at this level of essentially contested meanings, values and truth-claims that thinking is enabled to resist the desire for an access to some ultimate source of revealed truth which would then be just the product – the reflex image – of its own will-to-power over persons or texts. And we should not be too worried, Miller implies, if de Man pushes this doctrine to the point where it acquires anti-humanist (or indeed quite inhuman) overtones, as when he reduces the guilt-ridden language of that episode from Rousseau's *Confessions* to an 'allegory' of the undecidable relation between constative (supposedly truth-telling) and performative (self-exculpating) modes of narrative discourse; or again, when he treats ethics as the product of a certain persistent 'linguistic confusion', one that results from the 'structural interference of two value systems', namely rhetoric in its twofold (suasive and tropological) aspects. For Miller – as indeed for de Man – this seems to be the only way that ethics can go once deprived of those illusory values and beliefs that formerly held it captive. Irony is a crucial stage in this demystifying process since its high points in the history of speculative thought – from Socrates to Kierkegaard, Friedrich Schlegel and the German Romantics – have also marked the advent of a critical consciousness that cannot rest content with received forms of knowledge or conventional value-judgements. Thus 'ironic language', as de Man understands it,

> splits the subject into an empirical self that exists in a state of inauthenticity and a self that exists only in the form of a language that asserts the knowledge of this inauthenticity. This does not, however, make it into an authentic language, for to know authenticity is not the same as to be authentic. (1983, p. 214)

Hence the vain effort of those critics and philosophers – and de Man offers several examples, among them Wayne Booth – who would seek to place a limit on the workings of irony (or contain its more radically unsettling effects) by appealing to some ultimate ground of assurance, by treating it as the 'prefiguration of a future recovery', or as 'the reconciliation of the self with the world by means of art'. These thinkers make a 'morally admirable' mistake, but a mistake nevertheless, since they have to ignore the sheer *impossibility* of bringing this process to a halt once the ironist – or the reader alert to such discrepancies between overt and covert intent – enters upon the path that inevitably leads to a *mise-en-abîme* of endless duplicity and doubt. In de Man's words, the exercise 'may start as a casual bit of play with a stray loose end of the fabric, but before long the entire texture of the self is unravelled and comes apart' (1983, p. 215). And so it turns out that deconstruction – or the textualist 'ethics of reading' proposed by Miller and de Man – is that which necessarily waits at the end of every road travelled by theorists of irony, even those 'morally admirable' characters (like Booth) who would prefer not to go the full distance. For in the end one has to recognize that it is *language*, not consciousness, that provides the only court of interpretive appeal, and that language is itself so unstable a medium – so riven with conflicts between grammar and rhetoric, constative and performative functions etc. – as to place any final, authoritative verdict way beyond hope of attainment.

If Miller and de Man are right, then this applies most of all to those issues that are raised when ethics seeks to adjudicate in matters of ultimate human concern. For what emerges from a deconstructive reading of texts from Kant, Schiller and Hegel to the modern schools of existentialist thought or post-Romantic literary criticism is that ethical discourse finds itself confronted with a stark (and perhaps impossible) choice. It can *either* seek refuge in mystified notions of authentic self-knowledge, existential good faith etc., *or* take the alternative (more courageous) path of acknowledging its own 'linguistic predicament', accepting that ethical issues are structured on the pattern of this omnipresent conflict between logic, grammar and rhetoric, and thus winning through to an undeluded knowledge of the factors that prevent any direct appeal to a language of pure, self-sustaining principles and values. In which case, as de Man argues, the most rigorous and *ethically accountable* approach to questions in the domain of moral philosophy would be one that consistently rejected the recourse to wider (interpersonal or socio-political) contexts of human experience, and which focused its attention solely on those moments of textual 'resistance' or aporia which characterize ethical language in general. It is in this sense, according to Geoffrey Galt Harpham, that deconstruction 'might be seen most profitably, not as a product of ethical reading, but as a hyper-articulated instance of ethical discourse' (Harpham, 1987, p. 140). That is to say, it inherits the terms of that discourse to the extent of insisting – like so many moral philosophers from Plato to Kant and beyond – that any *truly* ethical act or maxim will involve a certain thwarting of personal desires, a check to our 'natural' inclinations and appetites, or a principled *resistance* to modes of fulfilment that would otherwise acknowledge no such constraint upon their freedom to follow the dictates of mere self-interested, pleasure-seeking will. Thus Kant and de Man '[b]oth posit on the one hand a "free" subject who would, if not coerced, follow its "desires"; and on the other, some utter and external rebuke to those desires, whether in the law or in the text' (p. 141).

So we should be wrong (Harpham thinks) to dismiss de Man's arguments out of hand, or to treat his and Miller's high claims for the 'ethics of reading' as just another version of the deconstructive ploy that reduces everything – truth, reason, history, politics, ethics – to the level of its own merely 'textualist' preoccupations. For de Man is still working with the same basic premise – the idea of *resistance* as an ultimate principle of truth, meaning and value – which has typified not only ethical discourse conceived as an autonomous mode of enquiry, but also the close relationship presumed to exist between ethics and the critical, truth-seeking interests of science, epistemology, political philosophy and other such self-disciplined modes of enquiry. Moreover, there is a sense in which de Man's constant talk of 'resistance' shows him still adhering to a Kantian (subject-centred) theory of ethical value, despite all his efforts to redefine that term in a strictly linguistic or textual register, and thereby to shift the whole ground of debate toward a deconstructive 'rhetoric of tropes'. For, as Harpham notes, it is a principle common to de Man, Kant and much recent thinking on the topic that 'the subject itself has a self-interfering, self-resisting, self-overcoming ethical "thickness", and that the moral law or [in de Man's case] the inhumanity of the text is no more external to the subject than are its "desires"' (p. 141). To this extent it would seem that deconstruction is indeed – in Harpham's striking phrase – a 'hyperarticulated' instance of ethical discourse, one that presses resistance to the point where it can only be defined in rigorous opposition to the terms, concepts and evaluative standards of first-order moral judgement.

On the other hand, Harpham is far from convinced that this 'ethics of reading' can really make good its principal claim, that is to say, the idea – embraced with such fierce determination by Miller and de Man – that rhetorical exegesis in the deconstructive mode is the best (indeed, the only) means of doing justice to literature's full range of moral, historical and socio-political concerns. His doubts are expressed in the following passage, which strikes me now – after much wrestling with de Man's work – as an admirable statement of the problems involved. 'The vexation many feel about deconstruction', Harpham writes,

> is an obscure reflection of the fact that deconstruction is both fanatically ethical and amoral. It does not sufficiently credit the drive for interpretation which literature also stimulates, and in fact treats this drive as though it were unethical and should therefore be resisted. What we prize most in literature may be, as I suggested, its 'unreadability'. But if literature were only unreadable, it would remain at the margins of human interest, in the position which deconstruction proudly cultivates. (p. 144)

Harpham's point here is one that leads back (not before time) to my argument concerning Empson's differences with just about everything that presently counts as 'advanced' literary theory. What is at issue is the question of how far criticism can rely on close-reading – or rhetorical exegesis – as a substitute for those other, more 'traditional' approaches that don't involve the same *de jure* veto on talk of authorial intentions, biography, historical context and so forth. For Empson, these latest super-subtle techniques were just another variant of the 'old' New Critical doctrine, the formalist idea (as promoted most zealously by critics like Wimsatt and Brooks) that the 'words on the page' are all that is required, or anyway all that *ought* to be required, since a critic who invokes 'extraneous' sources of information will thereby demonstrate either that the poem stands in need of such treatment – in which case it is a bad poem – or (more likely) that they have failed to read it with an adequate attention to matters of rhetorical detail. Where this doctrine went wrong, Empson thought, was in setting itself up as the one right method for interpreting literary texts, a method that regarded rhetorical close-reading as the only reputable game in town, and which could thus be used – as by critics like Wimsatt – for importing all kinds of dogmatic or unargued value-judgement under cover of a principled respect for 'the words on the page'. And this technique was rendered all the more effective by the formalist triple injunction: *not* to read poetry as entailing truth-claims, arguing a case or making sense in rational-discursive terms; *not* to take account of authorial intentions where this meant appealing to a larger ('extra-textual') background of reconstructed motives and interests; and *not* to make use of historical source-material unless it served merely as an anecdotal back-up for some reading arrived at through proper application of the standard New Critical methods. For the effect of these ideas – as Empson saw it – was to treat the critic as a privileged dispenser of truths known only through such expert procedures of arcane hermeneutical grasp, procedures which often (as in the case of Kermode) took on a divinatory, quasi-theological import. And from this point of view, expressed with increasing vehemence from the mid-sixties on, it seemed to Empson that 'new textualism' was really just old formalism writ large.

The main issue, once again, is that of 'resistance', or of whether – as de Man and Miller would have it – 'mere reading' in the textual-rhetorical mode can so effectively resist our settled expectations as to bring about a genuine shake-up in our habits of value-judgement, thought and belief. That this seems scarcely possible from the Wimsatt position of self-assured orthodox grasp is Empson's main reason for thinking such doctrines a melancholy sign of the times. Thus, to repeat: '[t]he idea that a piece of writing which excited moral resistance might be a discovery in morals, a means of learning what was wrong with the existing system, somehow cannot enter his mind; and yet surely this has often happened and provides the only interesting question for his article' (1987a, p. 126). Empson's point – here as so often in his later essays and reviews – is that any such 'resistance' will have to involve something more than textual close-reading in the manner that Wimsatt approves. For the willingness to grapple with complexities of language – paradox, ambiguity, irony, aporia and suchlike – is no guarantee that the critic won't end by 'discovering' some recondite meaning or moral, some latent truth of the text that perfectly matches her or his preconceived notions. After all, these methods had first been devised for the purpose of scriptural exegesis, and they still carried overtones – quite explicit in T. S. Eliot's case – of a technique that aimed to bring reading into line with the dictates of orthodox faith. 'I should think indeed', Empson writes, 'that a profound enough criticism could extract an entire cultural history from a simple lyric, rather like Lancelot Andrewes and his fellow preachers, "dividing the Word of God", who were in the habit of extracting all Protestant theology from a single text' (1987a, p. 107).

This remark occurs in a 1950 essay ('The Verbal Analysis') that Empson contributed to a *Kenyon Review* symposium, along with other prominent critics – Cleanth Brooks among them – who had been asked to offer some personal reflections on the current state of literary studies. At the time, Empson took a fairly relaxed view of the way things were going, albeit with apologies to his earnest colleagues for not having managed to 'raise the spirits to answer in the high tone which these questions deserve' (1987a, p. 109). But five years later, in the rejoinder to Wimsatt, he had clearly come to feel that this trend was doing great harm, and that rhetorical exegesis in the manner prescribed by Wimsatt, Brooks and their fellow New Critics was a positive hindrance to the teaching of literature as a source of genuine moral 'discoveries' about cultures, values and belief-systems other than our own. By now he had encountered many more examples of how the method worked out in practice, and the results struck him as uniformly bad, or at any rate worse than he had ever imagined when writing those passages of *Seven Types* – notably the analysis of Herbert's 'The Sacrifice' – which likewise pushed close-reading to the point where 'paradox' became a virtual touchstone of poetic value. And so Empson set about the uphill task of rescuing literary studies from what he saw as the two main corrupting influences at work among academic critics. One was the strain of neo-orthodox Christian thought – or the fashion for pious revisionist readings – which had come about largely through Eliot's influence on schools like the American New Criticism. And the other was that high formalist tendency, also much encouraged by Eliot, which treated poetry as a realm quite apart from the interests of plain-prose reason; which refused on principle to entertain matters of biography, history, authorial intention etc.; and which only took account of 'resistance' in so far as that idea could be construed in strictly immanent or textualist terms, that is, as a force-field of rhetorical tensions (ambiguity, paradox, irony etc.) whose import the critic was enabled to reveal through certain expert hermeneutical techniques. Their combined effect, Empson thought, was to shut down the workings of intellectual conscience and imaginative sympathy alike, so that criticism became nothing more than a sounding-board for this or that crampingly orthodox 'movement' decked out in the latest theoretical colours. And he would have had little reason to modify this view if presented with arguments for an 'ethics of reading' which took *resistance* as a programmatic key term, but which then made a point of defining that term so as to exclude any possible grounds of appeal to interests outside the self-insulated context of 'the man or woman face to face with the words on the page'. For in the end it is hard to see how Miller's formulation goes decisively beyond the formalist tenets of 'old' New Criticism, or makes out a case for regarding deconstruction – at least in its US-domesticated form – as a definite advance beyond the precepts and principles defended by critics like Wimsatt and Brooks.

As we have seen, Empson went various ways around to counter the disabling effects of this tendency, effects that were clearly visible (he thought) in the widespread regression to a style of textual exegesis with strongly marked theological overtones. Empson's argument is stated with maximum vigour and brevity in the following passage from his 1973 tribute to I. A. Richards, a critic whose work he now regarded – despite their various theoretical differences over the years – as a valuable corrective to this latest fashion for narrowly orthodox habits of response. 'The main purpose of reading imaginative literature', Empson writes,

> is to grasp a wide variety of experience, imagining people with codes and customs very unlike one's own; and it cannot be done except in a Benthamite manner, that is, by thinking 'how would such a code or custom work out?' In both countries [i.e., Britain and North America] this whole conception seems to have been dropped; and I should think it was done, again and again, as if in solitude, by university teachers wanting to retain good relations with school teachers – who naturally want to tell the children that all decent people agree with Teacher. The influence of Eliot would be a great help. (1987a, p. 218)

There seemed little hope of reversing this conformist drift if the only kind of 'resistance' that critics could envisage was the kind that arose from textual complications which their own interpretive methods and procedures were uniquely well qualified to expound. For Empson, on the contrary, one main requirement for making sense of 'codes and customs very unlike our own' was to read with a view to the different kinds of *argument* – the truth-claims, validity-conditions, structures of logico-semantic entailment and so forth – which the formalists made such a point of ignoring in their devotion to ever more exiguous techniques of rhetorical close-reading, and their adherence to an anti-cognitivist creed that ruled such interests strictly out of court. In *Complex Words* Empson puts this case at its strongest: that is to say, the idea that 'reading is an argument' *not* (as de Man would have it) because rhetorical figures always turn out to undermine or deconstruct the logic and the grammar of propositional meaning, but because – quite the reverse – our competence as readers, or our capacity to interpret any sort of language, depends upon our grasp of those verbal 'equations' whose meaning can only be analysed in terms of compacted propositional structures.

It is here – on this issue of relative priority between logic, grammar and rhetoric – that Empson differs most profoundly with theorists like Miller and de Man. For there is, so he would argue, absolutely no reason to suppose that rhetoric goes 'all the way down', or that verbal exegesis must always reach the point where logical explanations run out, where reason is brought up against its limits and where figures like paradox and aporia turn out to command the field. Such notions have acquired something like canonical status among the recent vanguard schools of literary theory, from New Criticism to at least one variety of deconstruction. But as Empson sees it, this just goes to show how easily critics can be led astray – or induced to accept all manner of irrationalist doctrine – when their geared-up methods of rhetorical close-reading get too far out of touch with the normative standards of our everyday competence as language-users.

Thus 'the trouble about modern criticism, a wonderfuly powerful instrument, is that it is always liable to be applied totally upside-down' (Empson, 1987a, p. 601). And never more so, he thought, than when the textualist imperative (the idea of extracting every last subtlety, every possible hint of irony or paradox from 'the words on the page') became joined to an orthodox movement of belief with thinly veiled religious overtones. That deconstruction is capable of just such a reading – despite the vigorous denials to be found here and there in Derrida's work – is clear enough from recent efforts (by Mark Taylor (1984), Thomas Altizer (1982) and others (e.g. Hart, 1989)) to annex it to a version of the 'death of God' rhetoric, the strain of so-called 'negative theology' developed by speculative thinkers in the 1960s. And although this involves – as I have argued elsewhere – a plain misconstrual of the passages concerned,[6] nevertheless it does indicate one major liability of any critical project that defines itself (like deconstruction) in terms of a rhetoric or generalized tropology conceived as surpassing all the powers and limits

[6] In his recent remarks on the subject Derrida has taken a more permissive line, tending to the view that 'deconstruction' is a multiple and culturally varied activity, so that no one should expect him – its nominal 'inventor' – to pronounce on the validity or otherwise of (e.g.) 'negative theology' and its current deconstructive offshoots. Nevertheless there are several passages in his earlier work that quite explicitly contest such claims, among them the statement that 'what is thus denoted as *différance* is not theological, not even in the most negative order of negative theology. The latter, as we know, is always occupied with letting a supraessential reality go beyond the finite categories of essence and existence, that is, of presence, and always hastens to remind us that, if we deny the predicate of existence to God, it is in order to recognize him as a superior, inconceivable, and ineffable mode of being. Here there is no question of such a move, as will be confirmed as we go along' (Jacques Derrida, 1973, p. 134).

of rational-discursive thought. It was this supposition that Empson found so suspect when confronted with its impact upon the teaching of literature through the highly effective pedagogical agency of the 'old' New Criticism. And he picked up more than a hint of the same unfortunate tendency at work in those later theorists, like Frank Kermode, who had once again fallen prey – as Empson saw it – to the creeping malaise of a 'textualist' obsession that blocked any appeal to historical realities or truths of human experience outside the endlessly duplicitous play of rhetorical figures and tropes. For if these critics were right then clearly there was no possibility of escaping from the much-touted 'hermeneutic circle', the idea that textual meaning could only be a product of the various sense-making codes, conventions, value-judgements or interpretive methods that happened to prevail within this or that community of like-minded exegetes. In which case the one and only lesson that literature had to teach was the knock-down neo-pragmatist argument advanced by Stanley Fish: that readers will always, inevitably, find what they are looking for in texts, and that no amount of theory, meticulous close-reading, rhetorical exegesis or deconstructive talk of textual 'resistance' can possibly make the least difference to this elementary fact about the nature of interpretive consensus-interests. Certainly it would leave no room for Empson's claim that the only good reason for reading imaginative literature was the scope it gave for making 'moral discoveries', for grasping 'a wide variety of experience' or for 'imagining people with codes and customs very unlike our own'.

It is worth bearing all this in mind when one comes across the footnote to *Complex Words* – seemingly a casual afterthought – where Empson comments:

By the way, the term Ambiguity, which I used in a book title and as a kind of slogan, implying that the reader is left in doubt between two readings, is [here] more or less superseded by the idea of a double meaning which is intended to be fitted into a definite structure. You can still have a doubt as to whether one or other of two structures is meant but this is much less common and belongs rather to peculiar states of dramatic self-conflict. (1951, p. 103n)

It is by way of these 'structures' – or forms of compacted propositional logic, condensing whole arguments into a single key-word like 'sense', 'honest', 'fool', or 'wit' – that Empson avoids the irrationalist tendency to elevate rhetoric over reason, or to single out some privileged rhetorical trope (whether 'paradox', 'irony' or 'aporia') as the end-point and veritable *ne plus ultra* of all critical endeavour. And he sticks to this principle even where the method comes up against problems, as with Wordsworth's use of 'deviant' Type IV equations which effectively collapse or short-circuit the normal structures of predicative thought, and which thus allow the poet to communicate his sense of a spiritual state transcending the antinomies of subject and object, mind and nature, God as a sustaining 'presence' in nature and nature (conceived in Spinozist terms) as an adequate synonym for 'God'. These ideas should generate at least some measure of resistance in the reader, Empson thinks, in so far as they exploit a rhetorical device which claims to give access to far-reaching truths about the human condition, but which in fact relies on the mechanism of 'false identity', a trick which can have more harmful effects when put to use in other (political or religious) contexts. Thus:

> It does not seem unfair to say that [Wordsworth] induced people to believe he had expounded a consistent philosophy through the firmness and assurance with which he used equations of Type IV; equations whose claim was false, because they did not really erect a third concept as they pretended to. (1951, p. 305)

And yet – as I remarked in discussing this passage before – Empson can still go on, after all these detailed reservations, to suspend his attitude of critical 'resistance' at least to the extent of declaring that 'the result makes very good poetry, and probably suggests important truths'. For it is a basic principle with Empson – more so in the later essays, but already quite prominent by the time of *Complex Words* – that verbal exegesis may not be enough, even if it tries to make decent (humanly intelligible) sense of the words on the page, and avoids raising 'paradox' (or the rhetoric of unreason) to a high point of orthodox faith. What critics also need to reckon with is the larger background of motivating interests that helps to explain why the author resorted to some 'deviant' structure of semantic equations that fails to hold up if one examines its workings more closely. In short, good reading always involves a willingness to stretch one's mind around problems – issues of interpretive method, maybe, but also questions of an ethical, religious or socio-political nature – that cannot be settled by a confident appeal to this or that standard critical procedure for making the problems disappear. Hence Empson's chief objection to the 'Wimsatt Law', or the New Critical veto on talk about authorial intention: that it acts as a regular screening device which allows interpreters to 'discover' all kinds of subtle irony, paradox, ambiguity etc., while stubbornly ignoring any challenge from moral codes or belief-systems other than their own.

Thus when Empson reads Wordsworth he doesn't – like de Man – concentrate solely on those moments of rhetorical self-undoing where the poet's high truth-claims turn out to be reliant on a mystified 'language of sense', a language whose symbolic or metaphorical workings the critic must then deconstruct, attending only to the words on the page and sternly disavowing any interest in the poet's life-history, motives or intentions. To be sure, Empson thinks it important that we shouldn't go along too readily with this strain of transcendental thought, since it may crop up in more virulent (or heavily politicized) forms when harnessed to a national-aestheticist creed which exploits the same kinds of rhetorical device. But one also has to appreciate Wordsworth's situation as a poet struggling to reconcile the tenets of Christian belief with his own, more humane (and at the time highly heterodox) form of pantheistic nature-mysticism. 'What is really in question', Empson suggests,

> is not any theory in Wordsworth's mind about the word [i.e., 'sense' and its structural-semantic resources] but a manipulative feeling of what he could make it do; a thing more familiar perhaps to poets than critics, and one which a poet easily forgets; the period during which Wordsworth could feel how to use this word was, I think, very brief. (1951, p. 293)

His point – here and throughout *Complex Words* – is that language can indeed be put to such 'manipulative' uses, sometimes in the service of religious or political propaganda, but also as a means of resisting such rhetorical effects through an effort of independent thought. Wordsworth's performance with the key-word 'sense' may be prone to metaphysical vagaries and assertions (or forms of compacted identity-statement) that gain their effect by simply 'jumping over' certain crucial stages in the logical grammar of the word. Thus '[t]he whole poetical and philosophical effect comes from a violent junction of sensedata to the divine imagination given by love, and the middle term is cut out' (p. 296). But if the poetry can none the less 'suggest important truths' – and provoke such strenuous sense-making efforts on Empson's part, over the long period from *Seven Types* to *Complex Words* – then this cannot be just a matter of its 'emotive' appeal, or its capacity to hoodwink gullible readers in quest of some vaguely uplifting mystical experience. Rather, it is the fact that Wordsworth was pushing language to the limits of intelligibility in his desire to envisage a decent alternative to orthodox Christian belief, an alternative which – as in Milton's case – met up with great resistance, not only in doctrinal but also in linguistic (or logico-semantic) terms. And here we are approaching what is perhaps the most crucial and problematical insight of Empson's later work: namely, his perception that this mechanism of 'false identity' can on the one hand give rise to all manner of irrational (and often vicious) beliefs, while on the other it provides at least the groundwork or the starting-point for a process of thought that can fight its way free of those same morally crippling effects.

Thus Wordsworth's vaguely adumbrated doctrine of 'sense' – his habit of using the word as a direct bridge between 'sense-data' and 'the divine imagination given by love' – may indeed present difficulties that are strictly insoluble ('aporias', in the deconstructive parlance) when treated from a logico-semantic standpoint. As Empson puts it: '[w]hen Wordsworth has got his singing robes on he will not allow any mediating process to have occurred' (1951, p. 304). But we also need to see that this doctrine provided an escape-route from the harsher forms of Christian-orthodox thought, especially the active false logic involved in the dogma of the Trinity, that is to say, the notion of God as somehow 'consubstantial' or identical with Christ, yet also as a vengeful executive deity, one who could be satisfied – 'bought off', in Empson's phrase – by the sacrifice of the Son, though only to the extent of allowing some small proportion of mankind to escape eternal torment inflicted on the pretext of Original Sin. In *Seven Types* Empson had treated such ideas with a certain quizzical detachment, or more in a spirit of anthropological curiosity, regarding them as inherently likely to turn up in those 'advanced cases' of psychic conflict – notably Herbert's 'The Sacrifice' – where his method achieved some of its most striking results. Thus 'Herbert deals in this poem, on the scale and by the methods necessary to it, with the most complicated and deeply-rooted notion of the human mind' (1953, p. 233). No doubt this reflects the young Empson's reading of Frazer and other pioneering anthropologists of the time, as well as his interest in Freudian psychoanalysis, offering as it did a whole range of supporting evidence for the existence of these 'deeply rooted' psychological tensions. In fact Empson never abandoned the idea that such mechanisms – paradox and false identity among them – could be found not only in extreme cases like the Herbert poem but also as a constant – maybe an intrinsic – aspect of human thought-processes in general. Where he did come to take a very different view was on the question of how far the conscious mind (or 'the public human mind as expressed in a language') could resist their more potent and mischievous effects by raising them to a higher intellectual or imaginative level, a level at which thought was no longer at the mercy of such atavistic drives and compulsions.

The point is made most explicitly in a passage from *Milton's God* where Empson remarks that 'our minds have a wonderful readiness to satisfy themselves with admittedly false identities', but then goes on to argue that 'any orderly schooling needs to drive the process into the background of its area of practical work' (1965, p. 244). *Complex Words* had been written mainly with the purpose of showing how these claims could be reconciled, that is to say, how a theory of language and interpretation that acknowledged the pervasiveness of irrational thought-forms could also – and without contradiction – defend a basically rationalist approach to issues of interpretive method. 'Regarded simply as a bit of our mental equipment', Empson writes,

> it [false identity] carries within itself a kind of recognition that the matter would bear looking into, or an impulse to do that later, though enough is settled for the immediate decision. Thus we should make terms with the process rather than struggle to renounce it; but educated people rightly suspect it, so that they recognize a familiar type of error, systematically misused, when they read an anthropologist's account of 'primitive thought'. The most staggering misuse of it is the doctrine of the Trinity. One can hardly discuss whether a man believes this doctrine, because it is merely a thing which his mind can be induced to do. To be sure, many good men have passed on from accepting the process here, feeling it as deeply subtle and noble, to the natural next step of forming some intellectual construct about the matter; and they have often been burned alive for it. But even without this result any such construct is precarious, because the mind so easily falls back on the primitive assurance that the Father and the Son both are and are not identical. (1965, p. 245)

This passage is perhaps untypical in the prominence it gives to Empson's gloomier thoughts on the topic, his belief that tolerance in matters of faith is a hard-won and always 'precarious' achievement, that the mind is deeply prone to revert to 'false identity' in its bad (paradox-mongering) forms and that language all too readily promotes such confusion through the ease with which it falls into 'primitive' (pre-logical) habits of thought. After all, it comes from the chapter 'Christianity' – Empson's most sustained and passionately argued attack on the religion – and follows some particularly gruesome citations from Augustine, Tertullian and other upholders of the faith. But even here the argument gives grounds for a different, more hopeful interpretation, one that would stress the mind's capacity to think its way beyond such irrational doctrines, as for instance by subjecting them to the processes of rational critique, or again – like the strong revisionist poets from Milton to Blake, Wordsworth and Shelley – devising an alternative (broadly pantheist) set of beliefs that still no doubt made use of 'false identity' as a source of imaginative strength, but which nevertheless managed to avoid the worst aspects of Christian-orthodox thought by substituting their own, distinctly heterodox versions of the received biblical account. Such was Milton's purpose, as Empson describes it: to 'cut out everything between the two ends of the large body of Western thought about God, and stick to Moses except at the high points that anticipate Spinoza' (1965, p. 145). And this despite the poem's manifest claim to 'justify' God's ways to man by taking on board all the mind-wrenching paradoxes of Original Sin, divine foreknowledge, vicarious redemption, the Father's 'satisfaction', predestined eternal torment and other such articles of faith.

This is what Empson so admires about *Paradise Lost*: its sheer intellectual nerve as a poem that faces up to the worst implications of the official Trinitarian teaching, but at the same time works this doctrine around into a humanized counter-mythology with much better claims upon our moral and imaginative sympathies. Thus with Milton, as with Wordsworth, one has to look beyond the localized symptoms of conflict, paradox or aporia and appreciate the strength and subtlety of mind that could handle such problems in a large-scale way without collapsing into pious conformism on the one hand, or deadlocked neurosis on the other. In the case of *Paradise Lost*, as Empson reads it,

> [t]he poem really does survey the Western half of civilization and express the conflict which arose from the introduction of Christianity into this great area, as a by-product of offering a solution to it which seems to him tolerably decent. The root of his power is that he could accept and express a downright horrible conception of God and yet keep somehow alive, underneath it, all the breadth and generosity, the welcome to every noble

pleasure, which had been prominent in European history just before his time ... [But] if you praise it as the neo-Christians do, what you are getting from it is evil. (pp. 276–7)

One can think of no other critic in the recent Anglo-American tradition who could possibly have written such a passage, or offered it as fitting conclusion to a work that ranged so far beyond the limits of conventional academic discourse. This is not just a matter of Empson's polemical stance, his fierce rejection of 'neo-Christian' values and his crusade against any variety of Lit. Crit. fashion that struck him as somehow lending support to those values. Much more, it is the attitude of sturdy 'common-sense' rationalism, joined to a knowledge that the human mind was liable to massive (at times quite disastrous) aberrations from this civilized norm, and a willingness – like Milton's – to test his own convictions against the most extreme kinds of counter-evidence or doctrinal challenge. This is why 'resistance' is such a basic notion in Empson's criticism, early and late; on the one hand that deep-laid resistance which he often encounters when striving to explicate the puzzles, paradoxes and aporias of poets like Herbert and Wordsworth, and on the other his principle that all good literature – on any adequate reading of it – is likely to resist our in-place convictions or settled habits of response, since the whole point of reading such works is to learn something of interest about other minds, other value-systems or cultural forms of life.

Hence his objection to the formalist (and post-structuralist) idea of reading as a basically hermetic activity, a decoding operation carried out on texts from a standpoint of self-assured method or theoretical grasp. Such criticism can learn nothing that it didn't already know, since it wields a whole range of orthodox safeguards (from the 'intentional' and 'biographical' fallacies, through the 'implied author' and 'implied reader', to 'intertextuality', '*mise-en-abîme*' and kindred rhetorical terms) which prevent the reader from ever coming close to an *argued engagement* with what the writer in question actually thought about this or that matter of genuine intellectual or moral concern. And this would also apply to a good deal of what currently passes for 'deconstruction' among British and US literary theorists. For although these critics (following de Man) make considerable play with the term 'resistance', their use of it is confined to a textualist register where one always knows *in advance* that metonymy will undermine the truth-claims of metaphor, that constative propositions will prove 'undecidable' on account of their suasive (or performative) character and that logic or grammar will self-deconstruct when exposed to that ubiquitous 'rhetoric of tropes' which close-reading always and infallibly brings to light. As I have said, there is a sense in which *Complex Words* is preeminently a work of critical 'deconstruction', a determined attempt to theorize (and thus resist) the more seductive kinds of confusion that come about when figures like paradox or 'false identity' get a hold on our normal machinery of interpretive thought, or when rhetoric imposes upon logic and grammar to the point of annulling any such rational resistance. But his argument is always that these cases are untypical – that they involve 'deviant' or aberrant forms of verbal equation – and moreover, that we couldn't make a start in understanding the results of this curious process except on the basis of a strong practical grasp of how language works in its normal (rational-discursive) mode. And where it doesn't so work – where the 'resistance' is greatest, as in Empson's readings of Milton and Wordsworth – then this is no cause to abandon the whole sense-making effort and embrace some variety of irrationalist creed wedded to notions of 'paradox' or 'aporia' as one's bottom-line terms of appeal. For in such instances there is a strong likelihood that the author is trying to cope with some deep conflict of judgements, values or beliefs, a conflict that can only be handled successfully on a larger narrative or mythical scale.

VII

This is the conclusion that Empson arrives at in the one chapter of *Complex Words* – '"All" in *Paradise Lost*' – which records something very like a defeat for his whole line of approach. The problem is that Milton uses this word in such a variety of contexts, and with so many vaguely 'emotive' meanings attached to it, that no amount of patient exegetical effort can get very far toward sorting out their logical grammar. Thus:

> the main occasions for using the word can be classed under the following Emotions: Combativeness (claiming all, arguing all else away, etc.), pride (ruling all, disdaining all etc.), love (offering all, disvaluing all but . . .) and self-sacrifice (standing as representative of all, giving up all for them). I think that equations may be drawn between any two of these, with the effect of defining a Miltonic type of character; the kind of man who would

feel in a wholehearted way that any one of these feelings entails any other is also the kind of man the style as a whole presents. But I think we can only connect the different uses in this vague and distant way; certainly there is no variety of Senses in the word, which in itself is merely a logical connective. (1951, p. 102)

This chapter is by far the shortest in the book – a mere four pages – and undoubtedly shows Empson coming up against resistance (or downright bafflement) as he tries, and fails, to avoid having recourse to a vague, all-purpose, emotivist account of the word. Not that its prominence is in any way suprising since, as Empson notes, 'the poem is about all time, all space, all men, all angels, and the justification of the Almighty', and besides, 'it seems to be suited to his [Milton's] temperament because he is an absolutist, an all-or-none man' (p. 101). But it is still a real problem for Empson's argument in so far as the word clearly carries a large – even crucial – weight of significance, while giving no handle for the kind of analysis which has up to now produced some impressive results, especially in the brilliant previous chapter on Pope's *Essay On Criticism*. In fact, he seems to have included the Milton essay as a kind of instructive limit-case, a fair indication that examples might always crop up 'where, so far from being able to chart a structure of related meanings in a key word, you get an obviously important word for which an emotive theory seems about all that you can hold' (p. 101).

However, there is another angle to the essay which allows it to be read – in more positive terms – as looking forward to *Milton's God* and the kinds of historical, biographical and socio-cultural interest that marked Empson's critical production over the next two decades. For if the logico-semantic approach hits bedrock with Milton's use of 'all', the question still remains as to just *why* this should be the case, or what might have been the conflicts of intellectual conscience and imaginative sympathy that drove the poet to adopt such a style. In other words, close-reading is simply not enough, since a narrow concentration on matters of language, style or 'technique' can tell us rather little when it comes to assessing the nature and sources of Milton's poetic power.[7] 'That his feelings were crying out against his appalling theology in favour of freedom,

[7] Empson makes much the same point – about the limits of 'purely verbal' exegesis or stylistic criticism – in his otherwise admiring review of Christopher Ricks's *Milton's Grand Style* (*New Statesman*, 23 August 1963, p. 230).

happiness and the pursuit of truth was I think not obvious to him, and it is this part of the dramatic complex which is thrust upon us by the repeated *all*' (1951, p. 104). Empson's point here – as so often in his later writing – is that verbal exegesis, no matter how acute or subtly responsive to the 'words on the page', can still go wrong in various ways if it gets out of touch with this wider background of motivating interests and concerns. Usually such failures of response came about through an over-valuation of rhetorical figures like ambiguity, irony or paradox, coupled with a formalist doctrine of poetic autonomy and – following from this – a fixed habit of simply disregarding any truth-claims, argumentative grounds, historical points of reference or whatever that would constitute a challenge, a standing affront to these orthodox rules of interpretive conduct. Empson's main purpose in *Complex Words* is to cut through the thickets of irrationalist dogma and aesthetic mystification that surround this formalist creed, along with other variants of the prevailing anti-cognitivist outlook that would fence literature off in a domain of 'emotive', 'paradoxical' or self-referential meaning, concerned only with pseudo-truths of its own elaborate creation. Hence his somewhat embarrassed resort to the various analytical 'bits of machinery', that is, the apparatus of logico-semantic equations, intended *not* as an exhaustive taxonomy – much less as a full-scale method for criticism – but rather as a means of restoring confidence in poetry's truth-telling character, its openness to the kinds of reasoned argument and counter-argument that operate in the realm of 'fair public debate'. Even so, as he concedes in the Milton chapter, this approach may run up against problems that indicate the limits of *any* such verbal-analytical technique, whatever its readiness to abandon the dictates of high formalist doctrine and treat poetic language as basically continuous with the interests and values of everyday communicative discourse. For with Milton – as indeed with any author, but most strikingly in Milton's case – interpretation will at some point need to take account of contexts, motives and circumstantial details beyond anything demonstrably 'there' in this or that key-word or isolated passage.

Not that Empson is willing to let the argument go by simply acknowledging defeat, or by admitting – what amounts to much the same thing – that the sheer range of meanings or associative overtones is such as to play all attempts at analysis completely off the field. 'The question I want to raise', he writes, is how far an exegesis of literary effects can go in terms of equations between connected meanings in single words, and how far we have to fall back on an Emotive linguistic theory instead. If this case is a fair sample, it looks as if one could say that the real contrast is between the different depths of unconsciousness which are being tapped. One could draw up equations for the effect of *all* in Milton, relating not so much senses of the word as whole contexts in which it has become habitual. But they would no longer be tracing a clear-cut, even if sub-conscious, mental operation, like those which let us talk straight ahead and get the grammar in order; they would be concerned with something more like a Freudian symbol. Even so, I think the critic would still be dealing with verbal effects to which a 'purely Emotive' linguistic theory could not be applied. Of course I do not mean to deny that a reader can best absorb them by accepting and trusting his own emotions as he reads. (1951, p. 104)

There are two main points that come across in this otherwise rather tortuous and groping passage of argument. One is Empson's firm distinction between 'unconscious' and 'sub-conscious' mental processes, a distinction that he clearly needs to uphold if the semantic 'grammar' of complex words is to be seen as analogous to – or perhaps even identical with – the operations by which we 'talk straight ahead' and make sense as competent language-users. Thus the reason for his evident fretfulness, here and elsewhere in the chapter, is that Milton's use of 'all' comes close to collapsing this distinction, suggesting that there may indeed be structures of associative meaning which lie so deep – or which originate so far back in the workings of 'unconscious' memory, motive and desire – that the analogy with grammar becomes quite implausible. But it is the second main point that offers at least the hint of an escape-route from this awkward situation. It has to do with the matter of *context*, or the question how far the interpreter must look 'beyond' or 'outside' the words on the page in order to appreciate the full range of significance carried by a problematic key-word like Milton's 'all'. Thus it may turn out – as Empson's later work would suggest – that the only alternative in cases like this is to draw upon the widest possible range of relevant 'background' information, and then put this knowledge to use in the reading of passages that otherwise resist the best efforts of close analytical commentary. In fact this seems to him such an *obvious* requirement – so basic an aspect of the critic's competence to write about any literary work – that the need to back it up with an argued defence on theoretical or principled grounds is just another symptom of the widespread malaise that has overtaken present-day 'advanced' Lit. Crit. opinion.

For the moment – in keeping with his relatively specialized interests in *Complex Words* – Empson is content to let this question ride and move on to address those other, more rewarding examples ('fool', 'dog', 'honest', 'sense' etc.) which offer less resistance to the structural-semantic approach. But having thoroughly explored that approach – having tried out its claims across a wide range of literary texts, often with impressive and convincing results – he clearly came to feel that a switch of emphasis was needed. For if there is one crucial but unresolved issue in *Complex Words* it is this problem of 'context' and the limits of verbal analysis, even when applied – as Empson applies it – with constant reference to historical source-material, notably the detailed case-histories provided by that 'majestic object', the *Oxford English Dictionary*. Still there was the difficulty of knowing just how much of this semantic history was actually carried by the key-words in question, as distinct from the larger socio-cultural context within which those words took on some definite (period-specific) range of associative meaning. At the one extreme is a case like Milton's 'all', bearing such a weight of diverse connotations that the appeal to context goes far beyond the limits of semantic or lexicographical research. At the other is Pope in the *Essay On Criticism*, making such consummately skilful play with the immanent possibilities of 'wit' and 'sense' that – in Empson's words – 'the style to which you have become accustomed is viewed as a sort of dialect with its own rules and structure of meanings, and the author partly fades out' (1951, p. 98). In both cases there is an obvious problem for the critic (like Empson) who stakes a great deal on the rational and ethical accountability of language, its resistance to the powers of rhetorical seduction and its capacity – when not so seduced – to make good sense of its own more obscure or hitherto 'sub-conscious' operations. Roughly speaking, these alternatives are signposted 'Heidegger' and 'Barthes': on the one hand an appeal to mysteries of language (or depths of preconscious signification) that elude all the efforts of reasoned commentary, and on the other a theory that reduces criticism to little more than an exercise in applied crypto-analysis, a structuralist decoding of sign-systems where 'the author' – or the notion of purposive, intelligent agency in language – appears just a figment of bourgeois-humanist ideology (see Barthes, 1977). Of course I am not suggesting that Empson uncannily predicted these trends, or that *Complex Words* can best be viewed as a work of anti-poststructuralist polemics *avant la lettre*.

But it does seem to me that he raises such questions with a degree of argumentative clarity and force that has not yet been matched among the apostles of recent literary-critical fashion.

In *Complex Words* this strikes Empson as basically a 'puzzle for the linguist', a problem best dealt with – he thinks – by consulting the dictionary wherever possible and then devising a logico-semantic 'grammar' for the key-word in question, that is to say, a fairly *ad hoc* piece of theoretical 'machinery' which would take account of *both* the background context (as established by instances of period-usage), *and* the author's specific intentions (as evinced by the various orders of equation or the degree of prominence assigned to this or that meaning from one such context to the next). All the same, as he admits, there remains the question

> [as to] how much is 'in' a word and how much in the general purpose of those who use it; but it is this shrubbery, a social and not very conscious matter, sometimes in conflict with organized opinion, that one would expect to find only able to survive because somehow inherent in their words. This may be an important matter for a society, because its accepted official beliefs may be things that would be fatal unless in some degree kept at bay. (1951, p. 158)

This is the real purpose of all Empson's theorizing in *Complex Words*: to explain how it is that language – including the most flat, colloquial, 'common-sense' or unassuming items of linguistic exchange – can put up a resistance to 'official' creeds and ideologies, especially where these demand a passive acquiescence in irrational doctrines or slogans. *Complex Words* goes as far as possible toward articulating a theory of these resistance effects, these structures or modes of oppositional discourse that constitute a kind of 'counter-public-sphere', a language with its own distinctive set of ethical and political values (see Negt and Kluge, 1972).

'Sense', 'honest', 'rogue' and 'dog' are all of them words which (in Empson's phrase) 'took their chance' with the emergence of a secular-rationalist ethos, and hence came to signify a range of attitudes at odds with the dictates of orthodox religious belief. Thus '"dog", it is absurd but half-true to say, became to the eighteenth-century sceptic what God had been to his ancestors, the last security behind human values' (1951, p. 168). And again, more explicitly:

> the feeling that the dog blows the gaff on human nature somehow attached itself to the ambition of the thinker to do the same, and this helped to make him cheerful and goodhumoured. His view of our nature started from a

> solid rock-bottom, a dog-nature, which his analysis would certainly not break in digging down to it; this made him feel that the game was safe, and the field small enough to be knowable. Whereas Shakespeare felt that 'there is no worst', and the corresponding depths to him were fearful degrees of lunacy; 'fool' was his earth-touching word, not 'dog'. (p. 169)

In such passages – to be found on almost every page of *Complex Words* – Empson is practising a form of jointly socio-linguistic and cultural materialist analysis which has scarcely been matched, let alone superseded by more up-to-date developments in the field. And this claim holds good, I would suggest, despite the various promising moves in that direction promoted by New Historicism, Bahktinian 'sociological poetics' or the work of Raymond Williams (himself much indebted to Empson's example (see Williams, 1983; and Empson, 1987a, pp. 184–7)). But one still has to recognize the decisive shift of priorities that led Empson to pretty much abandon the working methods of *Complex Words*, and devote his main efforts for the next quarter-century to the kinds of detailed documentary research that issued in the posthumous volumes *Using Biography*, *Essays on Shakespeare* and *Faustus and the Censor* (Empson, 1984, 1986, 1987b). What produced this shift was clearly his conviction – bolstered by the evidence of a looming 'neo-Christian' revival – that in the end verbal exegesis just wasn't enough to counteract the influence of obscurantist doctrines (among them the post-New Critical schools of *avant-garde* literary theory) that thrived on a narrowly 'textualist' approach and a taste for the kinds of hermeneutical technique that led straight back to the paradoxes of revealed religion. The only adequate response, he now felt, was to leave aside the business of close-focused textual explication and address himself to 'rescuing' those various authors – Shakespeare, Marlowe, Donne, Marvell, Milton, Fielding, Coleridge and Joyce among them – whose writings had already been 'kidnapped' by this movement of orthodox revisionist thought.

All the same it would be wrong to overstate the extent of Empson's 'break' with the interests and values – as opposed to the detailed logico-semantic 'machinery' – for which he had offered such convincing arguments in *Complex Words*. What chiefly carries over into the late essays is a generalized confidence in the sense-making powers of language, joined to a belief that reasons (good reasons) can in principle be given for any passage, any sequence of dramatic events, any issue of authorial intention or character psychology that critics might otherwise be tempted to regard as lying too deep for rational treatment or – in the typical 'symbolist' manner – as belonging to a realm of paradoxical wisdom where such explanations are entirely beside the point. It is this latter belief that he finds most repellent in moral and intellectual terms, especially when it is used – as by critics of Shakespeare like Derek Traversi (1954) – to insinuate some pious neo-Christian message which completely ignores certain crucial details of the plot, as well as saddling the author with political and religious views which are nowhere borne out by the text. To this extent Empson is fully in agreement with Stephen Greenblatt and other 'New Historicist' thinkers: that Shakespeare criticism has too often become a vehicle for conservative or downright reactionary creeds that exhibit a massive (and self-interested) blindness to what actually goes on in the two-way commerce between literature and its socio-cultural conditions of production (see Greenblatt, 1988a, b, 1990; Howard and O'Connor, 1987; Veeser, 1989). Indeed it is remarkable – unless one invokes some collective 'anxiety of influence' – that Greenblatt and his colleagues have managed to reinvent so many of Empson's arguments in the *Essays on Shakespeare* without even a token acknowledgement. For there is hardly a page in that volume where he doesn't 'anticipate' the New Historicists by asserting – as against myth-mongers like Traversi – that we can best make sense of the plays by putting them firmly back in their historical context, by drawing on the widest possible range of relevant source-materials, and ceasing to regard them as timeless monuments to some transcendental 'truth' enshrined beyond reach of such mundane secular interests. It is a curious reflection on the vagaries of current Lit. Crit. fashion that the one strong precursor of this 'back to history' movement should be pushed out of sight in the rush to engage with defenders of the orthodox faith.

Anyone who doubts this parallel between Empson and the New Historicists may wish to consult his essay 'Hunt the Symbol', reprinted in the 1986 Shakespeare volume. Here again the chief opponent is Traversi, and the main point at issue Traversi's argument that the late tragi-comedies (*The Tempest* especially) express a mood of mystical, transcendent, other-worldly wisdom, a placid acceptance of the paradoxes of Christian belief, arrived at after a long period of struggle leading up to this high point of achieved 'reconciliation'. What such readings display – as Empson very forcefully remarks – is a determined effort not to see what is there in the text, as well as a rigorous principle of exclusion when it comes to matters of social and historical context. In particular they cut out the whole vexed question of the play's colonialist bearings, a question much debated among the New Historicists and their Cultural Materialist cousins, but nowhere with quite the argumentative vigour that Empson brings to his essay. On Traversi's account we are supposed to see Prospero as a mouthpiece of the authentic late-Shakespearian vision, a figure who has at last renounced earthly power and thus entered a state of perfected spiritual wisdom. In Caliban, conversely, we are presented with a creature 'bound by his nature to service' (Traversi's words), and therefore very properly chastised by Prospero whenever his bad disposition gets out of hand. 'Please notice', Empson writes, 'that Traversi is here expressing the pure milk of the master-race doctrine, and it is presented with the usual glum sanctimoniousness as a traditional Christian moral, with no sign that it has ever been questioned' (1986, p. 239). As usual with such 'symbolist' readings, the interpreter manages to sound extremely high-minded while attributing the worst possible motives – or the lowest degree of moral insight and intelligence – to Shakespeare and his contemporary audience.

This leads on to Empson's main piece of argument concerning the play's political content and the reason why its point can so easily be missed by critics of a pious or conformist bent.

> [*The Tempest*] gives a very clear-eyed though grim picture of the process of colonization, which the first audiences would be bound to find interesting ... What they prove is that Prospero was not designed to symbolize the White Man's Burden, or to support what Macaulay called the nigger-driving interest; when Traversi argues for this symbolism in his high manner, taking it for granted that it is very 'religious', he does a moral injustice to Shakespeare and his audiences. They were not so bad as Traversi, who I take it was struggling to be as bad as God meant us to be, as bad as we were before the free-thinking Enlightenment. (pp. 241–2)

At this point clearly the New Historicist comparison breaks down, since it is impossible to imagine a critic like Greenblatt invoking the principles and values of Enlightenment reason, or launching so impassioned an attack upon the 'discourse' of any opponent whose views he happened to disagree with. For it is a leading tenet of New Historicism – as likewise of post-structuralism and other broadly affiliated schools – that 'discourse' (or rhetoric) goes all the way down, so that any such quarrel can only be a matter of competing language-games, cultural discourses or value-systems whose claims to truth are strictly incommensurable, and thus beyond reach of argued or principled debate. Hence the current (on their own terms unresolvable) issue between those who read Shakespeare as fundamentally an upholder of the values and social institutions of his time, and those who look sharp for the signs of subversive intent, or at any rate – since intentionalist talk is firmly ruled out – for points at which 'the text' subverts its own project through symptoms of ideological conflict.[8] In this respect the much-touted quarrel between New Historicism and deconstruction begins to look more like a local skirmish between rival versions of the textualist thesis. Thus 'history' as these critics conceive it is so completely redefined in discursive or rhetorical terms that its ritual invocation by one side as against the other amounts to just a slogan adopted for polemical or point-scoring purposes.

The contrast with Empson is, I think, enough to make the point: that any genuine 'return' to historical criticism will need to involve both a large amount of archival-documentary research (which the New Historicists are indeed willing to do, albeit often in a somewhat opportunist and quirky fashion) *and* a readiness to engage in the process of rational reconstruction where required, that is to say, the activity of working out what actually or probably happened on the basis of textual evidence which cannot in itself – as a matter of 'the words on the page' – serve to resolve the issue one way or another. This activity takes various forms in Empson's late essays, though always with the purpose of correcting or contesting some misconceived orthodox view. Its uses range from the large-scale reconstruction of social or historical contexts to specific questions of authorial biography, background situation, fictional character and motive, reader- or audience-psychology, critical reception-history and so forth. His point in each case is to uphold a strong version of the continuity principle, the argument – as against formalist or textualist doctrines – that interpreting literature requires the same skills, the same kinds of jointly cognitive, ethical and speculative interest, that are needed for the conduct of our practical, everyday lives. In this regard there is no great difference between making

[8] For discussion of this issue – often taken to divide the US New Historicists from their British 'cultural materialist' counterparts – see various contributors to Veeser (1989); also Jonathan Dollimore and Alan Sinfield (1985) and Terence Hawkes (1993).

sense of history as a record of documented actions and events, and making sense of plays, novels or narrative poems as a matter of humanly intelligible motives presented in fictional form. But there is – as I have argued – a crucial difference between this way of closing the literature/history divide and the way chosen by post-structuralism and its various textualist offshoots. Where they reduce everything (history and ethics included) to a force-field of contending rhetorical codes or textual representations, Empson makes a point of moving in precisely the opposite direction, refusing on principle to treat literature or criticism as a specialized activity cut off from other sources of knowledge and imaginative insight. And if this meant breaking the rules newly invented for the game, from Wimsatt's 'Intentional Fallacy' to the protocols of structuralist or post-structuralist method, then it seemed to him that they should indeed be broken as often and as flagrantly as possible, in the hope that criticism might yet be restored to some glimmering of rational sense.

One fine example – of the many that might be given – is this passage from his essay on *Tom Jones*, discussing the particular kind of 'double irony' that Fielding regularly uses when confronted with issues of class morality and conflicting ethical codes.

> What people found so entertaining at the time, when Fielding attacked Richardson in a rather explosive class situation (the eager readers of Richardson in French were presumably heading toward the French Revolution), was that the classes seem to have swapped over. The printer's apprentice was the gentlemanly expert on manners, indeed the first English writer to be accepted as one by the polite French, whereas if you went to see Fielding, they liked to say at the time, you would find him drunk in bed with his cook and still boasting that he was related to the Hapsburgs. His answer to Richardson was thus: 'It is useless to tell me what gentlemen do: I am one.' The real difference was about the meaning of the term; Fielding thought it should mean a man fit to belong to the class which actually rules in his society, especially by being a just judge. His behaviour eventually made a lot of people feel he had won the argument, though not till some time after his death. To die poor and despised while attempting to build up the obviously needed London Police Force, with obvious courage and humanity, creating astonishment by his refusal to accept the usual bribes ... this became too hard to laugh off ... Fielding presumed men ought to be promoted to the ruling class, as a regular thing; the point is merely that the method of promotion should be adequate to save it from contempt ... Of course, he does not mean that all gentlemen have it [i.e., 'liberality of spirit' or a decent magnanimity]; the total egotism of young Blifil, a

theoretically interesting case, with a breakdown into sadism, which critics have chosen to call unlifelike, is chiefly meant to make clear that they do not. But it seems mere fact that Fielding's society needed a governing class, however things may work out under universal education; so it is reasonable of him to take a reformist view, as the Communists would say, and merely recommend a better selection. (1984, pp. 154–6)

I have quoted the passage at length because it brings out so many characteristic features of Empson's later writing. These include the appeal to a broad-based historical and socio-cultural context; the use of biography as an obvious resource when trying to understand an author's intentions or – by much the same token – a character's imputed motives; the habit of constantly testing such hypotheses against a range of (sometimes conflicting) value-systems or ethical theories, regarded not merely as so many transient 'discourses' but as permanent options which exert (in de Man's words) a serious claim upon 'the shape and limits of our freedom'; the refusal to make these issues disappear by adopting some variant of the formalist doctrine that declares them strictly off bounds; and finally, the forthright tone of address that challenges the reader (not the 'implied reader' or other such phantom textualist entity) to judge how far their own responses measure up to Fielding's attitude of large-minded tolerant concern.

It hardly needs saying how remote this all feels from the kinds of question that currently preoccupy the more advanced sectors of Anglo-American theoretical debate. In fact, if one set out to trace the reception-history of Empson's work, it would register a series of deepening resistances and cross-purpose encounters, from the widespread critical acclaim for *Seven Types* – a response that was based, as I have argued here, on a highly selective, opportunist reading of that book – to the general failure to grasp what he was attempting in *Complex Words* and, after that, the frequent expressions of bafflement, strained understanding or downright hostility that greeted the output of his last three decades. Not that Empson found this in the least surprising, given his belief that academic Eng. Lit. (both its mainstream and 'radical' varieties) had for some time been drifting into an 'eerie cultural twilight', a condition of depressed intellectual and moral values where he had no wish to feel at home. 'As to the reader of a novel', Empson remarks,

Fielding cannot be bothered with him unless he too is ... prepared, in literature as in life, to handle and judge any situation. That is why the reader gets teased so frankly. The same kind of firmness, I think, is what makes the forgiveness by Tom at the end [i.e., his reconciliation with Black George] feel startling and yet sensible enough to stand up to Allworthy. I think the chief reason why critics have belittled Fielding is that they find him intimidating. (1984, p. 157)

Paul de Man has something rather different in mind when he remarks, apropos Empson's reading of Wordsworth, that 'commentators have had to forget Empson in order to carry on' (1984, p. 88). What impresses de Man about '"Sense" in *The Prelude*' is the essay's determined resistance to forms of premature interpretive grasp, its exemplary failure to construe the poet's meaning on terms that would offer a satisfying sense of achieved visionary power. To be sure, this is one major aspect of Empson's criticism; a proto-deconstructive 'hermeneutics of suspicion' which de Man is naturally quick to endorse since it falls in so readily with his own theoretical purposes. And yet, as I have argued, there is another whole dimension of Empson's work that goes clean against the formalist-textualist grain, and which de Man is himself obliged to forget – or pass over in tactful silence – if deconstruction is to carry on without disturbance to its programmatic aims and priorities. This is why his writing resists the current tendency to pigeonhole critics as being either 'for' or 'against' theory in some vaguely inclusive sense of that term. After all, as Empson wrote back in 1955, '[t]he English like to assume that they are sensible, therefore don't require abstruse theory, but one can't always gamble on that' (1987a, p. 141). It is a comment that the reader might usefully bear in mind when approaching the wide range of views on Empson's criticism contained in the present volume.

CHAPTER 2

Empsonian honesty and the beginnings of individualism

Gary Wihl

A philosopher of ordinary language might pose the topic of this essay as follows: what sort of world is made of human agents expressing themselves through verbal acts like approving and disapproving of other people's behaviour, lyricizing in plain verse their feelings without necessarily achieving authenticity or intimacy and knowing how to talk so that you gain people's trust and confidence without necessarily telling the truth? Two crucial verbal acts are excluded from this world, however: no one may deny things and no one uses hyperbolical diction. To imagine this world is to become part of the verbal universe of William Empson. I put forward the effort to imagine this world of limited verbal gestures to get at a central issue in Empson's work: for all his overt emphasis on verbal behaviour, his complete lack of interest in formal, aesthetic and stylistic resources in language, is Empson's verbal universe rooted in genuine social perceptions? As my short list might indicate, what seems to be excluded from the realm of verbal activity is a high degree of expressive autonomy, intimate personal understanding and anti-normative uses of language, as if these were impossibilities in face of the inherently social function of language. But Empson's faith in the socializing function of language runs into some serious problems. We posit values, question repressive conditions, affirm choices and legislate through verbal acts which rest on some principle of free agency, on the decision to pursue one course or another, and if any one of these acts results in harm, even violence, it may indicate the presence of a pseudo-social language that entraps and defeats agency, that is more propagandistic and rhetorical than rational and communicative. The social dimension of verbal behaviour remains a truism unless it defines a context for the questions of agency and decision-making. True, some social functions of language carry decisions internal to these functions, many of which need to be respected as the 'illocutionary' agreements discovered by speech-act philosophers, such as the verbal act of making a promise. One does not use the verb unless one is prepared to respect the obligations it names. But that is a minor definition compared to the pseudo-social language that deceives, misleads and gives us a false sense of our independence. To put the issue as strongly as possible: what if some of the most ordinary uses of language, like expressions of approval and disapproval, or confidential utterances shared in private between friends, circumscribed speakers within solipsistic fantasies and hallucinations which presented themselves as a social 'world'? I am suggesting that this question is of crucial importance to an understanding of Empson's entire socio-linguistic project.

These questions and issues can be focused so as to take on socio-cultural import for readers of Empson today in the context of Empson's discussion of the word 'honest' in Shakespeare's *Othello*, chapter 11 in *The Structure of Complex Words* (1951). 'Honest', an explicitly social value that directly connects a virtue with a way of speaking, attaches to one of the most recognizable vice-figures in English drama, Iago. Iago's 'honesty', Empson argues, marks a crucial historical evolution in the word, standing midway between an earlier code of honour and trust and a subsequent discovery of the Independent Self, verging on a potentially destructive cult of egotism and selfishness, something like being honest first and foremost about one's own impulses and desires.

In this essay I shall not be concerned with the overt historical logic of Empson's verbal analysis of 'honest', the apparent movement of the word from a stage of verbal and social stability (in Chaucer) to one of irony and rogue behaviour (in Rochester), a history that defines Shakespeare as the key transitional author. I doubt such pat developments could give an adequate account of the range of verbal motives in any cross-section of history designated by Empson as a semantic period. What centres upon Iago and the extensive discussion of 'honest' that is the keystone of *The Structure of Complex Words* is the development of the Empsonian logico-grammatical 'machine' (as in chapter 10 of *Complex Words*), which tracks the social evolution of discourse through key or complex words only to arrive at the most socially implausible conclusions. For instance, how does Empson arrive at the conclusion that Othello's suicide rests not on his discovery of Desdemona's innocence but on the collapse of Iago's 'honesty'? Apparently Empson would argue that the fundamental crux of the play rests on the complete destruction of an earlier code of honour which, somehow, Iago's peculiar 'honesty' partially supports. Without Iago, Othello has no characterizational claim to existence. Empson does not follow Bernard Spivack's dominant line of enquiry into Iago as a personification of Evil (Spivack, 1958); indeed, the morality of good and evil is largely irrelevant to Empson's working definition of 'honesty'. But should that imply a socially progressive Iago? One who makes possible the historical aftermath of a code of 'honest' individualism free of all considerations of honourable behaviour?

Consider also Empson's (outrageous?) suggestion that the reception of the play by a contemporary Elizabethan audience would have rested upon popular irritation with complacent cuckolds who obtained official preferment by sharing their wives (a view which makes Othello, proleptically, the antagonist of the naval officers who used to indulge Samuel Pepys):

> Othello's principles about the matter [of jealousy] were all wrong, let alone the way he applied them. The advent of contraceptives has taken a lot of strain off the topic, but I am not sure that the attitude of the Elizabethans was as simple as they pretended. I understand that murder of one's wife out of jealousy was not at all usual among Elizabethans, let alone usually condoned as *crime passionel*. Indeed the rancour of their incessant jeering at cuckolds is not easy to understand if these figures were simply considered ill-used; it has much more the air of a propaganda drive against a body [the cuckolds] which had excited popular resentment. They were too comfortable, if nothing worse; they must be made to do their duty; let them consider Othello, for instance; there's a really highminded man for you. (Empson, 1951, p. 245)

Here we have a further debunking of Othello's non-tragic honour, as it becomes a matter of propagandistic incitement – which conveniently leaves out the whole question of Othello's irrationality. Could so irrational an act of wife-murder be looked upon as highminded, especially when the audience would be fully aware of Desdemona's innocence? For Empson, Othello's excessive jealousy, which perhaps could never be rationalized, is easily dismissed; it takes second place to the jealousy at work in the truly popular figure, Iago. As I suggested at the outset, Empson's interpretation of social codes relies upon the criterion of approval; he can write off *Othello* as a tragedy because (obviously) it could not be condoned, although it could have served as propaganda. On the other hand, a generous theory of adultery, which leaves out the question of the honourable thing to do, would make it a matter-of-fact event which could be condoned. That is exactly how Empson interprets the conclusion of *Ulysses* in his essay on Joyce, published posthumously in the collection entitled *Using Biography* (1984). In the essay, he argues first in favour of the interpretation that sees Stephen return the next day for a liaison with Molly, then in favour of Joyce's tolerant view of human sexuality.

Christopher Norris puts the same point in the most generalized way when he correctly summarizes Empson's semantic analysis of 'honest' as nothing less than the dismantling of the entire concept of the tragic:

> Words like 'fool' and 'honest' have a down-to-earth quality of healthy scepticism which, Empson argues, permits their users to build up a trust in human nature based on a shared knowledge of its needs and attendant weaknesses. 'Dog' is the most cynical of the family, a rock-bottom term of mutual disillusion, yet at the same time a 'hearty' recognition of mankind's common predicament.
>
> There is not much room in this rationalist outlook for anything in the nature of a 'tragic' philosophy of values. (Norris, 1978, p. 86).

Othello as a rationalist study of the ethic of mutuality? How could Empson's clear-headed view of the socializing quality of words turn tolerance and mutuality into the most implausible of the play's interpretations?

Before I turn to a fuller examination of Empson's reading of *Othello*, I would like to emphasize that the collapse of mutual understanding into a private world of 'honest' fantasy is an essentially linguistic problem in Empson's discussion. There is no preventing this collapse by disproving the evidence or dismissing the charge against Desdemona, or by attempting any explanation simply 'outside' Empsonian linguistics. As Stanley Cavell would say, Empson is a critic who demands to be *answered*, not refuted. If there is a flaw in Empsonian theory it must be discovered and worked through from within Empson's perspective on a play like *Othello*. Otherwise, what is to prevent the Empsonian from replying that the critic has missed the point? Evaded what the play is all about? It is like Cavell's example of the 'yokel' who rushes on stage to Desdemona's defence, or the child whose fears are quieted by being told that it is just a 'play', or the sudden illumination of the house lights which breaks the play's spell without cancelling its meaning (Cavell,

1987). Such refutations of the play's events amount to a virtual negation of theatre itself, and with it what Cavell calls the 'honest' response the play is demanding. Similarly, the critic who would refute Empson must be in a real dialogue with Empson, must seek to understand what his position is really all about in the first place.

Empson's reading of the play is remarkable because it insists that the study of a complex word like 'honest' reveals exactly what is troubling about the play: *Othello* is about a new way of openly articulating private meanings, about the public honesty (real honesty, not ironic honesty) of the newly emergent self-seeker. To listen to the language of the play is to become aware of honest communications as the voice of a new individualism seeking its own form of approval. Such a reading far excels a number of existing limited approaches which cannot get 'inside' the play precisely because they sacrifice the linguistic analysis to a much less exact historical context. Another one of my brief lists would include the following:

(1) G. K. Hunter's examination of the historical context of Elizabethan colour prejudice, which results in a theory of Shakespearian articulation as the difference between appearance and reality (Hunter, 1978). A historical reconstruction of cultural prejudice makes possible an understanding of language as a transparent 'social organism' rather than an officially sanctioned code of verbal commands and performances. The barely noticed organic surface of language contains a 'multitude of tiny unnoticed assents' someone like Iago can exploit.

(2) Spivack's treatment of Iago as a personification, or allegory, of evil, an omnipotent force the literary tradition seeks to naturalize (Spivack, 1958). Literary expression reduces to a contest between literature's traditional allegorization of evil and the local, historically specific attempts to naturalize the allegory.

(3) Wyndham Lewis's discussion of Iago as the emergence of the average man's power for revenge, which undercuts shallow, conventional morality (Lewis, 1927). We are challenged to accept Iago as the manifestation of our own inner strength.

(4) F. R. Leavis's condemnation of Othello's magniloquent, figurative language as a form of tragic egotism which is bound to destroy itself (Leavis, 1952). In this interpretation language is self-consuming, charged with vanity; Othello's bombast fascinates us but it immediately suggests its own collapse.

(5) Even the highly sophisticated criticism of Peter Stallybrass (in Ferguson *et al.*, 1986), who is able to synthesize class, colour, gender and tragedy in a complex view of transgressive symbolic, ideological structures and contradictions (Desdemona as pure, chaste and noble but also foul, corrupt and debasing). Desdemona is the key 'symbol' of the play's ideological contradictions.

Empson is able to deal with the issues raised by each of these critics on the basis of another set of theoretical assumptions. Rhetoric is never merely egotistical, a vanity of words, because that would leave unanswered why we are paying attention to the language in the first place; neither would the assumption of the autonomy of literary conventions (even as a generalized form of literary tradition), which implies a severe limitation of literature's expressive participation in ordinary social discourse as a whole. Furthermore, Empson explicitly challenges the 'Victorian' legacy of finding the ethical significance of literature in the use of personifications or allegories. And the view of literature as a vehicle of liberationist transgression has yet to offer a clear connection between symbolic structure (an imaginary resolution of social conflict) and real, material, political change. This view of the 'in-between' status of the literary symbol, not quite a real source of change but still somehow expressive of an unconscious desire for freedom, seems to have had an adverse effect on contemporary Marxist theory and the New Historicism. Lee Patterson, in his excellent study of problems within historico-literary criticism, deliberately juxtaposes New Historicism and Marxism, showing how they form two sides of the same coin (Patterson, 1987). Historical understanding is either subordinated to a determinist materialism, no matter how sophisticated the symbolic analysis, or history seems to evaporate into 'sceptical self-cancellations', in spite of the extensive use of archival and primary source materials, since the theory fails to include an account of human agency as a cause of historical change.

Only Stanley Cavell's reading of *Othello* (1987) presents a forceful, immediate challenge, because it points to Empson's possible blind spot. From Cavell's perspective on Shakespearian scepticism, *Othello* is about the historical emergence of the isolated, profoundly uncertain, revengeful individual, who is so unable to recognize human otherness outside 'himself' that he risks destroying those around him. (Cavell notes that the revengeful sceptic is typically male-gendered.) A large component of Cavell's interpretation examines the act of denial in tragic language, which seems to be excluded from Empsonian theory altogether. In tracing Empson's analysis of linguistic structures of approval, which form the basis of speakers' mutual understanding, I shall try to discover why disapproval never becomes denial. Through denial, Cavell is able to touch upon the same concern as Empson, the emergence of the individual. But Cavell differs sharply from Empson in being able to maintain a primary interest in Othello rather than Iago and in his recognition of the tragic potential within everyday human life.

II

To enter into dialogue first with Empson and subsequently with Cavell, readers need to enter *Othello* in their particular way. Entrance cannot be gained through role-identification (or identifying with Desdemona, Iago or Othello, whatever that might mean in the first place), nor by having an emotional reaction to the play nor by aesthetically contemplating the play. *Othello* is switched on for us, as sentient social beings, when its meanings take on different levels of force: which meaningful utterances claim our approval (Empson)? Which utterances in the play demand to be answered so strongly that we discover something about the way we speak as we attempt the virtually impossible act of addressing a fictional character (Cavell)? Though the questions sound similar, they point Empson and Cavell to different key texts indicating very different socio-linguistic force-fields. These fields inevitably overlap at the (tragic) point of death, where we shall have the opportunity to assess the significance of Empson's entire project.

For Empson, Iago wins approval once 'honesty' serves as a basic social norm, but that does not mean he is truthful or praiseworthy. The issue has to do with the way meanings gain normative values in Empsonian semantics. Iago does not exemplify some normative value already at work in Elizabethan vocabulary, but rather the way in which norms are built up. In its pre-Shakespearian phase, 'honesty' is used to praise someone; it belongs to a courtly or chivalric discourse in which praise is a common form of address. But in the dozens of mentions it gets in *Othello* Iago is clearly not being praised; in fact, part of Desdemona's noblesse is revealed in her patronizing attitude toward Iago, 'praising' him like a good, common rogue or dog. If Iago reflects some normative 'honesty' and so deserves our approval, it is not because he is praiseworthy but because he is re-evaluating a more basic level of honesty, closer to the minimal standard of assumed truth-telling, which as a norm is not especially praiseworthy in and of itself. Many pre- or non-Empsonian readings of the play founder at this level in an attempt to substitute psychological motive for these discursive restructurings of honesty. Characterizational accounts of the Iago–Othello relationship provide poor explanations of the way they honestly communicate with each other.

A. C. Bradley (1905) or F. R. Leavis (1952), for example, in their opposing ways, search for the motives that drive Iago and Othello. Iago is a good companion, loyal and steadfast in his duty toward Othello, but so roguish and average that he does not merit appointment to higher military status, and is passed over in favour of the more chivalric Cassio. Iago then gains his motive for revenge, his envy of Cassio and secret hostility toward Othello. His revenge runs out of control, however, confirming his base character (Leavis), and thus his relative lack of didactic, literary value, or it becomes fascinating to watch in itself as it unfolds (Bradley). On the next level of analysis, we may consider the destruction of Othello as tragic because of the defeat of the code of honour, whether he or Iago is chiefly responsible for it. There are many variations on this interpretive theme. But what if the elaborate 'honest' exchanges between Iago and Othello are an attempt to mark the emergence of a new, post-chivalric mode of speech of a very different tragic nature, in which truth-telling or deceitfulness, and the older honourable code of behaviour which has become vulnerable, are not at issue. Or, to put it more accurately, what if honesty as a normative term for 'truth' and 'praise' is restructured as the approval of a norm based on individualism? To repeat: there is nothing to approve in Iago's dishonesty, as mere lying, nor in his destructive behaviour. But there is something to approve in his 'honest' individualism as it evolves into a doctrine of individualism through impulsive desire mixed with self-control.

Honest individualism has its own ethical paradoxes and dilemmas, of course. For one thing, to avoid Humpty-Dumptyism, 'honest' must carry the implication of truth somehow, but truth has shifted from 'troth' and openness to protecting, defending and exploring a new sense of self. One can honestly shelter oneself, maintaining an honest reserve, or one can be honest in the company of one's fellows, like 'honour' among thieves. The fundamental paradox is that the 'the selfish man is the generous one, because he is not repressed' (Empson, 1951, p. 192); he has a 'natural ease', which could evolve into either an Enlightenment Noble Savage or a Victorian Gentleman – which is not to say that people should trust either of these honest souls. The normative element rests on the resolution of the contradiction within individualism so as to make individualism typical, the 'measure of all things'. As Empson puts it, the typical individual man can 'recognize and fulfil both his own nature and his duties to society'; his impulses do not lead him away from socially constructive behaviour.

Honest individualism provides a better explanation of Iago's peculiar contradictions than two separately posited components of the play, psychological character plus literary expression. At the same time, with regard to my original set of questions, why does this more cogent, more participatory Empsonian reading yield implausible conclusions? One of the chief tasks Empson sets for himself is to make Iago 'plausible', typical of a new individualism in which we all share. But why is Iago the typical case instead of Herbert, or Pope or Gay's dramatic rogues? – all important contributions to the development of honesty but second to Iago, who gets the pivotal chapter of the entire book on complex words. How does Iago become the measure of all things in the play? Supposedly, it is because he shapes the new doctrine of individualism by reconciling its inner contradictions in a decisive way. After Iago, there is no turning back to honour. He presents no ideal worthy of emulation, but somehow we all become like Iago in our inner lives; he is our new 'average' as Wyndham Lewis noted (1927). Iagoism, which differs from Othello's egotism, has to do with discovering, checking and releasing impuses as we try to gain new forms of social intimacy and mastery between our much more spontaneous, unpredictable, 'natural' selves. But the claims of this new individualism, we must remember, are not in some scientific psychology of impulse. The intimacy, mastery and spontaneity are expressive categories, first and foremost properties of linguistic norms rather than psychological states. Iagoism is a new way of speaking. Here the implausibility of Empson's overall position becomes noticeable and contrasts with that of philosophers like Cavell or Michael Oakeshott (1959) who pay close attention to the tension between communion and individuality in different expressive norms.

As we follow Empson's exposition of three crucial dialogues in *Othello* we begin to see the arbitrariness and weakness of Iago's method of winning approval; it becomes a strategy for self-approval rather than self-reliance. Empson seems to be blind or indifferent to this strategy and seems to see value in forms of Iago's weakness as if they were a mark of a more rugged, more 'honest' individualism. Although he never asks us to approve Iago's immoral behaviour, Empson seems to think Iago's is the only form of speech that draws upon the general normative linguistic laws of approving and disapproving, so that we have to work through Iago's speech, like him or not, in order to socialize ourselves. From Cavell's perspective, this argument overlooks the completely unconvincing nature of Iago's pretences and schemes, which mask a much deeper crisis of dependency in the very concept of individualism; Iago is merely an excuse for a problem the tragically individual Othello would rather not confront. And from Oakeshott's perspective, verbal acts of approval and disapproval are wonderfully 'pragmatic' devices for reaching finite goals without having to acknowledge the complexity of other selves: 'One may indeed suppose a man able, perhaps, to perceive in the activity of others the operation of these moral categories [approval and disapproval] but regarding them as no more than a guide to the help or hindrance he may expect from such selves in the satisfaction of his own desires' (Oakeshott, 1959, p. 23). Genuine 'acknowledgement' of the operation of these categories pushes well beyond the categories themselves. Cavell's insistence on the burden of acknowledgement pushes us beyond them. Does Empson?

Consider Empson's unpacking of the densely honest discussion of Cassio held by Othello and Iago in Act III, scene 3, the discussion in which Iago supposedly begins to win the upper strategic hand. Cassio has already been dismissed for drunken brawling, has lost his precious 'reputation'. But now Iago discovers a further slight he must pay back in learning for the first time that Cassio had played the go-between for Othello and Desdemona, even as Desdemona now is playing the role for Cassio. Once again, Iago is made aware of his social inferiority, his exclusion from the confidential circuits of the higher nobles. And so he begins to capitalize on sexual innuendos about Desdemona's fidelity, sowing doubt in Othello, presumably, and assuaging his own injured feeling. It is a spontaneous turn around: Iago must cover his injury instantly, if his own 'honesty', or fellow-feeling for Othello is to be credible, and this involves a rather complex posture of *reserve* which becomes the crux of Empson's analysis. Iago's curious reserve, his deliberate hesitation in pouring poison into Othello's ear, is his resolution of his inner contradictions, his typifying gesture for winning approval. Empson's endorsement of this reserve, I suggest, begins to indicate what is wrong with his entire project. Iagoism is 'crucial', Empson says, because it is the first successful resolution of 'being ready to blow the gaff on other people and frank to yourself about your own desires' (Empson, 1951, p. 221). How do we know when someone is ready? The whole point of Iago's honesty is that he does not blow the gaff, ever; he simply gives the impression that he could dismantle the pseudo-honourable love of his betters in one stroke, but what he does instead is recode their behaviour in terms of honest/false confidence in their knowledge of each other, an increasingly implausible state of affairs because this either reduces them to fools, cancelling the tragedy as such, or it makes Iago more convincing than he really is. I believe Empson is misled into thinking the latter. Here is the crucial exchange for Empson, with his parenthetical glosses:

Oth: Is he not honest?	(Faithful, etc.)
Iago: Honest, my lord?	(Not stealing, etc. Shocked)
Oth: Ay, honest,	('Why repeat? ...')
Iago: My lord, for aught I know.	('In some sense.')

Iago: For Michael Cassio
I dare be sworn I think that he is honest.
Oth: I think so too.
Iago: Men should be what they seem,
Or, those that be not, would they might seem none.
Oth: Certain, men should be what they seem.
Iago: Why then, I think Cassio's an honest man.

(Empson, 1951, pp. 221–2)

Empson suggests that the point of the dialogue is for Iago to praise Cassio for being 'frank about his own [sexual] nature', his youthful vigour, but simultaneously condemn him for letting others see this, for lacking in public decency, as for example in the intrusions of Bianca which come later. Iago thus appears to understand Cassio's nature, one man to another, but as a more skilled, mannered, gentleman he has the 'honour' not to discuss Cassio's behaviour in too much detail. Thus: 'Iago can hide what reservations he makes but show that he makes reservations; this suggests an embarrassed defence – "Taking a broad view, with the world as it is, and Cassio my friend, I can decently call him honest''' (p. 222). To understand Iago is to accept this view of human nature while leaving room to criticize, with tolerance, those whose nature interferes with proper appearances in public. The 'honest' thing to do is lean on this common wisdom instead of prying into people's private affairs. The wild effect of the exchange, then, is for Iago to shift the feeling of candour from Othello and Cassio on to Cassio and himself, leaving Othello in doubt about his previously reliable romantic confidante. And with the sexual twist, there is further room for doubt in Cassio's real motives in the proximity of women. Cassio's natural honesty is in conflict with a woman's honesty, her chastity. Finally, Empson suggests the whole dialogue is englobed by a heartier, 'manly' honesty, or fellow-feeling, built up between Iago and Othello, as they seem to share a mutual distaste for annoying sexual implications in the midst of their official business. This man-to-man honesty, this serious attitude toward business at the expense of sexuality, becomes stronger and stronger in Empson's reading, and helps to explain his conclusion that Othello is ruined by his discovery of Iago's falsehood, not Desdemona's.

Implausibility does not intrude into Empson's reading of the passage because he discovers (imposes?) so much semantic complexity. He reaches deeper than G. K. Hunter in finding 'be' and 'seem' to be part of a game that shifts the entire semantic register of 'honest' from honourable, trustworthy and non-sexual to trust in conflict with sexual knowledge, leaving each position in the game up for grabs. (It is useful to keep in mind Bradley's point that Iago suspects that he has been cuckolded by Othello; trust and sexuality never stabilize in any pairing of the play's characters.) The implausibility lies in the values Empson works into his discussion. We must recall the major task of the interpretation is to make Iago plausible. Empson wants him to share a level of intimacy with Othello: he is warmly, appreciatively filled in as a character in spite of his lack of truthfulness. Iago is a bit of a poet in that he cannot be said to have lied when he has affirmed nothing, and yet something clearly has been valorized of typifying significance: his reserve, the last vestige of honour that attaches to basic, minimal honesty.

On the theoretical plane, Empson usually argues that minimally defined norms, such as 'honesty equals not lying', can be valued by speakers only if special circumstances warrant it. If everyone basically tells the truth all the time, then one does not earn praise for conforming to this assumption. Looking at the special acts of approval, then, becomes the key to discerning the more complex values at work in social discourse. In the fragment of dialogue just considered, Iago wrests an appreciative, approving use of honesty as 'faithful, worthy of special confidence' from Cassio onto himself. But here the special circumstances that warrant the word-shift have a twist: what is not asserted is what is approved! And this turns out to be a pseudo-honourable distaste for the vulgarity of sexuality, a nascent puritanism, which begins to take over the mutually supportive/destructive relationship of Iago and Othello. Perhaps we may now call these characters 'individuals' in their isolation, interdependence, defensiveness, and in their effort to be hardy with each other, but it is not at all clear what exactly is of typical value about all this. Cavell will call this sort of individualism a fatal trap, worst of all in its deep sexual horror. Empson seems content with this state of affairs – he will go on to argue for Iago's 'purity' – as long as the language of the play seems to work, to get the messages across from character to character, even if we miss much of the implications of the words in any given exchange. But the failed coherence of the individual (or the independent self) and a normative set of values is the radical problem Empson's pragmatism ignores. As Oakeshott said, approval is of little value unless we succeed in approving what we also desire. This is not as easy as it sounds and in Oakeshott's work approving is a trope for hermeneutics. I suggest that the pragmatism built into Empson's theorizing from the start actually prevents the occurrence of this hermeneutical task and substitutes for it a much too functional view of language which does not accomplish the task of pinpointing individualism within a larger field of always operating, always relaying, always situating meaning networks, or complex words. The theoretical point may be reduced to the need to link linguistic agency with individualism in order to reconstruct an understanding of community. Cavell calls it submitting oneself to the task of becoming intelligible to others, anything short of which leads easily to a sceptical denial that others really count for oneself. I shall conclude with an elaboration of this point as it touches on contemporary literary theory, but for the moment the point alone is sufficient to round off the discussion of Empson.

Empson looks upon human individuals as they emerge and disappear against a background of fluctuant meanings and word-patterns. Individual articulations, from the micro-level of conversation up to the level of implied doctrines and normative assertions, are exchanged and altered through the forces of approving and disapproving. But these forces seem to offer a very limited account of linguistic agency, which makes individuals no more than momentary concretions of meaning or resolutions of contradictory meaning. Thc further implication of the theory is that individuals serve to typify larger structures, but that the structures themselves seem to circumscribe a potentially vast arena of linguistic expressiveness rooted in a more active, resistant, critical individuality. Iagoism as a mode of expression is 'social' in so far as it draws upon the semantic background of 'honesty', but it is 'typical' in so far as it focuses select features of that blurry background. My point is that the focusing process inadvertently becomes an end in itself in Empsonian analysis and does not lead us back to a greater understanding of the background of our assumptions; philosophers might wish to call it a categorical error.

Iagoism's reserve supposedly works because it can be filled in by the background of the word 'honest' itself. But as a non-assertion, lacking in its own individual linguistic force, it leaves us to decide whether to approve it as honour or reject it as wounded ambition. Though seemingly rich in semantic play, this decision is really a very narrow one in terms of hermeneutical understanding, as can be seen in the sexual cost it imposes even in Empson's utilitarian acceptance of human impulse. Two further examples from Empson's discussion reinforce this point and add to the theory's implausibility, now that the implausibility can be seen as an inadvertent reduction of expressive activity. The first concerns Othello's supposed 'humbling' before Iago's 'purity' when he confesses to Emilia that it was 'My friend, thy husband, honest, honest Iago' who informed him of Desdemona's falsehood (see Empson, 1951, p. 226 on *Othello*, Act v, scene 2). Empson says that the line mixes 'horror' with a 'hearty use' of the word 'honest'. There is no irony in calling Iago honest at this point, as if Othello is feeling the full measure of his deception. Just the opposite: there is a horrible realization but it lies in a final acceptance, even an agreement, with Iago, the supposed element of heartiness or fellow-feeling. As in the dialogue concerning Cassio, Othello continues to feel a prudish disgust at sexuality, and finds support for this aversion in Iago's analogous misogynist position. Thus the 'horror' is not a truth retrospectively revealed about Desdemona but a confrontation, still shared by Othello and Iago, with the inherent awfulness of female sexuality. Cavell makes the same point about an underlying sexual hysteria in Othello's character, and Stallybrass (in Ferguson *et al.*, 1986) points out Desdemona's victimization as woman. The peculiarity of Empson's reading, however, lies in the way he attaches the positive values of shared understanding, mutual feeling and common value to Iago and Othello by negating sexuality. Empson's semantic analysis of 'honest' opens its communicative possibilities, but closes down its expressive ones. What sort of human individual would actually talk in this way? What sort of individuality is dependent upon such a misdirected 'horror'?

Empson never asks these questions because there is no tragedy in this horror; it has been displaced by the heartiness he would argue. To hear Othello's lines as tragic an audience would have to allow for the possibility that an individual's utterance comes from somewhere deep in the state of individualism, of aloneness, self-recognition, affirmation of self. Othello, it is true, is affirming something, but it is not necessarily through an Empsonian structure of approval. He may be affirming something about his own lack of sexuality, and clutching onto Iago so as not to expose it. Without reference to this specific passage, individuals hiding their sense of lack comes much closer to Cavell's general account of what the Othello–Iago relationship is all about in the first place. Empson will allow Othello to perform his individual reconciliation of horror with heartiness, in itself a very plausible human reaction formation. But as soon as Empson adds that Othello thereby submits himself to a clearer, purer, ideal view of love without sex, he leaves us to wonder about the normative background these lines are supposed to evoke. Iagoism has become the background, the type, the measure, the average that defines Othello.

Iagoism in Empson's final phase of interpretation takes over Othello completely, or so Empson reads the double negation of honour and honesty in the lines Othello speaks before his suicide: 'But why should honour outlive honesty?/Let it all go.' Empson's reading deserves to be quoted in full because it offers itself as the only explanation of the 'force of the question':

> Outlive Desdemona's chastity, which he now admits, outlive Desdemona herself, the personification of chastity (lying again, as he insisted, with her last breath), outlive decent behaviour in, public respect for, self-respect in, Othello – all these are honour, not honesty; there is no question whether

> Othello outlives them. But they are not tests of an idea; what has been tested is a special sense of *honest*. Iago has been the personification of honesty, not merely to Othello but to his world; why should honour, the father of the word, live on and talk about itself; honesty, that obscure bundle of assumptions, the play has destroyed. (Empson, 1951, p. 229)

Since Othello's honour does not depend upon Desdemona's chastity, which, in Empson's view, is a minor form of honour specifically attached to women, it can outlive her. By contrast, male honour by this time is so intertwined with the male honesty typified by Iago that it cannot survive Iago's destruction. This quasi-homoerotic, sacrificial reading (does the father have the right to outlive the son?) is the closest Empson comes to admitting a tragic mood. The reading is a remarkable summation of the play: the ambiguous reserve noted in the dialogue about Cassio gradually fixes itself as a hatred of sexuality, which then becomes the foundation of reciprocal male understanding, and finally the measure of honour's faint historical afterlife, soon to reach extinction. Something has misfired in the course of honesty's structure of approved meanings. Although the theory is telling us that we have reached the fullest articulation of feeling, that we can speak more honestly about ourselves once we are freed of honourable reserve, the vocabulary that pours out has very little force; it makes practically no claim upon our attention, except perhaps as a semantic puzzle. Does this sound like the voice of an emergent individualism, even as it marks the collapse of personification? For all its emphasis on a genuine moment of historical change, Empson's interpretation lacks plausibility; or at least the two are in tension.

Another version of this misleading picture of the individual may be found in Stephen Greenblatt's reading of *Othello* as an exercise in self-fashioning (1980). Identity and a framework of social discourse involving the church and human sexuality are completely conflated in Greenblatt's discussion, with odd-sounding results, much like Empson's, richly suggestive of historical change yet strangely lacking in expressive substance. Thus Othello does things like come 'dangerously close to recognizing his status as text', specifically the Church's texts against adultery within marriage (i.e. being too lustful toward one's wife). And Iago becomes the 'principle of narrativity itself', who gains persuasive power over Othello because of his learned, casuistical manipulation of the church's doctrines! This complex, interesting effort to situate a self in some larger field of (always repressive?) discourse ends by sounding as implausible as Empson's male bonding of Iago and Othello. *Othello* becomes either a study in male fellow-feeling or a study in the male self's exploitation of its own field of sexual discourse. Empson and Greenblatt seem to agree intuitively that the play is about something new in the concept of the individual self and that this conception rests upon the peculiarity of the Othello–Iago relation. But both seem to undermine the category of the individual self they seek to reveal to us, either as inevitably misogynist in what it actually puts into practice in its new expressive activity or as abstractly 'textualized' (a fate worse than being sexualized?).

Empson's interpretation of Othello seems so advanced largely because his approach is not based in aesthetic categories; he correctly sees that Naturalism, Allegory, Symbolic Evil and Appearance are doctrinal side-effects of a socio-linguistic structure with its own historical logic. His complex verbal structures cannot be called formalistic, and he is right in saying that the play is fundamentally about self-articulation, the birth of individualism through the vehicle of a new honesty, no longer subservient to honour. The problem, as I stated earlier, is that individuality, if it is to mean anything at all, must include an account of agency. It is not enough to see individuality as a passive realization of an already structured, though indefinite, horizon of meanings. At the same time, I do not mean to say that individuality is antisocial, as if its existence is by definition unsituated, negatively defined against the social. The exclusion of agency, self-expression as a means of situating oneself, marking oneself, within a meaningful framework, seems to be a common philosophical oversight in the very conception of individuality within the predominantly male liberal tradition, as Naomi Scheman has argued (in Harding and Hintikka, 1983). A falsely polarized picture of introspective states as essentially private events set against holistic explanations of social phenomena tend to equate individuality with the 'aggregation' of special properties, such as 'intending to be more honest' or becoming 'popular' with one's peers. Such notions of individuals as aggregates of special attributes provide little opportunity for critical self-understanding because they seem to allow for unpredictable shiftings of levels of explanation, ranging from the most narrowly solipsistic and fantasized to the most self-effaced and generalized. I suggest that these extremes, represented for the moment, and only for the sake of convenience, by Empson and Greenblatt, would sound very different if a stronger account of agency were built in to the theorizing. The strength of Stanley Cavell's reading of *Othello* lies in the strength he attaches to the expressive agency of individualism, which he too sees as the problematic new discovery of the Shakespearian period, and which he calls 'scepticism'. Cavell's reading of the play departs in striking fashion from the readings we have seen so far. Here is his own summary of the significance of Iago's 'honesty':

> however far he believes Iago's tidings, he cannot just believe them; somewhere he also *knows* them to be false. This is registered in the rapidity with which he is brought to the truth . . . I am not claiming that he is trying not to believe Iago, or wants not to believe what Iago has told him . . . I am claiming that we must understand Othello, on the contrary, to want to believe Iago, to be trying, against his knowledge, to believe him. Othello's eager insistence on Iago's honesty . . . is not a sign of his stupidity in the presence of poison but of his devouring need of it . . . that the idea of Desdemona as an adulterous whore is more convenient to him than the idea of her as chaste. But what could be more terrible than Desdemona's faithlessness? Evidently her faithfulness. (Cavell, 1987, p. 133)

In one decisive stroke Cavell removes two problems that have been hampering interpretations of the play: the implausibility of Iago manipulating Othello; and Iago as a spokesman for some normative, puritan contempt for female sexuality. For the first time, a powerful element of denial is revealed for our consideration, which allows the play to claim a tragic effect. The play as tragedy is hardly plausible today if it aims destructive force at a widely abused social value such as chastity. Cavell does not see tragedy in the destruction of chastity but in Othello's refusal to accept it; Iago and all his schemes support rather than challenge this refusal. The reason Cavell explicitly terms this 'denial' rather than accept Empsonian 'reserve' is that it requires a deliberate effort, complete self-investment. Othello must do the work of denial, and in this Iago really provides very little help. Far from rationalizing the destruction of Othello in the emergence of Iagoism, one historically eclipsing the other, Cavell takes us back to Shakespeare to listen to Othello's voice, a voice it has become very difficult to hear because indeed we have become too Iagoish, caught up in our own little fantasies of individual initiative, unable to recognize the poverty of our desire compared to the individualism that Othello expresses.

Othello is the beginning of individualism in doubt, uncertainty, lack of perfect knowledge; philosophically, Othello is in the spirit of Descartes rather than Montaigne. In Descartes, the dilemma is put this way: 'if I were . . . the author of my own being, I would doubt nothing, I would experience no desires, and finally I would lack no perfection' (quoted by Cavell in Heller *et al.*, (1986) p. 283). The Cartesian self is the tragic self, because it is driven by an insatiable need to authenticate its own existence epistemologically, but finds its epistemology limited, open to doubt; it discovers its own insufficiency in reason. The tragedy is heard in these lines Othello utters:

By the world,
I think my wife be honest, and think she is not,
I think that thou are just, and think thou are not;
I'll have some proof . . .

(Act III, scene 3, quoted in Cavell, 1987, p. 128)

For Cavell, the word 'honest' is not part of some network of chastity, honour and impulse upon which the meaning of the utterance draws. Cavell reads these lines as the expression of 'possibilities that reason, unaided, cannot rule out' even as Othello seems to admit that he is beyond the aid of reason. Desdemona's honesty is not susceptible to visual proof. The farcical manipulations of the handkerchief or the comic-like scenes of eavesdropping already indicate the poverty of 'proof' in face of the sceptical individual's insatiable demand for certainty. These lines become intelligible to us when we begin to see that Othello's doubts do not depend on Desdemona, an insight Empson seems to have intuited from his own angle, but on a refusal to see Desdemona for herself. Her honesty and chastity would expose his *lack* of perfect individuality, would tie him to her, would impose a much greater demand on his psyche. The sceptic, argues Cavell, prefers doubt as the assurance of individuality rather than submit himself to the test of another person's affection. Hence we have Cavell's suggestion that Othello is refusing to accept Desdemona's chastity rather than her absurdly implausible adultery. To accept Desdemona is to submit one's all consuming doubt, the perverted assurance of one's proper individuality, to dependency on another person, to the acknowledgement that there are other individuals, rather than the endless retesting of the object world of epistemological sense-experience. This is also why Othello seems to put Desdemona to the final test as if she were an object, a piece of stone, as if his violence were directed at her as a product of *his* artistry, the necessary violence the sculptor wreaks upon the inanimate object to make it mean something for himself. Following Wittgenstein, Cavell believes that it is easier to defeat the sceptic's picture of his own accomplishments than to discredit its underlying appeal for all of us to this day. Tragedy at least discredits scepticism's destructive impulse, its ultimately self-destructive victory over its own accumulated doubt and denial of human otherness.

There is one more crucial feature of Cavell's picture of the sceptical individual, which returns us to Empson in one direction and moves us forward into deconstruction in another. There is no epistemological solution to the sceptic's self-entrapment, no certainty of sense that could not be open to further doubt, no epistemological 'yokel' who could rush onto the sceptic's tragic stage. That is because the sceptic needs to be *answered*, not refuted or disproved. A communicative channel has to be opened within individualism in the first place, and for Cavell this channel is language not sense-experience:

> What skepticism threatens is precisely irretrievable outsideness, an uncrossable line, a position from which it is *obvious* (without argument) that the world is unknowable. What does 'threaten' mean? Not that skepticism has in its possession a given place in which to confine and isolate us, but that it is a power that all who possess language possess and may desire: to dissociate oneself, excommunicate oneself from the community in whose agreement, mutual attunement, words exist. My work begins with philosophical defences of the procedures of ordinary language philosophy, of appeals to the ordinariness of our attunements in words as responses to the skeptical threat. (Cavell, 1987, p. 29)

The sceptical threat is a refusal to allow oneself to become intelligible to others through words, and it is a refusal to see that the primary task of language is to acknowledge the presence of other speakers. Scepticism consumes language's attunements in the form of epistemological doubt, which in effect circumvents the possibility of being answered or challenged by another speaker because the only response it seeks is one from the object world.

In an essay on individualism, a contribution to a volume of essays entitled *Reconstructing Individualism*, Cavell carries forward his project in a discussion of Descartes and Emerson on the self reaching individuality through linguistic performance (in Heller *et al.*, 1986). The self submits to the process of becoming intelligible to another speaker, takes up the challenge of mutual attunement in language, the challenge Othello has warded off as a threat. In this recent essay, Empson has dropped out as an oft-cited ally, even though the idea of attunement and communion in language seem to be very Empsonian themes. It is as if Cavell has concluded that Empson is difficult to read but finally too easy in what he prescribes: Empson's robust Cult of Independence does not require sufficient effort within the ordinary. Cavell's performative verbs include 'subjecting', 'mastering', 'obeying' and 'deciding' – a very demanding assertion of one's individuality within the linguistic field. This emphasis on agency is precisely what Empson seems to have neglected, perhaps because in underestimating tragedy he failed to consider the threat of sceptical denial. I was suggesting this blindness at the outset of this essay as the absence of denial and of hyperbolic language in Empson's world.

The attack on deconstruction is often made in the name of an attack on scepticism. Deconstructionists, we are often told, say that we cannot know essential truths, that meaning is undecidable, that speech is inauthentic, that the subject is a linguistic illusion, that there is nothing outside the text. So an answer to scepticism might as well be one to deconstruction. Indeed that is one of the tasks Cavell sets for himself in this essay on individualism, but not in so facile a fashion. Cavell is intrigued by deconstructionist indecision, but he is unsure how much of a claim it imposes on our ordinary use of language. If deconstruction is scepticism, it would have to have an equivalent force, a tragic dimension. And this is exactly what it seems to lack, since Cavell comes to the conclusion that its indecision is part of its playfulness, part of the perverse autonomy of language which is exactly what we need to overcome to individuate ourselves. We cannot let words mean for us. If the sceptic refuses to see that his individual structure of doubt works because he is refusing to become intelligible to another person, then the deconstructionist, in Cavell's view, does the opposite by playfully exercising his doubts *in language* so as to destroy individuality altogether. We seem to be back to self-consuming artifacts or self-fashioning textualists. But just as Cavell has an answer to Empson, so deconstruction has an answer to Cavell. The work of this dialogue is far from done, though I will finish with an intimation of this answer.

Deconstruction does need to become more intelligible, and it has already begun this task in its particular attention to the *prosaic* dimension of sublime language, as for example in de Man's last essays on the Hegelian sublime. I suggest that in the name of ordinary language Cavell is failing to see a more prosaic view of agency and expressiveness that deconstruction is bringing into view. Emersonian self-reliant individualism is wonderfully sublime, but that is the whole point. Is individuality sublime? Does it have to 'command', 'obey', 'submit' and 'create' to become authentically itself? The force of these verbs is lost when we pass beyond the sublime. Whatever its detractors may choose to call it, deconstruction is part of the passing of the sublime. Cavell's ordinary, sublime individual sublates Empson's honest individual, but is in turn sublated by the prosaic individual.

CHAPTER 3

Empson, Leavis, and the challenge of Milton

William E. Cain

William Empson's and F. R. Leavis's work on Milton exemplifies a form of oppositional criticism rarely practised today. To be sure, there is much emphasis at the present time upon criticism that somehow resists, argues against or opposes its subject. Fredric Jameson's investigation of theories of modernism and postmodernism, Edward W. Said's account of Orientalism, and Sandra Gilbert and Susan Gubar's exploration of the traditions of women's writing are notable cases in point. But what makes all of these scholarly arguments notably 'oppositional' is their insistent stress on institutional and disciplinary contexts that, so the critics propose, have led to misguided and distorted understanding of the subject at hand and that now need resourcefully to be re-examined and reconstituted. With the possible exception of certain branches of deconstruction, critics today no longer labour oppositionally in quite the manner that Leavis and Empson, in their different ways, demonstrate in their scrutinies of Milton. Both are keenly aware that Milton's lofty institutional status – Leavis once testily opined that 'Miltonists command the academic world' (1974, p. 68) – significantly influences the terms employed for interpretation of his poetry. Yet both Empson and Leavis focus primarily on the writer himself, on his language and the assumptions that motivate and shape it. They seek to describe but also to evaluate Milton, offering an appraisal of him as a writer and of *Paradise Lost* as a work of art.

Such an oppositional relation to the writer under study may not seem especially peculiar or eccentric: when we read, we often find ourselves – as Empson might say – in an 'argufying' mood that prompts us to take steadfast issue with the writer, querying his values and suspiciously or sceptically measuring his performance. But evaluative criticism has long been in decline. It survives only in the highly animated realm of literary theory, where combatants frequently assess one another with unsparing militancy. We simply do not encounter the kind of critical essay that the best critics of the 1930s and 1940s favoured, an essay like R. P. Blackmur's stringent commentary on the 'unintelligibility' of e. e. cummings's language (1962, p. 27) or Yvor Winters's analysis of Emerson's poetry, which frankly concludes that 'Emerson at the core is a fraud and a sentimentalist' (1947, p. 279).

Yet it is only partially accurate to link Leavis and Empson as 'oppositional' to Milton. Leavis does indeed state his verdict upon Milton – 'disastrously single-minded and simple-minded' (1936, p. 58) – and bluntly declares that the poet's egotism displays itself in the deadeningly insensitive verse of *Paradise Lost*. In a coercively strong-armed tone that seems akin to what he decries in Milton, Leavis says that the poet 'reveals everywhere a dominating sense of righteousness and a complete incapacity to question or explore its significance and conditions' (1936, p. 58). Milton's desolately repetitive language, Leavis emphasizes, exposes his defective intelligence; this poet could neither feel the sensuous vitality and resonance of idiomatic speech nor subtly, delicately, inspect the nature (and limits) of his own attitudes and commitments.

In *Milton's God* (1965), Empson proceeds differently, expressing not so much his opposition to Milton as to the monstrously cruel Christian doctrine that Milton attempts to justify and that he manages somewhat to modify and tame.[1] Because Milton believes in Christianity and builds his poem upon it, he is, in a sense, Empson's opponent, the figure whose faith in the Christian God Empson resolutely contests. But *Milton's God* finally dramatizes Milton's resistance to Christianity, as well as his honesty, sympathy, fairness and, above all, generosity (a key word for Empson in this book). At

[1] In his cogent Introduction to a gathering of Empson's creative writings, John Haffenden notes that Empson seems settled in his disdain of the Christian God by the late 1920s and early 1930s (Empson, 1988, pp. 33, 36). But there are few overt signs of anti-Christianity in either *Seven Types of Ambiguity* or *Some Versions of Pastoral*, Empson's two major works of the 1930s. Empson does refer in passing to 'Milton's appalling God' (p. 168) in the chapter on Milton and Bentley in *Some Versions*, but this is not at the core of his argument. Milton hardly figures at all in *Seven Types*, which takes most of its examples from metaphysical and Romantic poetry, though the lengthy analysis of Herbert's 'The Sacrifice' (pp. 226–33) may forecast Empson's later investigation of the meanings of the Christian atonement in *Paradise Lost*. See also Empson's poem, 'Reflection from Anita Loos', and his own detailed gloss, in his notes, on the provocative line 'Christ stinks of torture who was caught in lime' (1955, pp. 66, 114). Haffenden's Introduction to his collection of Empson's literary essays and reviews includes a trenchant account of Empson's attitude toward Christianity (Empson, 1987a, pp. 23–34).

moments Empson does state directly where he thinks that Milton has failed or gone in an unfortunate direction, as in the War in Heaven in book VI (pp. 54–5). Unlike Leavis, however, Empson credits Milton with a supple feeling for language and the rhythms of argument, and pays heed throughout to this poet's 'adventurous intelligence' (p. 190).

Readers have often complained about Empson's bitingly scornful references to the evils of Christianity in *Milton's God* – which, to them, distressingly clash with Empson's tributes to generosity and fellow-feeling – but the attacks on Christianity seem to me to loom disfiguringly large only in the final chapter specifically keyed to the doctrine itself. Here, Empson's embittered, subversive language gets the better of him, as when he asserts that 'the Christian God the Father, the God of Tertullian, Augustine and Aquinas, is the wickedest thing yet invented by the black heart of man' (p. 251). If man is 'black' at heart, then he cannot really be the source of basically decent, humane feelings – those feelings which Empson declares that Christianity has habitually disdained and destroyed. Empson's case against Christianity holds true only if man's heart is not a black one; he cannot persuasively claim that Christianity fundamentally inspires evil behaviour, corrupting otherwise good men and women, if we in fact harbour a 'black' heart to begin with.

Empson's and Leavis's fierce response to *Paradise Lost* becomes more understandable when one grasps the ideological struggles in which these critics participated. Some of Leavis's hostility to Milton in *Revaluation*, a book written in the mid-1930s, derives, I believe, from his opposition to fascism. The monolithic remoteness of the poem, and the arrogant certainties of its author, likely bore, for Leavis, an uncomfortably close resemblance to the fascist 'brutalization' he warned against in *For Continuity* (1933, p. 12) and in early pieces in *Scrutiny*. In Empson's case, the political dimension of his argument with Milton's Christian doctrine (and its modern spokesmen) is even more explicit, as his allusions to Orwell's *Nineteen Eighty-Four* and conviction that the 'picture of God in the poem' is 'astonishingly like Uncle Joe Stalin' attest (1965, p. 146). In Empson's view, Christianity and Stalinism mirror one another, producing similar sorts of rigidity, intolerance and murderous oppression. 'Young people often join a Church', Empson observes, 'because they think it is the only way to avoid becoming a Communist, without realizing that a Renaissance Christian State was itself usually a thorough-going police terror' (p. 10). *Milton's God* is thus an intriguing document in the cultural history of the Cold War, for Empson condemns communism even as he exhaustively assails the very Christian humanism that most anti-communists zealously promoted. He makes clear how much he loathes the 'Totalitarian State' (p. 146), yet also contemptuously dismantles the idea of a Christian society that totalitarianism was supposed terrifyingly to endanger.

This ideological point helps us to perceive the charged complexity of Empson's book. Empson is an ethical critic, not a political one, but he perceives the issues of *Paradise Lost* to matter crucially amid the politics of the Cold War. To worship the Christian God means to do the bidding of a tyrant and carry out his horrible designs; and it is this same unthinking fidelity to tyranny that Stalinist theory and practice mandate. Empson's belief in the extreme significance of *Paradise Lost* for the contemporary scene – warning as it does of the corrupting influence of both Christianity and communism – explains some of the forced interpretations that he supplies to reinforce his argument. These are often entertaining, as Empson amusingly – and knowingly – propels his claims beyond what the evidence of the text warrants. But of course the risk he runs is that he sometimes appears unfair, so determined to indict Milton's God – and trace the affinities between Christianity and communism – that he racks and strains the poem.

An example of this occurs in Empson's chapter on Satan, where he comments on the rumour of 'new Worlds' (I, line 650) that apparently circulated in heaven before the Satanic host rebelled against God (see Milton, 1957). 'We gather that the angels regarded this rumour', Empson remarks, 'as a threat to their status in the hierarchy, just as they did the promotion which actually caused the revolt. The source of a rumour in such a hierarchy on earth (a battleship, for example) is usually mysterious; but in heaven it is hard to see who could be the ultimate source but God himself, as part of a war of nerves' (p. 48). This is a good, grim joke, but Empson is merely tossing out a troublemaking guess that conforms to his own feelings about God rather than to the details of Milton's language.

The impatience and laxity in Empson's reading are tied, too, to an undue literal-mindedness that he displays. Admittedly his literal-mindedness does function well on occasion; it bracingly urges us to attend empathetically to the movements of the story – how would

WE feel if placed in Adam's and Eve's predicament? – and successfully brings into focus the unsettling moral demands of the poem. More often, though, Empson allows his literal interpretation of a passage to skew what Milton has written. In his chapter on Heaven, for instance, he deals with Raphael's description of the assignment God gave a band of angels to guard the gates of Hell. Raphael reports that he and his companions obeyed God's decree even though they were aware that God alone would decide whether the fallen angels would remain in Hell or escape from it – 'not that they durst without his leave attempt' (VII, 237). 'They knew', Empson irritatedly declares,

> and they knew that God knew that they knew, that this tiresome chore was completely useless. Apparently most of them did not want to see Adam emerge into consciousness, but Raphael says that he did, and also that he assumes God gave him a job at the time merely to disappoint him. I grant that Milton is on strong ground so far as the situation is a military one, because an army does get disciplined like this; but then, consider the morale of this army. They know that they failed to defeat the rebels, and that God need never have ordered them to try, indeed must have intended to humiliate them, because as soon as he chose he removed the rebels with contemptuous omnipotence. (p. 110)

In strictly literal terms, Raphael's mission seems futile, but the language of disappointment and humiliation is Empson's, not Milton's. Earlier, in book V, Raphael had defined for Adam the nature of the service that God expects both angels and men to perform.

> Our voluntary service he requires,
> Not our necessitated
> . . .
> Freely we serve,
> Because we freely love, as in our will
> To love or not; in this we stand or fall. (V, 529–40)

Empson would probably wager that Raphael's words illustrate the completeness with which God has brainwashed his servants: they tell themselves that the jobs they know to be foolish are, in fact, jobs that they happily undertake because they love their stern taskmaster. But if Empson pitched his interpretation in this way, he would be seizing once more upon the literal fact of meaningless work while neglecting the language of love and gladly given obedience that depicts the work, for Raphael and Adam, as splendidly meaningful. Invariably Empson stresses that Christian notions of faith and obedience lead men to act absurdly or viciously; he never takes seriously, never pauses even to imagine, the possibility that Christianity might make good men better, and bad men good, as well as turn good men bad.

The strength of *Milton's God* is Empson's generous responsiveness to the poet's engagement with hugely difficult material, and its weakness arises whenever he presses his case against Christianity (and Milton's belief in it) against the action of the poem. At his best, Empson seeks to understand and articulate what Milton likely intended; as the key guideline, he recommends that we keep in mind Milton's first audience, for we can only 'impute' meanings which that audience could conceivably have recognized (p. 28). But Empson does not altogether abide by this theory, and often elides it with another one. 'A critic ought to use his own moral judgement, for what it is worth, as well as try to understand the author's, and that is the only way he can arrive at a "total reaction"' (pp. 204–5). Empson is driven to propound his own judgements, as when he grouses at the task assigned to Raphael, and these regularly enliven his book, if in sometimes exasperating fashion. Such judgements of his own, however, jostle against his admirable effort to enquire into the judgements that Milton probably intended. Is it Milton or Empson who highlights the humiliating pointlessness of Raphael's obedience?

By deftly enquiring into Milton's likely intentions, Empson does often fasten upon major complications in the poem. He notes very nicely, for example, the 'republican' ideas and attitudes that the Puritan rebel Milton had embraced during the years of the Revolution and that he furnished Satan: 'surely the first readers must have found this intriguing; the only good writer who had defended the regicide was ascribing to the devils the sentiments still firmly held by himself and his proscribed party' (p. 82). At these moments Empson pays homage to Milton's honesty and sympathy. It is testimony to Milton's artistic skill and power, says Empson, that he makes certain to provide his evil figures with strong arguments. Milton is determined to make his own task of 'justifying' God's ways an extremely difficult one; he is intelligent enough, and scarred enough by the failure of the Revolution, to see that defending God is hard. He is, Empson maintains, 'searching' and 'struggling' to justify God's dealings with mankind (p. 11), and this daunting enterprise often leads Milton into 'moral confusions' when he unflinchingly tallies the merits of Satan's revolt and discloses the forbidding unreasonableness of heavenly justice (p. 13).

Empson is inclined always to give Milton, not God, the benefit of the doubt. If a passage in the poem seems perplexing, it is probably because Milton is facing up to ambiguities in Christian doctrine, or to the inordinate burdens imposed on human minds by 'imperturbable Providence' (Hartman, 1970, p. 115), which a lesser writer would have glossed over or shunned. During his days as Cromwell's propagandist, 'Milton always remained liable', Empson states, 'to defend his side by an argument which would strike his employers as damaging; his style of attack is savagely whole-hearted, but his depth of historical knowledge and imaginative sympathy keep having unexpected effects' (p. 123). Unlike Leavis, Empson grants Milton an exploratory, and frequently critical, relation to his project of justifying God's ways. To Empson, Milton is distinctive for his inveterate ability to peer 'all around the issues that were being raised' (p. 153; see also pp. 177, 181).

Again, unlike Leavis, Empson trusts the sound and movement of Milton's verse. Where Leavis perceives only numbing monotony, Empson finds powerful feeling that clarifies the moral points of the poem – and clarifies them sometimes by undercutting the official truths of Christian doctrine that the language 'on the surface' (see p. 93) appears designed to promote. Empson refers approvingly to the 'force and music of the poetry' (p. 49); he alerts us to instances where Milton – his 'feelings' deeply engaged – is writing 'frightfully well' (p. 118); and he frequently celebrates the 'beauty' (e.g., p. 182) of particular passages. Empson is aiming to contest Leavis's (and behind him, T. S. Eliot's and Ezra Pound's) dismissal of Milton's language; and he is, furthermore, seeking to recuperate the infirm, if appreciative, terms employed by an earlier generation of impressionistic men of letters, who had invoked Milton's 'beauty' and 'music' in uncritical ways that Leavis in particular had angrily rebutted.

Milton's God, then, is especially noteworthy for its generous openness to Milton. Empson judges that Milton's language in *Paradise Lost* is complex, risk-taking, sometimes provocatively puzzling, and he nimbly sketches the poet's challenging confrontation with the thrust and harsh implications of Christian doctrine. But in order really to understand *Paradise Lost*, one needs not only to draw upon

Empson's illuminating account of Milton's search and struggle, but also must strive somehow to couple it with at least a modulated version of the arrogant, wilful Milton that Leavis blocks out. Leavis errs, in my view, in his description of Milton's language and in his flinty refusal to allow that Milton delves into and reflects upon his own poetic strategies and doctrinal values. On these matters, Empson is much more insightful, largely because he recognizes the supreme difficulties of the subject that Milton has chosen. As Empson says at one point, 'Dr Leavis seems to assume that Christianity must be at worst a neutral literary topic, so that anything ugly or confused in the poem must be the fault of the author' (p. 12). But Leavis does catch something of the unrelenting quality of *Paradise Lost* and the unyielding nature of the man who composed it. Sometimes Milton strikes us, as Empson tellingly argues, as generous and sympathetic, but he is also adamant, I think, about making his readers face the tough logic of Christian belief. On these occasions, Milton directly registers the impact of doctrinal truth, and he seems immensely uncharitable not only to his characters but to his poem.

This is especially true in books XI and XII, which describe God's forgiveness of Adam and Eve and present the panorama of history. Professional scholars have canvassed these books thoroughly, listing analogues and sources, as well as the doctrinal rationale, for them. But most of Milton's readers have not taken much pleasure in the final stages of the poem. C. S. Lewis, one of Milton's staunchest defenders and one of Empson's opponents in *Milton's God*, stamped books XI and XII as markedly inartistic stuff, an 'untransmuted lump of futurity' (1942, p. 128). Empson himself speaks of them as 'glum' (p. 190), and, in a new chapter for the 1981 paperback edition of *Milton's God*, reaffirms that he finds them 'dismal' (1981, p. 334). Leavis would have likely judged them to be plagued even more egregiously by the lifeless, wearying rhythm he observed elsewhere in the verse. But whatever their lapses in style and mood, these books reveal kinds of starkly challenging meanings in *Paradise Lost* that have figured in it all along and that now simply emerge with unmistakable clarity.

Book X concludes with Adam's and Eve's reconciliation after their stormy quarrel and with Adam's prayer of contrition for their faults, a prayer that the narrator recapitulates, in the final lines of this book, as a means of showing his human sympathy with (and bonds to) the characters (lines 1097–1104). Milton's narrator thereby profoundly endorses the love that Adam and Eve have demonstrated for one another and that they, furthermore, have shown for God by admitting their sin and appealing for his mercy. In an important sense, Adam and Eve have seized the initiative; they were responsible for disobeying God, and now they acknowledge their wrongdoing. As Empson remarks in passing in his chapter on Eve, 'it is important to realize' that 'there is a total absence of heavenly aid at this crucial point' (p. 168). But the beginning lines of book XI, which Empson touches upon but does not sufficiently probe, slant the scenes we have just witnessed in a painfully different direction:

> Thus they in lowliest plight repentant stood
> Praying, for from the Mercy-seat above
> Prevenient Grace descending had remov'd
> The stony from their hearts, and made new flesh
> Regenerate grow instead, that sighs now breath'd
> Unutterable, which the Spirit of prayer
> Inspir'd, and wing'd for Heav'n with speedier flight
> Than loudest Oratory. (1–8)

It has been 'prevenient grace' that has inspired Adam and Eve to feel contrite for their sin. While perhaps unobjectionable in doctrinal terms, these words limit and diminish human effort, sapping the powerful feelings that the ending of book X expressed. On the one hand, Milton labours to depict and honour human dignity: Adam and Eve sin and yet manage to recover from their failure to obey God and win through to renewed faith in his ways. On the other hand, Milton no sooner defines this area within which Adam and Eve had acted responsibily – and to which the narrator, repeating his characters' words, has apparently committed himself – than he abruptly eliminates it.

Milton turns the screw even tighter when the Son 'intercedes' on behalf of fallen man a few lines later:

> See Father, what first fruits on Earth are sprung
> From thy implanted Grace in Man, these Sighs
> And Prayers, which in this Golden Censer, mixt
> With Incense, I thy Priest before thee bring,
> Fruits of more pleasing savor from thy seed
> Sown with contrition in his heart, than those
> Which his own hand manuring all the Trees
> Of Paradise would have produc't, ere fall'n
> From innocence. (22–30)

The narrator's earlier lines had attributed man's act of contrition to God; later, God himself summarizes that man repents because of 'my motions in him' (line 91). Now, in a manner that is simultaneously mild and inescapably insistent, the Son exalts the prayers which Adam and Eve speak (thanks to God) after they have fallen and suddenly, curtly, lowers the value of the prayers they had uttered while still innocent. The effect is very damaging to the poem. As Arnold Stein has pointed out, Milton here retrospectively denigrates the work that Adam and Eve undertook in the Garden and the prayerful attitudes that informed it (1977, p. 162).[2] It is as though the Garden were second best all along.

Towards the end of book XI, Milton delineates how little the Garden means, and in the process he treats his own imaginative creation with striking severity. This can be seen clearly in his description of the Flood and the dreadful fate that overtakes Paradise. In his goodness, the archangel Michael tells Adam, God allows the 'one just man', Noah, to escape the Flood and save himelf from a 'world devote to universal rack' (XI, lines 818, 821). 'No sooner he with them', Michael explains,

> of Man and beast
> Select for life shall in the Ark be lodg'd,
> And shelter'd round, but all the Cataracts
> Of Heav'n set open on the Earth shall pour
> Rain day and night, all fountains of the Deep
> Broke up, shall heave the Ocean to usurp
> Beyond all bounds, till inundation rise
> Above the highest hills; then shall this Mount
> Of Paradise by might of Waves be mov'd
> Out of this place, push'd by the horned flood
> With all his verdure spoil'd, and Trees adrift
> Down the great River to the op'ning Gulf,
> And there take root an Island salt and bare,
> The haunt of Seals and Orcs, and Sea-mews' clang.
> To teach thee that God attributes to place
> No sanctity, if none be thither brought
> By men who there frequent, or therein dwell. (XI, 822–38)

Here Milton forecasts, through Michael, the destruction of the Mount of Paradise, and he does so by aligning himself with perhaps his central ethical tenet – that only spiritually enlightened men and

[2] My interpretation of the opening of book XI is indebted to Stein, and also to the different readings astutely given by Greene (1963, pp. 407–8) and Fish (1967, pp. 19–20).

women can bring holiness to a place. But even more painfully to the point is that this passage displays the poet imagining the violation of what he himself has created – the Eden portrayed as a landscape of teeming vitality and wonder in the earlier books of the poem.[3]

Coleridge once observed that when we read Milton, we feel his 'presence' at each and every moment, and nowhere else is this fact brought home to us so vividly. These are inexorable lines; their surging energy drives the reader toward the doctrinal lesson that the poet uncompromisingly announces. Milton is, one could hazard, unfalteringly courageous in staging this spectacle for himself and his reader; he is, as well, hard-heartedly, self-punishingly, exposing the relative inauthenticity of Eden, however richly compelling it might have previously seemed. 'No poet compares to Milton', Harold Bloom once suggested, 'in his intensity of self-consciousness as an artist and in his ability to overcome all the negative consequences of such concern' (1975, p. 125). This self-consciousness is intimately connected to Milton's willingness to behave critically, even self-destructively, towards the writerly product he has made. He presents magnificent fictions and then undoes them as forcefully as he can, undoes them, in fact, with an awe-inspiring exuberance. In a brief commentary on *Paradise Lost* in *The Structure of Complex Words* (1951), Empson gestured toward a rendering of Milton's exhilarated hurtfulness toward his poem when he commented on the poet's 'delight in the harshness of a theme which makes all human history turn on an absolutely trivial action' (p. 101). 'Delight in harshness' gets at an essential feature of Milton's writing.

A passage like this one from book XI calls, however, for the terms that both Empson and Leavis utilize. Empson enables us to glimpse the exploratory relation of Milton to his own craftsmanship and Christian loyalties, whereas Leavis valuably underscores the uncurbed egotism – humility paradoxically empowered by pride – that impels Milton toward drastic reappraisals of his workmanship. But we need to proceed even further with this line of enquiry. In his urgent honesty, Milton comes, by the close of *Paradise Lost*, to misrepresent not only his poem but also the very doctrine he has sought through his poetry to legitimate. In his final exchange with Michael, Adam declares that he has now learned 'that to obey is best' (XII, line 561) and that Christ is his redeemer. Michael com-

[3] I present a similar reading of this passage in *Crisis in Criticism* (1984, pp. 183–4).

mends these words as 'the sum of Wisdom' (lines 575–6) and adds that Adam must supplement this knowledge with Faith, Virtue, Patience, Temperance, and Love:

> Then wilt thou not be loath
> To leave this Paradise, but shalt possess
> A paradise within thee, happier far. (585–7)

As the poem moves quickly toward its conclusion, we may tend to overlook this feature of Michael's teaching, or else briskly accept it as part of the general pattern of spiritual sustenance and affirmation that Michael and Adam voice. But the accent on the 'happier' Paradise that awaits Adam is disconcertingly based on a false distinction between life before and after the Fall. While Adam and Eve lived free from sin in Eden, they enjoyed a harmonious relation to the external landscape, one that reflected their inner happiness and pleasure. Milton is now saying that life after the Fall is indubitably far better because of the luminous interiority that defines it, as though no inner happiness were possible before. This is false to the poem and to Milton's own doctrine, for it is the poignant lost eminence of Eden that enabled mankind to integrate inner and outer life. In order to celebrate the new dispensation, Milton seems crudely, certainly reductively, to imply that there was no kind of paradise 'within' before the Fall. If that were true, then Paradise would be exactly the bland, unchallenging, languid, empty environment that Milton took exorbitant pains, in the earlier books, to show it was not. He had laboured to represent Paradise as a site for moral testing and growth, and he did so very effectively. Now, in effect, he devalues the representational work he has done, setting aside any possibility for paradisal plenitude and highlighting Eden's essential human poverty and spiritual thinness.

But from another point of view, this apparent failure on Milton's part may stand as a powerful reason for praising him. Milton exalts the fallen world, the world of pain, suffering and limitation, the world in which men and women make mistakes yet in which they also find their happiness. Empson would probably have approved of the cast of these lines from book XI, however much he might have baulked at the doctrinal context in which they are layered. They likely would have appealed to the 'dissident rationalism' (Norris, 1978, p. 3) that always characterized his thought. Neither God nor man lies beyond the fair rule of reason; as Empson once remarked in an essay on Marvell, we must always 'fall back upon the use of reason' (1984, p. 43). No person (and no deity) can remain exempt from the inspected play of motives and the codes of decent conduct. We live in the world, and are happier for it.

When Milton, then, says through Michael that Adam will be 'happier' after the Fall, he is challenging the terms of the earlier books of *Paradise Lost*, but doing so in a manner which an Empsonian would doubtless admire. Here, as elsewhere, Milton shows his hostility to his own formidably buttressed dogma; he manifests sharply his unease with the conditions of the Edenic life, even though Christian truth declares – and he has seemingly agreed – that this life blended inner contentment with external order. Milton, one might suggest, here reveals to us how we ought to approach his poem. If we take it as built upon unimpeachable doctrine, we will end by judging it highly unattractive, or else we will continually be led to rebuke ourselves for our upset responses to the scenes that Milton presents and that we believe we ought simply to tolerate as fundamental to Christianity. But if, instead, we honestly admit the nature of our response, and seek as best we can to articulate the reasons for it, we will be grateful for, as well as profitably disturbed by, what Milton has resolutely wrought. *Paradise Lost* will not be a distant or repellent monument, but a wonderfully human work that struggles against dogmatism, mocks assertions of sheer (and never-to-be-questioned) will, and refuses any impulse to gain perverse pleasure from the misfortunes of others. Though officially dedicated to justifying God, the poem breathes, for Empson and conceivably for us, with an honourably high valuation of reason and respect for persons.

CHAPTER 4

Empson's Satan: an ambiguous character of the seventh type

Paul H. Fry

'My attitude in writing it was that of an honest man erecting the ignoring of "tact" into a point of honour.' Thus, with the word 'tact' in ironic quotes, William Empson looks back on *Seven Types of Ambiguity* in the 1947 'Preface' to the second edition. There is a remarkable self-awareness in this sentence, which concedes that there may have been an element of pose, perhaps of defensiveness – of tact, in short – in the author's cultivation of expository insouciance. Just where he was most slapdash and most offensive to scholarly method, just there, he says, he imagined himself to have been most honourable. Thus he confirms what we knew instinctively, that his unbuttoned rhetoric embodied the tactless tact of the gentleman's fireside conversation, 'using tact about the assertion of class' (1951, p. 205). But decidedly the conversation of a Dissenting Gentleman: the person Arthur Mizener in 1938 called 'the revolutionary critic in the guise of a correspondent of the T.L.S.' (1938, p. 58).[1] In Empson's style as in his chosen subject, the bluff squire, with his keen English nose for nonsense, almost completely obscures another character who is deeply sympathetic with Romantic attitudes. (It is as though Percy Shelley were to disguise himself as the father who had threatened to disown him.) The tension between these *personae* is what I wish to emphasize in this essay.

When an honest man in any case erects the ignoring of tact into a point of honour, the word 'tact' becomes hard to assign a '$' value, to use the notation of *Complex Words* (1951, p. 17). Empson views tact as a kind of self-inhibiting, veiled insinuation meant to cushion the potential shock of what one has to say (see Empson, 1965, p. 66), especially in a 'social situation calling for some tact and delicacy'

[1] Gentry, yes, but coded for eccentricity rather than propriety, appearing (for his honorary degree at Cambridge) 'as a country gentleman, a reformed Tom Jones in a canary yellow waistcoat' (Bradbrook, 1985, p. 115).

(1953, p. 130: this is impishly let drop during one of his tactless, indelicate readings of Herbert). It is tact of this deployed kind which for Empson controls the structure of irony: A speaks with veiled derision to B about C in the presence of C, who must then choose either to seem unimplicated but obtuse or alert but guilty as charged (see 1987a, p. 178). I am tempted to say even that this sense of tact as manipulated communication brings one as close as one can get to what Empson means when he skirts the idea of literary form, as when he says, 'It is partly this tact which makes Marvell's puns charming and not detached from his poetry' (1953, p. 106); and if this is so, then his preference for ignoring tact may suggest a connection between his restiveness under social constraints and his customary indifference to questions of overarching literary structure.

Both his own prose style and his typical interpretive emphases isolate the 'logic', the common but also complex sense, of the discrete instance; and a 'purely logical point' – again concerning Herbert – 'can be made more clearly if it is not muffled by a sympathetic tone' (1953, p. 184n). Hence Bentley, whom Empson admired for refusing to rest satisfied with symbolizing explanations, becomes 'the Man who said the Tactless Thing' in trying to impose a prose logic on Milton's poetic flights (1935, p. 149). For Empson himself ignoring tact becomes a question of offsetting one kind of shock, the arty *o altitudo*, with another kind, the slurred sound of unedited talk:

> Then [someone at a party] said, 'How do you manage to get it as loose as that? Do you dictate it?' I explained I used beer, but that when I saw the stuff in print (I had to admit) it shocked my eye as much as it did his . . . One thing is, I have to read so much Mandarin English Prose now, especially in literary criticism, and am so accustomed to being shocked by its emptiness, that I feel I must do otherwise at all costs. (1954 letter to Janet Adam Smith, cited in 1987a, p. 395n)

If 'tact' then can mean either cant or – less unequivocally – doing the humane thing, it puts us in the grips of an ambiguity of the seventh type, 'when two meanings of the word, the two values of the ambiguity, are the two opposite meanings defined from the context, so that the total effect is to show a fundamental division in the writer's mind' (1953, p. 192). This is just the form of ambivalence one sees in Empson's attitude toward Romanticism: ignoring tact he calls it cant, or tactfully he declares it the latest period flowering of humanism.

Itself a fissure in tact (as in Wordsworth's inadvertent registering of the tactility or lack thereof in the Complex Word 'sense'), Romanticism as Empson understands it discloses the historically growing urgency, as theme and crisis, of mental division. Thus Empson can show us by example that the modernist ethos which shaped and alienated his mind was only an antithetical chapter in the continuing story of Romanticism. Strategically situated in this way, Empson pioneered in the rescue of the Romantic poets from the disfavour of high modernism, and in pursuing this issue I would like to follow his lead and 'use biography' – to show how he settles into this role, intermittently and at times reluctantly, by finding in certain literary heroes a likeness to himself. As Martin Dodsworth and others have been at pains to remind us, Empson was a landed gentleman (Dodsworth, 1985). He liked *Tom Jones* because Fielding could judge character as a magistrate, and the fact that Shelley was a landed gentleman too is what accords that poet, still much derided in 1961, the complexity of attitude Empson requires in order to invoke his authority (citing the 'Preface' to *Prometheus Unbound*) for the qualified vindication of Milton's Satan: 'Shelley does not speak as an Underdog or Outsider, tormented to hysteria by his wrongs, but as the heir to an estate who may expect to do a good deal of administration himself; he takes for granted that he ought to learn to be a good judge, not that he is a victim' (1965, p. 20). 'Fortunately we have had Empson', wrote Harold Bloom, who was well placed to recognize that passage as a turning-point in literary history, 'with his apt rallying cry: "Back to Shelley!"' (Bloom, 1973, p. 23).

Like Bloom, whose emphasis has always likewise fallen exclusively on character, Empson finds models for his hero as readily among the poets as among their creations. And no wonder, for, as many have pointed out (with condescension from the thirties through the fifties, with admiration since then), Empson reserves no impermeable aesthetic realm for literature but reads it as though it were continuous with life.[2] He sees, as Christopher Ricks finely says, 'in real terms the situation out of which the person speaks' (in Gill, 1974,

[2] Both the *Scrutiny* reviews (by James Smith and others) and the mixed reviews by such American critics as Ransom and Brooks had this caveat in common. Cleanth Brooks interestingly qualifies the complaint in imagining that between *Ambiguity* and *Complex Words* Empson loses track of the distinction: 'an equation has its origin in the history of the language whereas an ambiguity is the result of the stylizing of language by an individual writer' (1952, p. 670). Censure becomes approval in, e.g., Jonathan Culler: 'for Empson ambiguities derive precisely from the continuity between language in poems and language in other situations' (1984, p. 327).

p. 145). While he claims in 1961 that it has taken him some time to 'get out of' the fashion for attacking character analysis (1965, p. 69), it seems clear looking back that his criticism was always passionately human-centred and sceptical of any claim that literature may symbolize, intimate or inhabit realms of being inaccessible to human life. Indeed, what he can never be found admiring in Romanticism, in common with T. E. Hulme, is its oceanic tendency, its leakage of concrete material personhood into the circumambient gas.

Authors and poets then are at once texts to be read and characters living among us. The hero of this community, viewed from the middle distance, is everywhere typologically the same: 'He stood for "honour", pride rather than humility, self-realization rather than self-denial, caste rather than democracy' (1935, p. 85); and in Empson's view the sort of Romanticism which is rooted in the progressive Enlightenment simply transfers this Theophrastean character-type to the poet, whose being an 'outcast and unacknowledged legislator, equally strong in Byron and Shelley, puts him exactly in the position of the mythical tragic hero' (p. 207). Hence for every Faustus ('the demigod rogue ... the ideal drinking companion, the great fixer, who can break taboos for you and get away with it' (1987b, pp. 46–7)) or Falstaff ('the scandalous aristocrat' (1986, p. 72)) or even Stephen Dedalus ('not less than archangel ruined' (1984, p. 212)) there was a Rochester ('only in real high life could a man learn to talk so that anybody could understand him at once' (1987a, p. 275)) or even, in his moments of brave disorder – rhyming 'delight' with 'Wit' – a Pope:

> no one but the broad, unspecialized and in a way careless person (the well-born soul) can recognise a new development of the imagination even when it is thrust under his nose, and ... even he only does it by rejoicing. The whole world of the Rules and the 'slight faults' is dwarfed and trampled upon, and the bad rhyme is meant as a brave illustration of the virtues of carelessness which are being praised. (1951, p. 96)

A slant rhyme as Empson reads it is as assuredly as anything else a sign of character. In this regard Hugh Kenner is right, for all his hostility, to point out that not one of Empson's Complex Words is an 'image', with the partial exception of 'dog', which immediately becomes a person (Kenner, 1958, p. 256).

But despite his mistrust of the 'image', which would appear to suggest an affinity with the Romantic idealist tradition, Empson's is decidedly the empiricist Romanticism one finds also in the work of his Cambridge contemporary Basil Willey; hence for him the keyword for 'unhappy consciousness' is the very word which ambiguously designates the site of the image, 'sense'. Honestly sensual, honestly sensitive, honestly sensible: 'I should say the English could claim that their present extreme muddle with this family [of meanings] came from having faced first the realist and then the romantic issues with more of the permanent human balance than their neighbours' (1951, p. 253). Only for the inattentive reader does Empson's having called 'Tintern Abbey' a 'muddle' and the Grecian urn a 'pot' render him indifferent to the divided Romantic character. Sharing his generation's distaste for 'undisciplined squads of emotion' (T. S. Eliot, 'East Coker'), Empson as late as 1972 thus discriminatingly endorses Coleridge's sonnet to Schiller: 'Not *any* extravagance of emotion is being praised but the kind which purges and renews, because it prepares you to resist tyranny' (Empson and Pirie, 1972, p. 16). In 1930 the influence of Hulme via Eliot was still less easy to escape; hence Empson at that time dutifully deplores 'the apparently direct sensory image' in Romanticism 'which cannot be attached to any of the senses' (1953, p. 175).

What he does not openly acknowledge is that this hovering among intentions and referents is just the sort of muddle that characterizes the ambiguity of each and every type. Intent on suppressing the *tone* of Romanticism, Empson does not notice that his own acerbic iconoclasm reflects the same degree of disaffection. One voice of the character he fashions for himself can repeat the most full-blown sentiments of the tragic hero and the Romantic poet-rebel, but with the epigrammatic calm of an *ancien régime* moralist: 'About anything established there settles this curious double sentiment, that it is both right because it is customary and customary because it is right; and the idea of what is normal, since both are contrasted with the confusion of actual occurrences, allies itself to the ideal of what is best' (1951, p. 315). The effect is an oblique, at times perhaps self-deluding mode of identification with the aristocratic republican tradition, adopted by one whose allegiance to the modernist revolution in literary taste, with its apprenticing of the individual talent to tradition, was never wholly shaken off despite his growing horror at the implied politics and religious abasement of this movement.

But Empson is far too cagily self-conscious to be a historical exhibit merely, as Hulme for all his brilliance has become. Evidently

Empson's purpose from the beginning was to straddle the canonical fence, to find a way of reading that made the Classic–Romantic distinction, given prominence especially by Hulme, seem artificial. 'It seemed', he writes of the task he had envisioned in *Seven Types*, 'that one could only enjoy both groups by approaching them with different and incompatible presuppositions, and that this was one of the great problems which a critic ought to tackle' (p. viii). One way of solving the problem was to acknowledge that 'complexity of the order of . . . mind' is not a partisan virtue (aligned in Empson's day along the classicist-modernist axis) but a quality which only the sympathy of an interpreter can securely distinguish from its near cousin, the dreaded 'muddle' (see p. 154). Reviewing the history of English literature from this standpoint, one can see in Empson's ransacking of the whole tradition the assumption that whatever else may set the periods apart they nevertheless have in common, even in the eighteenth century ('the very sanctuary of rationality' (p. 68)), the ambivalence – typically between principle and experience, theory and practice – to which humane intelligence falls prey.

To illustrate Empson's saving 'division' of mind, we need only our first sentence: 'My attitude in writing it was that of an honest man erecting the ignoring of "tact" into a point of honour.' As we have seen, not only is 'tact' double-edged, but there are also two potentially divergent points of honour, the school-tie code and the politics of humaneness. There are also – in this case – two types of 'honesty': Empson's early self as 'honest man', he now knows, is at once naif and ironist, fool rushing in and sage looking askance, opposites who meet in the common task of blowing the gaff. Finally there is the seventh-type Ambiguity of the word 'erected': Futurist, architectural and therefore tactful as a Marinetti machine or steel trap, but also the organic phallus, deconstructive, disseminative and therefore tactless. It was enough to rise higher and higher. The young Empson skiing would have encountered English leftist journalists and German rightist filmmakers in equal profusion on the slopes, perhaps acknowledging a little of each in himself, but above all, I believe, though *Milton's God* was three decades hence, he would have seen himself as Satan on Mount Niphates.

I want to reinforce this identification in part with reference to themes, but also, at closer range, by stressing the typical movement of Empsonian interpretation. Like his structureless, *trouvaille*-bedizened arguments, Empson's ambiguities are neither architectonic nor resolvable: rather they are open-ended meditations on the dialectic of signification and force, the conflict between the available paraphrases of a word and the atmosphere of tone and feeling that leaves paraphrase in disarray. Perhaps more continuously than he knows, Empson discloses violent motives that implicate both interpretation and the interpreted. Handled by Empson, the well-wrought urn becomes a broken pot, not only in specific outbursts of interpretation but also in the overall arrangement of the seven ambiguities in what he disarmingly calls 'states of advancing logical disorder' (1953, p. 48). For my case in point I shall choose what Empson calls a 'test case' for his method, the reading of Macbeth's 'Come, seeling night' (pp. 18–20), a reading in which Empson shows, as he says in his best deadpan style, how Macbeth 'imposed the pathetic fallacy on the reader by means of an ambiguity, and tricked him into an irrational or primitive mode of thought under colour of talking about the view' (p. 38). Empson's theme here, which I shall attempt to read as an allegory of Empsonian interpretation, concerns the loneliness of being cut off, that state in which tact is irrelevant and in which one can speak with what Empson elsewhere calls, referring to Lear on the heath, a 'disregard for dignity' (p. 46).

There is much in this reading that must have encouraged the American New Critics. In Empson's 'particular irrelevance' Ransom may have found his 'texture of local irrelevance'. Neither Empson nor Ransom of course mean that anything they find worth mentioning is truly 'irrelevant', a word they choose merely to make us take notice, but Empson *is* allowing for a certain looseness of connection, a dissolve into 'atmosphere', and this distinguishes him both from Ransom and from his own mentor I. A. Richards, whose entirely unironic concept of 'irrelevant association' in *Practical Criticism* Empson's wilder and more tactless assault on poems is meant precisely to rehabilitate. A more genuinely Hartleyan Associationist than Richards, Empson typically suggests the impossibility of irrelevance. The suspicion that there are subterranean links between every point on the compass of signification informs what can legitimately be called Empson's semiotic. We can easily look forward to Roman Jakobson's infinitely extendable 'axis of selection' when Empson shows in *Seven Types* how one word 'supplants' another – the verb is his – in an author's mind, or when he wonders how, 'if one's mind does not in *some* way run through the various meanings of a word', it 'can ... arrive at the right one'. 'Shakespeare actually intended', he writes, 'by putting down something a little removed from any of the approximate homonyms, to set the reader groping about their network' (1953, pp. 82, 64, 83).

Notice, though, that it is not just Shakespeare who is accorded an 'atmosphere' here, a palpable but indeterminate sphere of implication; Empson himself says things at his most challenging that one cannot quite track to their lair. What *is* this 'something physiological and odd', picked up later in 'the whole frame of body'? These expressions are motivated, I think, by Shakespeare's word 'thickens', and they perhaps inadvertently evoke the Russian Formalists' 'palpability of the sign', not, however, with the iconographic, concretizing aim of Formalism but rather to effect the irrational crossing over of language into reality and vice versa that undoes the binarism of semiotics and slides the signifier inextricably and once for all under the signified. Again and – I would argue – as always, Empson's every move can be domesticated within a Formalist aesthetic only to deconstruct itself in that setting, and Formalism with it.

Without programmatic staging, Empson's prose reflects an openness to ambiguity or division within the self. The result is a more or less continuous ambiguity of the seventh type that I am calling 'tactless': a word which – to recur to it once again – within itself plays out the dramatic conflict between tactility ('the "tact" of an exploring fingertip' (1987a, p. 105)), bodily presence, and disappearance into the thickening light, the wooded overgrowth, of association. But the drama at bottom – to move closer now to the *Macbeth* passage – concerns association itself considered as community:

Come, seeling Night,
Skarfe up the tender Eye of pitiful Day
And with thy bloddie and invisible Hand
Cancel and teare to pieces that great Bond
That keepes me pale.
Light thickens, and the Crow
Makes Wing to th' Rookie Wood.
Good things of Day begin to droope, and drowse,
While Night's black Agents to their Prey's doe rowse.
Thou marvell'st at my words, but hold thee still;
Things bad begun, make strong themselves by ill:
So prythee go with me. (III.2. 47–57, quoted p. 18)

Empson reads the pathos of Macbeth's speech as an indecisive reflection on the marginal but perhaps fatal difference between crow and rook, predator and colony: as a tragedy, that is, of the imperfect semantic overlap that reflects Macbeth's longing to return to the fold from which the word 'crow' has banished him. 'He is anxious . . . to be at one with the other *rooks*, not to murder them; that he can no longer, or that he may not yet, be united with the rookery; that he is murdering Banquo in a forlorn attempt to obtain peace of mind.' To be 'at one', to forge a union only by cutting off the relevance of whatever is exiguous to the group, the preferred thicket of meaning – this is a tempting choice for Empson the critic (everyone scolded him for spurning it), here reflected in the reluctance of Macbeth's alienation. In the force of Empson's readings, their transgressions, there is antagonism toward orders both social and hermeneutic which he still in part wishes to confirm and rejoin. What is involved is the scapegoat principle which he calls, in *Some Versions of Pastoral*, 'the tragic king, comic people convention' (p. 43). 'Thou marvell'st at my words', Macbeth tells his wife, 'So prythee go with me', as though by way of consolation a plurality of destructive 'black agents' (in the foregoing lines there was only one such agent) could form an alternative rookery of their own.

What authenticates individual consciousness for Empson is the belief here teased forth but elsewhere proclaimed, that the mind is itself a – potentially divided – community: 'the mind is complex and ill-connected like an audience, and it is as surprising in the one case as the other that a sort of unity can be produced by a play' (p. 68) – whence comes the issue which unifies the *Essays on Shakespeare* more than anything else, Shakespeare's obsessive fear of civil war. It is the rebel Empson's humane longing to be reunited with the rookery which makes him loathe those adversarial roles that can only be transumed in bad faith, paramount among them the nightmare drama of Christian sacrifice looming everywhere in his later work. These convictions about the mind as frail polity explain his lifelong enthusiasm for the playwright's many voices and his suspicion, which anticipates the Bakhtinian vein of so much current criticism, that Romantic lyricism at its worst is monoglossal as well as monocular. Yet it is in Romanticism (in this case, the *Rime of the Ancient Mariner*) that for Empson the 'totem and taboo' anomalies of Christianity are alone confronted through '[a]cceptance of the ethics of Jesus, but revolt against the Father who enjoyed sacrifice' (Empson and Pirie, 1972, p. 34; and see 1984, p. 117). If *Some Versions* can be read as an effort to redefine ambiguity in literary works as the reciprocal critique of the social classes, as a 'double plot' delimiting the horizons of classes and 'worlds' (unity being preserved by the paradox that our common humanity resides in nothing other than our inescapable partiality), and to extend our awareness of this practice into non-theatrical modes, we should not be surprised that one of the main tenets guiding this argument, 'that you can say everything about complex people by a complete consideration of simple people' (1935, p. 137), hearkens back directly to a founding text of British Romanticism, Wordsworth's re-situation of pastoral in his 'Preface to the *Lyrical Ballads*'.

To return to the *Macbeth* passage, it is clear that what accomplishes the movement toward an antithetical community ('prythee go with me') is not reconciliatory but rather, more dangerously, like the Christian sacrifice, a rationalization of evil. As Empson astutely argues in his analysis of the crow, Macbeth's commingling of light and dark – focused again in the word 'thickens' – attempts unsuccessfully to invest black agencies with legitimate authority. Theirs is the power, the force made strong by ill, while the good things of day, for all their 'great Bond', are anaemic, studies in the pallor and lassitude that in our allegory of reading we can refer to as 'weak'. Like a Bloomian weak reading, with its synecdochic 'tender Eye', day is unified, kept safely in bondage, only by taking a monocular view, while the 'bloddie and invisible Hand' of night, a violently disjointed metonymy – bloodied as much by amputation as by guilt – deconstructs the thin-blooded tissues of order. This it manages by the Möbius Strip effect that typically undoes logical progression: being invisible, the bloody hand must have scarfed up itself along with the tender eye, suppressing any and all fragments of the human that would have retained the 'Bond' of signification, in place of which there then appears a repetition in the register of the inhuman, a crow's wing for a man's hand. The mystery that emerges amid these mangled traces of community is the one that I think is in the back of Empson's mind just as probably as this passage from *Macbeth* was at the back of Milton's mind: the mystery of 'darkness visible'.

If one rereads *Seven Types* with these emphases in mind, and with the understanding that they exaggerate when taken in isolation, bringing out a strain of 'romantic diabolism' (1935, p. 167) which is at odds with Empson's aristocratic but sociable republicanism, it comes as a surprise to see how steadily the themes of revolt, alienation and darkness recur in his exhibits. *Macbeth* keeps coming back as an example in key places: ambiguity itself is made to 'float', with Macbeth, 'on a wild and violent Sea / Each way, and move' (1953, p. 101); and the words of the play are always (as Empson says in advance of Cleanth Brooks's great essay humanizing this theme) 'words which must be swaddled in darkness' (1953, p. 49). While in *Seven Types* Shakespeare is the author who most consistently transmits these themes, both in their diabolical and their reconcilable forms, if we look ahead in Empson's career we will find an increased, increasingly fascinated attention given for similar reasons to Milton, culminating in the sympathetic chapter on Satan in *Milton's God*.[3] Just as Macbeth embodies the decentralized feudal order Duncan has tried to weaken by creating new and more centrally answerable titled ranks, so Satan, prince of the North, is presented by Empson as a Norman baron rebelling against the tyranny of central authority and the parvenu pretensions of the Son. I think Empson would not have objected to being told that Macbeth and Malcolm help to shape his impression of Satan and Christ. He says that Satan is 'not so much a Scotsman, though that has been proposed, as a Yorkshireman' (1965, p. 77) – like Empson himself.[4]

Readers of *Milton's God* will recall the stunningly tactless personal anecdote Empson tells (pp. 66–7) of a time in 1939 when he landed at Los Angeles on his way from China to England, climbed to the top of a hill and screamed out loud. Overheard by a group of boys with airguns, Empson suddenly found he was being shot at, and so left the hill and resumed his journey, by train, to San Francisco. The experience, he claims, afforded him some satisfaction. Empson tells this real-life story in order to counter the idea that a soliloquy being overheard is implausible and belongs only to the realms of theatre and literature; and in turn to defend the plausibility of the rebel mountaineer Satan's speech on Niphates. But in the story Empson continued, unlike Satan, homeward towards his place of birth, there

[3] His preoccupation with Milton actually shows up earlier in his poetry, as R. E. Pritchard has very astutely said in a note on one of the poems: 'almost every poem of [1928–30] has an echo of or allusion to Milton, particularly *Paradise Lost* and its vast cosmic structure of immense distances and powers, and uncertain observers, seeking, like Empson, to find their place' (Pritchard, 1987, p. 60).

[4] Empson's pride in his regional identity has been remarked by Muriel Bradbrook, who sees that it is Marvell 'the Yorkshire M.P.' who interests him most in *Biography* (1985, p. 114), and by Frank Kermode, who reminds us that Empson's decision to teach at Sheffield was influenced by its location (1989, p. 117).

to join forces as a propagandist against what must then have seemed the true rebel angels abroad in the land. The irony to which I am trying here to call attention, as evidence of Empson's division of mind concerning the implications of Romantic divisiveness itself, can be expressed perhaps as follows: this strategically unguarded autobiographical moment of Empson's defence of Satan stands curiously apart from the cultural iconoclasm of *Milton's God* and becomes historically recognizable, rather, amid the fiercely traditionalist wartime propaganda of quite another book on Milton, ostensibly so foreign to Empson's purposes that he can find nothing to say about it, Douglas Bush's *'Paradise Lost' in Our Time*.

It would be wrong to imagine that Empson's championship of Satan was unique in its day or that it would necessarily have entailed, in itself, a turn to Romanticism. By the time of *Milton's God*, C. S. Lewis almost alone was arguing unequivocally that the devil is an ass.[5] Empson *needs* the Lewis argument, just as he needs Dover Wilson as a foil for his qualified defence of Falstaff ('he need not throw the drama away by pretending that the bogey was always ridiculous' (1986, p. 68)); and his enthusiasm in insisting that 'Satan is Milton as rebel' (1935, p. 169) is never secure enough to warrant suppressing the awkwardness of defending a view which he deems old-fashioned, not forward-looking: 'before we began to worry [in the Victorian period] about Milton's God being wicked, we had a long period [dating from Blake] of suspecting that his Satan was in some romantic way good' (1965, p. 17). It is important then to see just what it is that sets Empson's position apart from a view that has always been very widely held. What this is, I think, is a certain aspect of Satan's self-justification which will carry us forward to a sufficiently specific understanding of Empson's partial alignment with Romanticism.

What Empson likes about Satan is that he knows no time when he was not as now. He has no idea, as Empson says over and over, whether God created him or not, and naturally prefers to imagine that he made himself. Hence '[i]f Satan believed God to be a usurping angel there is no romantic diabolism at all in giving him our heartiest admiration' (1935, p. 167). But there is plenty of

[5] It may come as a surprise that John Crowe Ransom reviewing *Some Versions* (1938–9, p. 327) and Cleanth Brooks reviewing *Complex Words* (1952, p. 674) both second Empson's view of Satan as a heroic 'champion of progress' (Ransom), dissenting only from the view that Satan's author shares his sentiments.

Romantic autarchy. Empson is always distressed by arguments from simple causation which tend to place individual consciousness in a chain of determinacy. He is much more comfortable with immediate appearances, being willing even to speculate wildly about them (as in his giddier reconstructions of probable motives), trusting to circumstantial evidence, like Satan when he looks around him from his new bad eminence, takes stock and denies that the true conditions of his past life can ever be known. This is the most all-pervading trait that Empson shares with Milton's rebel angel; it does not extend to the simple Gnostic inversion of believing in diabolic creation, but it does embrace that more sceptical Gnosticism which doubts the existence of any truly originary creative intelligence (see 1965, p. 86, for both these views), leaving each and every individual consciousness – and conscience – freely self-emergent. (It follows as a matter of hermeneutic principle, for example, that the critic need not be wholly subservient to his author, at least not to the point of suspending his own world-picture, especially his ethical sense, in deference to the mere priority of alien ideas (see 1965, pp. 204–5).) It is owing to his conviction that individuality must generate itself unrestrainedly that even in his most Marx-influenced book Empson does not shrink from the heresy that 'the most valuable works of art ... often have a political implication which can be pounced on and called bourgeois' (1935, p. 20).

Even here, however, the link with Romanticism must be forged by inference. So great would be the strain on his literary loyalties were he to associate this indispensable outlook, the sense of the individual as autochthonous which is the basis of his politics, decisively with Romanticism that Empson appears most comfortable proclaiming it through his expositions of Buddhism, especially the concept of *dharma* or self-actualizing 'nature' – in place of a 'transcendent God' – which he derives in part from Aldous Huxley's *The Perennial Philosophy*. (He is also interested in the rather similar-seeming Confucian concept of 'nature' expounded by I. A. Richards in *Mencius on the Mind*. But even in such places as these he cites the 'Nature' of Wordsworth (see 1951, pp. 69–71).) However, the metaphysics of Romantic subjectivity are always less important to him than its politics, and his anthropocentric suspicion of grounding such beliefs in nature understood as mere landscape, belittled as 'the view' (1953, p. 38) or 'scenery' (1951, p. 298), was unvarying. In contrast with Wordsworth especially, by whom Empson was always for this reason both fascinated and put off, the self-realization of the individual for Empson made sense, was free of muddle, only as a political idea.

It is tempting to ascribe the less interestingly equivocal, more tendentious later work of Empson to the getting of Satan behind him. While he never ceased ignoring tact, while Marlowe's Promethean Faustus can be said to have become his last hero, and while he laboured mightily to rescue Donne and others from the tender eye of orthodoxy, Empson in the end seems to have returned to the taste of his earliest youth, the taste of Eliot which survives in *Seven Types*, though it is broken in upon by the dissociations of ambiguity itself. Be this as it may, whenever it is at full strength Empson's work requires that strain of Romanticism which is first and best reflected for a specialist in the Renaissance by the drama of Protestantism, Dissent and Revolution shaping the character of Satan. It is ironic, perhaps, that Empson was driven away from these themes as they have developed since the Enlightenment and back into that more homogeneous epoch in which the sole imaginative alternatives were some form of received religion or atheism by the very finality of his alienation from the Christian rookery. Tact gives way to tactics, and there is no place for ambiguity among such decided feelings.

CHAPTER 5

Compacted doctrines: Empson and the meanings of words

Alan Durant and Colin MacCabe

> The primary aim is to clear up confusion, so the author describes not only the varieties of meaning in a word but the various controversies in which they get used. Also he recognises that these different meanings within one word are liable to interact, so that they form 'compacted doctrines', as when *native* was taken to imply 'all subjected peoples are biologically inferior'; and he decides that many of our common words regularly tempt us to accept wrong beliefs, usually political ones. (Empson, 1987a, p. 184)

Coming across this passage for the first time, a casual reader might assume that this is someone writing about William Empson's *The Structure of Complex Words*. But in fact it is Empson himself, reviewing Raymond Williams's *Keywords* for the *New York Review of Books* in October 1977.

Besides the term 'keywords' itself, someone looking for likeness between the two books might highlight the shared idea of analysable structures of lexical meaning (especially the sense of embedded or compacted social doctrines inherent in the histories of words). There is also a common interest in the strengths – but also the limitations – of the *Oxford English Dictionary* (often referred to by Empson under its name at the time of first publiction, in instalments, between 1884 and 1928: the *New English Dictionary* (*NED*)). Williams approvingly cites Empson's assessment of the *Dictionary* as a 'majestic object' (1983, p. 39);[1] and for both writers, any work on the historical meanings of words is heavily dependent on it. More generally, too,

[1] What is now generally known as the *Oxford English Dictionary* was first published, in parts, as *A New English Dictionary on Historical Principles* (Murray *et al.*, 1884–1928). It was later reissued in a corrected form, with Introduction, Supplement and Bibliography, in thirteen volumes (1933); the *Dictionary* continues to undergo revision. For a detailed account of the planning, initial production and difficulties of the *OED*, see K. M. Elisabeth Murray (1977).

the two writers share a concern with public susceptibility to political complexities and possible distortions of the meanings of words, and an insistence on the social importance of greater critical awareness about language and its operations.

What makes such questions of likeness and divergence between the two writers more than usually interesting, however, is the peculiar combination of the clear importance of the issues they investigate with the lack of systematic attention usually given to them. While a great deal of research has been done on how the mental lexicon is organized, on how lexical items are disambiguated in parsing, on processes of metaphorical usage, and on other sensitive areas in the workings of vocabulary,[2] little attention has been given even now – forty years after *The Structure of Complex Words*, and fifteen after *Keywords* – to connections between the complex ways in which subtly shaded senses of individual words are used in discourse and changing structures of perception and thought. Empson's and Williams's work – along with Leo Spitzer's *Essays in Historical Semantics* and John Danby's *Shakespeare's Doctrine of Nature* (both first published in 1949), and C. S. Lewis's *Studies in Words* (1960) – marked out an area of concern with what Empson, reflecting on Wordsworth's use of 'sense', described as a 'concentrated richness of single words' (1951, p. 289). But this fresh area of concern has not been subsequently developed. Rather, it might be said that even now Empson's and Williams's work in this field is more admired than understood, which is why in this essay we confine ourselves to the primarily expository tasks of illustrating Empson's approach and comparing it with Williams's; only then do we begin to draw attention to unresolved issues which remain.

UNLOCKING *KEYWORDS*

Despite the many areas in common concern between his own work and *Keywords*, Empson did not like Williams's 'vocabulary of culture and society' (the sub-title of *Keywords*). There seem to have been two main reasons why.

[2] Detailed accounts of the main linguistic theories of word-meaning can be found in John Lyons (1977). An analysis of word-meaning consistent with the larger claims of Relevance Theory is Dan Sperber and Deirdre Wilson (1986, pp. 90–3). Practical work on the semantics of words can be found in James Hurford and Brenda Heasley (1983, pp. 177–231). A good introductory account of language-processing and interpretation is Judith Greene (1986, esp. pts 1 and 2).

Firstly, Empson points out that influences from a word's past do not always survive into later meanings. Citing as evidence the link between Jane Austen's predilection for puns and the fact that she never made a pun on the word, Empson challenges Williams's account of the word 'interest'. Williams argues, in effect, that the word always carries a substratum sense to do with money. But in his 1977 review of *Keywords*, Empson – who evidently felt his critique worth repeating in his 'Comment' for the third edition of *The Structure of Complex Words* published in the same year – argues that 'a pun of this sort can only impose a doctrine upon us if both meanings arise naturally in one context' (1987a, p. 185).

Empson's second criticism concerns what he sees as an undervaluing, in Williams, of possible resistance to biased use of words. According to Empson, Williams exaggerates the power of words to influence and direct thinking in ways that put language beyond self-critical thought. Williams's introduction, as Empson sees it, 'offers very little hope from the technique he provides' (1987a, p. 184). In his own writing, on the other hand, Empson prioritizes a more direct idea of the enabling power of awareness of language, especially as regards resisting propaganda. As is well known, although Empson worked alongside Orwell in the Far Eastern section of the BBC Foreign Service, as Specialist Adviser to the Indian and Burmese Section during the Second World War, he drew very different conclusions regarding the propagandist power of words. Empson shared with Orwell the sense, exemplified most clearly in *1984*, of how language can create new forms of truth which fundamentally contradict earlier truths, thus brainwashing people with varieties of Newspeak. But pushed too far, such a view challenges Empson's deep commitment to human beings' rational capabilities, and the possibility for self-understanding inherent in powers of the human mind to distinguish and analyse meanings.

Summing up his arguments against *Keywords* – and in effect justifying the different terms of his own project in *Complex Words* – Empson concludes his review:

> What he [Williams] needs to consider is the structure relating two meanings in any one of his chosen words, so that they imply or insinuate a sentence: 'A is B'. Under what conditions are they able to impose a belief that the speaker would otherwise resist? As he never considers that, he is free to choose any interpretation that suits his own line of propaganda. (p. 188)

To decide how far this perhaps surprisingly forceful critique of Williams is justified – and to understand the relationship between Empson's views on words and more recent perceptions – we need to understand much of the detail of Empson's arguments. But we also need to understand how these arguments fit in with larger critical concerns and priorities. In this essay, therefore, we combine an outline of Empson's main arguments in *Complex Words* with an illustrative case study (of the word 'wit'); in doing so, we compare Empson's account with other available studies (including C. S. Lewis's, and our own readings). Finally, on the basis of the two interconnected descriptions, we conclude with more general remarks about issues of compacted doctrines in the meanings of words.

WRITING *COMPLEX WORDS*

Empson believed that a key word – any recurrent but also peculiarly ambivalent or highly charged word – not only functions, as he puts it while describing 'all' in *Paradise Lost*, like 'a Wagnerian *motif*' (1951, p. 101), but also involves kinds of embedded 'semantic equations'. Words accumulate strata of senses and implications and assert propositions or arguments, even as they conceal such complexities by appealing to common-sense understanding. This is true not only of 'ordinary language', but also of poetry, which for Empson does not (as Richards and others had claimed) by-pass questions of truthfulness with its own forms of 'pseudo-statement'. On the contrary, poetic language in Empson's view simply extends the resources of sense-making characteristic of language use more generally (though Empson works through his own complex qualifications to this position in relation to the meanings of the word 'sense' in Wordsworth, and 'all' in Milton).

Working from these general premises, Empson seeks to analyse the 'logical structure' of words. At the simplest level, such analysis is desirable because, as Empson puts it in his account of C. S. Lewis,

> Readers need to be warned that a writer often means by a word something other than what their own background leads them to expect; a working understanding of the historical process of change of meaning, by giving this awareness, may be enough. (1987a, p. 143)

This is another way of putting the argument Lewis himself makes with his idea of a word's 'dangerous sense'. If a text makes tolerable sense our tendency is to go merrily on. We are often deceived. In an old author the word may mean something different. I call such senses dangerous senses because they lure us into misreadings. (Lewis, 1960, p. 13)

Despite the great detail of Empson's arguments, however, and the wealth of illustrations he presents, *The Structure of Complex Words*, as its author rather dismally observes in the preface to the third (1961) edition, was to a certain extent a failure. He seems to presume that this failure was the result of his unwillingness to observe the academic proprieties, and publish in specialist magazines (a course of action partly explicable in terms of the fact that in such publications Empson would not have been able to be as rude as he wanted to be). It is certainly possible that the book's failure was partly due to this; but it also has two other causes. One concerns the style of the book, which is highly idiosyncratic: Empson is writing to convince only one person, himself; and his exposition and argument are tailored to that audience. The other cause is the state of linguistics at the time the book was published: many of the linguistic premises with which Empson chooses to argue (especially those in the work of Gustav Stern, or in I. A. Richards's psychological theories of meaning, which divided the word into a cognitive meaning and an emotional charge which was to be measured by some future psychology) were already considered slightly old-fashioned. In addition, the behaviourist attack on psychology led by the American linguist Leonard Bloomfield – about whom Empson writes critically at various points in *The Structure of Complex Words*, and whom he challenges at length in Appendix III of the book – carried the day; and Empson's book was published in a decade (the fifties) in which few major linguists concerned themselves with semantics, and even fewer (if any) with historical semantics.

Departing dramatically from the behaviourist paradigm, Empson's investigations start from intuitions about meaning:

Till you have decided what a piece of language conveys, like any literary critic, you cannot look round to see what 'formal features' convey it; you will then find that some features are of great subtlety, and perhaps fail to trace some at all. (1951, p. 437)

This emphasis on prior judgements of what a word or passage means leads Empson to a view of analysis which

assumes an agreement, among those who seem most likely to know, as to what effect a bit of writing produces, and goes on to argue that this can only have been produced by a curious but demonstrable process of interlocking and interacting structures of meaning.[3]

It is the interpretative competence such intuitions derive from which makes possible analysis of what Empson, slightly depreciatively, often calls a word's or text's 'tricks' and 'machinery'.

Beyond the local points of clarification that such historical analyses can offer, however, there is a more general thrust in Empson's analyses: that we can begin to understand the historical processes of creating meanings by bringing into the public domain, for investigation and discussion, the changing and complex senses of the words we use. Philological enquiry is in this respect connected with a larger ethical purpose, which Empson emphasizes in his attention to the idea of public debate and in the confident view he takes of social understanding, by comparison with Orwell's apparent pessimism, or the analogous despondency as regards understanding and change Empson attributes to Williams. For Empson, many questions of political priority and direction spring from a need to think through, as clearly as possible, the way particular uses of language direct structures of thought:

> Roughly, the moral is that a developing society decides practical questions more by the way it interprets words it thinks obvious and traditional than by its official statements of current dogma.[4]

STATEMENTS, FEELINGS AND MOODS

Because of Empson's concern to demonstrate that much more is carried in a word than its cognitive meaning, he begins *The Structure of Complex Words* with an analysis of feelings in words. In many respects, his account is dependent on Richards's study of emotions; it also takes up and argues with aspects of Gustav Stern's *Meaning and Change of Meaning*, and is generally shaped by a debate over emotions which held particular significance for thinkers of his generation. Commenting, in fact, on this importance of the analysis of emotions for Empson's generation, C. S. Lewis argues towards the

[3] From a radio talk on the use of Basic English in teaching criticism (dated 1939, and, according to Haffenden, 'probably written as part of a series he [Empson] broadcast on Radio WRUL in Boston, when he needed money for the onward journey home from China'). Quoted in introduction to *Argufying* (Empson, 1987a, p. 9).

[4] Quoted in Stanley J. Kunitz, ed. (1955, p. 308). Discussed by Haffenden in introduction (Empson, 1987a, p. 7).

end of *Studies in Words* that Empson's great achievement – on a scale comparable with the achievements of Richards – is to have demonstrated that 'the conception of emotional language can be very easily extended too far. It was time to call a halt' (Lewis, 1960, p. 303). Since Empson's greatest originality lies in working on the logical structures of word meaning rather than on their emotional dimensions, it is appropriate, before reviewing his analysis of emotions, to introduce Empson's account of how words make statements, or how

> a word can become a 'compacted doctrine', or even that all words are compacted doctrines inherently. (1951, p. 39)

To describe how words create equations, Empson distinguishes five distinct ways in which a word can carry a doctrine, classifying them on the basis of 'both how the two meanings are imposed and which order they are given' (1951, p. 46).

The first and simplest way Empson calls the Existence Assertion. This simply states that what a speaker is talking about is presumed to exist. To say things about astrology or God, in the absence of some obvious statement to the contrary, is to imply that you believe these things to exist.[5]

But Empson moves on from this idea to more complex aspects of meaning, which he characterizes specifically in terms of equations:

> I think the same feeling of assertion is carried over to an entirely different case, which I shall call an 'equation' and propose to divide into four types. Two senses of the word are used at once, and also (which does not necessarily happen) there is an implied assertion that they naturally belong together, 'as the word itself proves'. (1951, p. 40)

While the notion of Existence Assertion may seem uninteresting, Empson's first example of what he calls an equation is not. He takes for analysis the sentence of a Victorian matron, 'You can't take Amelia for long walks, Mr Jones; she's *delicate*' (1951, pp. 44ff.). The primary sense of 'delicate' here is 'refined' or 'well brought up'; but the context demands a lesser but nevertheless independent sense: 'sickly'. The word poses an equation of the sort A = B, 'refined' = 'sickly'. As Empson puts it,

[5] Empson's Existence Assertion corresponds closely to what might now more commonly be thought of as existential presupposition, or the existential commitment presumed as a felicity condition on acts of assertion. For discussion, see Stephen Levinson (1983, ch. 4). See also Gerald Gazdar (1979, pp. 45–8). For an account which relates presupposition to a body of socially constructed, ideological assumptions ('interdiscourse') see Michel Pecheux (1982).

No doubt the trick of the thing is to pretend that the two ideas are identical, but they are also recognised as very distinct; in effect the matron packs in a syllogism; the relation imputed is 'A entails B', with *refined* as 'A' and *sickly* as 'B'. (1951, p. 45)

Later, in examining the history of 'delicate' (pp. 76–7), Empson indicates that such an equation is only possible in the nineteenth century, not the eighteenth, because of the word's older meanings of 'fastidious' and 'luxurious or self indulgent'. Further, the equation only goes one way ('sickly' does not entail 'delicate', in the sense of 'refined'). Also, the equation can be shown to be articulated around a certain repression of the body (what Empson refers to as 'chastity and the consequences of tight stays' (p. 77)) – a fact which Swinburne was able to use to good advantage in the poems Empson analyses at the end of the chapter.

Empson's second type of equation (pp. 48–50) is not between two separate senses, but between a sense and its implication. Empson understands an implication as rather like a word's connotation: something that goes with the word in certain contexts but not in others. 'Honest', in older forms of English, will typically carry an implication of courage, when used of a man (it still carries that implication if used of a horse). In cases such as that of 'honest', the implication is equated with the sense; and Empson illustrates this with another example: 'native' starts off as simply a descriptive word, meaning 'indigenous inhabitant'; but through constant colonial use the term comes to carry the implication of 'inherently subjected' or 'racially inferior'.[6] Eventually, Empson argues, this implication was integrated into the sense of the word.

The third type of equation (pp. 50–1) – of which Empson suggests there may not be very many clear-cut cases (and the difficulties of his description do not make it easy to be sure of finding more) – is in some respects similar to the first, in that it involves a main meaning and a meaning demanded by the context. But the order of terms is reversed; the meaning demanded by the context, so Empson claims, is such that 'the word can only be applied to the referent in view by a kind of metaphor' (p. 50). For this usage, Empson gives the example of Shakespeare's use of 'fool', in which, whatever other meaning it has, Empson argues that such other meanings are equated with 'clown'. Empson argues, in this case, that

[6] See also the entry in Raymond Williams, *Keywords* (1983).

the trick is that one part of the range of the word is treated as the 'key' or typical part of it, in terms of which the others are to be viewed. The rest of the meaning indeed seems to be remembered rather by treating it as a Connotation of the selected part, and to that extent Type III is analogous to Type II rather than Type I. (p. 51)

For all its difficulties of definition, Type III is important; Empson suggests that 'in most controversies where both sides agree on using a key word, the word is given two rival equations of Type III' (p. 51); and he suggests that using words such as 'worker' or 'business man' inevitably involves drawing on potentially controversial prototypical concepts of the terms, or stereotypes, which are based on this type of equation.

In the fourth type (pp. 51–2), order does not matter; and Empson hazards a guess that examples of the type are to be found mostly in 'individual theorists and stylists'. What constitutes a Type IV equation is that two terms are brought together in either order, but as though united under some third term ('in a similar relation to a third meaning of the word' (p. 52)), rather than discursively stated. Empson's examples are 'law' (encompassing both human and divine 'law') in Hooker, and 'sense' (encompassing both sensation and imagination) in Wordsworth. Problematic cases arise, for Empson, when there is doubt about whether the two terms create a superordinate third term, or not.

There is, of course, a possible fifth type of equation. But Empson rejects this, claiming to be concerned only 'with the kind of suggestion in a word which seems to cling to it and can affect opinion, so that nonce-equations by jokers and poets are not what I am looking for' (p. 54). He illustrates his rejection of a fifth type with an example from book IV of Pope's *Dunciad*:

> Where Bentley late tempestuous wont to sport
> In troubled waters, but now sleeps in Port. (201–2)

What we have here is two words ('port' in both cases) rather than two senses; and Empson dismisses such cases as not forming equations partly on the basis that two words are involved, and partly because of the evident existence of an intention to hide a meaning, such that sudden discovery of the sense is part of the contrived effect.

Together, these brief descriptions illustrate the range of Empson's characterization of the forms of statement carried in words, and give a sense of Empson's classificatory matrix for the detailed case studies which fill the following four hundred pages of *Complex Words*. In some passages, Empson presents his classification as being straightforward; in others, he recognizes difficulties with the system, as, for example, when he acknowledges that there is

> a certain amount of shuffling possible among the types according to the way the thing is received, and this seems rather untidy, but I should say that it only recognises the facts of the case. (p. 64)

To complete the general picture of Empson's account, we need now to return to Empson's analysis of Feelings. First, there are implications carried by a word (as, for example with 'honest', above). Empson notates such feelings as A/I; thus, 'honest' carries the implication 'brave'. But there are several other ways of controlling the sense of a word with feelings. One is to rule out certain meanings: when a history teacher says 'a bloody battle', the intensifier sense is ruled out in favour of the lexical adjective. Equally, the sense of a word can be altered by signalling approval or disapproval. This is achieved by what Empson calls Appreciative and Depreciative Pregnancies (pp. 16–17). Alongside more common currencies, the word 'kitsch', for example, can be used with an appreciative pregnancy, in which case it confers a positive evaluation on the object; the term 'art', with a depreciative pregnancy, confers negative evaluation.

Following on from these simple guides to what is included in a word's sense over and above its cognitive meaning, Empson moves to perhaps the single most valuable concept in *Complex Words*: that of a word's Mood (pp. 17–20). The term is taken from the grammar of sentences, where it indicates the speaker's relation to the sentence, and is carried over to individual words. Empson's sign for Mood is the £. So, for instance, A £ I gives the first mood of sense A, identifying the speaker's relation to someone else (Empson gives the example of a simple quotation 'A' which can mean 'what they call so and so but I don't' or vice versa). More important than the £, however, is the ?. This indicates that the speaker is using the sense under cover of using it about someone else, or negatively: what might be described, following Empson's colloquial mode of presentation, as 'these people are not like me'. Finally, Empson adds the o, for what is left over as emotion.

'WIT'

Wit is widely recognized as one of the most difficult words in the English language. To chart its usage from Shakespeare to Samuel Johnson is to follow the intellectual, literary, political and scientific conflicts of the time. How 'wit' was used, the discourse in which it was formulated, determined both what a speaker thought of the word and of the self – as well as the relation between the two. Indeed, C. S. Lewis suggests that 'if a man had time to study the history of one word only, *wit* would perhaps be the best word he could choose' (1960, p. 86).

Empson's analysis, therefore, is a suitable place to test out the scope and procedures of the analytic framework he presents in *Complex Words*. Problems can be examined in Empson's own acount, as well as in the parallel account offered by C. S. Lewis in *Studies in Words*; and we can go on to investigate difficulties left over from both.

Wit's etymology is simple. It is derived from the Anglo-Saxon 'wit' or 'gewit', which means 'mind, reason, intelligence'. From this early sense, you get a variety of complications. Roughly, it is possible to say that the word refers to the faculty of understanding. In the plural, however, it also refers to those who possess the faculty – perhaps the only clear remnants of this sense in current English are formulaic phrases such as 'at one's wit's end'.

Two associated senses then emerge. The first is associated with the kind of medieval psychology in which a person was understood as having five outward and five inward senses. The five inward senses were: memory, estimation, fancy, imagination and common wit, or common sense. What needs to be retained from this meaning, to follow the word's complex history, is that 'judgement' is a part of wit. The phrase 'I was frightened out of my wits' relates both to this meaning and to another meaning by which the mental faculty of 'wit' is understood to go implicitly with its proper or usual operation. There is a similar related sense with 'mind', which indicates the mental faculty and then, by an established implication, its normal or correct use; thus, 'out of my mind'.

The senses of 'wit' referred to so far are (except for the specific phrases cited above) now obsolete. But while they were still in circulation, an upward valuation took place: 'wit' comes to mean good or great mental capacity; and, in general, the word begins to indicate not the simple faculty but its quality (significantly, an analogous upward valuation took place in the word 'quality' itself). This use of 'wit' becomes dominant in the Renaissance; and C. S. Lewis suggests that the development may well be linked to the fact that 'wit' comes to be used as the standard translation for the Latin word *ingenium*. *Ingenium*, in Latin, starts off by meaning the nature or quality of something. Then, applied to someone's intelligence, it comes to imply a favourable interpretation. But *ingenium* is also opposed in Latin to another mental quality, 'judgement'; and Lewis states that this is also true of the development of 'wit' in English. The idea of *ingenium* in Latin being close to insanity, for example (as in Seneca's maxim 'Nullum magnum ingenium sine mixtura dementiae', or 'No great ingenium, without a dash of insanity'), is glossed by Dryden as 'Great wits are sure to madness near allied'.

But if Lewis is right to see an opposition between wit and judgement in neo-classical criticism, this opposition had been worked for and to a large extent attained by way of Locke's distinction between wit and judgement. If we go back earlier in the seventeenth century, it is doubtful whether this particular opposition can be found. Certainly Lewis is right to see some paralleling (a semantic calque) with *ingenium*. But if we look at Ben Jonson's remarks on the subject, entitled 'Ingeniorum discrimina' ('The Discrimination of Wit', part of *Timber* published in 1640), we see that Jonson's use of the word is still labouring to make the distinction. He starts his passage:

> In the difference of wits, I have observ'd; there are many notes; And it is a little Maistry to know them: to discerne what every nature, every disposition will beare: For, before we sow our land, we should plough it. There are no fewer forms of minds, than of bodies amongst us. The variety is incredible; and therefore wee must search. Some are fit to make Divines, some Poets, some Lawyers, some Physicians; some to be sent to the plough, and trades.
>
> There is no doctrine will doe good, where nature is wanting. Some wits are swelling, and high; others low and still; Some hot and fiery; others cold and dull; One must have a bridle, the other a spurre. (in Jonson, 1947, VIII, p. 584)

This passage is, in fact, almost a word-for-word translation from Quintilian, with 'wit' taking the place of *ingenium*. But the content of the rest of the passage is a working-out of Jonson's theory of the correct way to study and write. In the course of his description, Jonson denigrates those who do not possess sound judgement and scholarship – those, above all, who think their native talent will get them by:

But the Wretcheder are the obstinate contemners of all helpes and Arts: such as presuming on their own Naturals (which, perhaps are excellent) dare deride all diligence, and seem to mock at the termes, when they understand not the things; thinking that way to get off wittily, with their Ignorance. (p. 586)

The context of 'wittily' here, involving a sense above all of 'to mock', suggests that Jonson is using the word in roughly our modern sense. 'Wit' can be understood, as in *OED* Sense 7, as 'Quickness of intellect or liveliness of fancy, with capacity of apt expression, talent for saying brilliant or sparkling things, particularly in an amusing way' (the substantive has gone but the adjective, 'witty', remains). Jonson is using the sense of 'wit' which involves passing from the faculty of understanding to the *quality* of that faculty (in both cases, also taking in holders of the faculty), then passing on to a particular *expression* of that quality.

There is also a further sense of the word, which shows a similar development while resulting in a different content. The *OED* defines it (Sense 8) as follows:

The quality of speech or writing which consists in the apt association of thought and expression, calculated to surprise and delight by its unexpectedness (particular uses in 17th and 19th century criticism) later always with reference to the utterance of brilliant or sparkling things in an amusing way.

But here we must begin to doubt the *OED*. We can agree on the passage from the faculty to the quality of that faculty, and then to the particular products or results of the faculty. But the way in which those products are then understood simply pushes the issue back to the faculty itself; the *OED* seems to have conflated different notions of product under the influence of neo-classical criticism. What the *OED* foregrounds is the efforts made by late seventeenth and early eighteenth-century poets and critics to come to terms with difficulties around the notion of 'wit' inherited from the Metaphysical tradition. But there is a conflict between two senses of the products of 'wit', which the dictionary elides. For Shakespeare and Donne, 'wit' involved verbal dexterity but also a more serious kind of association, the conceit, which found its justification in a particular way of understanding the word closely linked with the rediscovery of hermeticism during the fifteenth and sixteenth centuries. Hermetic thought does not depend on a division between experience and language (in which one represents the other); in this sense, it differs fundamentally from the view which becomes a precondition of the scientific procedures developed by Bacon and the Royal Society. Rather, in hermeticism everything in the world including language, is linked in a system of correspondences. Wit can then be understood as that product of the reasoning faculty which discovers unlooked-for analogies and similarities; these analogies are then understood as belonging to the realm of truth. Much writing and thinking during the seventeenth century – we might think particularly of Hobbes and the Royal Society – is concerned to deny any notion of truth which would grant such an effectivity, or capability for *producing new kinds of truth*, to language. Language cannot generate truth through the identifications created by metaphor and simile, but only in relation to its description of the world (for Locke) or its own strict definitions (Hobbes).

Only by bearing in mind epistemological debates of this kind as we contemplate changes in meaning – as well as the institutional sites on which such debates were fought out – can we understand changes in the word 'wit'. Effectively what took place was the narrowing of a wider meaning, which kept within its range verbal felicities ranging from what we still call 'wit' to those conceits which, in their play on words, were believed to reveal a truth about the reality with which they were connected. Examples of the kinds of consideration the dictionary tends to ignore can easily be found. One of the first examples of Sense 7 in *OED*, for instance, comes from Falstaff's speech at the beginning of *Henry IV Part 2*, Act I Scene 2, in which Falstaff bandies insults with the page Hal has sent to him before engaging in more serious insults with the Lord Chief Justice (see Empson, 1951, p. 85; Lewis, 1960, pp. 98–9). Falstaff's claim is that 'I am not only witty in myself, but the cause that wit is in other men' (I.2.9–10). That the main sense here is close to our modern sense is made evident by Falstaff's preceding lines. The whole speech, before the use of the word 'wit', runs:

> Men of all sorts take a pride to gird at me. The brain of this foolish compounded clay-man is not able to invent anything that intends to laughter more than I invent or is invented on me. I am not only witty in myself, but the cause that wit is in other men. (1.2.6–10)

If we simply take the meaning 'humorous' in this context, we miss the element of *symbolic disorder* Falstaff represents. Not only is Falstaff a constant threat to the political system; he also threatens the order of the play and the kingdom at a symbolic level – sexually in his polymorphously perverse and bisexual body, and dramatically as the representative of an older stage tradition. The scene in which Falstaff proclaims himself 'witty' is only one example of the danger taken to be latent in his power over language; and this dimension of symbolic danger, rather than mere verbal frivolity, can only be appreciated if we bear in mind the contemporary linguistic theories of the day, and the way the word 'wit' is articulated in them.

As regards the way 'wit' develops in the seventeenth and eighteenth centuries, what is particularly significant is the emergence of theories regarding the relation between language and reality which underpin Bishop Thomas Sprat's famous pronouncements, in Section xx ('Their Manner of Discourse') of his *History of the Royal-Society* (1667). Sprat announces that all the rhetorical figures and, in particular, the arch-fiend metaphor, have been banished:

> They have therefore been most rigorous in putting in execution, the only Remedy, that can be found for this *extravagance*: and that has been, a constant Resolution, to reject all the amplifications, digressions, and swellings of style: to return back to the primitive purity, and shortness, when men deliver'd so many *things*, almost in an equal number of *words*. They have exacted from all their members, a close naked, natural way of speaking; positive expressions; clear senses; a native easiness: bringing all things as near the Mathematical plainness, as they can: and preferring the language of Artisans, Countrymen and merchants, before that of Wits or Scholars. (Quoted in Barber, 1976, pp. 132–3)

Sprat's identification of 'Wits' as those who, along with scholars, use figurative language indicates that Sprat is condemning a whole system of rhetorical education and study which allows language powers of its own. The strictures of the Royal Society, and the dominant theories of language after the Restoration, necessitated the narrowing of the symbolic capabilities of 'wit', if both a kind of pleasure and joy in words and yet also the dominant theories of the day were to be upheld. It is not surprising, therefore, that the new notion of a possessor of 'wit' emerges at this time. The relevant *OED* definition (Sense 10) runs

> A person of lively fancy who has the faculty of saying smart or brilliant things, not always so as to amuse; a witty person.

The growth of this new meaning accompanies the emergence of our modern sense of 'wit' as the major one; but it is only by holding in mind the quality, as well as the possessor of that quality, that we can understand this phase of the word's development.

The distinctions established during this phase of *wit*'s development are historically significant. If the notion of a truth inherent in language's own created connections is destroyed, the possibility of allowing 'wit' to be more than verbal play is excluded. Another word is needed, generally 'sense', to describe any judgement which is made of the quality of the mental faculty that is not dependent on its relation to language. What needs then to be noted is that adopting such a position denies virtually any effectivity to poetry in the realm of truth, and relegates it to the realm of delight; poetry becomes merely decoration. It is this problem that neo-classical criticism, and poets like Dryden and Pope, wrestle with; they are confronted by a conflict between their desire to conform to the epistemology of the age, and on the other hand their wish to claim serious investigative and epistemological rights for poetry.

Such claims – in effect, claims for poetry's capability to explore and construct, rather than simply represent and reflect, truth – are made difficult to sustain by developments in philosophical and scientific thought. But this does not mean it cannot be done. Poets like Dryden and Pope went on using the word 'wit' because they still wanted as far as possible to claim rights for poetry that had been denied by philosophy and politics: 'wit' becomes a focus of contradictions through which poets can both accept and disavow the reign of Newton and Locke. While it may be impossible intellectually to reconcile the claims of poetry to be more than ornament with the claims of the Royal Society to the royal share of truth in logic, this does not mean that attempts at such reconciliation are precluded from creative use of language. Indeed, one of the main achievements of Empson's subtle and delicate analysis of 'wit' in Pope's *Essay on Criticism* is that Empson shows how the word is balanced between two fundamentally opposing conceptions. In one conception, 'wit' is to be understood as 'conceptual force, range of imaginative power'; in the other, it is 'the power to make neat jokes or ornament an accepted structure'. Empson's analysis suggests that we should understand this hesitation between senses as one of the final attempts in English to articulate 'wit' in both the old way and the new.

In order to understand precisely what Pope is doing with the word 'wit', we need to draw attention in Empson's analysis to the structure of the first two equations he sketches out and the notion of a mood. Roughly speaking, Empson understands the development of Sense 10 of 'wit' as a mood attached to Sense 9. Pope's *Essay on Criticism*, in this view, becomes a prolonged definition of 'wit', together with a mood (or attitude towards the word and those who use it) which leaves the poet both defined and undefined. Pope's use of mood in the word parallels the whole strategy of the *Essay*: to distinguish rules poets must follow from rules they must not.

If we look at the opening passage of the poem, we see three of the different senses of 'wit' we have considered above; and we can also find a use of the head sense. While most of the equations which define 'wit' or a 'wit' are equations of Type I, there is one use which Empson describes as being of Type II (equations between a sense and its implication). While Empson himself does not consider this use to be fundamentally important, it is quite possible to argue that it serves as the focal point for the whole sequence of equations. The equation in question comes when Pope is inveighing against those who make one element in poetry predominate over the rest; Pope chooses 'wit' to start his condemnation off (the other elements he discusses are language and versification):

> Some, to conceit alone their Taste confine
> And glitt'ring Thoughts struck out at ev'ry Line;
> Pleas'd with a Work where nothing's just or fit;
> One glaring Chaos and wild Heap of Wit. (289–92)

Pope is clearly alluding here to Metaphysical 'wit'. But rather than using an equation which brings the head sense in, in what Empson calls the predicate position (what the speaker is putting forward, rather than the already established topic (see Empson, 1951, pp. 45–6)), this use seems to place it in the subject position and equate it with its implication. The purpose of this appears to be that of *bringing together* the sense of 'power to make neat jokes or ornament an accepted structure' with the sense of 'conceptual force, range of imaginative power'. By equating the two senses, the equation belittles 'wit' but also preserves for it a certain dignity. As such, the equation accomplishes the logically impossible holding together of the power of wit and its belittlement. Interestingly, therefore, it is just after this crucial equation in the poem that Pope produces his most famous lines on wit, when he writes

True Wit is Nature to Advantage drest
What oft was Thought but ne'er so well Exprest,
Something, whose Truth convinc'd at sight we find
That gives us back the image of our Mind. (297–300)

In these lines, there is a fresh attempt to integrate human beings, nature and language; and in his description, C. S. Lewis focuses on an unusualness, or strain, in Pope's usage: the way the modifier 'true' before 'wit' suggests that Pope is 'twisting the noun into a sense it never naturally bore', rather than repeating a current and dominant sense (Lewis, 1960, p. 107). But finally, there is no justification for wit except in 'expression', divorced from thought. Despite the memorability of the lines, their attempt to hold together Wit and Nature – and what Pope means by 'Nature' would need separate consideration – this is finally doomed, in the sense that the very splitting-out of a Metaphysical sense of 'wit' does not allow its re-integration into the predominant Restoration sense which is set up in opposition to it. This is very clear when Pope writes the *Essay on Man* some twenty years later, and concludes:

Shall then this verse to future age pretend
Thou wert my guide, philosopher and friend?
That urg'd by thee, I turn'd the tuneful art
From sounds to things, from fancy to the heart
For Wit's false mirror held up Nature's light
Shew'd erring price, WHATEVER IS, IS RIGHT. (389–94)

Subsequently, although 'wit' continues as a critical term, it has lost virtually all life in the old sense. This is what allows Samuel Johnson to come back and gloss the debate around 'wit' with a metalanguage which makes it possible to distinguish between the word's various uses. In the *Life of Cowley*, Johnson writes:

If Wit be well described by Pope, as being 'that which has been often thought, but was never before so well expressed', they certainly never attained, nor even sought it; for they endeavoured to be singular in their thoughts, and were careless of their diction. But Pope's account of wit is undoubtedly erroneous: he depresses it below its natural dignity, and reduces it from strength of thought to happiness of language.

If by a more noble and more adequate conception that be considered as Wit, which is at once natural and new, that which, though not obvious, is, upon its first production, acknowledged to be just; if it be that, which he that never found it, wonders how he missed; to wit of this kind the metaphysical poets have seldom risen. Their thoughts are often new, but seldom natural; they are not obvious, but neither are they just; and the reader, far from wondering that he missed them, wonders more frequently by what perverseness of industry they were ever found.

But Wit, abstracted from its effect upon the hearer, may be more rigorously and philosophically considered as a kind of *discordia concors*: a combination of dissimilar images, or discovery of occult resemblances in things apparently unlike. Of wit, thus defined, they have more than enough. The most heterogeneous ideas are yoked by violence together; nature and art are ransacked for illustrations, comparisons, and allusions; their learning instructs, and their subtlety surprises; but the reader commonly thinks his improvement dearly bought, and, though he sometimes admires, is seldom pleased. (Johnson, 1968, pp. 403–4)

The position of 'wit' in Metaphysical thought is by Johnson's time well understood; and it is clearly recognized as being distinct from the neo-classical use of the term. But the loading of Metaphysical 'wit' has become for Johnson mere 'occult resemblances': 'wit' has had its day.

SPEAKERS AND THEIR WORDS

It is worth noting at this point that C. S. Lewis gives a rather different history that the one we have presented here (which is based largely on Empson's). Lewis would have us believe that the progression within the word 'wit' is primarily brought about by confusion. Because people who possessed the wit-quality would also be likely to make witty remarks, he suggests, the whole issue became confused during a period of transitional meanings for the word. Lewis surmises that a speaker

would slip in and out of the different meanings without noticing it. It is all ordinary and comfortable until one of the meanings happens to become strategically important in some controversy. A bad linguistic situation then results. (1960, p. 103)

Some of the major discrepancies between Lewis's account and Empson's – which are discussed directly by both writers (see Empson, 1987a, p. 144; Lewis, 1960, p. 96) – focus on whether the 'joke' sense of 'wit' can be found throughout Pope's *Essay* or not. As Lewis puts it,

The question between Professor Empson and me is whether that slowly rising tide had yet reached all Pope's uses of the word. I believe it had not; the insulating power of the context still protected them. (p. 96)

But what is more important than matters of detail such as this within the history of 'wit' is a more important watershed between Lewis and Empson which emerges. For Lewis, illustrating his argument with discussion of 'courtesy' and 'curtsy' (p. 99), rigorous distinction is needed between a word's meaning and a speaker's meaning (Empson, by contrast, rejects the distinction in anything like a clear-cut form). For Lewis, whenever the distinction between speaker-meaning and word-meaning is thrown into doubt, language is somehow going wrong. In the case of 'wit', he recognizes the movement of the word from the sense of *ingenium* to the sense associated with 'witty'; but he views this as just a sloppy use of language in which product comes to replace quality without anybody really noticing. At the same time, nevertheless, Lewis demonstrates that he is unaware of both the critical and epistemological debates which precipitate the change, while somehow continuing to consider them separate from the word itself.

To understand the originality of Empson's work, what needs to be emphasized in Lewis's arguments regarding 'wit' – which significantly uphold his more general belief that words have meanings and speakers simply use or adapt those meanings – is that they ignore the extent to which the selection of the modern meaning for 'wit' *is the product of* the epistemological debates, and the specific theoretical and institutional struggles, of the seventeenth century. Yet as we have suggested above, it is only when we take such debates regarding the power of language seriously that we can begin to see how speakers and writers of the period oppose, on the one hand, theories which allow language an effectivity and reality of its own (such that truth is as likely to appear in words as in things), and, on the other hand, theories devoted to denying any such thing.[7]

Empson's account incipiently recognizes a dimension of word-meaning altogether absent in Lewis; an unacknowledged significance of the changes which take place in the word 'wit' is that the

7 If we want to relate the history of 'wit' either to a history of reason or to a history of poetry, the particular positions and beliefs would need to be distinguished. Roughly these are, on one side, the hermetic theories of language of a Bruno or a Campanella, which understand language's relation to reality not as that of representation but of a kind of reproduction in which language literally figures reality; on the other side, those Augustinian theories of language which entail that in certain uses words can lose the conventional relation to reality and become 'the audible and visible sounds of a direct apprehension of invisible and inaudible truths'. Both kinds of theory – though differently – grant the poet some kind of access to truth. For descriptions of Renaissance theories of language, see, for example, R. H. Robins (1967, pp. 94–132).

epistemological debates which produce the narrowing in meaning had institutional sites which related the struggle over ideas to more obvious forms of political struggle. The successive definitions and re-definitions of 'wit' are not, therefore, easily divisible into a word-meaning and a speaker-meaning; and it is simplistic, as Lewis seeks to do, to identify a definite meaning and then say that someone was just using that meaning for a specific purpose. What begins to be visible in Empson's writing is that 'wit' provides a focal point at which meaning and identity collapse into the material of language, but in a way which nevertheless prevents them being produced, unproblematically, as mere effects. To use or define 'wit' around the end of the seventeenth century is not just to choose a meaning; it is to attempt to establish a meaning and an identity.

This issue of the connection between the formation of a word's meanings and the formation of the speaker leads to a far more important divergence between Lewis's account and Empson's than the issue of the precise rate of change between senses of 'wit' which they acknowledge. While Lewis seems unable to bear the idea that questions of the speaker may be integrally involved in a word's meaning, Empson's whole project in *Complex Words* can be seen as an attempt to produce a theoretical account of exactly such relationships, showing how, in the case of 'wit', new definitions of truth and the relation between reality and language are to a large extent worked out, or fought over, through meanings for the word.

STRUCTURES OF MEANING

We have discussed Empson's analysis of the word 'wit' at some length because it illustrates possibilities, but also difficulties, in the analytic frameworks that Empson and others have devised to describe the complex histories of words. Above all, our account suggests that, rather than talking of words and the meanings given to them by individuals, we need to think of discourses and the practices that accompany them: practices which generally find their existence and articulation in institutions. It is this view of structures of meaning in words which begins to emerge in *Complex Words*, and which is arguably the most original aspect of Empson's analyses.

Some of the implications of such a view are worth comment. One is that meaning and identity become kinds of effect or produced relation, rather than elements from which to start. This does not mean that we should do away with words as units; we simply need to recognize that they are not themselves units of meaning, but material units *whose articulation produces meaning*. It is because the material units are not finally tied to any one meaning that they can function not only as central or 'key' words, but also as points of disruption, controversy and change in a discourse.

The notion that key words act as points of disruption and controversy, as well as of change, is indispensable if we are to understand how *Complex Words* fits in with Empson's work as a whole. It is also the main point at issue in Empson's reservations about Raymond Williams's project in *Keywords*. So to compare the relative merits of Empson's and Williams's positions, as models for the further kinds of analysis that seem necessary within contemporary English studies, we need now to draw out our own cautions about Empson's theories and relate these to his criticism of *Keywords*.

A first caution regarding Empson's analyses is that, although Empson claims it does not matter how many meanings for a word are conscious, he has a habit of writing as though the poet is consciously *choosing* all the meanings. The difficulty with this view is that it resurrects the notion of a subject unproblematically outside language at a further remove than Lewis's simple distinction between what a word means and what a speaker means by that word. Given the close connection Empson's case studies indicate between use of words and the formation of meanings and identities, this ambiguity is problematic; what seems needed, in order to connect the two conflicting senses of subjectivity, is an additional emphasis on the role of the *social* in meaning – an emphasis which can occasionally be found in asides Empson makes in the course of his exposition.

One such aside introduces the notion of the institutional site of a text. In explaining how a meaning can attach itself to a word, and how connotations (or Implications) can even overtake a word, Empson suggests that an Implication

> will come from an habitual context of the word (not from its inherent meaning) and will vaguely remind you of that sort of context. The context is presumed to be usual among some group of people; a merely [private] fancy would be called an Association of the word. (1951, p. 15)

A more general notion of the sociality of meaning also makes itself felt at the beginning of Empson's discussion of the concept of Moods. He writes that the main argument in its favour is sufficiently obvious; language is essentially a social product and much concerned with social relations, but we tend to hide this in our forms of speech so as to appear to utter impersonal truths. (p. 18)

In stressing the social dimension of meaning in Empson's work, however, we run straight into the fundamental conceptual problem of how to reconcile notions of the historical formation of individuals and their autonomous existence. Crucial in thinking through this problem is the development of a concept of a social unconscious. Empson sets himself pointedly against any such notion, of course, insisting that the processes he describes are conscious and intentional:

I am trying to write linguistics and not psychology; something quite unconscious and unintentional, even if the hearer catches it like an infection, is not part of an act of communication. (p. 31)

The deep conflict in Empson's position is that it is difficult to believe he takes speakers and writers of English to be conscious of the syntax and lexis of English as they write – especially given his justification for the structure of *Complex Words* in the confidence and speed of routine human interpretation. On the other hand, given Empson's evident respect for literary artifice and argumentative control throughout his work, it is difficult not to believe he attributes a great deal of the subtle effects of words to deliberate choices consciously made by the speaker or writer. If we are ever to resolve this conflict, we appear to need much more sophisticated notions of intention than Empson seems to be working with: notions which have to allow an existence to a social unconscious.

Something of what might be needed can be glimpsed by looking again at Empson's disagreement with Williams. Empson is enraged by Williams's claim that all uses of 'interest' are saturated with money relations because many uses of the word 'interesting' cannot be parsed in any way that brings out a reference to money at all. It is because of problems of this sort that Empson makes his crucial claim that 'what Williams needs to consider is the structure relating two meanings in any one of his chosen words so that they imply or insinuate a sentence "A is B"' (1987a, p. 188).

The important point, however, is not that a speaker is consciously saying 'A is B'; he or she may not *want* to say A is B. What matters is that use of the word inevitably leads the speaker to subscribe to the implication. In doing so, the speaker is defined as much as the word; and this accounts for the potential for embarrassment and anxiety when the implication is drawn out. In one sense, use of an equation is unconscious: Williams effectively conceives of a social unconscious working independently of the individual's consciousness. It is important, nevertheless, that the equation can be *made* conscious; and by focusing on the relationship between social dimensions of word-meaning and cognitive processes involved in interpretation, Empson – arguably more interestingly than Williams – points to the torque between individual and social.

As regards the ethical and political consequences which follow from these two positions, the key question is exposed in C. S. Lewis's idea (quoted above) that, in uses of different meanings,

> it is all ordinary and comfortable until one of the meanings happens to become strategically important in some controversy. (1960, p. 103)

As is perhaps especially evident in Empson's essay 'Argufying in Poetry' (1987a, pp. 167–73), Empson consistently valued the capabilities of reason more than emotive but finally non-argumentative symbolic understandings of what is at stake in moments of controversy; and as regards the processes of interpretation involved, he sought to displace what he dismisses as traditions of 'evasiveness and false suggestions' with 'another tradition, that of fair public debate' (p. 168). Considering differences of perception and understanding in particular, Empson seems committed to an idea of shared human rationality which underpins even what may turn out to be conflicting interpretations; he constantly distances himself from the idea of distinct, socially constructed regimes of meaning which are beyond the horizons of any individual speaker's or writer's understanding or intervention.

Unlike Empson, Williams does not engage much with questions of cognition or the exact processes involved in individual interpretation. Rather, his memorable image at the beginning of the Introduction to *Keywords* is of people simply 'not speaking the same language' – a view which almost invites Empson to consider that Williams sees language-users as shaped by the words they use, thinking *in* more than *with* them, and being finally at the mercy of slogans and catchwords pressed on them by larger social forces. The conflict in Williams's position, in this sense, lies in the precise degree to which he takes it to be possible to learn and communicate across languages of different social formations, even with the 'extra edge of consciousness' that can be gained from historical awareness.

In view of the scale of difficulty involved in thinking through questions of this kind, however, it can seem unduly dismissive of Empson to have objected so decisively when Williams writes,

I believe that to understand the complexities of the meanings of 'class' contributes very little to the resolution of actual class disputes and class struggles. (1983, p. 24)

Empson's critical reaction that this passage 'makes our minds feebler than they are' (and that it contributes to a 'gloom' he detects in *Keywords* (1987a, p. 184)) ignores the larger development of Williams's argument. The passage which immediately follows the quotation that so clearly antagonized Empson captures – possibly better than anything in Empson's own writings – a sense of connection between individual formation and social formation:

It is not only that nobody can 'purify the dialect of the tribe', nor only that anyone who really knows himself to be a member of a society knows better than to want, in those terms, to try. It is also that the variations and confusions of meaning are not just faults in a system, or errors of feedback, or deficiencies of education. They are in many cases, in my terms, historical and contemporary substance ... What can really be contributed is not resolution but perhaps, at times, just that extra edge of consciousness. (Williams, 1983, p. 24)

The final section of the same paragraph, too (which closes Williams's discussion of the aims of the book, as he turns to problems of layout and method) brings together what appear to be all the major concerns which unite Empson's and Williams's work. For all the divergence between the two writers, emphasized by Empson and by others since, a casual reader coming across the passage in question for the first time might take it as a statement of the main points of common cause, rather than the beginnings of unresolved disagreement, between the kinds of important critical work outlined in both *Complex Words* and *Keywords*:

This is not a neutral view of meanings. It is an exploration of the vocabulary of a crucial area of social and cultural discussion, which has been inherited within precise historical and social conditions and which has to be made at once conscious and critical – subject to change as well as continuity – if the millions of people in whom it is active are to see it as active: not a *tradition* to be learned, nor a *consensus* to be accepted, nor a set of meanings which, because it is 'our language', has a natural authority; but as a shaping and reshaping, in real circumstances and from profoundly different and important points of view: a vocabulary to use, to find our own ways in, to change as we find it necessary to change it, as we go on making our own language and history. (Williams, 1983, pp. 24–5)

CHAPTER 6

Figural narrative and plot construction: Empson on pastoral

Pamela McCallum

No one who reads *Some Versions of Pastoral* (1935) can deny that William Empson made a significant contribution to the development of literary theory. Empson's reading of 'heroic' and 'pastoral' in English drama works out a new conception of plot – what he calls the double-plot 'device'. He focuses on the distinction between the surface or manifest content of a given literary text and its deeper, underlying structures. Such a distinction allows him to disengage those techniques, mechanisms and devices which are to be discovered beneath the surface of the literary work. With Empson's innovative constructional model literary criticism takes on a new form which relinquishes the realm of everyday experience for systematic theoretical investigation (he uses the term 'critical theorizing'). He brackets out the common sense and everyday 'natural attitude' that takes for granted the surface content of a literary text. He is then able to discern certain deep structures which have eluded traditional content analysis. Of course, it is indisputable that new and much more rigorous theoretical models have been refined since Empson published *Some Versions*. But his writings were one of the first systematic attempts to elaborate a theory of double plot which is independent of immediate experience and the natural object.[1] Thus formal literary analysis still owes much to the distinction he drew between the manifest content of texts and their hidden deep structures.

This formal procedure which puts in parentheses the 'naturalized consciousness' of common-sense experience and everyday life is what

[1] Certainly Empson's texts are not free from the serious shortcomings of an English empirical tradition which fails to advance to a systematization of experience in new theoretical categories (Eagleton, 1986, p. 164). However, to the degree that Empson's writings contain an implicit 'structural' or synchronic model of double plot – to that degree his book on the pastoral has a genuine critical significance, especially in the context of 1930s English literary studies.

is new in Empson's *Some Versions*. His complex theory of double plot always and everywhere stresses the inner-textual or deep structural elements of a given dramatic work. As Paul de Man points out, Empson's pastoral convention is based on an opposition between 'the mind that distinguishes, negates, legislates, and the originary simplicity of the natural' (de Man, 1983, p. 239). Ultimately Empson's constructivist approach projects a model of the a priori 'conditions of possibility' of double plot (or, what is synonymous here, the hidden structural principles of the double-plot system and its universal laws). My discussion is divided as follows. In the first part I shall attempt to outline two essential elements of the problematic which informs Empson's overall theoretical model: (i) the theory of cognition and (ii) the theory of plot. In the second part I shall try to determine the structural limitations imposed by the extra-temporal character of his synchronic theoretical orientation. I shall argue that his methodologically suggestive work on double-plot systems can be taken as having critical implications for the processes of narrative figuration. I shall also argue that the methodological advance embodied in this new theory of double plot is strategically recontained within the limits of an ahistorical formalism.

The first idea which I want to stress relates to Empson's theory of cognition. He begins by showing that critical theorizing is opposed to the common-sense view of the literary work and the naïveté of the natural attitude. He distinguishes between the manifest content of a text and its deep structural forms. Common-sense thinking and traditional literary scholarship simply take at face value the surface appearances which conceal the deeper dramatic structures. They always fail to detect the double-plot devices which lie hidden in the natural object or the immediately given state of things. As Empson explains in the opening paragraphs of his chapter on double plots: '[double plot] does not depend on being noticed for its operation, so is neither an easy nor an obviously useful thing to notice' (1935, p. 27). The 'obvious effect' of an Elizabethan play is to make the audience believe that the dramatic performance 'deals with life as a whole, with any one who comes on to the street the scene so often represents' (p. 27). What the audience is accustomed to taking for granted is that the play depicts the whole web of English life. The double plot of an Elizabethan drama – half heroic and half pastoral – is felt to be about the immediately vital matters of daily existence.

Accordingly, one may say that the play only assumes the appearance of having referential content. Actually, the experienced reality is a technical effect produced by the operation of the double-plot device. As I have mentioned above, Empson's isolation of the intrinsic 'laws' which govern Elizabethan drama brackets the ostensible or surface content of a given text. This bracketing of commonsense experience suspends the simple and straightforward natural attitude which makes the audience believe 'this is true about everyone' (1935, pp. 195–6). If the assumption that the text mirrors a commonsense external 'reality' is discarded, it then becomes possible to concentrate on those basic deep structures which can be recognized beneath the surface of the text. For it is no longer a question of a surface creation that makes us feel part of reality as a whole; now it is rather a question of the deep structural devices and techniques that produce this effect. We may put it this way: Greene or Shakespeare or Webster do not aim at a dramatic mimesis that transparently reflects the immediacy of life; on the contrary, they aim at producing a technical effect which fully exploits the possibilities of the double-plot device. Without such technical devices there would be no illusion of content, no feeling of completeness. From an epistemological point of view the major weakness of conventional theories of plot is that they cling to a pseudo-reality. Access to the double-plot devices latent in the changing data of immediate experience is made impossible. It is quite otherwise with Empson's new and suggestive theoretical categories. By an insistence on the primacy of double plots he is able to articulate the essential mechanisms or deep structures which are buried somewhere within the dramatic form itself. His method of cognition dissolves the false appearances that hide the stock device; it uncovers and disengages the more fundamental double-plot system that underlies the apparent content of a given text. This inherent formal requirement, that of manifest text and deep structure, is what grounds and generates Empson's theory of cognition.

The other idea which I want to emphasize relates to Empson's theory of plot. We have seen that Empson ascribes much importance to the technical device of double plot in the development of the pastoral. There can be no doubt that he locates himself considerably beyond the surface appearance of the dramatic work. For the problem is to determine the operation of the hidden devices which have gone unnoticed and unremarked by traditional literary criticism; it is to determine the deep structures of double plotting which necessarily inform the dramatic text. As might be expected from his overall constructional model, Empson reproaches those critics who take appearances at face value and 'miss the connections' (1935, p. 27) which are designed to hold together the double plot. This oversimplified view of double plot tends to neglect what he designates as 'the interaction of the two plots' (1935, p. 30). From the very start Empson presents his formulation of double plot in terms of a series of correspondences, interrelationships and juxtapositions. Here it is worth pointing out that an identity of opposites is central to Empson's theory of plot. He undertakes to establish this identity by combining the two opposite parts within the larger double-plot system as a whole. The character of a double-plot system, Empson says, can be viewed as a unification of opposites, since there is a reciprocal interaction between the two structural components. What is crucial for him is that the two separate parts of the theatrical double plot are somehow systematically connected; for then, in their reciprocal interactions, in their reciprocal correspondences, both parts are made identical, both are made the same. Initially, no doubt, the two dimensions seem to be completely separate and isolated from each other (or as Empson puts it, the two plotlines are believed to 'have nothing to do with each other' (1935, p. 31)). But what had taken on the appearance of two unrelated parts turns out to 'form a unity by being juxtaposed' (p. 31). In Empson's theory of plot the two conflicting terms lose their independence and autonomy: they come to coincide within and through the correspondences, juxtapositions etc. that organize the new and enlarged double-plot system. Two sets of characters, two distinct plotlines, two antithetical themes are united by their mutual interaction.[2] This reciprocal interaction then ensures the identification of the main plot with the sub-plot, the heroic with the pastoral, the serious with the comic. When, for example, Empson analyses Greene's play, *Friar Bacon and Friar Bungay*, he is able to show how the main plot interacts with the sub-plot, how the two elements become identified in a single double-plot structure. It is the same deep structure of

[2] It is in this sense that double plot is formally quite similar to the seventh type of ambiguity where 'the two meanings of the word, the two values of the ambiguity, are the two opposite meanings defined by the context'. Both the device of double plotting and the seventh type of ambiguity imply 'relational opposites [in which] one cannot be known without the other' (Empson, 1953, pp. 192, 195).

double plotting which subsumes at once both the main plot and the sub-plot; it is the same basic underlying double-plot laws which bring together the two very different plotlines. Thus in Empson's new synchronic model the organizing category of double plot takes precedence over the older main plot–sub-plot convention.

After these preliminary remarks, let us look at a few of Empson's examples of double plot in *Some Versions*. We may begin with one of the earliest instances, a comic interlude which occurs in the Nativity play. The scene can be summed up in the following way: Mac's wife, who has stolen a lamb, hides it in a cradle and calls it her newborn child. When the searchers who are looking for the missing lamb find it, they 'think this a very peculiar child, a "natural" sent from the "supernatural"' (1935, p. 28). They begin to question Mac's wife. In this predicament she tries to conceal her theft by protesting that if she has deceived them she will eat the child in the cradle.

Here we encounter the organizational device of double plot in its elementary form. The centre of Empson's preoccupations is the Christ child-become-sheep (or sacrificial Paschal lamb). How can this inexplicable gift of heaven be understood? How did such a drastic change come about? From what did the sudden alteration and abrupt reversal derive? This is what Empson attempts to explain. Two phases are to be distinguished in his analysis of the Nativity play: first, reciprocal relationships are established between Logos and animal (supernatural and natural, newborn child and Paschal lamb); second, these relationships are displaced and inflected in the direction of Logos and humanity (Christ and Mac's wife, the Incarnation and the parody of it). In the first phase the accent is on the transformation of the Logos into an animal form, on 'a newborn child ... kept among animals in a manger' (p. 28). Supernatural spirit appears in the strangely distorted and disguised shape of natural spirit, or, in Empson's words, 'The Logos ... takes on the animal nature of man which is like a man becoming a sheep' (p. 28). What happens is that the Logos is absorbed into natural life. However, such an emphasis on the naturalist content of religion is unsatisfactory; it is much too closely related to a god-animal and not a god-humanity. Precisely for this reason the scene in the Nativity play involves a second phase. Through an unexpected twist, the 'man become sheep' acquires a human consciousness. By parodying the eating of the 'lamb' in the Sacrament Mac's wife, a thief who has stolen a lamb, elevates herself above the animality into which she had fallen. This new humanity of the human is no longer submerged in nature, but achieves self-consciousness in a 'powerful joke on the eating of Christ in the Sacrament' (p. 28). The effect of this parodying of belief in the Incarnation is to make 'the humorous thieves into fundamental symbols of humanity' (p. 29). This is ultimately due to the emergence of a third term, one which is neither Logos nor nature, but which is able to hold together the two distinct terms. To put it somewhat differently, the Logos becomes accessible in the form of universal humanity.

Another striking and more elaborate illustration of the double-plot convention is provided by Shakespeare's *Troilus and Cressida*. The play begins in Troy with the love intrigues of Troilus and Cressida which dominate the action of the first scenes. Cressida's uncle, Pandarus, arranges for her to spend the night with Troilus, a night in which they swear fidelity to each other. Next comes her removal to the Greek camp where she is passed from hand to hand and kissed in turn by all the generals in a parody of the opening love scene. She breaks her vow with Troilus and takes Diomedes as a lover. This sexual disloyalty runs parallel to political disruption in the Greek camp. Agamemnon, the Greek leader, needs the support of Achilles and Ajax whose military expertise is necessary for a Greek victory over Troy. He cannot win the war without them. But Achilles and Ajax, who are at odds with each other, have withdrawn their loyalty from the Greek cause. Their petty jealousies threaten to disrupt the Greek camp.

One of the remarkable features of Empson's chapter on double plots is the reconstruction of the complex relations between love and war, between personal and state loyalties, between private and public sphere in *Troilus and Cressida*. He describes this reciprocal interaction as follows:

> The two parts make a mutual comparison that illuminates both parties ('love and war are alike') and their large-scale indefinite juxtaposition seems to encourage primitive ways of thought ('Cressida will bring Troy bad luck because she is bad'). This power of suggestion is the strength of the double plot; once you take the two parts to correspond, any character may take on *mana* because he seems to cause what he corresponds to or be Logos of what he symbolises. The political theorising in *Troilus* (chiefly about loyalty whether to a mistress or the state) becomes more interesting if you take it as a conscious development by Shakespeare of the ideas inherent in the double-plot convention. (1935, p. 34)

The purpose of Empson in this passage is to stress the dynamic system of interrelationships between the two contradictory elements – that of love and that of war – which constitutes double plot in *Troilus and Cressida.* These two opposed terms are quite different from each other. They, however, can be taken to correspond and this correspondence is what comprises the double-plot system. In *Troilus and Cressida* two separate and relatively independent plotlines are brought into contact through a sudden coincidence of the sexual and political spheres when Cressida is transferred to the Greek camp. What began as a private love affair is transformed into a public orgy. Suddenly the faithful Cressida has passed over into the unfaithful Cressida. On the basis of this semic reversal the audience is compelled to connect the two plots: the sexual disloyalty of Cressida is made to correspond to the political disloyalty of Achilles and Ajax. Passionate love then becomes like war between states; the sexual plotline becomes indistinguishable from the political plotline. The force of double plot lies in its 'power of suggestion' which makes Cressida's broken vow 'symbolize' or 'cause' the fall of Troy. The decisive step taken by Empson here is to link the main plot and the sub-plot of Shakespeare's play by relations of reciprocity. He foregrounds the double-plot system of *Troilus and Cressida* which develops by the contradictory dynamics of the two opposed plots. In this sense it is obvious that the love plotline becomes meaningful only through its reciprocal relationship to the political plotline. Thus Empson's new constructional model allows us to restore to the surface of the text a deep structure which reunites the two opposed plotlines within the broader unity of a double plot.

Yet for Empson the most conspicuous instance of double plot in English drama remains Middleton's *The Changeling*. Here again he emphasizes the inextricable relationship between the tragic main plot and the comic sub-plot. The tragic plotline dramatizes the sexual intrigue between Beatrice, the daughter of a nobleman, and De Flores, her father's servant. At first Beatrice rejects his advances but once he has murdered an unwanted suitor for her, she finds herself drawn into a world of manipulative politics and sexual appetite. Although she is about to marry a worthy and dutiful nobleman, Alsemero, the calculating and perverse De Flores is able to force her to become his lover. The aristocratic plotline of sexual seduction and cynical *Realpolitik* is re-echoed and parodied by the sub-plot which takes place in a madhouse. Antonio, the 'changeling' from whom the play derives its title, disguises himself as a madman in order to woo Isabella, the jealously guarded wife of the asylum's doctor. But Isabella is not caught in the trap of amateurish schemes and 'mad' machinations which surround her. Her virtue, steadfast in the asylum's chaos, succeeds in convincing both her jealous husband and would-be lover of their folly.

Traditional literary critics have been unable to deal with the sub-plot of *The Changeling*. Generally speaking, the scenes with the lunatics, the brutal and obscene punning, the mockery of the wedding are thought to be vulgar and coarse. All this, they contend, is out of place and irrelevant to the inner structure and meaning of the drama. Such a view presumes that the main plot is wholly different and distinct from the sub-plot.[3] But Empson focuses on the interrelatedness of the two plotlines within the new synchronic framework of double plot. Instead of assuming the main plot and sub-plot to be separate from each other he relocates them in a system of reciprocal relations which constructs a structural unity by connecting and combining the two heterogeneous plotlines. His characterization of double plot then underlines the dynamic interaction between the tragic or heroic plotline and the comic or pastoral plotline. As he remarks, 'however disagreeable the comic part may be it is of no use to ignore it; it is woven into the tragic part very thoroughly' (1935, p. 48). He continues: 'Certainly if the chorus of imbeciles here was merely convenient or merely funny the effect would be disgusting; but the madhouse dominates every scene; every irony refers back to it; that is why the play is so much nearer Webster than either of its parts' (p. 49).

This is the perspective in which Empson uncovers the double-plot structure that informs and organizes *The Changeling* – a double-plot structure which requires that the mutual relations between main plot and sub-plot be articulated. For him, the higher and lower worlds of the court and the asylum coincide in the anti-masque that the madmen perform for Beatrice's wedding: on the one hand, there is present the metaphorical madness of love, sexual passion and unbridled will; on the other, the literal madness of the sub-human, terrifying disorder and senseless irrationality. There is, moreover, the suggestion that the mocking chorus of madmen in the sub-plot

[3] See, for example, T. S. Eliot's forced distinction between 'the grandeur of the main plot and the nauseousness of the secondary plot' (1933, p. 41). See also Una Ellis-Fermor's oddly one-sided comment that the sub-plot could be entirely left out of the play (1936, p. 144).

ironically alludes to the sins of Beatrice and De Flores in the main plot, drawing them into the insanity. Empson puts it in striking terms when he says that 'the effect of the vulgar asylum scenes is to surround the characters with a herd of lunatics, howling outside in the night, one step into whose company is irretrievable' (1935, p. 52). The anti-masque is the strange place where court and asylum mingle, where the madness of love is joined to literal madness, where heroic and pastoral are brought together. In an unexpected alteration the court and asylum are now reversed: the court becomes an asylum in which madness and murder are unleashed, the asylum becomes a court in which the mockery of the madmen indict these crimes. What Empson's insistence on the importance of the anti-masque underscores is that the two phenomena – the madness of love and literal madness – are interwoven in the same double-plot system. And if his observation that Beatrice and De Flores are both 'changelings' is taken into account, it is even more apparent that the two plotlines cannot be isolated from each other. At any rate it is clear that the ultimate precondition of *The Changeling* is the double-plot convention which incorporates the two divergent plotlines within the same deep structure.

To recapitulate briefly: common-sense thinking and traditional literary scholarship always take for granted that the two components of a double plot are isolated phenomena. In this context it seems clear that the achievement of Empson was to have linked together the two apparently discontinuous, independent parts. Strictly speaking, his more complex synchronic model of double plot must be seen as a relational system of mutually conditioning elements. Through the reciprocal relations between main plot and sub-plot he reveals the dynamic identity of opposites which characterizes double plot as such (the ceaselessly repeated and perpetually resumed juxtapositions and correspondences between the main plot and the sub-plot). This fundamental identity, insofar as it is achieved by the interaction of the two parts, is what makes up the very locus of Empson's theory of plot. Critical theorizing uncovers, as it proceeds further in disentangling the laws of double plot, such typical formal features as semic inversions, sudden reversals and so on. For it should be understood that the mode of action of an Elizabethan play (unexpected reversals, abrupt changes of scene, sudden about-faces) is constituted in and by the double-plot structure; it is the a priori formal condition which presides over what happens to the individual characters in a play. No wonder, then, that for Empson the real issue becomes how the heroic plotline is redoubled and inverted in the pastoral plotline. Thus it can be said that in *Some Versions* everything depends on a synchronic double-plot system whose essential structural characteristic is the dynamic and contradictory relations between main plot and sub-plot.

Worth noting too is the new formal concept of literary character that is implicit in Empson's chapter on double plots. In the older, more familiar, notion of character stress was laid on the acts and choices of a human individual. But it is important to realize that anthropomorphized characters are retheorized in *Some Versions* as bearers or supports of the double-plot system. What Empson's new constructional model implies is that the surface content of 'character' must be reread in terms of a synchronic system of reciprocal relations. On the superficial and immediate level a character may seem to possess an integrated personal identity or autonomous centred self, but in fact the so-called 'character' is the product (really the 'effect') of the double-plot structure and its internal dynamics. For instance, motivation and consistency cannot be expected to explain Cressida and indeed are undermined by the dramatic ironies and brutal puns which surround her representation. As Empson comments on the famous scene in which she kisses the Greek generals, 'The incident is nonsense, surely, as character study; it is not the Cressida who was embarrassed by her own tongue in the love scenes' (1935, p. 38). Elsewhere he makes a similar observation about Bianca in *Women Beware Women*: 'she is first the poor man's modest wife, then the Duke's grandiose and ruthless mistress; the idea of "development" is irrelevant to her' (1935, p. 55). Such a 'decomposition' of character (a term Empson borrows from Ernest Jones's essay on *Hamlet*) stems to a surprising degree from the deeper and more fundamental laws of the double-plot system. This is to say that Cressida or Bianca cannot be viewed as ethically free and responsible individuals who are capable of intellectual and moral development. Rather they are structurally subordinate to the unalterable laws of a double-plot system which imposes itself on them. It is clear, therefore, that for Empson the *dramatis personae* of theatrical double plots can never be anything other than ciphers or puppets: they are always subject to that overriding double-plot system which evolves according to its own strictly determined laws. In this connection it is significant that

Empson's categories of investigation anticipate the current theories of plot which have been outlined by such contemporary structuralist critics as Vladimir Propp and A. J. Greimas (Propp, 1968; Greimas, 1970).[4] Their notion of character as 'function' (Propp) or 'actant' (Greimas) permits us to grasp character as the surface manifestation of underlying semic relations and reversals. Of course, both Propp and Greimas would probably argue that Empson failed to construct a sufficiently formalized interpretive model. But it would not be too much to say that Empson's earlier formulation of double plot looks ahead to the new and sophisticated analytical categories of structuralism.

In the preceding section the basic concepts of Empson's theory of double plot have been briefly delineated. The problem now is as follows: what are the methodological limitations which characterize his theory of double plot? How is this methodological closure linked to his theory of cognition? As I have already had occasion to point out, Empson believes that the everyday world of natural appearances and immediate experience to be a game of illusions. He makes much of the distinction between the surface content of the text (the deceptive mirage which seemingly depicts English life as a whole) and its deeper, underlying structures (the double-plot device which is hidden from common-sense thinking). Here we should notice that Empson's critical theorizing contains at least four essential elements. First, he sets aside the manifest content of the play with its appearance of wholeness – that is, the audience's naïve way of experiencing and responding to a dramatic performance. He undermines the feeling of completeness which makes the audience take for granted the play as a portrayal of real life processes ('the whole of English life at some date'). Second, he replaces this psychology of audience response with an isolation of the double-plot device itself. Beneath the surface content of a play there is to be found the informing power of the double-plot structure (or, to put it another way, the synchronic unity of two distinct plotlines which gives a play the appearance of completeness). Third, he assembles a wide range of examples from English drama to support and illustrate this overall

[4] There are indications that Empson later repudiated his theory of the 'decomposition' of character (1965, p. 69). But methodologically the potential usefulness of this definition of literary character is clearly apparent in current discussions of the decentred subject. An application of the theories of Propp and Greimas may be found in the work of Fredric Jameson (1979, pp. 49–50; 1981, pp. 119–29). Of interest too are Catherine Belsey's remarks on 'subject-positions' in Renaissance drama (1985, pp. 149–91).

theory of plot. The Nativity play, *Troilus and Cressida* and *The Changeling* are clearly meant to be exemplary expressions of double-plot structure. Fourth, he elaborates and presents those indispensable formal prerequisites which preside over what happens in a given play. In Empson's scheme of things, double-plot structure comes to be seen as an invariant that subsumes under it all individual variations of double-plotting in English drama. Thus disengaged from the natural attitude of everyday life and common-sense experience, disengaged from the immediately given empirical substratum, the double-plot system becomes an objective a priori which embraces the whole content of English drama.

Such a deliberate stress on construction and method is reminiscent of Edmund Husserl's *Formal and Transcendental Logic* and *Cartesian Meditations* which are also based on an epistemological formalism. For in some respects Empson's literary criticism has surprising affinities with Husserl's transcendental philosophy.[5] Indeed, one is tempted to say that the metacritique Theodor Adorno has made of Husserl's phenomenology also applies to Empson:

> Husserl assumes that ... the transcendental precedes the empirical by definition and as a constitutive condition ... [He] turn[s] to 'form' in a very Kantian and traditional manner and make[s] the transcendental ego the abstract condition for the 'possibility in general' of the empirical without any content at all, even the accompanying content of the empirical ego. But what directly belongs to the 'transcendental' conditions of pure consciousness ... is the constitution of the ego in itself which presupposes above all temporal and thus content-filled experience. It makes no sense to speak of a timeless consciousness, whether objective or subjective, for a concrete structure of consciousness, such as the Husserlian reductions are supposed to dissect (*herauspräparieren*) cannot be thought as other than temporally determined in general. (1982, pp. 225–6)

In Husserl's philosophical texts the *epochē* of the phenomenological reduction is described as a suspension of the 'natural attitude' which prevails in the 'real' spatio-temporal world of everyday life. This 'crossing-out' or 'bracketing' of empirical reality serves to distinguish a pure transcendental subjectivity from the naïve positivity that constitutes the insurmountable horizon of the empirical ego and common-sense experience. In this purification of consciousness,

5 Christopher Norris has noted the parallel between Empson's philosophy of literary criticism and Husserl's 'critique of the naive and self-defeating assumptions of positivism' (1978, p. 99).

instead of presupposing the existence of the immediately given world, instead of accepting it as an existing real object, the 'experiencer' (Husserl's term) puts in brackets all thoughts, valuations, actions which have been made in the natural attitude that characterizes everyday life. He/she no longer considers the spatio-temporal natural appearance of a given object. On the contrary, he/she considers the a priori conditions that constitute and ground a given object (i.e. those more basic structures which make possible conscious experience of a given object in general). Once all judgements about the natural object have been suspended, a purified theoretical consciousness is then able to construct the 'possible conditions' of the forms of scientific knowledge (now conceived not so much as empirical but rather as transcendental). In this way, an a priori determined scientific paradigm – and the systematic variations which can be included in it – is substituted for the naïve psychologism of the natural attitude. From the point of view of Husserl's transcendental philosophy, what this means is that the phenomenological *epochē* affords a way to a residuum which becomes the ultimate basis for all possible scientific representation of the world (or in Husserl's words, 'the essence common to all, the universal by which all imaginable variants of the example ... are restricted' (1978, p. 248)).

For Adorno, however, this residuum tends to eliminate 'temporal' and 'content-filled' experience. When Husserl says that the pure transcendental ego has removed itself from psychic facts and the natural attitude, he means that his phenomenological *epochē* has identified and constructed an objective a priori which 'precedes the empirical by definition and as a constitutive condition'. This rigid system of fixed categories, according to Adorno, cannot be seen to articulate a dialectical relation between consciousness and its object. Rather it is a 'timeless consciousness' which downplays 'temporally determined' subject–object relationships. Under these circumstances, Husserl's universal and essential laws congeal into a static and reified 'system' that disregards the contingencies of historical existence. Adorno emphatically insists on this: '[Husserl's transcendental philosophy] as a "system" ... so thoroughly determines all ostensible individual objects, that in fact its "essence" can be read off every singular trait of the system' (1982, p. 209). The more Husserl's epistemological model of cognitive purity approaches a transcendental a priorism, the more it assumes the character of objective and unvarying laws of identity – so much so, indeed, that it seems to be hypostatized into a closed ahistorical system.[6] On this view, then, Husserl's epistemological formalism culminates in an objectivistic scientism which has been cut off from 'the fullness and movement of its object' (Adorno, 1982, p. 70).

The same tendency is to be observed in *Some Versions*. Like Husserl's transcendental philosophy, Empson's critical theorizing tries to make available a deeper knowledge of the objective laws which govern the construction of the literary text in general. His anti-psychological analyses also aim at determining the a priori conditions which make it possible to understand the inner dynamics of literary form. As I have repeatedly emphasized, Empson redefines the surface content of the dramatic text in terms of a more fundamental deep structure – that is, double plot. He starts by emancipating consciousness from the false world of accidental appearances, from the natural attitude of everyday life. He then firmly establishes those 'conditions of possibility' which enable the critic to analyse the dramatic text as a deeper unity (or double-plot structure). This new formal a priori, and not the unreflected immediacy of the natural attitude, is what makes Empson's investigations capable of constructing an interpretive model that articulates the reciprocal relations between main plot and sub-plot. For with Empson's central discovery of double-plot structure it becomes possible to read and apprehend the inner form of English drama as a synchronic system of reciprocal relationships. Within this new horizon, then, those plays which serve as his privileged examples (the Nativity play, *Troilus and Cressida*, *The Changeling*) become in each case accessible as various exemplars of a double-plot structure that develops according to its own laws. A theoretically satisfactory understanding of any particular play depends on an understanding of the deeper double-plot mechanism which unites main plot and sub-plot; it requires that the critic become conscious of the fundamental laws which guide the construction of the double-plot system. For unless the actual events dramatized are transferred into the essential 'laws' of the double-plot system there can be no technical analysis of a play's inner dynamics and reciprocal relationships. In this respect a Huss-

6 See Adorno's metacritique of identity theory in Husserl's transcendental phenomenology (1982). For another recent discussion which reproblematizes the excesses of Husserl's 'heroic rationalism' see Jacques Derrida (1973). Common to both Adorno and Derrida is a distrust of 'laws of identity' or 'logocentric hierarchies' which issue into closed, self-validating systems.

erlian 'structure of objective lawfulness' (Adorno, 1982, p. 209) is basic to *Some Versions*. Thus Empson's critical theorizing is able to uncover and determine a formal a priori of a wholly new kind, the formal a priori of the double-plot system.

Here the resemblance between Empson and Husserl is striking. For both, a pure transcendental subjectivity (or to put this in Empson's language, 'critical theorizing') suspends the natural attitude which accepts as valid the everyday world as it appears in common-sense experience. Both undertake to ascertain those formal prerequisites which must be made known before the specific object of study can be discussed. This would all seem to suggest, however, that the conceptual schema for the analysis of empirical materials must be given in advance. For the important point here is that the apprehension of a given object of experience is dependent on the construction of a synchronic model which organizes the empirical data. In other words, what is extolled is the set of global systematic categories which facilitate a formal articulation of the undiscovered or buried meaning of cultural phenomena.

The methodological limitations of such ahistorical laws and systems are connected with the peculiar difficulties presented by Husserl's transcendental a priorism (what has been described above, following Adorno, as a 'structure of objective lawfulness'). When Empson brackets out the disparate materials of everyday life he constitutes an autonomous double-plot system that develops according to its own laws and dynamics. His primary reason for this is that he wants to construct a theoretical model which maps the contradictory dynamics of the double-plot system. However, what Empson finds attractive in this new constructional model is what Adorno criticizes as the essentially abstract character of Husserl's transcendental a priorism – that is, the effacement of temporal specificity and lived experience in a closed ahistorical system. This is how Adorno assesses the limitations of the synchronic thought which characterizes Husserl's transcendental philosophy: Husserl's formal-epistemological assumptions 'can never sustain the claim of an unvarying "structure of pure consciousness". Since it arises out of psychological observations in specific persons in specific situations, it refers back to them' (1982, p. 221). He also says that 'the [meaning] acts themselves still remain temporally determined "psychic phenomena" and, by Husserl's own account, real events' (p. 164). This is no less true of Empson's theory of double plot. Indeed, it is precisely to the extent that Empson's theory of plot ends up in formal and non-temporal laws that *Some Versions* is incapable of grappling with historical questions and problems.[7] Everything tends to be hypostatized into a supra-historical essence of art or aesthetic form in general (device, ambiguity, irony and so on). Everything tends to be transposed into the frozen immobility of a fixed and timeless structure. Thus the genuine diachronic dimension of drama cannot be disclosed, if by means of the a priori notion of the double-plot device, temporal phenomena are ranged under an all-embracing 'structure of objective lawfulness'.

It would seem, then, that Empson's new theory of plot produces a form of closure at the very point where the analytical framework should be modified and enlarged. Here, as in many other instances, his organizing category of double plot takes on a reified and static shape that is detached from the contingent circumstances of concrete history. But it must not be forgotten that Empson's new critical method played a very prominent role in twentieth-century Anglo-American literary criticism. From this point of view his synchronic account of double plot might be said to have opened up a place for a more adequately developed theory of plot. Indeed, it might even be said that *Some Versions* invented a wholly new formal strategy for the reading and interpretation of dramatic texts. Unlike traditional literary critics, Empson was able to bring to the surface the deep structure of double plot which is latent and implicit in the dramatic text. His distinction between the naïveté of the natural attitude and the pure ego of conscious life allowed him to make visible the double-plot mechanisms that remained hidden from traditional scholarship. This was already the case with Husserl, for whom the real nature of an object can be determined only on condition that we suspend valuations, judgements and thoughts made in the natural attitude. Because everyday 'naturalized' consciousness is immersed in the unreflective practicality of the empirical world, because it

7 It is strange that no regard is paid to Renaissance historical developments in the chapter on double plots. For instance, Empson seems unable to articulate the specific historical tensions and conflicts to which his text alludes (why is double plot such a predominant aesthetic form in the drama of the sixteenth and seventeenth centuries?). Paul Alpers has argued that for Empson 'pastoral has a unifying social force, is a means of bridging differences and reconciling social classes' (1978, p. 101). However, it is Raymond Williams, and not Alpers, who has noticed the hegemonic and legitimizing function of pastoral ideology in Renaissance England. Commenting on the pastoral motif of a golden age in the literature of the period, he writes: 'An idealisation, based on a temporary situation and on a deep desire for stability, served to cover and to evade the actual contradictions of the time' (1973, p. 45).

naturally accepts the validity of this empirical world without question, it posits it as somehow existing, as somehow 'obvious' or 'self-evident'. For this reason everyday 'naturalized' consciousness cannot locate those mechanisms, techniques and devices at work within the form of the play as such. It cannot detect the operation of the double-plot system beneath the surface of the text. If an understanding of a particular play is to be possible, there must first be a crossing out or bracketing of the insubstantial appearances which characterize the natural object. The critic must suspend the common-sense and everyday attitude which assumes the play mirrors the appearance of things ('the whole of English life'). He/she must then reconstitute the self-sufficient and autonomous double-plot 'system' which defines itself by the interaction of the main plot and the sub-plot. Where an older generation of literary critics restricted themselves to commentaries on the content of a particular play, Empson's new theoretical model was able to generate an unexpected formal innovation (what he designated 'double-plots'). It is this formal virtuosity which enabled him to develop beyond the unthematized historicism of a Tillyard or the vitalist intuitionism of a Leavis. It is this synchronic orientation which enabled him to devise an explanatory model structurally capable of unravelling the complexities of English drama. Thus it becomes clear in what sense Empson's 'critical theorizing' reminded the nascent discipline of English studies that literary criticism could not limit itself to traditional methods and analyses but had to come to grips with new kinds of formalization.

CHAPTER 7

More lurid figures: de Man reading Empson

Neil Hertz

Late in *Allegories of Reading*, towards the end of his chapter on Rousseau's *Social Contract*, Paul de Man writes, 'We have moved closer and closer to the "definition" of *text*, the entity we are trying to circumscribe' (1979, p. 268) and many of his readers must lean closer to the page: here it comes!

We can think of other such points in works of criticism where analytic questioning is, for a moment, made to feel like a quest-narrative, the critic pausing to invite the reader to share a sense of mounting anticipation, of getting 'closer and closer'. There is Maurice Blanchot, on the opening page of *L'Espace littéraire* (1955, p. 5), gesturing at what he takes to be the region towards which his writing is moving, the pages on the gaze of Orpheus, on Orpheus' trip to the Underworld, his climb upward and then his turning to look back at Eurydice. Those pages have been frequently cited in recent years. Less familiar is an oddly apposite moment in William Empson's writing, another descent into Hell towards another woman. He is beginning his entry into the zone of maximum – that is, Type VII – ambiguity and has been discussing what Freud called the antithetical sense of primal words, citing Freud on how the primitive Egyptians used the same sign for 'young' and 'old'.[1] Now he catches himself up, mock-apologetically, grants that all this talk about the Egyptians is 'in some degree otiose' and writes:

[1] Empson goes on to cite Freud's claim that the Egyptians 'only gradually learnt to separate the two sides of the antithesis and think of the one without conscious comparison with the other', then comments: 'When a primitive Egyptian saw a baby he at once thought of an old man, and he had to learn not to do this as his language became more civilised. This certainly shows the process of attaching a word to an object as something extraordinary; nobody would do it if his language did not make him ... ' (1953, p. 194). The passage, for all its throwaway quality, is worth comparing with de Man's linking of the 'advent of theory' in literary studies to the 'introduction of a linguistic terminology . . . that considers reference as a function of language and not necessarily as an intuition' (1986, p. 8).

I have been searching the sources of the Nile less to explain English verse than to cast upon the reader something of the awe and horror which were felt by Dante arriving finally at the most centrique part of earth, of Satan, and of hell.

> Quando noi fummo là, dove la coscia
> Si volge appunto in sul grosso dell' anche,
> La Duca con fatica e con angoscia
> Volse la testa ov' egli avea le zanche. (1953, p. 196)

Empson leaves untranslated these lines from the last canto (xxxiv, lines 76–9) of *Inferno*: 'When we were where the thigh turns, just on the swelling of the haunch, the Leader with labour and strain brought round his head where his legs had been' (Dante, 1961, p. 425). Drawing out the analogy, Empson then adds cheerfully: 'We too must now stand upon our heads, and are approaching the secret places of the Muse' (1953, p. 196).

No one sounds less like Blanchot than Empson, but the two passages are thematically comparable. It is common, in end-of-the-line texts[2] of this sort, for movement towards one's goal to be allegorized in terms of the pull of desire, the fear of the law. So Blanchot can write, 'Regarder Eurydice, sans souci du chant, dans l'impatience et l'imprudence du désir qui oublie la loi, c'est cela même, *l'inspiration*' (1955, p. 231), and Empson can, still more insouciantly, superimpose 'the secret places of the Muse' on the shaggy loins of the character Dante calls 'the Emperor of the dolorous realm'. But what of that moment in *Allegories of Reading*: can a similar figuration be read there as well?

At first glance, it would seem not: the pages we are concerned with (pp. 266–70) move back and forth between lengthy citations of the *Social Contract* and careful interpretive paraphrase. The argumentation is compact, the diction a combination of Rousseau's own and de Man's conceptualized linguistic vocabulary. What governs the movement of these paragraphs is not a quest-narrative but the elaboration of an analogy between law and grammar with respect to the categories of the general and the particular. De Man begins with Rousseau's statement that 'there can be no fundamental Law that is binding for the entire body of the people' and glosses this as implying that 'the meaning of the contractual text has to remain suspen-

[2] On the movement of a text towards 'the end of the line' see Kenneth Burke (1957, pp. 56–75), and my own discussion of such scenarios in 'Afterword' (Hertz, 1985, pp. 217–39).

ded and undecidable' (p. 266). He then notes Rousseau's insistence on the separation of the particular members of the body of the state from the state as a whole, noting the paradox that 'to the extent that he is particular, *any* individual is, as individual, alienated from a law that, on the other hand, exists only in relation to his individual being' (p. 267). This is paraphrastic, dry and demonstrative. But what de Man concludes from this passage of argument is put more intriguingly:

> From the point of view of the legal text, it is this generality which ruthlessly rejects any particularization, which allows for the possibility of its coming into being. Within the textual model, particularization corresponds to reference, since reference is the application of an undetermined, general potential for meaning to a specific unit. The indifference of the text with regard to its referential meaning is what allows the legal text to proliferate, exactly as the preordained, coded repetition of a specific gesture or set of gestures allows Helen to weave the story of the war into the epic. (p. 268)

I will take up the allusion to Helen shortly. For the moment I would note that nothing in Rousseau – or in de Man's earlier argument – would seem to require that the legal text here be characterized, anthropomorphically, as 'ruthless' or 'indifferent'. One effect of this diction, however, is to link a discussion of the law with de Man's later consideration of excuses in the final chapter of *Allegories of Reading*. There, Rousseau's claim that his lie about Marion was unintentional, an *effet machinal* of his timidity, leads de Man to note that the excuse is both fiction and machine, referentially detached, implacable in its repetition of a preordained pattern, comparable in this respect to Heinrich von Kleist's marionettes, 'capable of taking on any structure whatever, yet entirely ruthless in its inability to modify its own structural design for nonstructural reasons' (p. 294). That de Man had the later discussion in mind while he was working on the *Social Contract* is clear from another reference to Rousseau's lie in the pages we're considering: 'as we know from the *Confessions*', de Man writes, 'we never lie as much as when we want to do full justice to ourselves, especially in self-accusation' (pp. 269–70). In both chapters of *Allegories of Reading* and elsewhere – *passim* – de Man's language personifies the agency of the text, but personifies it as impersonal, often fiercely so.

But to return to Helen: where did she come from? What is shc doing *duns cette galère*? Like Rousseau's lying excuse, de Man associates her with both fiction and machine. Years earlier, in 'Criticism and Crisis', he had written:

All literatures, including the literature of Greece, have always designated themselves as existing in the mode of fiction; in the *Iliad*, when we first encounter Helen, it is as the emblem of the narrator weaving the actual war into the tapestry of a fictional object. Her beauty prefigures the beauty of all future narratives as entities that point to their own fictional nature. (1983, p. 17)

There Helen served as a figure in a *mise en abîme*, hovering somewhere between standing in for the narrator and standing in for the aesthetic object. In the later text she figures less as an emblem of the narrator than as the locus of a set of gestures, her own agency enabled by, but also submitted to the imperious control of the text. But I am flattening out what is in fact a more interesting formulation in de Man: the analogy his sentence insists on is between 'the legal text' and 'Helen' – the ruthless indifference of the one rubs off on the other, and we are reminded that Helen is at once the accomplished artist of the beautiful, the weaver passively rehearsing the weavers' code, and the woman whose beauty initiated the Trojan War and 'brought death to so many brave men'.

The last quotation is not from de Man, but from what I would speculate was de Man's source for this allusion to Helen, a remarkable paragraph in Empson which I shall cite, in the interests of thickening up the texture, and raising the stakes, of this discussion.

We know that when de Man read *Seven Types of Ambiguity* in the 1950s he found its first and seventh chapters particularly compelling. Appended to the first chapter is an 'Annex on Dramatic Irony' illustrative of what Empson calls 'a sort of dramatic ambiguity of judgment which does not consider the characters so much as the audience' (1953, p. 43). In this case the characters are Portia and Bassanio in *The Merchant of Venice* – Empson is writing of the scene of the three caskets – and his point is that the song Portia sings while Bassanio is deciding which casket to choose ('Tell me where is fancy bred ... ') hints in its rhymes at the proper choice without exactly suggesting that Portia is intentionally tipping him off. The scene allows us to entertain some doubt as to Portia's honesty, but leaves the question unresolved. Empson goes on:

Irony in this subdued sense, as a generous scepticism which can believe at once that people are and are not guilty, is a very normal and essential method; Portia's song is not more inconsistent than the sorrow of Helen that she has brought death to so many brave men, and the pride with which she is first found making tapestries of them; than the courage of Achilles, which none will question, 'in his impregnable armour with his invulnerable skin underneath it'; than the sleepers at Gethsemane, who, St Luke says, were sleeping for sorrow; than the way Thésée (in Racine), by the use of a deity, at once kills and does not kill Hippolyte. This sort of contradiction is at once understood in literature, because the process of understanding one's friends must always be riddled with such indecisions and the machinery of such hypocrisy; people, often, cannot have done both of two things, but they must have been in some way prepared to have done either; whichever they did, they will have still lingering in their minds the way they would have preserved their self-respect if they had acted differently; they are only to be understood by bearing both possibilities in mind. (1953, p. 44)

I set down this paragraph in part as a contribution to the recent polemic about Paul de Man's behaviour during the war, about which I shall have more to say later in this essay. One could wish that Empson's 'generous scepticism which can believe at once that people are and are not guilty' were as widespread as he generously believed it to be. But I also imagine that, coming upon this soon after the war, de Man may very well have been struck – both entertained and gratified – by the matter-of-fact shrewdness with which Empson could take up loaded questions of innocence and guilt. That those questions were on de Man's mind as well, and remained there as questions to be taken seriously, nobody who has read *Allegories of Reading* can doubt.

But my more immediate reason for citing *Seven Types* is to suggest that the way in which Empson links the image of Helen weaving to a thematics of indecision, machinery and guilt may account for the allusion's surfacing where it does in de Man's essay, in the middle of a consideration of machinery, guilt and indecision – what de Man calls undecidability and figures as suspension. Helen, he says, is like the legal text, and that text, as we noted before, 'has to remain suspended and undecidable' (1979, p. 266). The paragraph that begins 'We have moved closer and closer to the "definition" of *text* . . . ' concludes in this way:

But just as no text is conceivable without grammar, no grammar is conceivable without the suspension of referential meaning. Just as no law can ever be written unless one suspends any consideration of applicability to a particular entity including, of course, oneself, grammatical logic can function only if its referential consequences are disregarded.

On the other hand [the next paragraph begins], no law is a law unless it also applies to particular individuals. It cannot be left hanging in the air, in the abstraction of its generality. (p. 269)

That final image, of the law 'left hanging in the air', coming as it does just after the repetition 'suspension'/'suspends', could have been included in my essay 'Lurid Figures', where I commented on the recurrence in de Man's writings of what I took as a kind of idiosyncratic punning, in which certain terms he relies on conceptually – words like 'suspension' and 'disfiguration' – often turn up in proximity to images of hanging or of physical defacement or mutilation, producing an odd but characteristic pathos (Hertz in Waters and Godzich, 1989, pp. 82–104). I labelled it the 'pathos of uncertain agency', and, since I need to say more about that notion, and cannot assume a reader's familiarity with the earlier essay, I shall briefly rehearse some of its claims here.

I tried to show that lurid figuration in de Man was not wilful or gratuitous but a necessary by-product of his theoretical concerns, a function of his attempt to dwell, speculatively, on what he called a 'permanent disjunction' (1986, p. 92) in language, the 'radical estrangement between the meaning and the performance of any text' (1979, p. 298). I cited what was already a much-cited pronouncement of his – 'No degree of knowledge can ever stop this madness, for it is the madness of words' (1984, p. 122) – setting it alongside some bizarre writing of his own that seemed to me to qualify as sufficiently mad to illustrate his point. The idea that the particular pathos in de Man's text was linked to a sense of uncertain agency I derived at first from a reading of a paragraph in his essay on Walter Benjamin's 'The Task of the Translator', which I shall set down again here:

All these activities – critical philosophy, literary theory, history – resemble each other in the fact that they do not resemble that from which they derive. But they are all intralinguistic: they relate to what in the original belongs to language, and not to meaning as an extralinguistic correlate susceptible of paraphrase or imitation. They disarticulate, they undo the original, they reveal that the original was always already disarticulated. They reveal that their failure, which seems to be due to the fact that they are secondary in relation to the original, reveals an essential failure, an essential disarticulation which was already there in the original. They kill the original by discovering that the original was already dead. (1986, p. 84)

What is noticeable here is that a familiar deconstructive turn – the claim that the activity of disarticulation is discovered to have always already taken place – is given an unfamiliar twist: the construal of disarticulation as murder and murder as, paradoxically, 'discovering that the original was already dead'. This, it seemed to me, adds, if only fleetingly, a pathos of uncertain agency. The prose conjures up a subject – 'perhaps a killer, perhaps only the discoverer of the corpse – who can serve as a locus of vacillation: did I do it? or had it already been done?' and thus introduces another version of undecidability (or suspension), this time between judgements of a subject's passivity or activity, innocence or guilt (see Waters and Godzich, 1989, p. 86).

It may be worth recalling that in the pages we are considering, pages en route to a definition of 'text', the ruthless or indifferent activity of the law – or the text – is set over against a counter-force, a form of covert or subversive agency attributed in the legal model to the individual and in the textual model to the referent. De Man notes that 'the logic of grammar generates texts only in the absence of referential meaning, but every text generates a referent that subverts the grammatical principle to which it owed its constitution'. Similarly, glossing Rousseau's argument that 'all citizens constantly desire the well-being of each [because] no one exists who does not secretly appropriate the term *each* and think of himself when he votes for all', de Man characterizes this as an 'act of deceit', a theft which 'steal[s] from the text the very meaning to which ... we are not entitled, the particular *I* which destroys its generality'; and it is at this point that he links this discussion to the *Confessions*, to the motifs of guilt, lying and self-accusation (1979, p. 269). The basis for that link should now be clearer: it is in the traces, in the language of this page of argumentation, of the figure of an undecidably guilty subject and/or referent who can be imaged as facing off in specular fashion with a powerful but vulnerable (that is, flawed, disarticulated, already dead) law and/or text.

This section of 'Promises (*Social Contract*)' concludes with the promised 'definition' of text as an 'entity' that must be considered from a double perspective: from the perspective of grammar it is a 'generative, open-ended, non-referential' system; from the perspective of figure it is 'closed off by a transcendental signification that subverts the grammatical code to which the text owes its existence' (1979, p. 270). We can see that half the chapter's title refers to the grammatical system, to the structure of promising, the other half to the particular 'allegorical narrative of [the text's] impossibility', the paradoxes of contractual society that de Man has teased out of Rousseau. The indirection of allegory was necessary, de Man had argued, because 'what remains hidden in the everyday use of language, the fundamental incompatibility of grammar and meaning, becomes explicit when the linguistic structures are stated, as is the case here, in political terms' (1979, p. 269).

In 'Lurid Figures' I tried to demonstrate that yet another narrative could be read out of de Man's writings about textuality, one that had been suggested to me by a biographical anecdote, the story of de Man's mother's death. Because I had been told this story in confidence the anecdote does not appear in 'Lurid Figures'; however, one result of the recent interest in Paul de Man's youth has been the publication of the story, or a version of it, so I feel free to discuss it here. The story, as a university friend of de Man's, Edouard Colinet, tells it, goes like this:

> Paul's father, Robert (Bob) de Man, was a businessman, manufacturing and selling medical instruments and x-ray equipment in Antwerp. Paul's elder brother died in an accident and, after that, his mother committed suicide: Paul had the bad luck of being the first to find her hanged – he was about 15 years old at the time. Paul's father was so disturbed by these two violent deaths that for a time Paul had to be taken care of by his uncle Henri. (in Hamacher *et al.*, 1989, p. 427)

I would stress the fact that this is an anecdote, one account of how something may have taken place; there are other versions. According to Paul de Man's cousin Jan – Henri's son – it was Robert who found his wife's body, and it was not the case that Paul 'had to be taken care of by his uncle'. That never happened, says Jan de Man: Paul was seventeen, not fifteen, at the time and didn't need taking care of.[3] Jan de Man has the dates right, that much can be confirmed: the elder brother was killed 20 June 1936, when Paul was sixteen; his mother hanged herself exactly a year later. But as to who found her body, all that can be said is that the story Paul de Man told Edouard Colinet and some other Belgian friends is the same story he told, in later years, to various members of his family.

What he chose to tell provides the germ for what I find obliquely inscribed at various points in his writings – a tableau of uncertain

[3] Letter from Jan H. de Man, 27 June 1988.

agency, of someone confronting a suspended body, himself suspended between feelings of matricidal guilt and of the intensified innocence of the bereft, immobilized in the act of having 'kill[ed] the original by discovering that the original was already dead'. Its appearance in de Man's texts may be read as another example of end-of-the-line figuration, to be contrasted with the passages from Blanchot and Empson with which we began. As each of these theorists approaches an elusive centre – named variously as *text* (De Man), as the articulation of *l'œuvre* and *l'ombre* (Blanchot), or as 'the most complicated and deeply-rooted notion of the human mind' (Empson) – they find themselves spinning gendered allegories of law and desire. In this passage of Blanchot's, the object of desire and the law that forbids its realization seem distinct: Orpheus in the impatience and imprudence of his desire to look at Eurydice, must forget the law, we are told (1955, p. 231). In Empson, things are less clear-cut: Satan and the Muse don't occupy the same imaginary space, but rather are juxtaposed metonymically, seemingly at the critic's whim. More remarkably, at the equivalent point in de Man's text, the law – at once ruthless and vulnerable to subversion – is impossible to differentiate from the object of ambivalent desire: the law is like a hanging woman. The structure is not triangular and static but specular and unstable, and, precisely because of that instability, it is available to figure the textual operations that de Man will follow in one essay after another.[4]

I am proposing that Paul de Man's writing bears the traces of a particular, thoroughly contingent event in his life, but the form

[4] Compare de Man's account, in 'Lyric and Modernity' (1969) of the non-filial (or, at least, non-Oedipal) relation of Mallarmé to his predecessor Baudelaire: 'The truly allegorical, later Baudelaire of the *Petits Poèmes en Prose* never stopped haunting Mallarmé, though he may have tried to exorcize his presence. Here was, in fact, the example of a poetry that came close to being no longer representational but that remained for him entirely enigmatic. The darkness of his hidden center obscures later allusions to Baudelaire, including the *Tombeau* poem devoted to the author of the *Fleurs du Mal*. Far from being an older kinsman who sent him on his way, Baudelaire, or, at least, the most significant aspect of Baudelaire, was for him a dark zone into which he could never penetrate' (1983, p. 184). In Mallarmé's 'Le Tombeau de Charles Baudelaire' that 'dark zone' is named 'un immortel pubis'.

De Man is engaged in contesting the appropriateness of thinking in terms of genealogical lines of descent, whether of critics of modern lyric (e.g., Otto Friedrich as 'father' of Hans-Robert Jauss, who, in turn, 'fathered' Karl-Heinz Stierle) or of poets (e.g., Baudelaire as 'father' of Mallarmé and 'grandfather' of the surrealists). Here, representational poetry is aligned with genealogy and a reassuring, if conflictual, pattern of Oedipal lineage, the 'truly allegorical' with 'a dark zone into which [one] could never penetrate': a figure that blurs differences – of position and of gender, of figures of law and desire – much as does the passage in *Allegories of Reading*, or Empson's evocation of Satan at the 'most centrique part of earth' which is somehow also the site of 'the secret places of the Muse'.

those traces take is bound to be overdetermined. The figure of the hanging woman has a long history that pre-dates de Man's encounter with it in 1937; indeed, we can be sure that de Man's own relation to that figure must pre-date its actualization for him at the time of his mother's death. For the figure recurs in fantasies of matricide and abjection that inform texts from classical times to our own.[5] If we would speculate that de Man's witnessing an externalized version of one such fantasy was traumatic, we must also add that such a witnessing would necessarily place him in a different relation to the contents of the fantasy, a relation we can know nothing about but which need not have been merely disabling.

If one is persuaded that there is this strand of figuration in de Man's writings there still remains the question of what can be made of it. Can it be shown to function in ways that invalidate the general bearings of de Man's work or, alternatively, can it serve to deconstruct his more abstract theoretical arguments? Here the model would be de Man's remarks on Nietzsche's *The Birth of Tragedy*:

> [T]he deconstruction does not occur between statements, as in a logical refutation or a dialectic, but happens instead between, on the one hand, metalinguistic statements about the rhetorical nature of language and, on

[5] On the particular association of death by hanging – and of other forms of suspension – with women in classical texts, see Cantarella (1985, pp. 91–101). Cantarella cites among other sources the work of Loraux: 'Le corps étranglé' (1984, pp. 195–224), and *Façons tragiques de tuer une femme* (1985).

Marc Redfield has pointed out to me an intriguing modern instance in *Great Expectations*, where the reiteration of the word *figure* loads a macabre scene with a further, rhetorical burden. In chapter 8 Pip wanders into an abandoned brewery on Miss Havisham's property, sees Estella in the distance, then suffers this hallucinatory moment:

> It was in this place, and at this moment, that a strange thing happened to my fancy. I thought it a strange thing then, and I thought it a stranger thing long afterwards. I turned my eyes – a little dimmed by looking up at the frosty light – towards a great wooden beam in a low nook of the building near me on my right hand, and I saw a figure hanging there by the neck. A figure all in yellow white, with but one shoe to the feet; and it hung so, that I could see that the faded trimmings of the dress were like earthy paper, and that the face was Miss Havisham's, with a movement going over the whole countenance as if she were trying to call to me. In the terror of seeing the figure, and in the terror of being certain that it had not been there a moment before, I at first ran from it, and then ran towards it. And my terror was greatest of all when I found no figure there. (1961, p. 77)

Dickens will have Pip recall this moment twice later in the novel, each time in connection with his unsuccessful attempts to grasp the secret of Estella's face: whom does she remind him of? That the answer turns out to be Magwitch, Estella's literal and Pip's figurative father, complicates the bearing of the hallucination: a dimly discerned admonitory man's face is superimposed on the vision of a hanging woman, the law blurred into the lineaments of the ghastly bride of desire, and all under the sign of resemblance and figuration.

the other hand, a rhetorical praxis that puts these statements into question. (1979, p. 98)

Are we dealing with such a rhetorical praxis here? De Man would say we are not, and offer another name for what we are pursuing: he would call it an obsession and he would have no trouble accommodating it to his understanding of how texts work. He knows about obsessions, his own and other people's, and can be wryly witty on the subject, as in these remarks about Michael Riffaterre:

It would be all too facile to point to the psychological implications of Riffaterre's model, in which the mathematical as well as the maternal implications of the 'matrix' are obvious, or of his literary examples, with their obsessional stress on death, on sarcophagi, on a not altogether simple sexuality, on hallucination and on obsession itself. If morbidity happens to be one's measure of theoretical audacity, Riffaterre is second to none. (1986, p. 40)

De Man's reader, picking up the allusion to the maternal, noting de Man's own interest in 'death ... sarcophagi ... obsession itself' might be tempted to read this as veiled autobiography, but that would not dismay de Man. He could acknowledge writing of this sort as telling – telling of his own obsessions – and still insist that obsession-in-general plays only a secondary and derivative role in the motivation of texts.[6] Obsessional concerns will find expression in what I have been calling lurid figures, and the covert narratives of violence or eroticism these imply are, de Man has argued, 'defensive motion[s] of the understanding', ways of imposing intelligibility on otherwise baffling operations of language.

That is the burden of the last pages of 'Anthropomorphism and Trope in the Lyric', where de Man reads the relationship between Baudelaire's sonnets 'Correspondances' and 'Obsession' as the 'construction and undoing of the mirror-like structure that is always involved in a reading' (1984, p. 252). After the symmetries between the two have been established, de Man goes on to demonstrate the several ways 'Obsession' translates 'Correspondances' into 'psychological and therefore intelligible' equivalents for elements in the

[6] See the foreword to the revised second edition of *Blindness and Insight*: 'I am not given to retrospective self-examination and mercifully forget what I have written with the same alacrity I forget bad movies – although, as with bad movies, certain scenes or phrases return at times to embarrass or haunt me like a guilty conscience. When one imagines to have felt the exhilaration of renewal, one is certainly the last to know whether such a change actually took place or whether one is just restating, in a slightly different mode, earlier and unresolved obsessions' (1983, p. xii).

more enigmatic poem. Although he had begun his reading by warning that to arrange the two sonnets 'into a valorized qualitative hierarchy' would be 'more convenient than it is legitimate' (1984, p. 254), he will nevertheless insist that the more 'perfectly and quickly' understood 'Obsession' is the less commanding text. Even if, contrary to fact, it had been written first, it could not be taken as either the origin or the cause of 'Correspondances'. '"Correspondances" implies and explains "Obsession" [he goes on] but "Obsession" leaves "Correspondances" as thoroughly incomprehensible as it always was.' What emerges from these pages is that obsession (in Baudelaire's poem and in general) will always operate as a 'defensive motion of the understanding' – like figuration, it is a mode of intelligibility. De Man concludes:

> Whenever we encounter a text such as 'Obsession' – that is, whenever we read – there always is an infra-text, a hypogram like 'Correspondances' underneath. (1984, p. 262)

If the specular figures we have been noting are thus obsessive, if, following de Man, we cannot hope to find in them the source or origin of the more difficult turns of his text, how then might they function? Perhaps as signs of a defensive wish for just such a source and origin, the confirmation of self (purchased at whatever cost) that a traumatic recollection could provide? De Man would seem to imply something of the sort in the last chapter of *Allegories of Reading* when he considers the threat that a writer may lose control of his text, a threat that contains within it the possibility of 'the radical annihilation of the metaphor of selfhood and the will':

> This more than warrants the anxiety with which Rousseau acknowledges the lethal quality of all writing. Writing always includes the moment of dispossession in favor of the arbitrary power play of the signifier and from the point of view of the subject, this can only be experienced as a dismemberment, a beheading or a castration. (1979, p. 296)

But in the pages that follow an interesting complication is developed, one I was unable to take account of in 'Lurid Figures', but which bears on our earlier discussion. The threat just described is not, it seems, the most threatening of threats, for it remains tied, de Man argues, to the metaphor of text as body. He will then go on to treat of the 'more directly threatening alternative of the text as machine' (1979, p. 297). Recalling the moments in Rousseau's *Fourth Rêverie* that conjure up a dangerous machine, he adds:

The threatening element in these incidents then becomes more apparent. The text as body, with all its implications of substitutive tropes ultimately always retraceable to metaphor, is displaced by the text as machine and, in the process, it suffers the loss of the illusion of meaning. The deconstruction of the figural dimension is a process that takes place independently of any desire; as such it is not unconscious but mechanical, systematic in its performance but arbitrary in its principle, like a grammar. This threatens the autobiographical subject not as the loss of something that once was present and that it once possessed [that is, the threat is not one of castration or beheading], but as a radical estrangement between the meaning and the performance of any text. (1979, p. 298)

In 'Lurid Figures' I had simply conflated these two accounts, and, glossing what I took to be a 'moment of madness', had cited both of them as well as a third, similar formulation of de Man's:

[F]iguration turns hallucinatory [I wrote] in an attempt to render intelligible what, according to de Man, cannot be rendered intelligible, the 'radical estrangement between the meaning and the performance of any text' (1979, p. 298). Or again in the language of *Allegories of Reading*, it is the moment in which 'the writer severs himself from the intelligibility of his own text', one that 'has to be thematized as a sacrifice' (1979, pp. 205–7), or that, 'from the point of view of the subject . . . can only be experienced as a dismemberment, a beheading or a castration' (1979, p. 296). (Waters and Godzich, 1989, pp. 99–100)

But it now seems clear that only two of these citations – the last two – describe the same moment, a moment that is figured as sacrifice or castration, and that these in turn are meant to be contrasted with a more dangerous moment, that of the radical estrangement of meaning and performance. If that is so, how are we now to read the passage on Rousseau's *Social Contract* with which we began? With its allusions to the 'fundamental incompatibility of grammar and meaning', to the 'impersonal, machinelike systematicity' of the *Social Contract* (1979, p. 268), it asks to be read as a figuring of the text as a motiveless machine. Yet threaded through these pages, I would argue, in the allusions to the social body and its members, in the specular struggle between a quasi-personified ruthless generality and a deceitful, thieving particular *I*, and in the images of the hanging text or law, is just the sort of figuration de Man associates with text-as-body. Could the more lurid figures – because lurid and because figural – mark a defensive motion of understanding? Would the simultaneous conjuring up of text-as-body shelter the subject from the more threatening aspects of text-as-machine? That would be like saying one finds the sonnet 'Obsession' threaded through 'Correspondances'; and indeed that is one way of reading de Man's pages on those poems. Or it would be like saying that the appearance of Helen in the text – her beauty, her equivocally active and passive relation to the motions of weaving – similarly conflates the object of desire and the law so as to veil the threat to meaning in luridly attractive metaphoricity. It may be possible to proffer a theoretical distinction between these two metaphors for text, body and machine, but it may not be possible to write of the text-as-machine without drawing on the idiom of text-as-body, that is, without calling upon lurid figures.

It may seem that the only interest of the appearance of these figures in de Man's writings lies in the ways they might serve as clues to the unfolding of a drama of engagement and defence – engagement with problems of textuality and defence against the risks attendant on such thought. But obsessions may serve as promoters of thought as well, and I think that can be demonstrated by looking at pages de Man devoted to two thematically related poems, one by Rilke ('Quai du Rosaire' (1979, pp. 40–3)) the other by Hugo ('Ecrit sur la vitre d'une fenêtre flamande' (1986, pp. 45–51)). Both concern the motif of a Flemish carillon, the 'Glockenspiel, das in den Himmeln hängt', in Rilke's plangent final line, and de Man will refer to the Rilke poem, nine years later, in 'Hypogram and Inscription', where he offers a reading of the Hugo poem to give focus to his critique of Riffaterre's semiotics.

De Man turns to 'Quai du Rosaire' in the course of a discussion of figuration in Rilke, and concludes his brief account of it by locating the poem's 'true interest' not in its 'thematic statements' but rather in 'the intricacy and wealth of movements triggered by the original chiasmus'. One can acknowledge this and still note that the thematic statements, which de Man does not ignore, are loaded ones for him. Or rather, that de Man's paraphrase and selective citation of the poem loads it with a secondary, lurid interest that is neither dissimulated nor fully confronted. The poem, written in German, is a description of the city called Brugge in Flemish, but by referring to the francophone Flemish poet Georges Rodenbach, de Man can name the city in French, not once but three times in the space of two pages, as 'Bruges la morte'. It is as if the sound of that feminine ending – *la morte* – were particularly compelling, set as it is in an interpretation that dwells on 'the seductive but funereal image of a temporal annihilation which is enjoyed as if it were a sensuous pleasure, "der Süssen Traube / des Glockenspiels", which actually is the death knell that reduced the city to a ghostly memory'.[7] De Man will locate the poem's thematic appeal in its combining 'the audacity of a paradox with a promise of beauty or even, in the image of the grapes, of sensuous gratification on the far side of the grave', then, in a characteristic gesture, draw back from the seductions of his own paraphrase: 'Yet the true interest of the poem does not stem from these thematic statements.' What is missing from de Man's critical account is any thematization of the reader-critic's own fascination. In the terms he would later adopt, de Man refuses to 'give a face' to the suspended carillon;[8] hence he can find no way of inscribing his own face in this text, as he will in the later essay, with the help of Victor Hugo's remarkable image of the mind as 'l'esprit, ce veilleur fait d'oreilles et d'yeux' (1986, p. 49).

But the need for just such an inscription is signalled further along in the Rilke essay, in its concluding paragraphs. There, after commenting on the way in which certain of Rilke's poems represent a 'renunciation of the euphonic seductions of language', a 'denunciation of the ultimate figure, the phonocentric Ear-god on which Rilke, from the start, has wagered the outcome of his entire poetic career, as error and betrayal', de Man cites, as a valediction, these lines from one of Rilke's French texts:

> Masque? Non. Tu es plus plein,
> mensonge, tu as des yeux sonores.

7 References in de Man's texts to authors other than the ones he is directly concerned with are rare enough to prompt some curiosity when they occur. In this case there is an immediate warrant for the allusion: as de Man points out in a footnote (1979, p. 42, n.22), Rilke was familiar with Rodenbach's novel *Bruges-la-morte*. Indeed, turning to the novel, one finds that much of its action takes place in a house on the Quai du Rosaire. There are other resonances of Rodenbach in de Man's work, however, that are not mediated by Rilke, but seem rather to have been effects of Rodenbach's importance as a cultural touchstone, especially for francophone Flemish readers. As a participant in the literary revival associated with the review *La Jeune Belgique* in the 1880s, then as a Belgian Symbolist poet and novelist living in Paris and associated with Mallarmé, Rodenbach represented the possibility of high art that was at once cosmopolitan in its modernity and rooted in the particularities of Flemish history and geography. De Man's articles in *Le Soir* testify to his own youthful investment in this ideal.

8 De Man's insistence on the importance of the trope of prosopopoeia is first formulated in a summary fashion in 'Autobiography as De-Facement': 'Our topic deals with the giving and taking away of faces, with face and deface, *figure*, figuration and disfiguration' (1984, p. 76). On de Man's use of the term 'face', more particularly on his reading of Wordsworth, see Catherine Caruth (1985, pp. 935–48), and Cynthia Chase, 'Giving a Face to a Name' (1986, pp. 82–112).

'At the moment of its fulfillment', de Man comments, 'the figure announces itself by its real name', that is, as *mensonge* (1979, pp. 55–6).

If we had any doubts that here, at the end of the Rilke essay, de Man is belatedly and surreptitiously addressing the suspended carillon, they disappear when, in 'Hypogram and Inscription', he writes, of Hugo's poem, that the 'carillon's relation to time has to be like the relationship of the mind to the senses: it is the sonorous face, the "masque aux yeux sonores" (Rilke) which, by metonymic substitution, links the sound of the bells to the face of the clock' (1986, p. 48). Precisely by dwelling on his own version of the figure Wordsworth calls the 'speaking face' (1984, p. 89), by untying the knot named 'masque aux yeux sonores', a knot by which, in the language of 'Shelley Disfigured', 'knowledge, oblivion and desire hang suspended' (1984, p. 107), de Man has been able to press his understanding of figuration past where it was in the Rilke essay to the explicit and rewarding discussions of reading-as-prosopopoeia that characterize his work after *Allegories of Reading*. In 'Hypogram and Inscription' the gain is registered in two ways: in the critic's embedded signature – the mystery guest signing in as 'a bizarre waking monster', 'l'esprit, ce veilleur fait d'oreilles et d'yeux' – and in the lucidity of the discussion that accompanies this signature, in which de Man articulates the link between the hallucinatory aspect of prosopopoeia and the arbitrary or 'catachretic' imposition of meaning (1986, pp. 48–9).[9]

With this in mind, I want to return to the question of de Man's wartime writings and their relation to his later work, a question that takes on a somewhat different look (or ring) when it is posed against the background I have been sketching in. And I want to link it to another historical question, that of de Man's interest in the work of William Empson. More particularly, I shall offer a speculative account of what de Man found in *Seven Types of Ambiguity* when he set out to introduce Empson's work to the French reading public in 1956.

[9] Appropriately, the critic's signature is inscribed in what de Man calls a 'seduction scene', a scene in which questions of cognition are played out 'in the erotic mode of "mere" sense perception' (1986, p. 49). The scene prompts de Man to append an uncharacteristically La Rochefoucauldian footnote: 'Rather than being a heightened version of sense experience, the erotic is a figure that makes such experience possible. We do not see what we love but we

De Man's discussion of *Seven Types* concentrates on Empson's remarkable seventh chapter, for it is there that he finds both the boldest theoretical formulations and the most intriguing illustrative material. We have already noticed Empson's way of figuring his path through his book: coming to the seventh type, that is, coming to terms with radical ambiguity is like reaching Satan, like Dante's reversing direction at the centre of the earth, like approaching 'the secret places of the Muse'. As the chapter goes on the implications of this playful language are developed into a darker thematics of incest, sacrifice, hanging and gender confusion. For example, glossing the last lines of Keats's 'Ode on Melancholy' – 'His soul shall taste the sadness of her might / And be among her cloudy trophies hung' – Empson writes:

> *Her trophies* (death-pale are they all) are *cloudy* because vague and faint with the intensity and puzzling character of this fusion, or because already dead, or because, though preserved in verse, irrevocable. They are *hung* because sailors on escaping shipwreck hung up votive gifts in gratitude (Horace, III,i.), or because, so far from having escaped, in the swoon of this achievement he has lost life, independence, and even distinction from her. (1953, p. 217)

This swoon into indistinction, into a hanging which is also a fusion with 'Veiled Melancholy', resonates with the lurid figuration I have been tracing in de Man's writing. Moreover, in these pages, the swoon is made to feel like a mode of sacrifice, as, further along, Melancholy is replaced by the figure of Christ depicted, in Empson's account, as a 'monstrous hermaphrodite deity'. The phrase occurs in the course of a discussion of an epigram of Crashaw's improvising on the biblical verse 'Blessed are the paps that thou hast sucked' (Luke 11:27). Crashaw had written:

> Hee'l have his Teat e're long (a bloody one)
> The Mother then must suck the Son,

and Empson comments:

> The ... couplet is 'primitive' enough; a wide variety of sexual perversions can be included in the notion of sucking a long bloody teat which is also a deep wound. The sacrificial idea is aligned with incest, the infantile pleasures, and cannibalism; we contemplate the god with a sort of savage

love in the hope of confirming the illusion that we are indeed seeing anything at all' (1986, p. 53, n.23).

chuckle; he is made to flower, a monstrous hermaphrodite deity, in the glare of the short-circuiting of the human order. (1953, p. 221)

What Empson is tracing is what he calls 'something weird and lurid' in the seventeenth-century mystics' 'apprehension of the sacrificial system', which he will characterize as 'a true sense of the strangeness of the mind's world' (p. 222). The drift of the chapter is towards a reading of George Herbert's 'The Sacrifice', in which the Crucifixion is held up as *the* privileged manifestation of a Type VII ambiguity. Empson moves through the poem slowly, glossing various stanzas, stressing the 'fusion of the love of Christ and the vindictive terrors of the sacrificial idea' (p. 228) until he reaches what he calls 'the final contradiction':

> Lo here I hang, charged with a world of sin
> The greater world of the two ...

as the complete Christ; scapegoat and tragic hero; loved because hated; hated because godlike; freeing from torture because tortured; torturing his torturers because all-merciful; source of all strength to men because by accepting he exaggerates their weakness; and, because outcast, creating the possibility of society. (pp. 232–3)

Left out of this litany of paradoxes is an odd equivocation concerning the gender of the voice that speaks in Herbert's poem, one Empson had noted earlier in his commentary. The refrain with which each stanza ends – 'Was ever grief like mine?' – and whose repetition contributes more than any other verbal device to what Empson calls the poem's 'strange monotony of accent' is a quotation from the Old Testament that, as Empson remarks, 'refers in the original not to the Saviour but to the wicked city of Jerusalem, abandoned by God, and in the hands of her enemies for her sins' (p. 227). Empson's pronouns convey the shift of gender, though he does not comment on it; his remark is made very much in passing. But it is worth our dwelling on for a moment. It is one thing for Jesus on the Cross knowingly to echo the Psalmist – 'My God, my God, why hast thou forsaken me?' (Matt. 27:46; Ps 22:1) – and another, somewhat more puzzling thing for Herbert (or the liturgical tradition he was drawing on) to have the hanging Christ ventriloquize the lament not *for* but *of* a sinful and abandoned woman.[10] Here are

[10] Rosemond Tuve would contest this statement. In 'On Herbert's "The Sacrifice"' (1950) she had taken Empson to task for ignoring the poetic and liturgical traditions that informed both the figuration and the tone of Herbert's poem. Empson had replied briefly in 'George

the verses from Lamentations (1:8–9, 12, 16), first the words of the poet, traditionally taken to be Jeremiah, describing Jerusalem, then the plaint of Jerusalem herself:

> Jerusalem hath grievously sinned; therefore she is removed: all that honoured her despise her, because they have seen her nakedness; yea, she sigheth, and turneth backwards.
>
> Her filthiness is in her skirts; she remembereth not her last end; therefore she came down wonderfully: she had no comforter. O Lord, behold my affliction: for the enemy hath magnified himself.
>
> . . .
>
> Is it nothing to you, all ye that pass by? behold, and see if there be any sorrow like unto my sorrow, which is done unto me, wherewith the Lord hath afflicted me in the day of his fierce anger.
>
> . . .
>
> For these things I weep; mine eye, mine eye runneth down with water, because the comforter that should relieve my soul is far from me: my children are desolate because the enemy prevaileth.

With his usual offhandedness, Empson doesn't quote the passage, merely identifying it as 'a quotation from Jeremiah' (1953, p. 227), which may well have led some readers to the wrong book of the Bible. But Paul de Man, in 1956, seems to have taken the trouble to

Herbert and Miss Tuve' (1950; repr. Empson, 1987a), and Tuve had gone on to extend and further document her disagreements with Empson in the opening section ('"The Sacrifice" and Modern Criticism') of *A Reading of George Herbert* (1952, pp. 19–99). There, in the fuller version, she addresses, among many other passages, Empson's reading of 'Was ever grief like mine?'. Adducing a medieval lyrical genre, the Monologue or Complaint of Christ, she writes:

> One group of these monologues is formed by the *O vos omnes qui transitis* poems. Christ's first words, as in Herbert, will be some variant of these phrases from Lam. i.12, where, of course, they are said by the city of Jerusalem. They are twice repeated, as if by Christ, in the Good Friday and Holy Saturday responsories, and it is liturgical convention, not Herbert, which makes 'any grief like unto my grief' apply to *Christ's* sorrow. . . .
>
> Both in liturgy and in lyric the conventionalizing of a situation, for one thing, fixes certain words and ideas inextricably in a particular frame of reference – as the 'attendite, et videte Si est dolor similis sicut dolor meus' become inescapably Christ's own words, for Herbert or for Handel, so that we must be chary of interpretations based on a lively sense of their being rather said by the city of Jerusalem 'in the original.' . . . Herbert's 'original' was not a verse in Lamentations, but a well-known and effortlessly accepted tradition which made a double reference to both Old and New Testament, with all the resulting implications, absolutely inescapable. (p. 34)

Although her stress is on how 'inextricably' or 'inescapably' certain meanings are fixed within 'a particular frame of reference', Tuve seems to be granting that 'double reference . . . with *all* the resulting implications' is also 'inescapable'; the question seems to come down to whether one's sense of a particular implication was 'lively' or subdued. My claim in the following pages is that there are signs de Man responded to Empson's 'lively' reading of 'Was ever grief like mine?' when he encountered it in 1956.

track down the allusion to Lamentations, to give the appropriate reference and to quote one of the verses, which then figures at the conceptual centre of his praise of *Seven Types*. Empson's 'less serene mind', he writes, was not content with I. A. Richards's 'reassuring notion of art as the reconciliation of opposites', for he understood, de Man goes on, that

> the text does not resolve the conflict, it *names* it. And there is no doubt as to the nature of the conflict. Empson has already prepared us by saying that it is 'at once an indecision and a structure, like the symbol of the Cross', and ends his book on George Herbert's extraordinary poem entitled 'The Sacrifice', a monologue uttered by Christ upon the cross, whose refrain is drawn from the 'Laments of Jeremiah' (1,12) (1983, p. 237).

And de Man copies out the biblical verse ('Is it nothing to you, all ye that pass by', etc.) before going on to assimilate Empson's theory of poetic ambiguity to a Hegelian account of the Crucifixion:

> This conflict can only be resolved by the supreme sacrifice: there is no stronger way of stating the impossibility of an incarnate and happy truth. The ambiguity poetry speaks of is the fundamental one that prevails between the world of the spirit and the world of sentient substance: to ground itself, the spirit must turn itself into sentient substance, but the latter is knowable only in its dissolution into non-being. The spirit cannot coincide with its object and this separation is infinitely sorrowful. (1983, p. 237)

The propriety of de Man's translating Empson into the idiom of Hegel's Unhappy Consciousness has been questioned recently (Eagleton, in Nelson and Grossberg, 1988, pp. 619–31; Norris, 1985a, pp. 70–96), but more interesting than this debate, from my point of view, is the fact that the language de Man chooses to give voice to by introducing the biblical verse into his text is not to be found in either Empson's chapter or Herbert's poem. The voice de Man summons up, in an act of prosopopoeia, is that of an allegorical figure in Lamentations, an afflicted woman called 'Jerusalem', and it echoes that of another afflicted woman, the central character in a poem de Man reviewed in *Le Soir* in 1942, a poem about the ravages of war in Belgium which takes as its epigraph these verses from the gospel of Matthew:

> Then was fulfilled that which was spoken by Jeremy the prophet, saying,
> In Rama was there a voice heard, lamentation, and weeping, and great mourning, Rachel weeping for her children. (Matt. 2:17–18; allusion to Jer. 31:15)

The poem, 'The Massacre of the Innocents', was by Hubert Dubois, a Belgian Catholic poet de Man had earlier written of admiringly.[11] It is, in the words of de Man's review, 'a meditation on the guilt that has led humanity to the dreadful state in which it finds itself for the moment', a meditation structured as a narrative of the abjection and redemption of that figure of Rachel who, the poet claims, is to be found within all his readers as they cry out, with him, against the horrors and injustices of war. Because de Man's review is interested exclusively in the poem's ethical themes and its formal mastery, a brief rehearsal of its plot is necessary, if the connection I would propose, between this piece of wartime journalism and de Man's later writings – on Empson and Herbert as well as, more generally, on the economy of sacrifice – is to make sense.

After an introductory stanza personifying the Rachel 'within each one of us' – representing her drunk with grief, cradling a dead child in her arms and demanding justice of the Lord – her pitying and powerfully accusatory voice is heard until it is interrupted, first by the poet, shocked by the 'impudence' of her address to God, then by a downpour of blood and a chorus of voices from heaven, identified as the dead voices 'of children or of angels':

> Assez crier, assez mentir! Allons, Mère, à genoux!
> Assex fonder sur Dieu ton injuste courroux.
> . . .
> Allons, Rachel, tu sais que si l'on prend tes fils,
> Toi-même les perdais, toi-même en fis jadis
> Périr . . .
> Il pleut leur sang sur toi, coupable mère.

The voices go on to recount why Rachel bears this blood guilt, and the accusation turned against her reads like an indictment of heedless loose-living during the *entre-deux-guerres* period, the sort of indictment familiar to readers of right- and left-wing anti-plutocratic, anti-parliamentarian tracts of the 1920s and 1930s. Rachel has turned men away from virile and arduous pursuits towards 'les biens caressants . . . les biens donnés, / Les biens charnels.' She is responsible, moreover, for their losing the desire to transmit life, to propagate sons – and here the poem takes on a tone of pro-life fervour familiar to us these days but not always present in pre-war denun-

[11] De Man's review of 'Le Massacre des Innocents' appeared in *Le Soir*, 1 September 1942 (repr. de Man, 1988, pp. 265–6). His review of Dubois's earlier work, 'La poésie au bois dormant', appeared on 9 September 1941 (repr. de Man, 1988, pp. 143–4).

ciations of capitalist decadence: Rachel is blamed for denying her vocation as mother, and for counselling young brides not to bear children, hence for murdering the unborn, the very children whose voices are now denouncing her. The voices press Rachel to abandon her hypocritical self-pity and to acknowledge her implication in evil, and this set of stanzas closes with a chilling celebration of war – 'Temps du meurtre, ô temps pur!' – as an unmasking of the death that had been dissimulated during a corrupt peacetime.

Now Rachel can be seen for what she is, not a victim but a drunken Amazon, 'plus sombre que la mort et comme elle, brulante', and abruptly Rachel confronts this image of herself mirrored in a blood-red fiery sky. This is the poem's turning-point, a moment of specular apotheosis that is also Rachel's salvation: the instant she sees herself 'la mort reçoit sa face' and when death recognizes itself it is, says the poet, by the grace of God no longer Death. The poem ends with Rachel transformed, singing of the promise of peace in an apocalyptic landscape still bloodied with war: 'il pleut toujours le sang sur mon temps déchiré; / Mais un jour il sera le ciel en vérité.'[12]

Like 'The Sacrifice' (as Empson read it), this is a poem in which the plaintive and unjustified voice of a fallen woman is redeemed. On the evidence of his seeking out and citing the verses from Lamentations in 1956, I would guess that the memory of his involvement with Dubois's text was stirred when de Man came upon Empson's discussion of Herbert. More interesting than this historical footnote, however, is the fact that none of the various aspects of Dubois's poem that I have been drawing attention to – the figure of the victimized but also guilty mother who is both abjected and recuperated, the ways in which sexual, familial and socio-political elements are blended in the poem's plot and imagery, the fable's

[12] Hubert Dubois (1903–65) was to publish another poem during the Occupation similar in its apocalyptic setting, in its contempt for pre-war decadence and in its voicing of an acceptance of Belgium's defeat: *Le Chant dans les ruines* (1944). I have been unable to discover whether or not Dubois was prosecuted for collaboration, although reviews of his works in the 1950s suggest that he may have been. One critic, reviewing his career, after referring to 'La poésie au bois dormant', writes of him: 'Que cette prescience trop lucide se soit ensuite égarée dans le temporel, sous la poussée d'événements extérieurs, importe peu sur le plan supérieur où nous entendons à présent juger une œuvre qui a finalement retrouvé son vrai sens. . . . C'est que nous avons dépassé, par une étrange purification, le massacre et les ruines' (André Gascht, 1953, pp. 496–7). The last sentence alludes discreetly to Dubois's wartime publications, titles that are sometimes included in, sometimes omitted from his post-war bibliographies. (My thanks to Ortwin de Graef, Tom Keenan and Chantal Kesteloot for their help in locating copies of Dubois's poems and of writings about him.)

turning on a scene of specular reversal – had, in 1942, found its way into de Man's review of 'Le Massacre des Innocents'. Neither the lurid setting nor the particular actions of Rachel and her accusers is commented on; instead, de Man insists on reading the poem as a rigorous movement of thought, a 'logical reflection' aimed at bringing out 'principles and abstract tendencies'. The fundamental element of Dubois's poetics, de Man claims, is 'the word with its rational content'; the miracle of the poem – and de Man is unstinting in his praise – is that Dubois can make his thought come alive 'without recourse to any of the standard poetic artifices – allegory, symbol or metaphor', relying rather on 'that most difficult of forms, the direct expression of his thought'. And that thought is, as de Man summarizes it, comprehensive and generous in its elevation, ethical in its content:

> Complaint and lamentation cannot be justified, even in a situation as pitiable as this. For all that is happening now is not the blind and pitiless action of destiny, but the consequences of a fault, of an accumulation of moral faults committed down through the ages. The utility of such an ordeal is to oblige people to become conscious of this guilt, to make the masses see that they have acted badly. Consequently, the more severe the punishment, the greater the hope of at last witnessing the growth of those true values which should allow life to be lived harmoniously, in the place of the false facilities which have led to this catastrophe. (1988, p. 266)

This is powerfully wishful writing, as any formulation of the 'utility' of sacrifice, the salutary or expiatory or compensatory value of suffering, is bound to be. Equally wishful, I believe – and obscurely related to the wish for sacrifice to serve some purpose – is de Man's odd insistence on the rational, direct, non-figurative nature of Dubois's poetic language. In a closed sacrificial economy, there would be no leftovers, no pains unaccounted for, nothing that couldn't be subsumed under a governing aim; in the closed economy of the text of reason, the sort of text de Man emphatically wants Dubois's to be, the 'standard poetic artifices – allegory, symbol or metaphor', with the possibilities for ambiguity or equivocation attendant on their use, must also be ruled out. And it is just these questions – of sacrifice, of figurative language, of a lurid thematics – that surface again when de Man reads Empson, and which are there taken up in a significantly different way.

But there is something else missing from de Man's discussion of Dubois's poem, and missing, so far, from our own consideration of it:

the word 'Jew'. Like other readers of de Man's writings for *Le Soir*, when I first came across the headline on the *Chronique littéraire* for 1 September 1942, 'Le Massacre des Innocents', I read on to see if it represented the sort of subversive gesture I had occasionally found elsewhere in de Man's articles. I knew that the deportation of Belgian Jews had begun in the summer of 1942 (I subsequently learned that raids resulting in mass arrests had taken place in Antwerp in mid-August); it seemed possible that de Man's choosing to review this particular poem at that particular time was a surreptitious act of protest and solidarity, an encoded naming of the crime he saw taking place around him. Other readers have entertained that possibility,[13] but I found this hoped-for interpretation didn't survive my reading of the article or, later, of Dubois's poem. Both poem and review, although each acknowledges the horrors of wartime Belgium, shift the responsibility for those horrors away from the Nazi occupiers – in Dubois's case, onto the pre-war sinfulness Rachel is made to represent; in de Man's, onto a more diffusely characterized 'accumulation of moral faults committed down through the ages' or 'repeated crimes against the human person'. Neither Dubois nor de Man appears to make any attempt, coded or not, to differentiate the degrees of suffering felt by various elements of the population, unless the simple title of each text, 'The Massacre of the Innocents', could be counted on to be read with such a message in mind. I am not convinced it could and find both poem and review disconcerting to read. If either is in any way about the Belgian Jews, it would seem to testify to a blank disregard for what was happening to them in 1942, or – if the concern was there but forced to dissimulate itself – to what from our current perspective looks like astonishingly bad timing.

Without seeking to soften this judgement of de Man's review of Dubois, it is still possible to pursue the question of how that article may have come to take the form it did. I would approach it by focusing on what I noted had been excluded from de Man's discussion of the poem – call it, emblematically, Rachel, in her three aspects: Rachel as Jew (that is, as possibly giving voice to the plight of the Belgian Jews in 1942), Rachel as *coupable mère* (that is, as

[13] Shoshana Felman, for example, in 'Paul de Man's Silence' (1989), argues for the 'latent resistance connotation' of the poem and of de Man's review of it (pp. 714–15). That seems mistaken. Other readings of Felman's, however, in particular her use of de Man's discussion of Rousseau's *Confessions* to illuminate his own refusal to speak of his wartime activities (pp. 729–34), strike me as persuasive and valuable contributions to the current debates.

embodying a complex of feelings about mothers and sons, and the real and fantasmatic exchanges between them), and Rachel as metaphor (as the central figure of Dubois's poem, standing in turn for the uncomprehending, pitying reaction to war, the self-pity of its victims, the self-indulgence of the pre-war democracies, Death, Hope, and so on). It is very unlikely that de Man, in 1942, could have read 'Le Massacre des Innocents' without both experiencing and bracing himself against what he would later call 'the seductive powers of identification' (1979, p. ix), in this case the pull of Rachel, the temptation to a pitying and self-pitying, thoroughly ambivalent act of identification with a victimized woman. That drama of seduction and resistance would be played out in silence: the connotative resonance of Dubois's figurative language, along with its possible bearing on the situation of the Jews, would go unrecognized and not appear in the text, suppressed along with the figure of the guilty mother. Instead, language would be found to stave off that temptation, first by analysing the poem as a 'logical reflection', then in the form of a final, idealizing tribute to Dubois:

> The man capable of sublimating the suffering that daily wrenches humanity at war, capable of seeing, despite an immense pity, that this pain is salutary because it expiates repeated crimes against the human person, exhibits that fundamental superiority of being that is proper to all true artistic talent. (1988, p. 266)

That sentence may strike the ear now as both hyperbolic in its celebration of the artist's superiority and callous in its willed sublimation of suffering; but it is worth noting that it is also an act of fervid identification. We can take it as a reminder of the difficulty of resisting one sort of identification without falling into another. This is by no means Paul de Man's problem alone, but it is very much a problem he turned his mind to thereafter. His post-war writing can be thought of as an extended study of the stakes and the mechanisms of identification, which is another way of saying that the puzzling knot that binds uses of figurative language to specular structures and to gestures of sacrifice would explicitly occupy his attention.[14]

One can see signs of this in de Man's writing immediately after the

[14] On the appearance of the concepts (and words) *renunciation*, *sacrifice*, *temptation*, *seduction*, and *identification* in de Man's writings, see Minae Mizumura (1985).

war. Notions like that of the utility of sacrifice, the compensatory rewards of suffering – notions that governed his reading of 'Le Massacre des Innocents' – have disappeared from articles like 'The Dead-End of Formalist Criticism'. There, Empson's choice of Herbert's poem as his climactic example is read not as a transcendent reconciliation of the conflicts he had been exploring but as a demonstration of the impossibility of reconciliation, hence of the delusory nature of those poetics de Man labels 'salvational'. De Man's language has its own pathos, but his interest in sacrifice is less in its pathos than in its structure and dynamics: 'sacrifice' is read as a figure of incommensurability, a thematic gesture at a linguistic problem that won't go away. That's why the first sentence of de Man's gloss on Herbert's poem – 'This conflict can be resolved only by the supreme sacrifice' – is followed immediately by one shifting the emphasis away from any conceivable resolution: 'there is no stronger way of stating the impossibility of an incarnate and happy truth' (1983, p. 237). If we were to ask why these two atheists, Empson and de Man, should meet at the foot of the Cross, de Man would say that they were led there not in the imitation of Christ but through their shared interest in radical linguistic ambiguity, in the sort of contradiction that could be thought of, in Empson's words, as 'at once an indecision and a structure, like the symbol of the Cross'. An indecision and a structure – that is, now taking up de Man's idiom, an impasse, or dead end, or aporia, a moment of suspension or, in the lurid thematics I have been tracing, a specular encounter with a hanging figure.

A hanging 'figure'? Or a hanging woman? The figure on the Cross is a man, isn't he? We have seen that in Herbert's poem the answer to that is yes and no. The plangent refrain of the poem is, equivocally, that of Christ and Jerusalem. And I have been suggesting that the equivocation is a productive one, an element in the sort of ambiguity both Empson and de Man are concerned with. A final glance at the divergence of Empson's path and de Man's after their imaginary meeting in 1956 should bear this out.

Empson spent a great deal of wit and energy, most memorably in *Milton's God* (1961), but throughout his post-war writings, inveighing against what he called 'neo-Christian lit. crit.', a complicity – sometimes he made it seem like a conspiracy – of theologians and close-readers to foster piety and subservience to a system of unnatural values centred on God the Father, whom Empson liked to call 'the torture monster'.[15] His chief objection to this god was that he took 'satisfaction' – not just satisfaction in the acknowledgement of a redeemed debt, but the sensual satisfaction of a sadist – in the crucifixion of his son, thus setting an example of finding delight in human suffering that, Empson thought, had perverted Western behaviour for two millennia. This stance would seem to have obliged him to reconsider his discussion of 'The Sacrifice', which he did, in 1950 and again in 1963, chiefly in response to Rosemond Tuve's criticisms. Characteristically, he both does and does not recant:

> I put 'The Sacrifice' last of the examples in my book, to stand for the most extreme kind of ambiguity, because it presents Jesus as at the same time forgiving his torturers and condemning them to eternal torture. It strikes me now that my attitude was what I have come to call 'neo-Christian'; happy to find such an extravagant specimen, I slapped the author on the back and egged him on to be even nastier ... Rather to my surprise, Miss Tuve agreed that the poem carries the major ambiguity, which was traditional and noble; after rejecting most of my illustrations, she seemed disposed to treat me as a pagan stumbling towards the light. Clearer now about what the light illumines, I am keen to stumble away from it. (1987a, p. 257)

There was a time when Empson could describe 'what the light illumines', his primal scene of Christianity, in language that captured the disorientations – of feeling and thought – that his encounter with radical contradiction had provoked:

> The sacrificial idea is aligned with incest, the infantile pleasures, and cannibalism; we contemplate the god with a sort of savage chuckle; he is made to flower, a monstrous hermaphrodite deity, in the glare of the short-circuiting of the human order. (1953, p. 221)

By the 1950s, this flashing vision had been discarded, the 'monstrous hermaphrodite deity' replaced by 'the torture monster', a more comprehensible figure of the Law as a sadistic father engaged in tormenting an innocent son. Empson has stabilized the vacillation implicit in the earlier scene – a vacillation of position and gender – that had made the scene adequate to the bewildering nature of the linguistic problem he was engaging. Of the 'hermaphrodite deity' only a trace remains in the later writings. It occurs in an

[15] Empson's quarrel with Christianity is usefully summarized by John Haffenden in his introduction to a posthumously published collection of articles (Empson, 1987a, pp. 21–40).

unpublished piece ('The Satisfaction of the Father' (*c.* 1972)), in the course of a summary of Thomas Aquinas' discussion of the Crucifixion: 'Aquinas plainly knew', writes Empson, 'that the most intimate place of the religion was a horrible one' (1987a, p. 624), a sentence in which we can hear a flickering acknowledgement of what it was that had earlier led Empson to associate radical ambiguity not only with sacrifice, but also with Satan and with 'the secret places of the Muse'.

I have quoted enough of Paul de Man's post-war writings to suggest that his understanding of sacrifice took a different turn from Empson's, a turn that precluded any stabilization of the concept. Consider, as a final example, the last pages of 'Wordsworth and the Victorians' (1984, pp. 88–92) which contain, coincidentally, another endorsement of Empson's work. This time de Man cites 'Sense in the Prelude',[16] the 'one essay [that] stands out from the fundamentally harmonious consensus that unites, for all their apparent disagreement, all contemporary writers on Wordsworth'. Specifically what de Man admires is Empson's arguing that if one traces Wordsworth's uses of the word *sense* one discovers that 'the emerging confusion cannot be reduced to any known model of trope that would control an identifiable semantic field'; 'it is impossible', de Man concludes, 'to make sense out of Wordsworth's sense'. As a reader capable of sophisticated rhetorical analysis, Empson is then compared to Wordsworth himself who, in one of his Prefaces, had produced an analysis of the word *hangs* equally astute but with absolutely opposite results: *hangs*, de Man notes, accurately, is 'by Wordsworth's own avowal, *the* exemplary metaphor for metaphor, for figuration in general', hence precisely for the possibility of making sense.

Having thus positioned *hangs* and *sense* at opposite poles, de Man now introduces a key word of his own, *face*, a term that, as we have seen, has been implicit in his thinking from the earliest written chapter of *Allegories of Reading* to his latest texts on prosopopoeia:

> Masque? Non. Tu es plus plein,
> mensonge, tu as des yeux sonores. (1979, p. 56)

The force of de Man's reading of 'face' in *The Prelude* is developed out of his understanding of the tensions between the cognitive and

[16] Originally published in *Kenyon Review* 13 (spring 1951), pp. 285–302, then as chapter 14 of *The Structure of Complex Words* (Empson, 1951, pp. 289–305).

performative aspects of language, tensions which are both stated and enigmatically enacted in the climactic sentence of his essay: 'How are we to reconcile the *meaning* of face, with its promise of sense and of filial preservation, with its *function* as the relentless undoer of its own claims?' In 'Lurid Figures' I discussed the strangeness of this sentence, pointing out the way its language draws at once on the lines of Wordsworth's de Man was analysing – the Blessed Babe passage – and on Yeats's rhetorical (or maybe *not* so rhetorical) question 'How can we know the dancer from the dance?' (Waters and Godzich, 1989, pp. 98–9).

But the sentence can also be juxtaposed instructively with some of the language of *Allegories of Reading* I cited earlier; for example, with de Man's characterization of 'Quai du Rosaire' as combining 'the audacity of paradox with a promise of beauty or even . . . of sensuous gratification on the far side of the grave' (1979, p. 43). The two promises (of 'sense and filial preservation', and of 'sensuous gratification beyond the grave') resemble one another, but we can note a telling difference in tone between the earlier lugubrious account of 'Quai du Rosaire''s imagery as 'seductive but funereal' and the more difficult language and explicit violence with which the facing-off in Wordsworth is described.

Or we might align this allegorizing of meaning-and-function as mother-and-child with the pages on the *Social Contract* with which we began: 'There can be no text without grammar: the logic of grammar generates texts only in the absence of referential meaning, but every text [read: mother] generates a referent [read: child] that subverts the grammatical principle to which it owed its constitution [read: relentlessly undoes its own claims].'

In each of these passages – from 'Wordsworth and the Victorians' and from 'Promises (*Social Contract*)', as in his later writing generally – the language of Demanian theory coexists in a state of high tension with the obsessive figuration I have been following. Positioning himself so as to feel the force of that tension – as if acknowledging that he could occupy no other position – was clearly productive for de Man. Its value to him can be read obliquely out of the last paragraph of the Wordsworth essay:

[O]ne can find, in Wordsworth's text, lexical continuities which are perfectly coherent; despite the somewhat ominous overtones of the literal predicament it invokes, the word 'hangs' is a case in point. Other words, such as 'sense' in Empson's essay, lead instead to near-total chaos. Somewhere in between, at the interface of these contradictory directions, words such as 'face' can be said to embody this very incompatibility. (1984, p. 92)

To embody an incompatibility: the phrase resonates with de Man's praise of Empson, years earlier, for having so forcefully demonstrated that what poetry was about was 'the impossibility of an incarnate and happy truth'. The difficulty and the interest of de Man's later work is in its idiosyncratic refinement of a theory and pathos of sacrifice: the 'incarnation' or 'embodiment' his later texts invoke is not that of a Christian god-in-man or of a Hegelian spirit-in-substance but of 'incompatibility' or 'incommensurability' in words. The reception of de Man's work suggests that such an understanding of sacrifice – and the strange combination of control and disorientation it exacts from its subject – may be considerably harder to take in than the sustaining paradoxes of theology.

CHAPTER 8

Fool and 'Pharmakon'

William Righter

'Ambiguity', like 'irony', has so long been a common instrument of modern criticism that its use may well have sunk into the totally routinized. Yet its capacity to find new forms of defamiliarization, to resurface through other conceptual languages such as the 'polysemy' of Barthes or Derrida, may show the ease with which certain underlying preoccupations about the nature of language may be naturalized in conceptual schemes of different sorts, with wider implications of quite different kinds. It is the echo of this naturalization, and what it tells us about the theoretical structure that uses it, that may help measure the force of such theories themselves, show something of their degree of reach, and their illumination of the richness and congestion of meaning to which they address themselves. For the exploration of the possibilities and limits of the multiple senses of 'complex words' has seemed part of our understanding of language in general, but most especially of the language of literature where that complexity seems a constitutive principle. And in an adjacent form of discourse Derrida sees something equally constitutive in the ambiguity that arises through translation and marks what he calls 'the very passage into philosophy'.

What happens when one tries to measure the passage by way of translation, with all of the multiple senses such a passage may contain – including the translation by which we express our understanding of a literary work – or the analogous path by which the exploration of the richness of language may be found in the cultural depth of a key word? If I am concerned here with two kinds of investigation, the analogy may have some use in giving intelligible dimensions to an enduring problem in critical thought. And a point of departure can be found in the difference between Empson's treatment of ambiguity in *Seven Types* and the effort to ransack fully the cultural matrix of more open contexts that characterizes *Complex Words*. For

Empson's treatment of the Shakespearian 'fool' goes beyond what a typological analysis can do and talk of types of equation tends to vanish in practice. For any strict application of this analytic mode will always have the somewhat reductive effect that its characteristic feature is distinctive boundaries. To set up a model of the relations between types would in turn imply a falsifying map that the open-ended procedures of the later book had to redraw, in following through to the end the fullness that a key word or concept in its multiple contexts can reveal, and doing so with respect to a great work where the resonance can be most grandly and consequentially felt.

Certainly one feature of this change in his own method is registered in the distinction between those meanings which are imposed by the immediate context – difficult as the criteria for establishing this may be – from 'the compacted doctrine', where the word itself 'seems to put the doctrine into our minds'. It is the difference between the variables that context may determine, and the further variables that lie within the word itself, like 'traces', one might say, of their many commitments. These words seem to carry what Empson calls 'equations' as an internal relation. These equations are certainly formulated in terms of another typology, but rather than the typology being the framework through which the possibilities of complex words are studied, it is, as he says, something devised after the case studies, so he is 'more sure of the general literary account than I am of the classifying fitted onto it' (1951, p. 74). In short, the investigation preceded the rationalization and ordering of its components. One effect of this *post facto* approach to the more general levels of argument is to suggest an almost arbitrary imposition of pattern. It suggests that the classification is given more as a helpful ground plan than as an operative principle. And certainly the relations between the types play no active part in the ways in which the equations themselves evolve, but are mentioned as reference points, rather in passing. One will invoke references as an aspect of the way in which they might illuminate context, rather than as interrelated features of a system. This seems partly an awkwardness which follows from an attempted resemblance to the model of *Seven Types*, when in fact the similarity is superficial.

An awkwardness also attaches to the notion of equations themselves. Here a mathematical, and sometimes almost mechanistic way of explaining the relation of a referent to its complex properties becomes an artifice most honoured in the omission. The two elements taken together seem like an experiment in scientific description which is evoked but seldom applied. And the same may apply to the nagging presence of I. A. Richards's distinction between cognitive and emotive language which looms so large in the more theoretical chapters. These somewhat misleading pieces of theoretical apparatus make it look as if the interest in the work is back to front, while the most important aspects of theory arise from the case studies where the implications of the particular can unfold. I do not suggest that this is akin to de Man's notion about critical blindness to one's presuppositions, but it does seem an example of the mistaken impression often given by attempting to formalize one's procedure in a counter-productive way.

The discussion of 'fool' is set naturally in historical context, and in the paradoxes that arise directly from it.

> 'This fellow's wise enough to play the fool, and to do that well requires a kind of wit' (*Twelfth Night* III . i . 67). The conception had to be built up gradually, both in his own mind and for his audience, before he got to the terrific uses of it in *Lear*. On the other hand the clown who bases his effects on 'you are a fool too' was certainly not a romantic invention of Shakespeare's ... To make the characters theorise about the clown was to insist that he was part of the play. This may also explain why Shakespeare tends increasingly to say *fool* rather than *clown*; the stage comedian was called a *clown* but the court clown was called a *fool*, and Shakespeare wanted to insist that he was representing a court fool not letting loose a clown on his stage. According to the N.E.D., something important had happened to the word just before the Elizabethans took it over; the earliest affectionate use for a dependent is dated 1530 and the earliest use for a mere imbecile is 1540. Now the introduction of these two further meanings into the word was necessary to complete it as an instrument. (1951, pp. 114–15)

It becomes an instrument in its subtle power to join opposites, to catch both the fusion and the distinction in these variants of wisdom and folly. The power implicit in its fully conscious use was created both from the ambiguity that Erasmus had already explored, and the steadily complicating uses that the *NED* records, in which the colloquial, courtly, legalistic and theatrical streams of use combine unevenly, and where the predominant sense shifts in the historical perspective. The effect of mapping this sequence of accumulating uses onto a non-English tradition is to develop a permutation system in which different uses combine, but selectively; and the reservoir of possible meanings is sufficiently present to enable us to ask which of a large number of possible meanings is predominant in any one case. Does 'fool' mean idiot, or clown or object of endearment? Is it used derisively or affectionately? The narrowly exclusive sense would hardly ring true in most of the Shakespearian instances, and the context can throw multiple aspects of the primary, secondary and 'trace' elements of the meaning into a variety of reliefs. The 'adventurous stage' of trying 'to codify the process of combination' (1951, p. 39) which relates the supposed 'head sense' to the 'immediate context' (p. 46) gives rise to the puzzles of which Empson is so immediately aware: both 'head sense' and force of context are impossible to state with any certainty in a clearly codifiable form for any occasion of a complex use.

The equation system in *Complex Words* goes some way towards establishing a relational pattern among the possible meanings, which can establish a degree of primary force in context which subsumes those pressures generated by the possibility of alternative or even quite opposed senses. There may in this be a superficial resemblance to the structuralist *combinatoire*, in which an analytic model is created for the relational functions within narrative or linguistic structures. However, the structuralist aim is at a higher level of generality, and the Empsonian equations do little more than condense a description into notational form. Rather than an analytic instrument they are a form of shorthand which aims at clarity through tightening the terms of the description by the very effect of numbering types. If one asks whether a certain use really fits under type II or type III one may be largely engaged in an effort to pin down the variables of context to define other variables so that they can be seen in terms of each other. The uses of 'fool' fit all types of equation by turn, and to some extent the confusion created by somewhat arbitrary classifications is acknowledged (1951, p. 117). But the seductions of this urge to system do little more than embroider some peripheral nuisance. The genius of Empson lies at least partly in his capacity to move from one context to another with a keen awareness of how they reflect and qualify each other. The combinations are not so much codified as lovingly and ruthlessly explored, with an eye to what takes flight and eludes as well as to the bedrock. And perhaps the very notion of open-ended permutation gives to any thought of system that very feeling of the mind in movement, travelling the circuits of possibility.

I have made two criticisms of the equation system itself. One is that the determinants of the particular uses are so elusive that 'head' and subordinate senses cannot be reliably fixed upon to provide a relational system that is both convincing and stable. The drawing in of another comparison or the seeing of another aspect of context would shift the combination like a kaleidoscope. And Empson's sensitivity to this comes out pervasively in the qualified language through which the system is operated: 'it seems to me', 'I suppose', 'we may suppose', 'I suppose it would be fussy to', 'not always in *quite* the same way'. This tentativeness is attractive insofar as it represents an exploratory, 'trying out' habit of mind which is then partially cancelled by the rigours of Empson's notational system. And this reflects the second criticism: once the pattern of accumulated meaning is translated into system-theoretical terms, those terms do not communicate anything of interest additional to the input. So the comment 'Such a twist of thought seems a fair case for the question-mark sign: $3c + ?2 = 1a - .1\pounds 1$' leaves the question mark buried in a formula that is only useful as part of a further explanation which will need to take a different form. Empson's notational codes have something of a Rube Goldberg quality, although they are perhaps not much more preposterous than Lévi-Strauss's efforts in the same line: they are merely abbreviations that are useless until decoded and even then add nothing to the argument.

With 'fool' the system is not worked very hard, and the schematic layout of the range of possible meanings for the Shakespearian repertoire of uses (1951, pp. 111–12) may at least have the value of a kind of display in which the elements to be combined can be spread out and seen in a sequence. This represents a development which is a series of qualifications of one sense by another. And the altering or piling up of combinations with the qualifications implied gives the ground of the possible 'movements of mind'. It is from the Erasmian tradition of praising folly that arises the paradox on which variations can be played. Upon this base the simple senses inherited from the older tradition may push against the paradox and insinuate the substitutions which multiply the variants. And part of the process of multiplication is created through the drama itself, in a growing audience awareness, where for example 'a new head sense could be established temporarily as part of the "style" of the play'. If common or legal usage is the source of a meaning, it is dramatic context that not only enables the deliberate transmutation of one sense of 'fool' into another, but places the fool upon the stage to comment. Action's fool is reflection's man of wisdom. And mixed folly and wisdom from the same source complicates the awareness of possible senses supposedly 'there' in the word.

In his normal practice Empson's method tries to determine which of the meanings from the original repertoire is primary (sometimes this is the 'head sense' but not necessarily), spelling out the multiple accretions to it, while at the same time selecting out those critical differentiae and perhaps even marginal aspects of the usage that give it its peculiar distinction and flavour. 'Clown' is on the path that leads from affectionate dependence and imbecility to 'fool', part of the development which leads towards the completed instrument. Yet judgement is all, and Empson's procedure moves from describing the accretion of complex meanings to selecting the prominent and those whose interest reaches farther. There is a double movement of mind – in this case Empson's own – between the growth of possibility of meaning through complexity, and the selective cutting across or breaking down of that complex amalgam of meaning. Both historically and procedurally it is as if synthesis preceded analysis. For analysis to take effect the variables must be assembled; this resembles a linguistic natural history which records and classifies the elements of a complex whole. Then one can begin to pull apart in various ways, discriminate according to a variety of interests and principles, or senses of relevance. The movement is from a general picture – itself carefully constructed – to an aspect with a more localized focus, which catches the figural force of important intersection points within the repertoire.

The problem of this figural force comes through the recognition that any one use can become a metaphor for any other, so that the simple substitutions of 'fool' and 'clown' create in the first instance a figurative expansion; for if you reflect about a foolish man that he is like a clown 'the effect is then that you call him a clown metaphorically'. The move from particular to general can be doubled, as in what he calls 'Mutual Metaphor', and the process of figuration seems to have no limit. But the choice between meanings that this opens to us must be determined by another principle, even if an unstable one. Even the movement in a single direction seems to push the meaning open in ways that otherwise must be shaped and contained. Consider the way in which one metaphoric movement presses against the Erasmian doctrine:

If then a Shakesperean use of *fool* is not a metaphor from the clown, I class it as a rather generalised memory of the Erasmus doctrine; but if it is, as most of them are, I maintain that it brings in the darker and more tragic picture that he got from his madmen. The two structures need not conflict, though they seem normally to be independent; and I think that *The Merchant of Venice*, which has a good deal of medieval feeling in its central allegory, gives a rather special case of a combination of the two. The negro prince represents pagan splendour and the lust of the eye; he chooses the gold casket, and finds only death in it, but nobody calls him a fool. The admittedly undeserving suitor who gives and hazards all he has (and all his friend has too) is apparently to stand for the triumph of the humble Christian. Only the conventional man between them, who chooses reasonable silver and is too much of a gentleman to ask for more than he deserves, is met by a picture of an idiot and a schedule calling him a Fool. Erasmus would no doubt have liked the thing as a whole, but I doubt whether he would have rubbed the idiot in so firmly. And what the allegory meant to Shakespeare was probably something rather different from the Christian interpretation; I think it was that you ought to accept the realities of life courageously even if rather unscrupulously, and not try to gloss over its contradictions and the depths that lie under your feet. I do not know how to symbolise a direct fusion of the two structures. (1951, p. 124)

I suppose the failure to symbolize represents a limitation of the equation system. But it also seems to indicate some larger conceptual difficulty. The relating of a 'darker and more tragic picture' to allegory opposed the disorderly open-endedness of metaphor to the 'generalised memory', which contains both traditional narrative forms and ordering conventions. So, what 'the allegory meant to Shakespeare' may be distanced from a Christian interpretation; yet there is something disturbing and unresolved about placing the Fool at the heart of the reasonable life. It is as if the allegory proposed a series of relations, an order of values. Yet that order contains an element that runs amok, that refuses to keep in its place, and in the end is not assimilable into the allegory. And this parallels the problem of the two structures.

If Empson fails to find a way of representing the disturbing or subversive force in this otherwise rather schematic and self-contained allegorical scene, the problem is more complex in *King Lear*. For if here 'Fool' suggests the uncontrolled element in an ordered scheme, in *Lear* it presses against the very uncertainty of order. Certainly the source of disorder is there: 'it is the Fool who causes the beginning of the storm against Lear' (1951, p. 129). The offence against Goneril is against that newly established and conventional order whose evil we will soon know. But he is the catalyst to a chain of disturbing consequences: fool offends; gentleman chides; Lear strikes; Goneril responds in the name of her own established rule and interest.

Of course the role of 'fool' in the uncertain order of *Lear* is developed by way of Empson's rejection, often implicit to the point of being taken for granted, of any overall allegorizing or Christianizing view of the play. This puts a number of possible determinations quite aside, and key terms lack that solidity and certainty of placing themselves that an allegorical scheme might have given. They lose precision of outline partly through the abandonment of any conceptual order which might lend itself to allegory. This relative indeterminacy may also help to account for a more open explanatory structure in the essay, largely abandoning the equation and permutation systems in order to engage with the colouration of that 'darker and more tragic picture' which derives from certain dimensions of 'fool'. The description of that colouration takes two general forms. One is an index of the degree to which the relation of oneself to one's world has gone awry: 'the natural fool of fortune' or playing 'fool to sorrow'. This is something of a rag-bag of uses for which Empson attempts no typology or precise genealogy. The family resemblance draws on the way in which a moment can reveal a gap or discrepancy; or an ironic perception of the action leads to the substitution of 'fool' for whatever the normal identity of a character might have been. The variety of effect is startling but somehow does not push the limits of resemblance: Edgar in disguise, Cordelia hanged, Kent in the stocks; and of course Lear himself, both identified by the Fool as 'fool', and in the end truly one – 'he is genuinely a Fool now and has a right to the title' (1951, p. 145). In what is called a 'universal accusation of folly' to become a fool is to deny or lose oneself, or step into something alien, an abyss. But there is also a normative element in it, a black alternative condition which draws on disparate meanings that join worthlessness to madness. Beyond this there may be worse, as the Fool implies to Lear: 'I would rather be anything than a fool, and yet I would not be thee.'

Much of the argument moves between alternative explanations of how this intricate reflexivity affects both particular uses and the 'head sense'. But the applications within a play are, of course, performed by its characters. In this perhaps the Fool may have a privileged role in his incarnation of the multiple displacements that calling others 'fool' implies. But the sense of any such use depends upon the understanding of its source, and, with the characters in a play, the construction of some form of hypothetical psychology, some general understanding of what their words and actions mean at any one point in the play. But there is also a fuller sense of what they would be like, if one could really have a comprehensive view, even if we see it only in fragments through the dramatic action. The implied whole is a construct, even more than the particular dramatic moment. And this differs for various readers for an obvious mixture of personal and historical reasons. Of course one might manage to see Lear much as Bradley, or much as Orwell (or Wilson Knight, or Jan Kott, etc.) saw him. But the 'much as' indicates that such sharing is qualified, if always imaginable. That a bent of mind, or feel for one's own contemporaneity, both shapes one's imagining and can be modified and manipulated, goes without saying. As does the possibility of self-deception and the counter-productive: 'The determination of Bradley to bring out the best in the good characters sometimes makes his judgements rather brutal, oddly enough' (1951, p. 131). This is also an example of trying to overdetermine and limit the possibilities, with an indication of its attendant cost.

So one dimension of the understanding of 'fool' works through the understanding of persons, but in a way which draws on dramatic circumstance, which makes the use more complex than Empson's 'machinery' can easily handle. For the use is qualified by the presumed understanding by the speaker of his object, a secondary and wider understanding of both speaker and reference, as well as the change of meaning as the action unfolds. That is, it might not only mean something rather different at the end of the play from what it meant at the beginning, but have gone through some fairly drastic transformations. But the single case can pose different kinds of variables. When Lear says of Cordelia, 'And my poor fool is hanged' the reading depends not only on the historical resources on which Shakespeare might have drawn, but presumptions about Lear's state of mind and present understanding, the alteration of Cordelia's fortunes, the relations of innocence, folly, madness and endearment – to pick only the main lines of possible significance. The most primitive grasp is a meta-fiction built on a fiction of Lear, trying to overcome its intrinsic opacity. And this construction no doubt requires the corresponding invention of an audience which will be a sounding-board for the diversity of this process. Here 'fool' becomes the focal point where understanding and confusion meet – relation and disorder.

While others are of great interest, there are two aspects of Empson's method that have consequences that I wish to isolate. One is that procedure through the invention of persons and their invention of each other that I have tried so briefly to describe. The other lies in seeing the metaphor from the 'fool' stretched to its farthest implications:

> The foolish Lear can compare the storm and the heavens to himself, and the stock metaphor from the clown and the lunatic can be extended to include the cosmos. Such is the impression from a literal reading, I think, and critics have either evaded it or hailed it as being anti-Christian. But, if you take it as simply a result of working out the key metaphor as far as it would go, you need not expect it to have a clear-cut theological conclusion; the problem for the dramatist was rather to keep such a thing at bay. The effect of the false renunciation is that Lear has made a fool of himself on the most cosmic and appalling scale possible. (1951, p. 155)

Here the use of dramatic form works in another way, to qualify and ironize metaphysical commitment. How specific this is to Shakespeare is unclear, and certainly the balance of effect in other dramatists is not entirely the same. There is a formal theological conclusion to Marlowe's *Dr Faustus*, yet it is rich in ambiguity and a strange openness strains against the allegorical, while the splendid carnival of punishments at the end of Jonson's *Volpone* leaves no doubt about the rigour of moral conviction. Perhaps this is one reason why, for all his brilliance, there is a residue of ugliness in Jonson which appears precisely in this literal-mindedness. Even at Shakespeare's crankiest (Empson is quite straightforward on the streak of sexual revulsion) a world is created which is not quite reducible to a hard-nosed moralizing stance. This raises the question of whether or not the Empsonian pursuit of metaphor would work as well in a world of more fixed and tidy views. (In *Complex Words* Pope is the case where the brilliant deployment of uses is not played out in a metaphorically extended way.)

In 'working out the key metaphor as far as it would go' Empson at least partly indicates that Shakespeare has used it at fullest possible stretch, that Lear has appeared as somehow the ultimate fool, which combines the notion of the most extreme case with that of the word as providing a focus for the widest possible range of meaning. Somehow they do not cancel each other out, although accretion may change its aspect as emphasis, selection and modification work within it. In this case 'as far as it would go' also suggests completeness, that all the possible resources have been ransacked, and that they are somehow all present in the supreme 'fool'. Yet this suggests an essentialism that is wholly avoided. Various criteria for the determination of 'as far as' are hinted or implied: extreme extension, saturation, completeness, etc., but no essential yardstick. What Empson's analysis chiefly conveys is the inexhaustibility of metaphor. And there is no fixed measure.

The inexhaustible possibilities of 'as far as' of course would not imply that some meanings are not suspect and that their marginality cannot be made clear. Empson rather shies away from the notion of the Holy Fool with its transcendental trappings, as he does from anything which might give the play too well defined a metaphysical force. The various *obiter dicta* with which the essay ends have a methodological diffidence which would seem to put such a force rather outside the reach of his own way of seeing, even if something is there that must be acknowledged: 'by being such a complete fool Lear may become in some mystical way superlatively wise and holy. It seems hard to deny that this idea is knocking about yet I think it belongs to the play rather than the character' (1951, p. 157). It is a view which pushes away from doctrine and belief and towards experience and desire. 'And the scapegoat who has collected all of this wisdom for us is viewed at the end with a sort of hushed envy, not I think because he has become wise but because the general human desire for experience has been so glutted in him. He has been through everything' (p. 159).

So the final terms are naturalistic and psychological rather than transcendent or metaphysical – glut more than understanding. These are given features of the human condition: hardly describable, much less encompassable, ready to resurface in unexpected ways with another surge of feeling or flicker of appetite. Yet wisdom and holiness are 'knocking around' in aspects of 'fool' that do not adhere to Lear, perhaps partly because if there were an aura of holy folly it could not be possessed by him alone. One may vaguely think that the play generates certain moral or religious atmospheres with which it then does nothing decisive. These things are felt and present, but hardly located with respect to any distinctive pattern of belief. And to go further by way of Empson would be pure speculation.

A more characteristic indication of how the method works is given through the selectivity of senses: 'What the key-word or "pattern" approach brings you to, I submit, is a fundamental horror, an idea that the gods are such silly and malicious jokers that they will destroy the world' (1951, p. 156). This is not quite akin to saying that the real force of the play comes through its subliminal message, but suggests rather that the cumulative effect of the language transcends particular occasions. Yet this too must be treated with reservation. He is sceptical of Caroline Spurgeon's more classificatory and additive approach, for the frequency of a figure may not be a reliable index of its importance. 'Gold' as an implied metaphor in *Timon of Athens* may outweigh the rarity of its direct use. On the other hand, he has not made an attempt to measure the cumulative effect of the forty-seven manifestations of 'fool' or to decide which act metaphorically and which do not, although he may assume that the substitutions implied are so pervasive that all of the manifestations are metaphoric to some degree, while the literal references to 'gold' in *Timon* are simply that.

The thought of accounting for implied metaphor takes us farther still from the clear contours of a method. The difficulty in extracting a programme from this comes out partly in the imprecise relations between 'key terms', 'master symbol', 'double symbol' etc. ('dog' is a double but not a master, while 'fool' is a master). Sometimes the force of these distinctions is clearly visible and sometimes not. 'Metaphor' is often used loosely for almost any sort of figure, although very good reasons could be given for this. He treats Richards's quite open definition as unduly restrictive (1951, p. 332). So 'working out the key metaphor as far as it would go' – which seems almost as programmatic as Empson gets, bar the equational system – has an openness both as to what constitutes the right sort of key, and as to how one determines how far one should go, as well as the liberality conveyed by the highly indeterminate 'working out'. All of these depend ultimately on the depiction of such aspects of context that 'what is important' is clearly seen. And in the depiction of these multiple contexts and the power of transformation which they enact, Empson's descriptive invention continually rediscovers the possibility of meaning.

In this the two great Empsonian themes of *ambiguity* and *irony* continually return to the foreground. Both derive their effect from an openness of possibility that goes beyond the particular case, yet which has not found a description at a more general level. Complex words are open to continuous mutation – the historical record is evidence enough – and employ a combinatorial freedom that contexts draw from them. It was through this that the creation of 'fool' as instrument became possible. What Empson's example shows is the degree to which the interest is rechargeable with that shift of context, with the discovery of the new dimension in an example, a way in which the background of the complex word opens to another shaft of light or turn of the screw. In the most direct possible way the ironies of 'fool' arise from such kinds of complication, where the most concrete version (clown) and the most grandiose implication (cosmic) serve as ironic comments on each other. The effect is to give further and further dimensions – like new vistas appearing as the stage and scenery changes – to the enormous complexity arising out of some particular circumstance, so as to provide another ironic contrast with the downbeat simplicity of the conceptual machinery and its absence of any general claims.

To relate this effect to Derridean irony is to evoke a different mode of the relational. If one looks to the 'complex word' *pharmakon*, the terms in which its transformations are seen have more precise lines of directional control, as if every element were part of a more structured design, even if the upshot is always to call that structure in question. For the design relates movement, change, uncertainty within a world of carefully controlled connection.

Hence, for example, the word *pharmakon*. In this way we hope to display in the most striking manner the regular, ordered polysemy that has, through skewing, indetermination, or overdetermination, but without mistranslation, permitted the rendering of the same word by 'remedy', 'recipe', 'poison', 'drug', 'philter', etc. It will also be seen to what extent the malleable unity of this concept, or rather its rules and the strange logic that links it with its signifier, has been dispersed, masked, obliterated, and rendered almost unreadable not only by the imprudence or empiricism of the translators, but first and foremost by the redoubtable, irreducible difficulty of translation. It is a difficulty inherent in its very principle, situated less in the passage from one language to another, from one philosophical language to another, than already, as we shall see, in the transition between Greek and Greek; a violent difficulty in the transference of a nonphilosopheme into a philosopheme. With this problem of translation we will thus be dealing with nothing less than the problem of the very passage into philosophy. (Derrida, 1981, pp. 71–2)

This sense of 'passage' derives partly from the transformational power in the ambiguous substance which denies its substantiality in a self-contradictory way. The account is rich in indications of transition, of multiple forms of movement from one state to another: passages through languages and cultures; through magic, alchemy, medicine into what may be health or death; from non-philosophical concepts into philosophy, from myth into truth. All of these transitions are representations of movement: 'from . . . into', 'from . . . to', so repeated that the movement itself seems to predominate over any final term or destination. And indeed 'The *pharmakon* is the movement, the locus, and the play: [the production of] difference. It is the *différance* of difference. It holds in reserve, in its undecided shadow and vigil, the opposites and differends that the process of discrimination will come to mark out' (Derrida, 1981, p. 127).

As in the created ambiguity of *différance* where the insertion of a temporal and logical gap into the distinction from which meaning is derived is conveyed by neologism, the cross-currents of *pharmakon* come from a calculated over-determination that does not arise from the *Phaedrus* in the same way that the ambiguities of 'fool' arose from *King Lear* – where the natural nexus of combinations created the complex instrument. There is a nexus, but its most important features are arranged through coordinates brought to bear. I don't mean that Derrida could have got his argument under way without natural ambiguity. And the ambiguity is rich enough without his re-invention of it. But of course it looks more tangential in the *Phaedrus* where it seems so often an indeterminate metaphor of transformation, and where its richness in context is but a distant point of allusion. That richness is re-inscribed so that the multiple natural meanings – 'remedy', 'recipe', 'poison', 'cure', 'drug', 'philtre', or even 'charm' or 'spell' – are all through the fact of translation the representations of the mysterious signifier in what can become alternative areas of understanding in structured lines of thought.

So the 'malleable unity' in question 'or rather the strange logic that links it with the signifier' is already shaped by the kind of self-consciousness that works through meta-languages. (Here I take the signifier to be the word itself, and the 'malleable unity' the collective possibilities of the multiple signifieds.) Are the ways of this 'strange logic' analogous to the process by which 'fool' has gathered its depth of meaning? If the latter has been followed through the wild course of natural process, subject to hazard and uncertainty, revealing glimpses of the unexpected through the unpredictable course a word has taken, the masked and obliterated unity will be the subject of something regular and ordered. Any such analogy will compare the description of a jungle whose rare fauna may be caught in flight with a more conceptually controlled environment, a philosopher's Garden of Adonis, perhaps, whose arranged magic is valid for a season – ultimately to be jettisoned like last year's ladders – and where the seeds and specimens have known identities and predictable promise, a controlled and ordered polysemy.

There seem to be two senses in which the understanding of such a polysemy is opened up. One lies in the sequence of more or less approximate translations that the various contexts may draw upon, thus evoking different decisions in the translation, sometimes as radical as the choice between the 'poison' and the 'cure'. In this sense the 'passage into philosophy' is similar to the breaking down of some mythic nucleus which can be dismantled into analysed components, involving us in discriminations, choices, critical procedures – deciding what something means. The other lies in those senses that involve a form of symbolic displacement, as in the identification of the *pharmakon* with writing. Of course the latter may work by way of the former, as is straightforwardly the case in the treatment of *Phaedrus* 274e where ambiguity so appears 'without hidden mediation, without secret argumentation'. But this process has begun with a reference to the written oration hidden beneath Phaedrus' cloak, where the hidden argumentation exists in Derrida's assertion, a step necessarily suggested through reading backwards: the riches of argument were already there.

This is only to suggest two rough tracks on which the polysemy might be deployed. Derrida's argument moves on quite other and more various paths. But the notion of translation poses questions that are not wholly resolved, or at least not in the instance of use, revealed. I mean that the *pharmakon* which lies behind its translated versions derives from them a mythical unity; it seems to stand behind all of its incarnations like an 'ur' concept, the guarantor of the unity. There is an assumption of something constant behind the translated terms that we have found in our own natural and conceptual language, so that however variable the possibilities of reading there is a point to which they return. Does this very presence of the underlying *pharmakon* imply at least a semblance of essentialism, even of that aspect of Platonism which does not wholly disappear with 'malleable'?

I should like to follow in a selective way some aspects of the various paths. But consider first certain of the conditions that govern them, like 'indetermination' and 'overdetermination', which themselves seem to imply the possibility of essential meaning which is either diffused in the indeterminate or over-narrowly specified in the overdeterminate. Overdetermination might have its ordered regularities if one saw it as the attempt to contain the possibilities of meaning, to give it the tidiness and distinctness of limitation. That any particular translation of *pharmakon* would require the terms of a determining context to give shape to the necessary 'head sense' would be understood. In the passage mentioned, 274e, Theuth clearly means that writing is a cure for the memory, yet Thamus' reply, which does not mention the word, argues that it is not. Is a deep indetermination introduced by this further consideration, which shows without saying so the danger hidden in the therapy, the poison in the cure?

Yet indetermination would seem to have no characteristic use of its own, but be simply the loss of determinate meaning in any one context; it introduces the shadow world of the many uses that we have for the occasion rejected, and whose existence as trace elements may appear to haunt us as the perspective changes, however slightly. But is the indeterminate only intelligible in terms of the failure of determination, and is there any way in which a regular and ordered account of it could be given? It is hard to see something that goes beyond simple structuralist oppositions: order and disorder, regularity and chaos, which co-exist as *definienda* of each other. After all, as Wisdom says, 'What is oneness without otherness?'. But it is otherness that poses the difficulty in having only a negative identity.

It is not part of Derrida's aim to remove such difficulties, or to unpack in a satisfactory way the contradictions in relating order to the indeterminate, which is merely inherent in the 'irreducible difficulty of translation'. There is no way in which 'irreducible difficulty' can be resolved in smooth re-arrangement. His method is to follow the stages and problematics of the irresolvable as Plato's text provides the ground of devious paths. 'Operating through seduction, the *pharmakon* makes one stray' (Derrida, 1981, p. 70); and, again, he notes 'the leading astray' (p. 71). This 'ordered' straying is in some senses Derrida's own literary form, and the relations between ordering and straying, between sequential and oblique movements, constitutes at least the external form of a game in which the nature of one's own discourse is continually, if not exactly systematically or seriously, put in question. The shifting of types of discourse within the essay enables a number of kinds of language game to co-exist, and to extend the treatment of *pharmakon*: analysis, description, side comment, narrative, parody, a mock fictionalizing; all play a part in the larger sense of language appropriate to its divine inventor. For 'his propriety or property is impropriety or inappropriateness, the floating indetermination that allows for substitution and play. *Play*, of which he is also the inventor' (p. 93). The effect of this is drawn out more fully in a passage that examines the non-substantial character of the *pharmakon*, which 'cannot be handled with complete security, neither in its being, for it has none, nor in its effects, the sense of which is always capable of changing' (p. 126).

The pattern of movement is from the 'floating indetermination' to the transformational possibilities of play to the systematic analysis of ambivalence. But this ambivalence is at least partly unlike the ambivalence of 'fool', in that it is not substantive. 'If the *pharmakon* is "ambivalent," it is because it constitutes the medium in which opposites are opposed, the movement and the play that links them among themselves, reverses them or makes one side cross over into the other (soul/body, good/evil, inside/outside, memory/forgetfulness, speech/writing, etc.' (p. 127). There seem to be two levels, not indicated separately. One is of primary ambiguity where two or more meanings may co-exist in an indeterminate mix. The other is a somewhat stricter notion of ambivalence as the conjoining of opposites, although the pairings mentioned include opposites of quite different sorts and hardly form an intelligible class. Certainly the primary ambiguities are subject to the further variables of being read according to context, where the predominance of one meaning may efface others, and in varying degree; or, as in the case of 'fool', carry their doubleness (or multiplicity) with them.

If one proceeded through an inventory of the relatively natural meanings, it would be moderately restricted in its possibilities, although contextual instances would, as with 'fool', qualify each other. To the process of symbolic identification there seems no limiting principle. However it is the non-substantive nature of the *pharmakon* that enriches the possibility of complication. 'Without being anything in itself', it is the 'medium in which opposites are opposed', as well as being the inexhaustible reserve, 'diacritical, different, deferring', from which 'contradictions and pairs of opposites are lifted'. Part of the problem of this arises in the passage of the *pharmakon* from what is essentially a substantive characterization – poison, cure, drug, spell, etc. – through a symbolic substitution – writing, forgetfulness, etc. – to the non-substantive matrix from which discrimination, dialectic and contradiction derive. And one will have to ask in the end whether or not in the course of this passage logical problems arise which are damaging to the enterprise.

This is clearly a highly figurative portrait of this matrix, of this beginning point which can hardly be described in itself, but must be located, researched, dramatized through what spills out of it. Only the consequences have the suitable degree of definition, are separable as identifiable pieces of language and argument – at least insofar as we take the notion of insubstantiality substantially to heart. The cultural, mythic, literary and philosophical components that have spilled out from the 'medium' unfold through their appropriate differentiation and are culturally specific according to their own modes. We can say all sorts of things about them. But theoretically, we can only reach the *pharmakon* through the products of this possibility. The 'medium', matrix, *chora*, etc. becomes a hypothesis only reached by way of what follows from it. Yet for Derrida it is incarnated in a word, '*pharmakon*', whose multiple uses and meanings, which echo through the Platonic dialogues in rich and varied ways, provide a medium of another kind, a ground of figurative transformations.

This means two kinds of development are directly possible. One is through the numerous Platonic instances of a word whose multiple meanings lead directly to the figuration that composes a substantial part of Derrida's own 'argument' about the nature of writing. Whether or not this development supports his general argument, or could do so, does not concern me. (I happen to think that it does not, and could not. But that is not my problem.) What does concern me is the intrinsic interest in the process of unfolding, in the complex and devious ways through which an 'instrument' is created. And the process may tell us enough about the nature of that instrument that we might have some sense of its further use. If it is the beginning point of a sequence of 'movements of mind' we might reach some understanding of the drift and consequences of such movement.

The other kind of development is the dark mirror of the first. It simply consists in a number of things that Plato did not say. They may come to us by way of Plato in that they are represented as arising in the interstices of what he did say. Or they may circulate more freely as implicit in the kinds of concepts in play: *pharmakos* does not exist in Plato's text, indeed is 'strikingly absent'. The 'forces of association' may powerfully suggest the importance of terms not actually present but communicated through the lexical system (cf. Derrida, 1981, pp. 129–30). And the 'pharmacy' of Derrida's title seems largely a construction of his own, an extension of the notion of *pharmakon*, something evoked by it to give a sense of the depth of meaning held in reserve. 'It is also this store of deep background that we are calling the *pharmacy*.' (This formula is interesting partly because the depth of background will bring the essay close at many points to the historical and etymological dimensions of Empson's 'complexity'.) So it is out of the extension of concepts, the elaboration of cognates, the construction of further members of the verbal chain, that the dimensions of meaning and possibilities of argument will move.

The justification of the evocation of *pharmakos* clearly gives some difficulty. More than one might expect, as one hardly took the essay to be a strict reading of Plato in the first place. The important move seems to be from the sense of the density of the textual setting to the metaphoric freedom that the construction gives, a freedom based on Derrida's awareness of the far-reaching use of Socrates as scapegoat. It is characteristic, of course, that this is a metaphoric step, another figurative aspect of the instrument.

Indeed, the whole method by which the unfolding of *pharmakon* proceeds is a process of figuration, which may or may not parallel a conceptual argument for which it provides the articulation, or which, if seen the opposite way, is followed by certain conceptual implications. Even if what Derrida is doing is a form of philosophy, he seems to begin 'within the limits of this tissue: between the metaphor of the *histos* and the question of the *histos* of metaphor'. That web may be the product of centuries, yet it is undone through the construction of a pattern of figures, a web in a sense of his own, and one in which a series of figures are described by others. A sequence of figural substitutions is inaugurated, in the first instance by reference to the role of example, which will be seen in terms of further examples. And so it will proceed through stories, myths, rituals, customs, visual instances from painting, family relationships, politics, gardening, and others, including the possible multiplications and subdivision of such categories.

Have the many stories become figures which may represent each other in such a way that the figuration of figuration dissolves all meaning in metaphor? We shall look at this possibility in the end. But certainly the openness of play as opposed to the closed circuit of the game is posed for Derrida both in terms of the Platonic appropriation of play, and its own openness as figure. The reduction to game means a subordination to rules, so that one can say 'It is part of the rules of this game that the game should *seem* to stop' (Derrida, 1981, p. 128). The force of 'seem' in this may blur the edge of a necessary decision. And indeed, is 'this game' *his* game? For the sense that the *pharmakon* is 'caught' by philosophy suggests that his own play has been tied to a game which, by its built-in rules, should have to stop. But is it illusory? Is Derrida caught in a game posing exit lines that he knows are arranged, 'overdetermined'? It might be a consolation compared with the indetermination of play. Does one sense that there is no end to the multiplication of metaphors and so much figuration is a weariness of the mind's eye? Or is it the vertigo of freedom in the face of implicit overdetermination?

It is tempting to see in this an analogy to the Empsonian problem of where to place common-sense limits on the open-endedness of permutation. But Empson's 'system' is conceived in what can be expressed as quantifiable terms, and its limits are those that a natural historian might find in counting specimens, or deciding how many more examples were necessary to establish a general rule. Mutations may continue but they are not infinite in number at any one point, nor precisely and finitely containable. Derrida suggests rather a closed system in which new meanings are generated through contrast and opposition, something which may reflect fairly directly his Hegelian and structuralist inheritance.

The empirical habit of mind, of seeing things as much as possible for what they are and not what they are not, finding one's way among the individual cases with a close eye to their circumstantial character and carefully discerned uniqueness, contrasts sharply with seeing things defined by opposition and by positioning within a relational system. This suggests that there is, to put it paradoxically, a systematic indetermination built into the empirical approach. A new example might turn up, a new circumstance alter the perspective on what had seemed like more limited uses. And the 'post-structuralist' character which seems clearly identifiable in the treatment of *pharmakon* conveys some measure of determination through this very fact, which inserts a certain element of game in any movement towards play.

Yet, if in Empson there is no stopping-point other than the exhaustion of interest – in seeing that the permutations run into the sand as there is less and less critical light to be found in looking to further cases – the difficulty with the proliferation of figure lies less in its diminishing returns than in the centrifugal force of the further dimensions its recreation involves. The movement into a predominantly figural expository mode makes narrative, myth and metaphor shift so radically that one game seems to have become another. We cannot decide whether or not the same rules would apply, or where in the series of substitutions we feel that the connections have become lost, and irrelevance or inanity yawn before us. So the other face of 'overdetermination' is metaphor roaring out of control, and the 'ordered' yet indeterminate polysemy has produced a self-conscious but none the less problematical conjunction of randomness and design.

Rather than following a metaphor as far as it will go, the multiplying of metaphors in a sequence of substitutions outflanks each game as the shape of the game begins to seem determined. Is the creation of the semblance of a stopping-place in effect to describe the metamorphosis of the game, and hence the reality of the stopping-place? Or is there no final outflanking movement by which the others are contained? For if the very nature of the game lies in a limitless re-invention of itself, the possibility that the game stops is ruled out. The seeming stopping-point will simply be the lightly touched pencil marking which indicates what we hope is an intelligible segment, a point at which we at any rate have to stop, and where the flow of games is punctuated by some appropriate sign, like the curious little fiction with which Derrida's essay ends. There is no end, only the semblance of an end.

Arguments of this sort exemplify two of the principal difficulties that are frequently pointed out in what has come to be called 'deconstruction'. One is that the possibility of endless substitution leads to an infinite regress in which nothing is ever finally explained, nor can ever be. One moves from the semblance of an argument through a story, a myth, metaphor or related figure and back without a sense of where the satisfactory level of explanation may be found. Even if one restricted oneself to steps which were of roughly the same form there would still be no way of saying *this* is the point at which we now have an understanding. This is clearly the message intended, but can it be coherently stated and held?

The second difficulty lies in the element of implicit reflexivity. For Derrida's own text must itself enter into the game – or even play – and its own authority cannot be other than assimilated to the same standing as the text on which it comments. There is no way in which the comment can stand outside the process it describes and claim any form of privilege with respect to it. These considerations lead far beyond the present case to what has been thought the implicit nihilism in these games within games, founded on nothing but each other and caught up in a contingency of language which is recognized in a 'playing on the play within language'. The consequence is best described by one whose idiom is close to that game, J. Hillis Miller:

> 'Deconstruction' is neither nihilism nor metaphysics but simply interpretation as such, the untangling of the inherence of metaphysics in nihilism and of nihilism in metaphysics by way of the close reading of texts. This procedure, however, can in no way escape, in its own discourse, from the language of the passages it cites. This language is the expression of the inherence of nihilism in metaphysics and of metaphysics in nihilism. We have no other language. The language of criticism is subject to exactly the same limitations and blind alleys as the language of the works it reads. The most heroic effort to escape from the prisonhouse of language only builds the walls higher. (in Bloom, 1979, p. 230)

The verbal gyrations which follow and try to indicate the way in which deconstruction may yet point to a region beyond metaphysics need not concern us. It is the question of interpretation that does.

We have been looking at a reading of certain aspects of the *Phaedrus*, or at least at the exploration of certain issues by way of that dialogue. Beyond a series of seemingly tentative manoeuvres which combine diffidence with assertiveness, the text is gradually reached through, among other things, a recognition of the impossibility of its being directly perceived. The 'rules of the game' are hidden. And the text itself is lost to the present except for the regenerating power of reading, that tissue of decisions which undoes the web of centuries. 'By the logic of play', we must enter into a necessary game which we can never master. We take and follow a thread – continuing the figure – creating a web, a supplement if one likes, playing a game without known rules. Is our reading, like Derrida's, like any other, created through decisions, discriminations even, which sketch that fragmentary understanding called interpretation, which must in the end be identified with the text in question, in effect the only text we have? Perhaps in Derrida's case the philosopher and critic have become one in the making of the web, in this meta-commentary become speculation which remains text. If so, what has happened to the passage into philosophy? For the philosophy we have reached through being caught in discrimination, dialectic, etc. seems no different from interpretation. This in turn ends in the ironic tale in which the echo-chamber disarticulates speech into the illusion of a dialogue 'Full of meaning. A whole story. An entire history. All of philosophy' (Derrida, 1981, p. 170).

Such re-invention is less a violation or re-arrangement of the text than a signal that the original ground is incomplete. The normal procedure through much of the essay is to take the philological, historical and anthropological evidence quite seriously in a perfectly conventional way, while shifting the angle from which the text is seen so that the necessity of interpretation forces a more and more radical figurative characterization. After all, the philosopher moves through multiple games and interpretations, from the simple breaking apart at the beginnings of dialectic to the indistinguishable blur of buzzing voices which surround the last incarnation of the *pharmakon*: the doubleness of an attack of demonic possession and the cure against such attack. The philosopher's recognition of his contradictory self is a form of madness, which bears within itself its cure: one keeps writing.

The ambiguities that surround acts of philosophical utterance, the passage into philosophy by the simultaneous assumption and demolition of its own myth, do not make it easy to decide how such a commentary – interpretation as Hillis Miller says – fits any version of critical understanding that is consonant with itself. Insofar as it was perfectly clear that Empson was involved in a critical reading, one must acknowledge the degree to which such a reading accepts the authority of an historical conception of meaning: but contingently so, and not in the sense of claiming some special epistemological character for history. And the lowest level of implied metaphysics would be hard to identify beyond an Enlightenment rationalism that is attached to process and not to substance, or to an experimental outlook that is relatively humble in the face of its given. Derridean interpretation in a sense has no given. What one interprets becomes something else in the moment of mentioning it.

Derrida's works are neither philosophical nor literary. His strategy refuses to be governed by concepts of ends ('a teleo-eschatological horizon'); rather than ordered relations of means and ends his strategy refers to the play of the strategem itself. Rather than names having a precise conceptual meaning they represent a 'system of predicates', a conceptual organization centred on a predicate, with the use of a name (indeed old words, old names) being 'a kind of *lever of intervention*' through which such organizations are grasped and transformed.

Hence the extended use of *pharmakon* as both conceptual centre and lever of intervention. It is an old word of course, and one which attaches by *écriture* to others, one which has been carefully surrounded by the radiating circles of multiple meanings, by its mysterious past, cultural exoticism, its innate capacity to be used against itself, the old word made banal by familiarity, eroded by use, yet requiring its own rediscovery as the guarantee of philosophy's only possible 'ultimate' term of reference and point of departure.

I am quite aware that I have avoided in substance any consideration of the ostensible theme of Derrida's argument concerning the relation of *logos* to *écriture*, or any consideration of his elaborate dismantling of the Platonic assumptions: words name things, which are so nameable because they in turn represent essences which in turn have their metaphysical foundations. From this a long tradition of metaphysical realism with respect to universals follows. There are two reasons for this omission. For one I am convinced that there are other ways of disposing of this metaphysical baggage without going by way of this contrast of *logos* and writing. Secondly, I am not convinced that the reasoning about supplements and so on succeeds in its own terms. But for my purposes it is not necessary to argue this case. It enters only indirectly through the characterization of *pharmakon* as the antidote to that metaphysical primacy. For it is the figural centre of a descriptive system, an account of the non-essential nature of naming, of the non-substantive picture of language, and my concern is not with whether or not such an account establishes what it set out to do (in fact I think it does not) but with the nature of this figural instrument.

But if of the making of figures there is no end, the vehicle for such figures is writing; and there is no stage at which the comment on a text naturally exhausts itself, or reaches a point where the account, or our understanding, if you will, is complete. Rorty remarks: 'For Derrida writing always leads to more writing, and more, and still more – just as history does not lead to Absolute Knowledge or the Final Struggle, but to more history, and more and still more. The *Phenomenology*'s vision of truth as what you get by reinterpreting all the previous reinterpretations of reinterpretations still embodies the Platonic ideal of the Last Reinterpreter, the *right* interpretation at last. Derrida wants to keep the horizontal character of Hegel's notion of philosophy without its teleology, its sense of direction, its seriousness' (Rorty, 1982, pp. 94–5).

As with figures, so with interpretations. There is no way in which the lever of intervention can make a move that is more decisive than other moves. Interpretations are not justified, but simply are. They may serve our understanding if we accept their relational and transitory nature. But then, if no criteria for justification can be given, no criteria for failure are present either. For indeed, if all teleological considerations are abandoned there is no end by which comparisons might be made. The way in which a figure may illuminate another may be seen, but hardly explained. That there should be any difference between 'the right interpretation at last' and relative rightness in limited contexts, for which at least partial criteria would be statable, could not occur to Derrida or enter into his project in any way. It would be too dimly quotidian, too deeply dispiriting altogether.

Yet if *pharmakon* is a lever in a flux where no leverage is possible, 'fool' is a key where in the end there is no lock. In Empson there is no riddle, and in his own way, no end. The pursuit of 'fool' leads to something quite different from the buzzing in Plato's head, but as deeply palpable: the experience of pain. Or perhaps it is an end of a most unanalysable Anglo-Saxon kind to find the terminus of an analytic process in experience itself. So our two cases may point in quite different ways, with the instruments of ambiguity and polysemy shaped by quite different procedures; yet in the comparison there are valuable analogies to be drawn. Empson has moved through the pathless wilds of a natural language, where the uncertainties of connection, qualification or predominance of an aspect leave judgement or decision on a 'darkling plain', where the glut of experience has no precise measure. Derrida works through the artifices of hypothesizing and then eroding such structures of containment.

Both have moved through radical uncertainty of meaning with wholly different concerns in the management of its consequences. One takes the recognition of the randomness of things as a fortuitous and natural fatality which is the underlying condition of life. The other forces randomness upon us through dismantling the false structures and makings of sense which our fictionalizing mentalities have shored against our ruin. For Empson the dramatic irony of *Lear* is a mirror to men's hearts where the truth of folly is a concentrated and terrible moment on which the mind may come to rest. For Derrida the mirrors reflect each other in the endless exchange where nothing comes to rest and the eye must simply follow to the vanishing point.

CHAPTER 9

William Empson's cosmicomics

Jean-Jacques Lecercle

> Qu'une réalité se cache derrière les apparences, cela est, somme toute, possible; que le langage puisse la rendre, il serait ridicule de l'espérer.
> E. M. Cioran

LE COSMICOMICHE

The third piece (one hardly dares call it a 'story') of Calvino's *Le Cosmicomiche* is entitled 'A sign in space' ('Un segno nello spazio'). In it, an aged entity recalls how, in the virgin universe of the very beginnings, he made the first sign: 'What kind of a sign? It's difficult to say – if I say "sign", you immediately think of something that is distinct from something else, but in those days nothing was distinct from nothing' (Calvino, 1965, p. 41). The 'story' tells us how, having made the sign in one specific point of the universe (whereby this point became a point, being the only point different from all others, and he became, as the maker of the only sign, somebody), he had to wait for a complete revolution of the galaxy, a mere two hundred million years, to have a look at it. The rest of the story rings a tragic note. After this long wait, he found the sign erased by another, invidious, entity, took to making feigned signs, was imitated and found himself again in a universe without a point of reference, not for lack of a sign, but for an excess of signs, their multiplication having occupied all the available space and cancelled all differences between signs and things: 'In the universe, there was no longer container and contents, only a general thickness of agglutinated signs' (p. 51).

Before we interpret this away as an illustration *avant la lettre* of the conception of signs and language commonly attributed to Derrida (the original sign reads like a caricature of the arche-trace, and the ending could be rephrased, in a parody of one of his more cryptic formulas, '*il n'y a pas de hors-signe*'); or before we strike nearer home, and attribute the piece to the influence of Umberto Eco's semiotics, perhaps we should reflect on the structure of the text. It starts with three lines, printed in italics, which spell out a straightforward piece of vulgarized astrophysics: 'Situated as it is towards the outside of the Milky Way, the Sun takes two hundred million years to complete a revolution of the galaxy' (p. 41). This pre-text is immediately followed by the 'story' outlined above, narrated by one Qfwfq: 'Exactly so, that was the time needed for it, hardly less, – said Qfwfq'. And the narrative which develops out of this has a rather abstract quality: in those days there were no people, no things, no events – only the eternal laws of the cosmos, and it is only the male-chauvinist bias inherent in language which makes one refer to Qfwfq as 'he'. In other words, if this is a story, it has undergone the ultimate narrative *epochē*: Husserl's transcendental ego has suddenly become the main character in *Coronation Street*.

This is a strange way of beginning an essay on Empson's poetry. The implied comparison with Calvino which such a starting-point suggests is outrageous on innumerable counts. I seem to be comparing an Italian novelist of the sixties, writing from a (post)modernist point of view, and an English poet of the thirties and forties, one notoriously steeped in the great tradition of English poetry (sufficiently so to be commended by Leavis at the end of his *New Bearings in English Poetry* (1932)) and in the wit of the Metaphysical poets. No attempt will be made to present this comparison as an exercise in the postmodern game of anachronism (a well-known path to awareness of the hermeneutic circle), not even as a response to a sense of the outrageous in Empson's own poetry, for, after all, he is well known for his mischievous delight in provocation, witness the celebrated line 'I knew the Phoenix was a vegetable' (Empson, 1955, p. 36). I shall rather seek to justify my comparison by making two serious points.

The first is that, beyond the evident and unbridgeable differences, a common thread runs through both texts. Perhaps even two threads. As the title of Calvino's book indicates, his texts always start from a serious reflection on cosmology (or at least one presented as such), using the language of vulgarized science; and they always develop into comic narrations, where the seriousness of science gives way to tongue-in-cheek fictions. So that his pieces are all based on a passage from the serious to the non-serious, in its two senses of comic and fictional. This narrative strategy points towards a more general problematic, of the serious and non-serious uses of language, which surfaces in Derrida's critique of Austin in *Marges* (Derrida, 1982). Where does the frontier between the serious and the non-serious in language lie? Or, rather, is there such a frontier? Calvino's 'stories' tell us how scientific propositions can be insidiously destabilized by quotation, irony and punning. His texts purport to show us how one can make literary (and almost literal) fun of science. This is also Empson's problematic. There is no need to recall his early interest in maths or his admiration for I. A. Richards, who is the author of *Science and Poetry* (1926b). Any reader of the poems will have noticed the obsession with scientific theories (often indicated in the notes) and cosmic images ('Our bullet boat light's speed by thousand flies', (1955, p. 18)) – like Qfwfq, he can exclaim 'it is we soaring explore galaxies' (p. 18). And, as the title of one poem, 'Earth has shrunk in the wash' (p. 28), shows, those cosmic images are also, more often than not, comic. Empson's purpose seems to be not only to make poetry out of sheer fun (in both senses of the phrase), but also to make fun, and also poetry, out of science, without making fun of either poetry or science. Perhaps the most striking characteristic of his poetry is his serious non-seriousness – Erasmus Darwin turned upside down, or rather subjected to *Aufhebung*.

My second point continues the first in more detail. Beyond the play on words which it justifies, this strategy involves difficulties. The duality of the serious and the non-serious will threaten the stability of the text. The writing will be constantly attracted to opposite quarters, *tiré à hue et à dia*, in danger of disintegrating. Tragicomedy, which is clearly the source of Calvino's title, is not an easy genre. It is always possible to decide that the mixture of comedy and cosmology fails to take, to accuse Calvino of low and facile comedy, to dismiss Empson's effort as undergraduate wit – his taste for 'ideas' on the one hand, and his linguistic playfulness and poetic 'technique' on the other threaten the only seriousness that poetry must cultivate, that of moral feelings and emotions. This is roughly what Leavis has to say about the shortcomings in Empson's poetry:

> indeed the criticism of him would be that in his work the heat of creation is as yet too exclusively a matter of interest in technique and ideas; and that, however intense this interest may be, something more is needed before his

intelligence and his technical skill can be fully employed, and before one can predict for him confidently a career as a poet. (Leavis, 1932, p. 148)

This is recognizably Leavis, as an Empson poem is so recognizably Empson's. But apart from the critic's well-known *marottes*, which he attempts to foist on the poet, Leavis's text evinces an awareness of the tension between 'ideas' and 'technique' in Empson's poetry, a tension between potential incompatibles. This, I think, is the deepest thread common to Calvino and Empson. The cosmic and the comic do not, cannot go well together, and yet go together they must. The common strategy of our authors is to turn this potentially dangerous instability into creative tension, into the very structure of their texts. For duality is not only present in the themes – a rather contingent similarity – but in the strategy of writing. Calvino plays on the opposition between serious pre-text, or theme, and non-serious text, or development. In Empson's *Collected Poems*, the structure is the inverse of this: the cosmicomic poems are followed by notes so abundant (they are sometimes much longer than the poems they are supposed to be attached to) that explanatory prose comes back with a vengeance, and sometimes the reader has the feeling that the poem is only a fiction *entrée en matière* for the explicit expression of Empson's ideas, emotions and moral feelings (in other words, the notes would provide Leavis with what he failed to find in the poems). The prose writer turns out to be almost a poet in his imaginative fictions, whereas the poet eventually manages to express himself in the form of prose. The importance of the notes to Empson's poems becomes evident once we have noticed that the two poems in which he takes himself most seriously – even if he is also at his most playful – 'Bacchus' and 'China', are the objects of the longest notes by far. (My argument is, of course, circular: the very length of the notes is an indication of the importance Empson attaches to the poems.)

I shall abandon Calvino for a while. The detour through his narrative of sign-making has enabled me to focus on three aspects of Empson's poetry which I feel are central: the duality of science and comedy in theme and style; the tension between these two poles, as they are felt to be both unavoidable and incompatible; and the structural duality of poems and notes in the *Collected Poems*.

THE STRUCTURE OF COMPLEX TEXTS

My first task shall be to explore this generalized duality. If the tension between two opposite poles is the organizing principle of Empson's poetry, if his style is pervaded with it (whether this is the outcome of conscious strategy or not is immaterial – on the one hand the wit of his poetry gives an impression of total control, and on the other hand the slightly hysterical need to dot one's i's in the form of explanatory notes sounds like Freudian denial), one would expect the tension to invade the text at all levels. So it does. I shall concentrate on two of these levels.

I have not done yet with the strangeness of the notes. A rough computation (I promise this will be my only venture into the arid land of statistical criticism) gives a proportion of two-thirds text to one-third notes. The space taken up by notes is, it seems to me, enormous (all the more so as not all the poems are annotated). Nor do I think we can explain this away by the necessity of making a slim volume slightly plumper, even if such is the usual account for the most famous of poetic footnotes – one recalls that the notes to *The Waste Land* are said to have originated in the publisher's anxiety at the blankness of the *vide papier* at the end of the book. Empson's notes are not at all like Eliot's. They do not indicate sources but provide explanations in the etymological sense of unfolding of meaning. Besides, we do need them. They often provide meaning which is so close to Wittgenstein's 'private language' (that notorious impossibility) that we could hardly have expected to recover it. The reader of Empson's poetry is often hardly in a better position than the reader of Raymond Roussel's *Impressions d'Afrique*, where the extraordinary events find their source in the author's irrepressible punning on words, fragments of folk-songs, and even, in one instance, the address of Roussel's bootmaker. The notes are the equivalent of Roussel's explanatory essay, 'How I wrote certain of my books' – the main difference being that Empson's is a softer hermeticism, since he has entrusted us with the key to his meaning in the same volume, rather than making us wait, like Roussel, for a posthumous account of the innumerable tricks he has played on us.

I find Eliot's notes entirely straightforward, even if slightly tongue-in-cheek at times. But Empson's I find curious – both laconic and garrulous. This, for instance, is the note to 'Dissatisfaction with Metaphysics':

There was a myth that no element would receive Mahomet's body, so that it hung between them and would appear self-subsisting. The earth's orbit being an ellipse has two foci with the sun at one of them; one might have a complicated theory, entirely wrong, making the other focus the important one. I failed to make a pun on *focus*, and its original sense *hearth*. Two mirrors have any number of reflections (the self-conscious mind); a dotted line is used for 'and so on'. The mind makes a system by inbreeding from a few fixed ideas. Prospero's book of magical knowledge was buried deeper than ever plummet sounded, and the depths of knowledge which had previously been sounded became deepest during the disaster of the Flood. (1955, p. 95)

The strangeness of this passage is not merely due to the fact that I have unfairly treated it as an independent text, thus making it incoherent. To be sure, knowledge of the attendant poem helps, at least in most cases:

High over Mecca Allah's prophet corpse
(The empty focus opposite the sun)
Receives homage, centre of the universe. (p. 9)

The first four lines of the note adequately gloss these, the first three lines of the poem, even if the annotator's craft (we only have to compare this with the footnotes in an annotated Shakespeare) is superbly disregarded – the reader has to provide a link between text and note and decide what concerns what. Not always an easy task: the sentence 'two mirrors have any number of reflections (the self-conscious mind)', apart from the fact that it could itself be glossed, the passage from reflection to reflexivity being more problematic than it seems, fails to provide an apt commentary to lines 6 and 7 of the poem:

Two mirrors with Infinity to dine
Drink him below the table when they please. (p. 9)

There is a teasing aspect to the notes: more information is proffered than we could reasonably have expected, and yet some of the information we did expect – at times, most of it – is withdrawn. Nor is this, of course, a criticism of Empson: complete explanation would reduce the reader's effort towards understanding to nothing, insufferably constrain his or her freedom of interpretation, and make the act of reading somewhat boring.

We have reached an important point, for it appears that the notes themselves are a locus for tension – between the need to explain the correct meaning and the at least partial withdrawing of the explanation. In his notes, Empson sets himself too many, potentially contradictory, goals. He explains puns which we might have missed (see that rather coy denial: 'I failed to make a pun on *focus*' – once he has obligingly drawn our attention to the etymological meaning of 'focus', 'hearth', what has he done but make a pun on 'focus'?); he also explains the allusions to scientific facts and theories (usually – and enjoyably – false), indicates remote sources and often comments on his own performance in a Shandyan manner (the 'failed' pun on 'focus' is also meant as *captatio benevolentiae*). At the same time, he withdraws some of the required explanation or makes it sufficiently abstruse to need careful deciphering. The general drift of the notes, however, which this hesitant withdrawal resists, is from the esoteric to the exoteric. The aim appears to be to make up for the flippant obscurity of the poems by establishing their meaning, which must be the author's meaning. Empson loves to be his own hermeneut: he is obviously so much better at it than we ever could be, and it would be a shame to leave such an important task in our clumsy hands. The result, however, is somewhat unexpected. This tactic, far from diminishing the strangeness of the poems, increases it. We cannot but interpret the notes, as we read them after the poems, or at the same time, as an attempt at damming the free flow of our interpretation, at dictating the right meaning to us, at blocking the paths opened up by our own poetic imagination. I am grateful for a little enlightenment, for the texts are truly difficult – not for the imposition of a true, because authorial, meaning. In that respect, puns turn out to be falsely polysemic: they do proclaim that meaning is not in a one-to-one relationship to words; but because they can be explained, they place a strict limitation on the number of possible meanings, so that the essential notion of the *right* meaning is preserved. Besides, the decision to add explanatory notes raises a simple question: why bother to write esoteric poems in the first place, if the author himself is prepared to gloss them? The already suggested answer, which stated that the notes merely hint at the authorial meaning, that even the longest of them fall far short of real clarification, that the essential point is always left for the reader to discover (for instance, 'To an Old Lady' is addressed to the poet's mother), is by no means sufficient. True, the constraints on our own interpretation are not unbearable, and there is no cause to resent the pedagogic devices of a great teacher. But it is a question of all or nothing. If there is an author's meaning, then there is one (right and only) meaning, and the constraints are immediately maximal. Even one step on the road to authorized, because authorial, explanation will unavoidably lead to the explanation of everything. The obvious *fuite en avant* of the note to 'Bacchus' (where Empson gives a verse-by-verse commentary – line-by-line explication is not far) proves my point. But perhaps there is a more important justification for the author's tactics, although the practice may no longer be intentional, and therefore neither strategic nor tactical, but symptomatic. The very strangeness of the combination of poems and notes may be taken as a symptom of unresolved conflict. On the one hand we have a poetic style which seeks to protect itself from comprehension; on the other, notes which give with the left hand the knowledge the right hand has withdrawn. We seem to have the two Lacans, the esoteric scriptor of the *Ecrits* and the exoteric speaker of the *Séminaires*, in one text. Empson wants to have his cake and eat it – he is flirting with a Roussel-like private language, and at the same time recognizing its dangers and struggling to overcome them.

Duality, therefore, reigns not only between poems and notes, but within the notes. There is a second level on which it is also evident. What I have been reading is the *Collected Poems* (1955). But this volume collects two earlier ones, *Poems* (1935) and *The Gathering Storm* (1940), plus one or two previously uncollected pieces. This division would be entirely irrelevant, were it not for the drift in style from one volume to the other. In the last paragraph, we met the two Lacans – now we have the two Wittgensteins. And the movement within and between the two volumes is the same as from text to notes – it goes from the esoteric to the exoteric. Empson's later poems are often less 'difficult', less metaphysical in style than his earlier texts. This is a typical opening in Empson's first manner:

> Re-plyed, extorted, oft transposed, and fleeting,
> Tune from plucked cotton, the cat's-cradle pattern
> Dances round fingers that would scratch in meeting. (p. 12)

And this is typical of his second manner – the difference in style needs no comment (witness the fact that here there is no need for glossing):

> Slowly the poison the whole blood stream fills.
> It is not the effort nor the failure tires.
> The waste remains, the waste remains and kills. (p. 60)

Perhaps the mention of Wittgenstein is not irrelevant: like him, Empson appears to have moved from the asceticism of hermetic expression to a firmer confidence in the resources of language at its most ordinary.

If duality pervades the structure of Empson's poems, it would seem that it is not only a matter of opposition and tension, but also of movement from one pole to another, or rather of hesitation, advance and retreat, assertion and withdrawal. *Interruptus est*: the climax is never reached, and the notes and change in style are there to exorcize all danger.

That the danger concerns the mastery or control of meaning is now clear. The dualities of serious and non-serious, cosmic and comic, poem and note, early and late manner are all to be taken as displacements of the central tension: there is meaning, authorial and therefore accessible and susceptible of explicit formulation; and there is no single fixed meaning, but a fluid proliferation of amorphous and often partial meanings. This is how Empson himself expresses this idea:

> No, I'm afraid that the business of guessing what it means when there isn't enough evidence to tell the answer is one we've trained ourselves in. I just cut out the bits I thought were in bad taste and it didn't leave enough to make any sense really. That's what happened to 'The Teasers'. (quoted in Press, 1969, p. 203)

A reader of poetry is in the business of interpreting without any assurance as to the right answer – in other words, her freedom of interpretation is entire. On the other hand, she has to 'guess' – and therefore there *is* an answer (the author's meaning), even if, as in Roussel, it is impossible to reach it, the text being incoherent, not 'making any sense really'.

This quotation, in which John Press sees a statement of the essential nature of Empson's art, shows that the duality which structures the poem is highly unstable. On the one hand, we need authorial meaning, otherwise the poem dissolves in ever-renewed, free-wheeling interpretations. Ambiguity and punning, two central themes in Empson's critical work, appear as symptoms of this danger and ways of blocking it. What I have said of puns – which corresponds to Empson's critical practice when he accounts for them in the work of other poets – may remind us of the analysis of ambiguity in linguistics: meanings multiply, but they are always univocally determined and their proliferation is strictly limited to one meaning per deep structure origin of the ambiguous surface structure. In this respect, the notes play the same part as the syntactic derivation which explicates ambiguity: they help to fix meaning as varnish fixes paint. If ambiguity appears to unleash meaning, it is in a highly restrained and decorous manner. This, I think, is the source of Empson's obvious critical preference for ambiguity and punning over metaphor. All three phenomena find their common source in the dangerous potentiality of proliferation of meaning. The difference between them is that the first two only toy with the possibility, whereas metaphor, which is never, unless it has frozen into cliché, entirely determinable, lets language speak for itself and meaning escape the author's intention. The theory of equations in *The Structure of Complex Words* can be read as a rearguard action against the danger of metaphor (and here of course other philosophical ghosts loom up in the intertextual distance – if not the early Wittgenstein, at least Russell and Frege inveighing against the hopeless vagueness and nonsensicality of natural languages).

But reducing Empson to a poetic logical positivist simply will not do. As a poet, he cannot but be highly aware that language is irredeemably polysemic, that there is no origin, no fixed sense, that the author's intentional meaning is no privileged point of reference. In the middle of the long note to 'Bacchus', in which he goes to extreme lengths in order to make *his* meaning clear, he has the following, slightly disenchanted, comment: 'I was thinking of Mandevil when I wrote "so soon", though it would be absurd to pretend that this is part of the poem; he says that Adam was only in Eden for half an hour, "so soon he fell"' (p. 109). In the same sentence, a source is offered which takes the poem back to the author's reading, in the manner of Livingston Lowes in *The Road to Xanadu* (1927), and it is withdrawn as irrelevant. I spoke earlier of symptom: this sounds wondrously like Freudian denial. The result of course is that in the poems, it is language that speaks – the poems always precede and override (and overrule) the notes. Theirs is a hermeticism not of concealed, but of absent (or, which is the same thing, multiple) meaning. The notes appear as failed attempts at blocking the natural development of the poems, an empty gesture towards a form of control after the event. They assert that it is the author who speaks and deny that language speaks in its own right, at the very moment when, by their mere presence, they demonstrate that language does speak. That the two attitudes are deeply linked appears in this passage from Derrida's *Dissemination*, on the dialectics of polythematism and monothematism: 'Polysemy always puts out its multiplicities and variations within the horizon, at least, of some integral reading which contains no absolute rift, no senseless deviation – the horizon of the final parousia of a meaning at last deciphered, revealed, made present in the rich collection of its determinations' (Derrida, 1981, p. 350).

We understand Empson's admiration for the Elizabethan and Metaphysical poets, for their attitude to language is similar to his. A heroic attempt at imposing authorial control over language only shows, in the extreme subtlety of linguistic play, that language speaks on its own. A pun is always threatening to turn into metaphor (indeed, the two tropes are much closer in structure than tradition will allow – a live metaphor is a generalized, and therefore indeterminable, pun). Once we have realized that an author habitually uses punning, how can we fail to discover a potential pun in every word, for such is the inherent polysemy of language? The infinite layers of commentary on Shakespeare's less perspicuous passages will bear out this point. Empson's own theory of equations is a good instance of this drifting: the multiplication of equations announces the proliferation of meaning. His poems are so deeply divided because his conception of language is itself divided: he has in fact a conception – at times clear and at times denied – that language is deeply divided.

DIVISION

Duality has given way to division. Unresolved tension opens up the way to contradiction. I am treating Empson's text in the way Lévi-Strauss deals with myth. In a myth, he sees the expression of a false, or rather fictional, solution to a real contradiction (Lévi-Strauss, 1958). What this 'real' contradiction may be in the case of Empson will emerge later. But the poems can certainly be interpreted as the systematic combination of incompatibles. I shall explore various ways in which the text is divided against itself.

The latest reprint of *Collected Poems* (1984) opens on a photograph, taken in 1948, in which an earnest Empson, one almost wishes to add a comically earnest Empson, is putting a point to a pipe-smoking, reflective listener. This comes as an ironic contrast to the epigraph, a one-page extract from what appears to be an Indian myth, entitled 'The Fire Sermon'. The reader goes from the potential non-seriousness of the photograph to the (at least apparent) high seriousness of the myth. When he finally turns the epigraph page, he next finds an author's note, innocuous enough in its original version of 1955, but with a highly interesting addition, dated 1983, which describes the frontispiece, and adds:

When I. A. Richards saw the villanelle beginning 'Slowly the poison ...' (p. 60) he said it was the best comic poem I had done so far; and I must have betrayed my surprise, because he added, not to hurt my feelings, that of course it was *deep* humour. I was not hurt but relieved; denouncing the universe has never seemed a sensible thing for a poem to do, and I had feared my villanelle might be tainted with that pomposity. Much of the verse here is about the strangeness of the world, in which we are often tripped up and made helpless, and the first thing to do in that situation is to understand it. In such a case, it is usual for some to laugh and others not. I was feeling very earnest when I was snapped, though the effect is comical; and this makes it seem a suitable lead-in for the poems.

Since this makes the frontispiece an icon of the poems, it appears that the opposition between earnestness and comedy, high seriousness and humour, despair (the apparent tone of the villanelle) and exhilaration (the humour which I. A. Richards finds in it) are central to Empson's poetry. Richards's phrase, 'deep humour', is the name for the fictional, and unstable, solution to this contradiction: a drawing together of generic incompatibles. A closer look at the villanelle will confirm that the solution is indeed deeply unstable. The tone is that of a dirge – an impression increased by the repetition which is distinctive of the form; we are made to share an awareness, not so much of death itself as of the death of memory, of the weight and waste of the past. But at the same time, the text is riddled with inversions, which threaten to blur the tone, and account for Richards's reaction. Our traditional expectations are foiled. This is not a lament on missed opportunities, or the impossibility of remembrance of things past, but on the contrary on the abundance of the past, which will not fade away, and which therefore weighs us down. There is no renewal, the carcass of the old dog always remains:

> They bled an old dog dry yet the exchange rills
> Of young dog blood gave but a month's desire
> The waste remains, the waste remains and kills. (p. 60)

The use of grotesque images (the old dog) and *outré* co-occurrences, which give the impression of metaphors congealed into objects ('It is the Chinese tombs and the slag hills / Upset the soil, and not the soil retires') jar with the apparent lugubriousness of the tone, so that we eventually realize that the formal patterns of repetition, rhyme (the whole poem uses only two rhymes, '-ills' and '-ires', and all the rhymes in '-ills' occur in monosyllabic words, turning the poem into an instance of the comic game of inventory), and conversion ('shrill' is used as a verb in 'Not to have fire is to be a skin that shrills', a rare, but not unheard-of use, in which we perceive an echo of Tennyson) work against the solemnity of tone and diction. This is Empson in his typical cosmicomic belatedness: the poem does not deplore death, but rather the tragedy of prolonged life, of life eternal without eternal youth, condemned to Nietzsche's eternal return of the same, or to the plight of the heroine in Rider Haggard's *She* (if this allusion sounds slightly bathetic, let us recall that in 'The Scales', he makes poetic use of Haggard's *King Solomon's Mines*):

> Not to have fire is to be a skin that shrills.
> The complete fire is death. From partial fires
> The waste remains, the waste remains and kills. (p. 60)

The cosmicomic contradiction in tone sometimes becomes explicit, when the form of the poem is divided against itself. Thus, 'The Teasers', that deliberate piece of incoherence ('But a beautiful metrical invention, I do say', he adds in the above quoted commentary) demonstrates division in its strophic form:

> Not but they die, the teasers and the dreams,
> Not but they die,
>   and all the careful flood
> To give them what they clamour for and why. (p. 67)

And the grammar of 'China' is patently divided (a device typical of comic verse), the poem ironically playing one 'voice' against the other:

> The dragon hatched a cockatrice
> (Cheese crumbles and not many mites repair)
> There is a nature about this
> (The spring and rawness tantalise the air). (p. 70)

The poem is based on 'two main ideas' (comparing China and Japan as the offspring of the same culture, and forecasting that, in spite of her defeat, China will absorb Japan). These two ideas 'now seem to me false', but express 'a kind of ignorant glee' – then follows a four-page note which shows the importance Empson attaches to this 'falsity' and that the form is in accord with the proffered contents: 'the grammar is meant to run through alternate lines; I thought this teasing trick gave an effect of the completely disparate things going side by side' (p. 117).

Teasing, or the teasing out of contradictions through linguistic wit, is the essence of Empson's style. It is, after all, the subject of his most programmatic poem, 'Bacchus', where alcohol, like poetry, is presented as a way of access to reality (of which more later) in explicit terms:

> a mythological chemical operation to distil drink is going on in the first four verses. The notion that life involves maintaining oneself between contradictions that can't be solved by analysis, e.g. those of philosophy, which apply to all creatures, and the religious ones about man being both animal and divine. Drink is taken as typical of this power because it makes you more outgoing and unself-critical, able to do it more heartily – e.g. both more witty and more sentimental. (p. 104)

This is where we go further than Lévi-Strauss and his dialectics of myth and fiction. Maintaining oneself between contradictions in life does not involve solving them in language, but on the contrary giving in to them, translating them into another medium and playing with them, so that the serious becomes comic (Prometheus' tormentor, in verse three of the poem, is cirrhosis of the liver; the phrase 'lights of the god's car', at the very end, is fully integrated within the series of optical images, photons and foci, but conjoins, by way of a pun, the most down-to-earth contemporary object with the mythical glory of the god's progress). The web of language both makes the incompatibles co-present (for they are present in the same dictionary, in the same language) and at odds with each other (they remain incompatible in what Umberto Eco calls the 'encyclopaedia' – our culture as embodied in our words and phrases). Witness Empson's constant use of anachronism, paronomasia and punning (the poem makes extensive use of the polysemy of 'cope') – they are figures of inversion and contradiction, of the persistence and necessity of division. It takes drink or poetry to make the co-presence of the incompatibles bearable.

We are again close to the centre. The division is both *within* language, and *represented*, if not resolved, in it. It is not a matter of Wittgensteinian isomorphism, the syntax of language mirroring the syntax of the world, but rather a contamination, a lack of distance, which makes language share the instability of reality and at the same time project onto it, absorb it in a way, and assert its independence from both the reality it is supposed to refer to and the speaker who is supposed to master it. Only language speaks: *il n'y pas de hors texte*.

This instability of language (the impossibility of determinate reference and expression of the speaker's intentions) is what Empson's poetry is about. It emerges in the only prose poem in the collection, 'Poem about a Ball in the Nineteenth Century'. Empson is even more defensive and derogatory about this piece than he usually is: 'there is a case for hating this sort of poetry and calling it meaningless so I had better explain, to protect myself, that no other poem in the book disregards meaning in the sense that this does. At the same time it is meant to be a direct description' (p. 95). The first lines of the text will show what he means:

> Feather, feather, if it was a feather, feathers for air, or to be fair, aroused. Round to be airy, feather, if it was airy, very, aviary, fairy, peacock, and to be well-surrounded. Well-aired, amoving, to peacock, cared-for, share dancing inner to be among aware. (p. 10)

This is not an undergraduate's proto-Surrealist joke; it is the stuff that poetry is made of, the free flow of unstable language groping towards form – here at its most inchoate, although more controlled when it takes on metric shape or when polysemy is reduced to pun. The fundamental instability of language clearly appears in the possibility of two readings. One, induced by the title, will look, against considerable odds, for linguistic and narrative coherence – it will aim at interpreting the poem as a description: a ball in the nineteenth century. True, the description is a little 'direct', and what we are given is raw impressions: the whirling and the twirling and the swirling of the ball which dissolve the syntax of consciousness. This is the world of Hilaire Belloc's 'Tarantella': 'Do you remember an Inn / Miranda? / [. . .] And the Hip! Hop! Hap! / Of the clap / Of the hands to the twirl and the swirl / Of the girl gone chancing, / Glancing, / Dancing' (Belloc, 1938, p. 402). But Empson's strategy is not one of imitative harmony. The syntactic incoherence does not picture the incoherence of impressions in the outside world. It demonstrates the incoherence of language, by opening up the possibility – nay, by recognizing the necessity – of another reading. For repetition, alliteration and paronomasia show that the poem must be read as an instance of language speaking by itself. Those are not impressions, but linguistic series ('airy, very, aviary, fairy') developing on autonomous lines, be they phonetic (paronomasia) or semantic ('association of words'). The first reading is respectful of order – the order of Saussure's *langue*, the order of our world as we speak it, Eco's encyclopaedia. The second reading is faithful to the disorder of language, the instability of Lacan's *lalangue*, the violence of what I have called elsewhere the remainder (Lecercle, 1990). The poem must be read thus – twice, or in two opposite directions. But all Empson's poems ought to be read in this fashion, the essence of his wit being a compliance with the rules of *langue* which is also an awareness of the workings of *lalangue*. And *lalangue* operates, in Empson as elsewhere, by giving poetics the upper hand over grammar, and letting the dictionary (or the remainder) dominate the encyclopaedia. Thus, in 'Scales', the heavy intertext (*Alice in Wonderland*, the *Odyssey*, Rider Haggard, etc.), duly catalogued in the note, the function of which is to spell out the encyclopaedia, will not prevent the dictionary from upsetting this carefully constructed meaning, and in its free-wheeling plunge the meeting of lovers into eroticism:

> And though your gulf-sprung mountains I allow
> (Snow-puppy curves, rose solemn dado band)
> Charming for nurse, I am not nurse just now.
>
> Why pat or stride them, when the train will land
> Me high, through climbing tunnels, at your side,
> And careful fingers meet through castle sand. (p. 24)

A similar effect occurs in 'Camping Out', where the parenthesis '(that will could break)' (p. 18), evokes not only divine or human will, but also another William, and his 'will' sonnets, with the notoriously obscene punning.

The instability of language is not controlled by giving *lalangue* free rein: the poet speaks language; language speaks the poet: both these propositions are true, and neither is. We have both an attempt at communication as access to a referent (in the guise of a description of the poet's girl-friend in 'Camping Out', and also in the allusion to Shakespeare) and a giving in to the free play of independent language: both succeed, and neither does. Rather than the Heideggerian *die Sprache spricht*, perhaps de Man's formula, *die Sprache verspricht sich* corresponds to the situation – Christopher Norris glosses it as 'language necessarily misleads, undoes or betrays itself to the extent that no intention can entirely govern its effect' (Norris, 1988, p. 193). Perhaps we should insist on the '*sich*' and fully realize that not only does language betray intention, it also betrays *itself*. It is unable *either* to reach out to a referent *or* to do without one, and operate in a vacuum of its own. The poem is the embodiment of this necessary *aporia*. It is a type of text that seeks an access to reality which is denied to conventional language (the poet's task is always, in Mallarmé's phrase, to go towards reality by *donner un sens plus pur aux mots de la tribu*), and that at the same time thematizes the impossibility of such access – there is no limitation of reality in language. I shall end this section by giving an example of this in Empson. A reader of his poems looking for stylistic interpretation through Spitzerian intuition would be, I think, struck by the device of topicalization (or, to go deeper into the jargon of linguistics, left dislocation) which is so frequent as to be a signature. Were one to parody Empson – and the poems eminently deserve parody – this would be one of the elements to pounce upon. Two lines from 'To an Old Lady' will illustrate the device: 'Ripeness is all; *her* in her cooling planet / Revere . . . '; '*Years* her precession do not throw from gear' (p. 15). I have italicized the topicalized noun phrases. But this is no mere grammatical device, it is a stylistic one, rich in meaning at that. And this meaning is contradictory. On the one hand the inversion/dislocation enables the text to *present* the topicalized object to the reader's consciousness; it does not only focus on it, it makes it more real. '*Its glass of the divine* (that will could break) / Restore, beyond nature . . . ' (p. 18). Once presented thus, the metaphor (for the surface of the lake mirroring the sky), far from establishing a distance between word and thing, makes the word become the thing, gives us the impression of direct access to the object through the image which it so vividly suggests. But this, of course, is mere illusion. For on the other hand the object thus made present is caught in the web of grammar, in the constant shift of signifiers through ambiguity and punning: thus, this 'glass of the divine' is also the very material glass with the help of which the poet's girl-friend is 'cleaning her teeth into the lake'. Language (grammar) is so wily that it will sometimes withdraw the presentation of the object it seems to achieve, as appears in this line from 'Camping Out':

Soap tension the star pattern magnifies. (p. 18)

The preferred interpretation of the syntax of this sentence is Subject-Dislocated Object-Verb. But what prevents us, once dislocation is recognized to have taken place, from reinterpreting this as an instance of double syntax, and thus reading the sentence as Dislocated Object-Subject-Verb, a fine linguistic *abyme* of the mirroring process the line purports to reproduce? What has disappeared here is reality – nothing is presented any longer, there is no direct access to reality through language.

REALITY

Yet reality is what 'Camping Out' is about. The division which structures the poem is to be interpreted as an attempt at reaching towards reality, in spite of the impossibility of leaving language. 'Dissatisfaction with metaphysics': such a title must be taken as a joke, but a serious one. The poem is built on a duality of foci and mirrors, based as it is (so the note, as usual, explains) on the entirely false theory that of the two foci for the orbit of the earth, the other focus, not the sun, is the important one. Metaphysics is the natural ground for such fictions, and Leibniz is our best science-fiction novelist (Lardreau, 1988). Science, as opposed to metaphysics, is the home of true theories, and as such promises access to the real – it is also the historical locus of false, metaphysical theories, which in its progress it discards. The access to the real it affords is therefore doubtful, always being clouded by the language in which its theories are necessarily couched. The scientific, matter-of-fact (Husserl would say 'objectivist') access to reality through 'facts' is always threatened by the metaphysics inherent in natural language. The task of poetry is to propose a new approach to reality through purified language. Yet, as we have seen, this goal is impossible. This accounts for the poetic tension, in Empson's poems, between the free play of words, the (comic) wit, and the attempt to burst out of a self-enclosed language into truth, into (cosmic) reality.

In Douglas Day's biography of Malcolm Lowry, there is another photograph of Empson (1984, p. 113). It was taken in 1932, in Cambridge, in the garden of J. B. S. Haldane's wife. She is sitting between two unidentified persons, and above her a group of young men are standing, among them Lowry and a very youthful, almost adolescent Empson, who does not look his twenty-six years. I would like to take this chance encounter between poet and novelist as the sign of a common quest for reality. One theme they have in common, in 'Bacchus' and *Under the Volcano*: alcohol as a privileged path towards the real. I have already mentioned the power to smooth contradictions which Empson ascribes to drink. Towards the end of the note to 'Bacchus' he evokes the feeling of 'tragic exultation' the subject inspires in a fictional character. This is the Consul and his world – not the world of booze as a cheap escape from reality, not a world in which the drunken man loses his way by straying from the right path, but a world where there are no right paths any longer, because reality in its etymological insignificance (in its inescapable, meaningless and obtruding presence) pervades everything – a world in which extraordinary, mythical drunkenness lets reality dominate the subject. Which means that we must not interpret this alcoholic experience of the real as some sort of epiphany. Such is not the case either in Lowry's novel or in Empson's poems. The 'person feeling tragic exultation' through alcohol, on whom 'Bacchus' ends, is burning, Consul-like, from the invasion of reality as it is, not as an object of revelation, and from the triumphant exhilaration and despair which this fundamentally banal experience occasions:

> She whom the god has snatched into a cloud
> Came up my stair and called to me across
> The gulf she floated over of despair.
> Came roaring up as through triumphal arches
> Called I should warm my hands on her gold cope
> Called her despair the coping of her fire. (p. 44)

What 'Bacchus', in its highly non-serious seriousness, describes is alcohol as a means of remaining faithful to reality.

So far, I have used the two phrases, 'the real' and 'reality', indiscriminately. Deliberately so. But this is going against the grain of a long and venerable tradition of dualism, of which, for instance, the Lacanian school of philosophical psychoanalysis, where the two concepts are carefully distinguished, is a contemporary offspring. 'Reality' in this sense is the name of the constructed *Lebenswelt*, whether the construction is purely subjective or social (see Berger and Luckman, 1971). 'The real' is what lies out there, which is just what it is, indifferent and unattainable to humankind. The Kantian origin of this in the opposition between phenomenon and noumenon is obvious. The Lacanian 'real', like the thing-in-itself, is defined negatively: *le réel, c'est l'impossible.* Unlike Kant's, however, this real is not totally inaccessible – we are going further back to a tradition of theologians and mystics: it bursts in on us in epiphanies, in flashes of illumination or horror. In Lacan, close encounters with the real are mostly black epiphanies (as one talks of 'black magic'): death, hallucination, the psychotic crisis which tears the structure of the ego apart. There is no revelation, only danger, in such encounters. But there is another, older tradition of white epiphanies: the mystic's rapture, the Romantic poet's vision are also encounters with the real. Conrad's heart of darkness, where Kurtz's savagery and madness are for Marlow a crucial experience (and where Kurtz's state of mind is the result of a black epiphany), as well as what lies behind Shelley's painted veil, are literary representations of 'the real' thus understood.

Empson explicitly deals with this theme in 'This Last Pain'. On the face of it, the poem, based on the idea that 'human nature can conceive divine states which it cannot attain', seems to be arguing for a distinction between the constructed reality of our imagination and the unattainable real which alone gives it meaning. The unattainable character of the real is felt to be tragic, and accounts for the gloomy last line, which has provided the title for A. A. Alvarez's admirable essay on Empson's poetry (1958): 'And Learn a Style from a Despair'.

But a careful reading of the poem will show that the situation is more complex, and irony is at its usual work. The wit is as sparkling as ever:

> 'What is conceivable can happen too,'
> Said Wittgenstein, who had not dreamt of you. (p. 35)[1]

This, Alvarez points out, is not only a variation on the 'coy mistress' *topos*, it is the kind of thing which makes one exclaim: 'I wish I had said that.' But more is at stake than this: the nature of reality. Empson's note glosses the allusion to Wittgenstein rather flippantly: 'This touches Wittgenstein neither as philosophical argument nor as personal remark ... Wittgenstein is relevant because such feelings have produced philosophies different from his' (1955, p. 102). Am I

[1] What Wittgenstein (1961) actually said is, of course, rather different. See *Tractatus*, 3.02: 'What is thinkable is possible too', and also, perhaps, 2.012: 'If a thing *can* occur in a state of affairs, the possibility of the state of affairs must be written into the thing itself.'

mistaken in sensing the figure of ironic inversion in this? If Wittgenstein is mentioned because he is irrelevant, we may have to reinterpret the line not as a celebration of the Romantic powers of imagination (which is what the poem apparently is, although the sardonic overtones should put us on our guard), but as describing the unexpectedness of the real, which is always out of reach of imagination or conception – *la réalité dépasse toujours la fiction*. Perhaps everything conceivable can be made real, or rather constructed into a reality – but not everything is conceivable, and Wittgenstein could never have dreamt of the beloved's beauty. So that the apparently Platonist image of the magic lantern which pervades the poem takes a twist, and must be reconsidered. We start in a Shelleyan mood, in 'All those large dreams by which men long live well / Are magic-lanterned on the smoke of hell' (p. 32). 'Hell' here, the note adds, is meant for chaos, the eternal nothing: this is not Shelley's painted veil which we must not lift, for in Empson there is nothing behind the veil, which is the only reality. If the outcome is that imagination 'builds an edifice of form / For house where phantoms may keep warm' (p. 33), we must also realize that there is nothing else, no real either to disrupt or to safeguard the appearances or phantasms of reality:

> This then is real, I have implied
> A painted, small, transparent slide. (p. 32)

The real is being collapsed into reality. The frontier between the two, the magic-lantern slide, turns out to be the only reality. Before we interpret this as an *en abîme* celebration of the prison-house of language, we might reflect that the consequence is also that the duality of elements has disappeared. There is no need to distinguish between reality and the real, appearance and essence, being and Being. The task of the poet is no longer to leave the cave or lift the veil – there is no world of forms or of reality beyond, for there is no beyond.

Whether this monist reality is exclusively linguistic, or the immediate reality of the world around us (and the task of the poet to make us see again what we never saw because it was too close and obvious) remains to be seen. Empson's anti-Romanticism strives towards the second, which is, as we shall see, always already undermined by the first. But we understand why alcohol is not the means of an epiphany, whether black or white – there is no cause for epiphany, and addiction to drink must rather be understood as an ontological commitment, an acceptance of the world as it is, of the fact that we are unavoidably caught up in the despair of reality, which is also the joy of reality. A reality whose main characteristic does not lie in its concealment or uncovering of truth, but in its insignificance, its meaninglessness.

Perhaps the reference to the early Wittgenstein is not amiss in this context. The *Tractatus* bears the trace of the influence of Schopenhauer (see Hacker, 1986). And a similar concept of reality is to be found in a contemporary French philosopher, whose main sources of inspiration are Nietzsche and Schopenhauer: Clément Rosset (see Rosset 1967, 1977). His is a Manichean world, in which there is a positive pole, endlessly celebrated, of reality; and a negative one, ceaselessly inveighed against, the idea of the double or of representation. There is no distinction between appearance and essence, real and reality, because this would be another instance of the figure of the double, and as such hopelessly caught in the illusions it engenders. Reality is what there is, or rather what is there, around us, so pervasively obvious that we usually fail to see it and search, behind it, for non-existent essence. It is hazardous, monotonous and insignificant. It is also cruel (one of Rosset's books is entitled *Le principe de cruauté* (1988): a paean to a painful, unavoidable, incomprehensible reality). Not that we should interpret our destiny as tragic because of this cruelty – we should rather rejoice at its entirely contingent, but inescapable presence, and not imitate the philosopher, whose system is a rationalization of his quarrel with reality, of his compulsive attempt to deny it.

This world is also Empson's – it is what emerges from the ambiguities of 'This Last Pain'. Rosset's universe is a neighbour of Empson's comic cosmos. The comparison certainly casts a new light on two central characteristics of Empson's poetic style (the phrase 'fidelity to the real', which I have used, embodies this intuition). The first is the role ascribed to language. In a dualist system, its task is to construct the subject's reality. 'The limits of language mean the limits of my world', said Wittgenstein, who had not dreamt of Empson, in his solipsistic youth. It is also to welcome the epiphanies which it will vainly seek to record, the mystic's words having a sad tendency to fail him or her. Not so in Rosset's monist world. Language is on the side of representation, of the double, and its effect is to betray reality by producing a replica of it. Hence the *grandiloquence* of language – Rosset's essential concept in the field of philosophy of language. This grandiloquence culminates in the so-called 'performative verbs', which claim to state and act at the same time, thus betraying the fact that language poses as a substitute for reality. How to do things with words – the very programme of grandiloquence, whose aim is to replace the truly important (things) with the inflated but unimportant (words). The term Rosset uses is '*l'anodin*', 'the trivial', in which we must still read the old sense of 'anodyne', a drug to relieve pain or distress – language is the opium of the speaking masses. And the allusion to Marx is not without its point: this substitution, this anodyne, is a form of violence. *La parole grandiloquente fait violence au réel* (Rosset, 1977, p. 112) – the violence of paranoia and narcissism, the violence of representation which alone can turn an indifferent and insignificant reality into an immoral and intolerable image. At best the fate of reality is to escape language, of language to miss reality. All of this, I think, is very close to Empson's practice. His anti-Romanticism (which can be traced back to the influence of Eliot) is the expression of his rejection of grandiloquence. Instead of constructing a false reality in order to miss the real, his poems try to be instances of fidelity to it. His is not the language of grandiloquent imaginings, but of the most determined striving towards reality.

There is something paradoxical here – as indeed there is in Rosset – for this attack on the unavoidable grandiloquence of language is formulated in language, and therefore is unreliable. But let us not despair, another use of language is conceivable, one that tries to achieve fidelity, and whose task is not to represent. This is where the second characteristic of Empson's poetry comes in: the hermetic asceticism of his style is the very opposite of grandiloquence. The reader's painful attempt to reconstruct a meaning which always eludes her – a task imposed on her by a mischievous poet – prevents her from projecting the facile fantasies of imagination and cliché on to reality. The very abstraction of Empson's poetry, its use of conceit and fictional theory, is, paradoxically, the only path to reality at its most immediate, which is also its most concealed – reality as it is around us. Direct reference and 'communication' is, as we have seen, impossible. 'Camping Out' does not refer to the poet's girlfriend in any simple way. But its cosmic images and complicated web of wit and allusion are merely the necessary detour for the celebration of that simple perception, in which unmediated reality immediately obtrudes: 'And now she cleans her teeth into the lake' (p. 18). Such fidelity has its tragic aspect. Reality is cruel, the cosmos empty of meaning, earth has shrunk in the wash. It also has its comic aspect, for giving in to the contingent real provokes exhilaration – there is not only cruelty in reality, but also cause for *allégresse*. And exhilaration there is in Empson, what Richards so aptly called his deep humour. His is not only, as Alvarez says, 'a style from a despair', but also a style from a joy.

CONCLUSION

We must not, however, turn Empson into some kind of empiricist, striving to lose himself in immediate reality. As our reading of 'This Last Pain' has shown, his position is more complex, and implies a constant shuttling from reality to language. Hence the mixture of exhilaration and despair in his cosmicomics. And this is where the outrageous comparison with Calvino, who weaves the same threads into his text, is finally justified. He it is who enables us to formulate the contradiction that runs through Empson's poetry. On the one hand he does try to be faithful to reality. On the other hand, he has to do it in the only medium which can achieve this fidelity (bovine contemplation will hardly do), language, whose major function is to miss reality. In such a situation, what can one do but try to inveigle reality from its shy concealment, by making a sign which, giving direction to the universe, reveals to us that it is as it is, that there is nothing to reveal? But this, Calvino shows, starts a train of events which will end up in a world where signs have completely taken over reality and covered it in a veil of fictions. One strives to gain access to reality (a singularly immobile trip, since reality is always already not only put there, but right here) – one never manages to escape from language. Language is both the rope and the spikes on top of the wall, the smuggled-in file and the iron bars. The *aporia* of Empson's poetry is shown in his retreat from an esotericism which paradoxically is more open to immediate reality (it is not rife with potential revelation and concealed truths) into an exotericism where language is so dominant that reality is missed (in the two senses of the word). This is no criticism – merely the statement of a necessary failure which is the obverse side of a resounding success. We must take Empson's poems – this is the highest praise I can think of – in the same sense as Wittgenstein wishes us to take his *Tractatus*: as a piece of nonsense (in so far as it seeks to express in language what can only be shown), which nevertheless (or so he thought at the time) solves all the problems of philosophy still pending. Calvino is right: the world is made up of signs. Anti-Romantic asceticism cannot escape the garrulous failings of Romanticism: there is grandeur in this fall.

CHAPTER 10

Empson as teacher: the Sheffield years

Philip Hobsbaum

William Empson earned his living as a teacher of English Literature. What follows is an account of one man's experience as his pupil. This is limited, but it is better than no account, which is what we have had until now.

I first made contact with William Empson in 1959. After four years away from Cambridge, where I studied under F. R. Leavis, I had decided to research into an aspect of literary theory. This was an unusual topic thirty-three years ago, and Empson, with his range of interests and concern with theoretical problems, seemed the best person with whom to work. So I went to Sheffield.

After some preliminary discussion, Empson decided on a working title for what was to become my Ph.D. thesis: 'Some Reasons for the Great Variety of Response to Literature among Modern Literary Critics'. This was a discussion of critical divergences and controversies, with a view to finding whether there was a theory of value that could emerge from the practical consideration of literature. I worked full-time at this thesis between 1959 and 1962, and continued part-time until 1968, when my doctorate was conferred. Empson's technique of supervision was to encourage me to write as much as possible. I typed out draft investigations into critical controversies, and I called these 'enquiries'. I took care to leave wide margins on which Empson could write his comments. These were usually copious, sometimes abusive, but always in tidy handwriting. He would post these annotated enquiries back, often by return of post, making each time an appointment for a meeting in his office. There he would discuss my findings, and I his comments. Sometimes these meetings overflowed to a neighbouring hostelry. Since he associated me with Leavis, whom he detested, there was little chance of our agreeing on any particular issue. Whenever I found that Empson had damaged one of my arguments, though, I always dropped it. My opinions brought out some powerful ripostes, some of which are reprinted here, as an enlargement to the Empson canon.

These were the years when Empson was working on his book, *Milton's God* (published in 1961). He was particularly concerned to correct what he took to be my Leavisite assumption that *Paradise Lost* had broad areas of generalization rescued by passages of local coherence. My feeling about the description of Paradise, for example, was that the imagery was so sketchy as to allow of a wide variety of possible interpretations:

thus was this place
A happy rural seat of various view;
Groves whose rich trees wept odorous gums and balm,
Others whose fruit burnished with golden rind
Hung amiable, Hesperian fables true,
If true, here only, and of delicious taste:
Betwixt them lawns, or level downs, and flocks
Grazing the tender herb, were interposed,
Or palmy hillock, or the flowery lap
Of some irriguous valley spread her store,
Flowers of all hue, and without thorn the rose.

Empson replied to my strictures: 'The description only prepares for the story; it has therefore to fit all aspects of the story. [Milton] is recalling an Italian landscape painting, Venetian I should say. [The words] are merely in keeping; that is, so far as they make any suggestions, they make these ones. The style of *Comus* would be out of place.'

Complaints about lack of realization left Empson sceptical. I had quoted the first appearace of Adam and Eve in the poem:

Two of far nobler shape erect and tall,
Godlike erect, with native honours clad
In naked majesty seemed lords of all,
And worthy seemed, for in their looks divine
The image of their glorious maker shone,
Truth, wisdom, sanctitude severe and pure.

Empson chose to follow Walter Raleigh and C. S. Lewis, believing that the portraiture was best left to be filled in by the imagination. 'This is always true of mental images, that is why Imagism is completely wrong.'

I had suggested that *Paradise Lost* was uneven. Empson replied,

'This is true, except that with Milton "what he made of the story as a whole" has to be an important element in one's reaction to the glowing bits.' I had pointed out various difficulties in the structure. Empson replied, 'I think that this conflict between emotive associations is good because it is related to a theological problem. You take for granted that one can't be interested in what the poet and his intended audience found interesting.'

Here was the first indication of the difference concerning Intention that was to bedevil discussion between us. Empson felt, in the teeth of his own practice in *Seven Types of Ambiguity*, that critics who singled out individual passages of a text as having verbal energy were failing to join such passages on to the main narrative:

What I would say is that each of them interprets the poem in accordance with his theology or world-view but pretends to be making a purely Aesthetic judgement. If you realise that the poem is consistent in giving the basis for all these reactions, because it expresses the basic contradictions of Christian theology, you no longer think it a shapeless rag-bag. During the eighteenth and nineteenth centuries it was rather dangerous to say this, though the ideas were not at all obscure. Nowadays the hypocrisy has become mysteriously inborn, in that nobody can imagine there was any difference of opinion about Christianity in earlier times.

This comment led straight on to *Milton's God* which was published a year or so after these manuscript exchanges, in 1961. Here Empson worked hard to produce all kinds of inferences as a means of explaining contradictions in Milton's theology. To quote Empson's own conclusion, 'The reason why the poem is so good is that it makes God so bad.'

Surely there is a blur here, between moral and aesthetic considerations? It goes far beyond the interpretation of *Paradise Lost*. I went on to illustrate this critical blur by means of an enquiry into the dissensions among critics of Scott Fitzgerald. Even in 1960 there were signs that this writer, who seemed to me attractive but essentially minor, was in process of being inflated into the Great American Novelist. Following Empson's views on the critics of *Paradise Lost*, it seemed to me that many of the moral considerations put forward by admirers of Scott Fitzgerald were really aesthetic ones.

To some extent, Empson agreed. He found Fitzgerald's novels charming in their simplicity:

I think they are about 'what Americans feel about millionaires'. Gatsby has been wonderfully successful against great difficulties; why call him weak?

He feels that with Daisy he would lead a better kind of life altogether, though he can't yet tell how. Why should he not? How could he know [whether Daisy was worth it or not] till he had got her?

A good many critics were able to tolerate Daisy as a figure because they read the narrator, Nick Carraway, as a critical spectator capable of supplying a distancing commentary. Some such commentary would seem to be necessary, given the lyrical descriptions with which the book abounds: 'High in a white palace the king's daughter, the golden girl.' But John Farrelly, a critic Empson particularly despised, pointed out that these words are those of Carraway, the supposedly detached narrator. Carraway, in Empson's view, 'thinks Gatsby right to have such feelings, and likes him for it, while not surprised that he has picked on someone who doesn't deserve them. Why want more?' Of Gatsby's ostentatious display, Empson wrote, 'I think it delicious. He is much nicer for showing his shirts than his rubies ... Well, eighteenth century aristocrats often spent money, too.'

In reply to my central point in this enquiry, about the decorative qualities of the novel being mistaken by several critics for moral ones, Empson answered, 'Decoration is aesthetic; if it was a Baroque Palace you would treat it solemnly as art.' He went on to say, 'People have had this magical feeling about fashion for a long time; though I am not sure it didn't come in with the French Revolution.' In several passages, especially those concerning Daisy such as the one about the 'golden girl' already quoted, I had commented on Gatsby's romantic attitude. Empson replied, 'Of course romantic is always a rude word to you. I think this passage is so sweetly funny it startles, knocks you down.' He added, 'I don't believe her charm *was* only money. Both Fitzgerald and Gatsby are very likely to be wrong ... The decoration makes us feel what it is like to be charmed by Daisy; and you can still be impressed by the picture for other reasons, as you said.'

However, regarding Daisy and her set Empson conceded, 'It comes as the greater shock when they behave so badly', even though 'real aristocrats did this for two centuries before American millionaires'. He had in mind Daisy's treatment of her child. Empson granted Fitzgerald a considerable degree of authenticity. 'I expect he knew quite a lot about rich people after trying so hard ... I wouldn't love these millionaries, but I don't mind *him* doing it; and anyway I wouldn't try to blame him for doing it in such priggish question-begging formulas'; this last comment referring to remarks made by critics such as D. W. Harding, Marius Bewley and John Farrelly; and no doubt, by association, myself.

Empson did, however, say in conversation, 'Fitzgerald seemed to have no expectations that the rich could disappoint', and his concluding note, referring to the blur I had located between aesthetics and morality, reads:

I was much brought up on old Punches, where newly rich people like Mr Buggs and Sir Gorgius Midas are treated as pathetically funny; so the American habit of treating them with religious awe seems to me entertainingly strange, not an evil which needs attack. This kind of difference is probably what lies behind the choice whether to attack the book with supposed proofs using these extremely slippery technical terms.

The terms in question were mostly drawn by Fitzgerald's critics from the New Critical glossary: objective correlative, significance, negation of values, and the like. Empson objected also to the use of terms such as 'pathos' in such a manner as to seem necessarily pejorative.

The kind of sympathy Empson extended to the fictional character, Gatsby, was very much akin to his response to the poet, Shelley. I had assembled a set of critical opinions, mostly hostile, about the 'Ode to the West Wind', to see if they could be faulted. Such critics as F. R. Leavis, Yvor Winters and Allen Tate were among those whose evaluations were catechized. Empson joined in the debate vigorously, first of all declaring in favour of the much-disputed skyscape of the poem:

The clouds make *rain*, and this dissolves them but fertilizes the earth; hence they are *exactly* like the seed-bearing. Here all the critics you quote are just missing the point ... The rainclouds building themselves up from the Pacific Ocean were a marvellous sight from 20,000 feet; they looked like a field of beans, and of course were a major source of world fertility.

From this Empson argued that the wind itself was a current phase of evolution. Shelley 'believes God to be immanent not transcendent, to operate through the Spirit of the Age'. Empson interpreted the winter of the poem as 'the restoration of the Bourbons. Why can't anybody say so?' He considered that Shelley recognized the modesty of his own role. 'Why not remember all those Chinese landscape painters, up to a thousand years before, convinced that they were expressing a mystical view of Nature?' Referring specifically to the strictures of Yvor Winters, he said 'All this prosiness seems to me provincial.' Referring to the strictures of Allen Tate, he said:

'Irony' becomes a fatuous cliché with anti-romantic critics. Shelley says that his own poetry won't last, but it will affect the spirit of the age and thus have a permanent good effect on subsequent evolution. It is both more modest and more practical than usual among poets. Surely he doesn't suppose that this poem alone will reform mankind. *Prometheus* was the chief application of the method.

But, even here, Empson is nearer the world of Gatsby than one might expect. There is an extent of special pleading.

I think the Preface to *Prometheus* is where Shelley expresses the programme he is taking for granted in the *West Wind*. But anyway he was part of the movement which developed the doctrine of Read's *True Voice of Feeling*. He is to influence politics, but only indirectly by expressing elevated thoughts beautifully. The Romantic poet had a duty, to describe his own feelings sincerely, because this would relieve the others in his society who would unconsciously be feeling the same (being part of the same evolutionary movement). He is the unacknowledged legislator because he is like a fashion expert, who can feel what all the ladies are going to want to wear next spring, though they don't themselves know what they want till they see his collection.

To call the work of M. Dior 'self-indulgent' is already absurd misunderstanding; how much more the work of Shelley, who gave away a fortune and lived on bits of bread and was absorbed in struggles to better mankind.

With all this generosity of impulse, we can see the tendency, which was to grow in Empson's criticism, of deflection away from text and into biography. However self-denying Shelley's life, self-denial in itself would not make the 'Ode to the West Wind' any the better – or any the worse – a poem.

Empson identified a much less acceptable attitude when we came to discuss Sir Thomas Wyatt. But here, again, he tended to talk about personality rather than poetry. I had been sorting out the critical reactions to 'They flee from me that sometime did me seek'. This poem begins with an ambiguity that tempted Empson, even before I had begun, into repartee. 'I believe they were mice or rats he had been feeding in the dungeon. I advance upon this text hoping that you will prove that.' It seemed to me in 1961 that the situation in the poem was more complex than Empson's jocular remark would suggest. The inclusiveness of 'they' in 'they flee from me' gave a giddy sensation of being rejected; being rejected, it would seem, by one's known world. Empson personalized this, some might feel unduly, in his comment.

I cannot get away from the remark of C. S. Lewis: 'How unpleasant it must have been for a woman to have Wyatt in love with her.' Here he seems even more unpleasant than usual.

Arthur Waley describes a sheer genre of Chinese classical poems which pretended to be by a girl neglected by her lover and were by a statesman neglected by an emperor; he thinks the custom derived from the poems of one homosexual politician. However, this would only be useful as corroboration.

'Let Austin have his swink to him reserved' makes just the same type of rhyme and seems to me very good, but somehow I can't feel the last couplet of the Wyatt poem as anything but bad.

It struck me that our contemporary the poet Mr PORKER [*sc.* Peter Porter] is very like Sir Thomas Wyatt, because both of them threaten the universe that if it doesn't treat them well enough they won't let it pass its exam. They both treat it as if they were grumbling to the waiter in a restaurant. But really they both seem to live (on their wits) a good deal more agreeably than their neighbours ... You were beginning to ask in the pub why I thought bad temper unpoetical in itself; one could not say that in general, but the cool grumbling of the man who has found his niche and believes the universe holds nothing more must always feel pokey.

Yet Empson was not always hostile to 'the man who has found his niche'. A good deal depended on the attitude of the speaker. It has always seemed to me that 'The Garden', by Andrew Marvell, revealed a place not so much of rest as of recuperation. The critics had taken the poem too simply; from Frank Kermode, who saw it as a place of innocence, to Empson, for whom it was a place of concupiscence. Almost thirty years after his essay on Marvell's 'Garden' we find Empson qualifying his earlier account.

I am inclined to think we were all, including myself, too solemn about the poem to recognize the social realities of the case. As a Puritan Marvell would presumably feel he ought to be fighting against Charles, but he had found a splendidly cushy job which would obviously end in something better, improving his worldly prospects. As a papa myself I would be cross with a young man who said he didn't need to learn any skill, because all the experience in the world just soaked into him as he sat in the garden. It is impudent, just as the boast that he no longer requires women is impudent; in short, it really is witty. However, it is *like* being in a mystical state, and an intense desire to keep out of the sordidness of the world must I think be felt in that verse of 'Appleton House' 'Bind me ye woodbines ...'; he really did feel at any rate that he was living in an enchanted place.

However, this suits your interpretation very well, I think.

There is a Norwegian lady who has found that Fairfax was copying out a treatise on Hermetic philosophy, I forget what, so that Marvell might have been inserting definite mystical ideas to please his patron. But I think they would still only amount to a graceful compliment.

I don't quite agree with you that mystical states can't be expressed, but Marvell wasn't doing it – he implies that that would be an excessive claim for himself, and this modesty is what makes the impudent wit graceful.

One can see how, over the years, Empson moved from his analytical early work into a series of attempts to characterize his authors. Such characterizations, however, had little to do with the concepts I formulated. One of these was the Misreadable Poem. This is a poem so inadequate as an act of communication that it is impossible to show when it has been misread; no meaning can be indicated as valid. This was in contrast with a poem whose sense was determinable; a wrenching of whose sense could be shown to have taken place when the poem was misread. My contention was that some poems were misreadable and some were misread. The inference is that all texts are not equally available, even to the most interested reader.

One of the pieces I put forward as an example of the misreadable poem was 'The Nightfishing' by W. S. Graham. This seemed to me in 1961 to be a high-water mark of obscurity in modern verse. Coincident to the inception of my enquiry, Empson had received a manuscript article, on Graham's philosophy, by J. A. Stephens. The coincidence certainly stimulated Empson's interest; and, in his way, he spoke up for the poem. This involved him in some heavy reading-in. That is to say, he read into the vague suggestions provided by the poet interpretations that were very much his own.

I was by no means alone in my difficulties with this poem. Roy Fuller had demanded in a review of Graham's book, 'What can be the reason for these hideous and by no means untypical constructions?'. He quoted:

> Here, braced, announced on to the slow
> Heaving seaboards, almost I am now too
> Lulled.

Empson's comment is interesting:

I think it good, but only as a sketch of sea-sick feeling. Surely the man isn't pulling on a rope, merely trying to balance. ['Announced'] – as if on a stage about to speak. The next words 'my watch is blear' mean he is taking his turn as look-out and must go to sleep.

What we have here is almost a fiction in itself, a means of filling in or filling out Graham's printed indications. The passage is, as Fuller indicates, representative. Here is one very similar:

> So I have been called by name and
> It was not sound. It is me named upon
> The space which I continually move across
> Bearing between my courage and my lack
> The constant I bleed on.

The obscurity here seemed to me to derive from what I called a False Metaphor; that is to say, a dead metaphor that in this case works against a presumed meaning. The obscurity did not trouble Empson. One can observe him, so to speak, rewriting the poem.

> (It was not sound. It is me . . . It is this . . .). I think it is the microcosm idea; all experience is included in this instant – precisely symbolised by it. But *how* the precision is got we get no hint . . . ['So I have been called by name.'] Here the paradox is intended; a different process. 'Breathless mouths may summon'. ['It is me named upon / The space which I continually move across.'] The name is like colouring on a map – all the red parts are British. I don't think this 'false' – there is no word suggestion for it to conflict with.

This defence of the poem is bound to look more generous than an analytical criticism, but it depends on whether one is putting a regard for the author ahead of a regard for one's reader. I was making the point that the structure of 'The Nightfishing' was sacrificed to local poetic effect. This elicited from Empson the aphorism 'On the other hand, good texture can be seen first and makes one decide that a meaning is worth looking for.' This begs the question as to whether the local texture in this case is 'good'. One has to remember that the exchange of views between Empson and myself took place at a period just after one when the reigning monarchs of English poetry were Edith Sitwell and Dylan Thomas, apostles of darkness so far as meaning was concerned. Consequently, obscurity in verse was very much a subject of discussion.

It turned out, however, that Empson was not basing his interpretation on the text so much as on his regard for the author.

> He agreed to do a piece for the BBC about his home village, mostly in prose, and returned to the village for the purpose; but annoyed the BBC by failing to produce it after the hour had been advertised. Really I think he has been fighting like a cat to get out of the home village and being a fisherman, but he recognizes, in a way, that this is the only interesting

material he has, to make himself into an author with. I suspect that that conflict is what makes him incoherent, not anything about philosophy. A nice chap and a genuine talent, however distorted.

I think he could write good poetry, because this feels so like good poetry. But I have to agree with you I don't think it comes through.

What I was never able to get across to Empson was my concept of reading-in. When you have a good deal of sympathy for a writer as a person, it is often possible to make a case for him by building up a structure which may be based on his sketches but which essentially stems from one's own interests and preoccupations. Empson had emerged as a poet of great brilliance in his youth, but most of his life he had been a *poète manqué*. A considerable amount of his poetic brilliance seems to me to have been diverted into his prose. At times this takes leave of the basic necessities of describing a text. However, a tendency to fill in the author's sketched indications can lead to anarchic reading and wild over-valuation.

In the final version of my thesis, in the later 1960s, I included various interpretations accorded to a poem of Sidney Keyes by 118 A-level GCE candidates. Here we had controlled conditions and a homogeneous group. But the group was writing about what seemed to some of them, and certainly seemed to me, an obscure poem. I had better reproduce it.

The Bards

Now it is time to remember the winter festivals
Of the old world, and see their raftered halls
Hung with hard holly; tongues' confusion; slow
Beat of the heated blood in those great palaces
Decked with the pale and sickled mistletoe;
And voices dying when the blind bard rises
Robed in his servitude, and the high harp
Of sorrow sounding, stills those upturned faces.

O it is such long learning, loneliness
And dark despite to master
The bard's blind craft; in bitterness
Of heart to strike the strings and muster
The shards of pain to harmony, not sharp
With anger to insult the merry guest.
O it is glory for the old man singing
Dead valour and his own days coldly cursed.

How ten men fell by one heroic sword
And of fierce foray by the unwatched ford,

Sing, blinded face; quick hands in darkness groping
Pluck the sad harp; sad heart forever hoping
Valhalla may be songless, enter
The moment of your glory, out of clamour
Moulding your vision to such harmony
That drunken heroes cannot choose but honour
Your stubborn blinded pride, your inward winter.

The interpretations of the A-level candidates reading this poem varied from those who took it to be literal description to those who supplied a set of referents from their own imagination. Some of the latter saw the Bard as Hoder, the blind god who threw the mistletoe at Balder and so killed him, or as Death speaking to the upturned faces, or as two blind veterans of the Second World War playing and singing to soldiers in a hut. My own belief at that time was that, like Graham's 'The Nightfishing', and a great many other modern poems, this text could not be interpreted.

Empson, however, had a good deal of sympathy for the A-level candidates, and even more for the soldier-poet who wrote the piece under discussion. He therefore produced a version of 'The Bards' all of his own:

The bard of the poem (as history would demand) is not an aristocrat brought up to use expensive weapons but a plebeian who happened to go blind so that he had no other means of livelihood but to train as a poet. He had to imagine and praise deeds and virtues which were greatly against his own sympathies, let alone his experience. But he is proud that he has become such a professional man, and really can praise warriors with a splendour obvious to every listener in the hall. Yet at the bottom of his mind there is a leering hatred of the men he has to praise, even while he is jealously proud of the quality of the poetry which expresses it. This poem, you see, is actually about the astonishing powers of men to intuit one another's intentions. The bard knew exactly how the warriors felt, that was why he succeeded as a poet, and Sidney Keyes (a wartime conscript who was carried to his death when he wrote) knew exactly how bad the bard felt in a situation which might have appeared preferable to his own.

This is a better piece of writing, in my view, than the poem by which it was inspired; at least, it is linguistically more vigorous. But is it in any sense an interpretation? Phrases like 'a leering hatred of the men he has to praise' and 'the astonishing powers of men to intuit one another's intentions' seem to me to have more to do with Empson's situation than that of the Bard or of Sidney Keyes. The fact that Empson sympathized with Keyes and with all the young men who died in the war does not necessarily render any of them good poets.

The poetic vein that runs through Empson's comments on 'The Nightfishing' and 'The Bards' informs his view of the more far-reaching text of *King Lear*. I had been struck not only by Empson's pessimistic essay in *The Structure of Complex Words* but by his role in a correspondence that took place in *The Critical Quarterly* during 1961. Empson had written, 'I was trying to support the view of George Orwell, that the old man is "still cursing, still not understanding anything" at the end.' Orwell's essay, it seems to me, drains the play of poetry, and Empson's essay pours in, by way of compensation, a good deal of poetry of his own. My own view is that the character of Lear develops through the play and that in the last scene he is invested with a compassion and humanity he did not have before. In particular, the predicament of Cordelia leads him to think of another human being rather than himself. The tone seems to me curiously ecstatic.

LEAR.
And my poor fool is hang'd! No, no, no life!
Why should a dog, a horse, a rat, have life,
And thou no breath at all? Thou'lt come no more,
Never, never, never, never, never!
Pray you, undo this button: thank you, Sir.
Do you see this? Look on her, look, her lips,
Look there, look there!

Cordelia leads him to think of another human being rather than himself. If, as some commentators and as Empson in his *Complex Words* contended, Lear ended up unregenerate, the play would be meaningless. I put this point to Empson; his reply was vociferous:

We want, if we are interested in Lear's sanctification, to know whether it is genuine or trustworthy – what will happen if Cordelia is killed? Won't he stop being a non-attached Yogi and start cursing again? As this is what he does we do not feel that the sequence is pointless; it tells us something we wanted to know. To pretend that he is still a Yogi at the end seems to me an evident misreading of the text. In the final scene he is not a village idiot, simply no longer regenerated ...

... Surely there is no doubt that the intended audience, being Christians, were assumed not to believe in the pagan gods, but to believe that Lear did? Any other assumption seems to me mere homeless random sentiment ...

... The 'curiously ecstatic' tone comes because he believes she is recovering – as he says, and as we can see makes an analogy with the death of Gloucester ...

... I don't understand why you say Cordelia dies to prove there is virtue in suffering – or why Lear dies that others may not suffer ...

I think now that one of the factors sparking off Empson's tirade was a tendency on my part to adopt a reading of the play related to Christian doctrine, particularly that found in Roman Catholicism. Cordelia's role seemed to me that of an intercessor, showing by example the good life. Lear, in this interpretation, stood for the human soul as subject of the intercession. It is not my own philosophic view, which is agnostic, but it seems to me the only interpretation which makes sense of Cordelia's death. The union to which Lear and Cordelia aspire is not in this world. Empson, as a militant atheist, necessarily attacked that standpoint. But, in doing so, he forgot that it is possible to respect a work of literature with whose philosophy one does not agree.

Empson identified in my interpretation a number of attitudes to which he was hostile. He linked together Leavisitism, Christianity, Puritanism and Affective Theory, and wrote to me on 2 August 1969 with a vehemence that had become, by now, characteristic:

What is wrong with your whole position, I still believe, stems from the self-binding theory that a critic is never allowed to gauge the author's Intention. I must not make extravagant claims for a process which all persons not insane are using in all their social experience; I have only to say that the effect of renouncing it (in the unique case of the most delicate and intimate formulations of intention) produces dirty nonsense all the time, with a sort of tireless unconscious inventiveness for new kinds of nonsense.

My thesis was published as *A Theory of Communication* by Macmillan in 1970 and, in the same year, as *Theory of Criticism*, by the University of Indiana Press in the USA. However, my theoretical standpoint was put most explicitly in a chapter of my thesis that did not appear in the book but which was published separately in the *British Journal of Aesthetics*, April 1967: 'The artist's intention is only evident if it is inescapably realized in the work; and in such a case it makes more sense to talk in terms of artistic achievement.' Empson's comments on the draft of this chapter seem to me to constitute a crucial statement of his position:

An 'inescapable' work of art would be simply a man-trap, I suppose ... When you have decided what the author meant, why can't you decide that the meaning was bad (dull, etc)? ... To decide between two variants in a text, or two ways of producing a play, you need to consider which the author is likely to have wanted – to forbid that is merely silly . . .

. . . I feel strongly about Intentionalism, but in a psychological not a theoretical way. Maybe, as an intention is only known as it is shown, all references to intention can in theory be avoided. The same is true of forces, in dynamics, which never come into the equations – one might say, they live in the equals sign, where the cause meets the effect. But all the same nobody could learn dynamics without learning the rules about forces, and using them all the time. This, by the way, is not 'like' empathy but the same fact of our natures. Still, I couldn't really agree that other people's intentions are meant to be bypassed in this way; it seems to me that the chief function of imaginative literature is to make you realize that other people are very various, many quite different from you, with different systems of value as well; but the effect of almost any Orthodoxy is to hide this, and pretend that everybody *ought* to be like Homer or Dr Leavis.

At no point, of course, had I denied the existence of intention; but it seems to me that Empson underestimated the difficulty of knowing what it is. His viewpoint leads him to fill in the outlines of Adam and Eve in the fourth book of *Paradise Lost*, and this is the same process as creating a story-line for the amorphous poem, 'The Bards'. It leads him further to picture, in *Milton's God*, the child Milton sitting in a gallery at one of his father's city banquets; and to fantasize, in *Using Biography*, Tom Palmer, Marvell's presumed stepson, making no bones about allowing the poet minor sexual pleasures. This last, in particular, strikes me as a derogation from his earlier criticism.

As a critic, Empson remains for me the author of *Seven Types of Ambiguity*. Any tyro can fault its organization, but it is a treasure house of exploratory analysis. Empson in the autumnal phase of his career was still capable of dazzling insights, but he was moving away from analysis towards the prose version of a poetry that he did not compose as verse. He was still alert to the process of his own writing, which remained very spirited, and to faults in mine, which on occasion he drubbed vigorously. To this day I cannot use, nor can I let my pupils use, words like 'subjectivity'. My employment of New Critical terminology, which he called 'pedants' jabber', has become exceedingly sparse.

This essay is the last of my enquiries for Empson. For all my various purgations, I cannot feel that he would have liked it. But at least it has the merit of relaying some of his aperçus and epigrams, not hitherto ready of access. It may even convey the sense of being at the receiving end of a series of stinging, and almost unanswerable, ripostes.

References

Abrams, M. H. 1953. *The Mirror and the Lamp: Romantic Theory and the Critical Tradition*. New York, Oxford University Press

Adorno, Theodor. 1982. *Against Epistemology*. Trans. Willis Domingo. Oxford, Basil Blackwell

Alpers, Paul. 1978. 'Empson on Pastoral', *New Literary History* 10

Althusser, Louis and Etienne Balibar. 1970. *Reading Capital*. Trans. Ben Brewster. London, New Left Books

Altizer, Thomas (ed.). 1982. *Deconstruction and Theology*. New York, Crossroads

Alvarez, A. A. 1958. *The Shaping Spirit*. London, Chatto & Windus

Arac, Jonathan. 1987. *Critical Genealogies: Historical Situations for Postmodern Literary Studies*. New York, Columbia University Press

Auden, W. H. 1979. *Selected Poems*. London, Faber & Faber

Barber, Charles. 1976. *Early Modern English*. London, Andre Deutsch

Barthes, Roland. 1977. *Image/Music/Text*. Trans. Stephen Heath. London, Fontana

Belloc, H. 1938. *Stories, Essays and Poems*. London, Dent

Belsey, Catherine. 1985. *The Subject of Tragedy: Identity and Difference in Renaissance Drama*. London, Methuen

Berger, P. and T. Luckman. 1971. *The Social Construction of Reality*. Harmondsworth, Penguin

Blackmur, R. P. 1962. *The Double Agent: Essays in Craft and Elucidation*. Gloucester, Mass., P. Smith. (First published 1935)

Blanchot, Maurice. 1955. *L'espace littéraire*. Paris, Gallimard

Bloom, Harold. 1973. *The Anxiety of Influence: a Theory of Poetry*. New York, Oxford University Press

1975. *A Map of Misreading*. New York, Oxford University Press

(ed.). 1979. *Deconstruction and Criticism*. London, Routledge & Kegan Paul

Booth, Wayne C. 1974. *A Rhetoric of Fiction*. Chicago and London, University of Chicago Press

Bradbrook, M. C. 1985. 'Sir William Empson [1906–1984]: a Memoir', *Kenyon Review* 7

Bradley, A. C. 1905. *Shakespearean Tragedy: Lectures on Hamlet, Othello, King Lear, Macbeth*. London, Macmillan

Brooks, Cleanth. 1947. *The Well-Wrought Urn: Studies in the Structure of Poetry*. New York, Harcourt Brace

1952. 'Hits and Misses', *Kenyon Review* 14

Burke, Kenneth. 1957. *The Philosophy of Literary Form: Studies in Symbolic Action*. Rev. edn. New York, Vintage Books

Cain, William E. 1984. *The Crisis in Criticism: Theory, Literature, and Reform in English Studies*. Baltimore, Johns Hopkins University Press

Calvino, Italo. 1965. *Le Cosmicomiche*. Turin, Einaudi

Cantarella, Eva. 1985. 'Dangling Virgins: Myth, Ritual, and the Place of Women in Ancient Greece', *Poetics Today* 6. *The Female Body in Western Culture: Semiotic Perspectives*. Ed. Susan Rubin Suleiman, pp. 91–102

Caruth, Catherine. 1985. 'Past Recognition: Narrative Origins in Wordsworth and Freud', *MLN* 100

Cavell, Stanley. 1987. *Disowning Knowledge in Six Plays of Shakespeare*. Cambridge, Cambridge University Press

Chase, Cynthia. 1986. *Decomposing Figures: Rhetorical Readings in the Romantic Tradition*. Baltimore and London: Johns Hopkins University Press

Chomsky, Noam. 1957. *Syntactic Structures*. The Hague, Mouton

1966. *Current Issues in Linguistic Theory*. The Hague, Mouton

Collingwood, R. G. 1936. *The Idea of History*. London, Oxford University Press

1939. *Autobiography*. London, Oxford University Press

Culler, Jonathan. 1984. 'A Critic against the Christians', *Times Literary Supplement*, p. 1327

1988. *Framing the Sign: Criticism and Its Institutions*. Oxford, Basil Blackwell

Dante Alighieri. 1961. *The Divine Comedy. I: Inferno*. Trans. John D. Sinclair. New York, Oxford University Press

Dasenbrock, R. W. (ed.). 1989. *Re-Drawing the Lines: Analytic Philosophy, Deconstruction, and Literary Theory*. Minneapolis, University of Minnesota Press

Day, Douglas. 1984. *Malcolm Lowry*. New York, Oxford University Press

Day, Frank. 1984. *Sir William Empson: an Annotated Bibliography*. New York, Garland

De Man, Paul. 1979. *Allegories of Reading: Figural Language in Rousseau, Nietzsche, Rilke, and Proust*. New Haven, Yale University Press

1983. *Blindness and Insight: Essays in the Rhetoric of Contemporary Criticism*. 2nd edn. London, Methuen

1984. *The Rhetoric of Romanticism*. New York, Columbia University Press

1986. *The Resistance to Theory*. Minneapolis, University of Minnesota Press

1988. *Wartime Journalism, 1939–1943*. Ed. Werner Hamacher, Neil Hertz, and Thomas Keenan. Lincoln and London, University of Nebraska Press

Derrida, Jacques. 1973. *'Speech and Phenomena' and Other Essays on Husserl's Theory of Signs*. Trans. David B. Allison. Evanston, Ill., Northwestern University Press

1981. *Dissemination*. Trans. Barbara Johnson. London, The Athlone Press
1982. *Margins of Philosophy*. Trans. Alan Bass. Chicago, University of Chicago Press
Dickens, Charles. 1961. *Great Expectations*. New York, Harper. (First edition 1861)
Dodsworth, Martin. 1985. 'Empson of Yokefleet', *Sewanee Review* 93
Dollimore, Jonathan and Alan Sinfield (eds.). 1985. *Political Shakespeare*. Ithaca, NY, Cornell University Press
Dubois, Hubert. 1944. *Le chant dans les ruines*. Bruxelles, Editions de la Toison d'Or
Eagleton, Terry. 1986. *Against the Grain: Selected Essays*. London, New Left Books
Eliot, T. S. 1928. *For Lancelot Andrewes*. London, Faber & Faber
1933. *The Use of Poetry and the Use of Criticism*. London, Faber & Faber
Ellis-Fermor, Una. 1936. *The Jacobean Drama: an Interpretation*, London. Methuen
Empson, William. 1935. *Some Versions of Pastoral*. London, Chatto & Windus
1951. *The Structure of Complex Words*. London, Chatto & Windus
1953. *Seven Types of Ambiguity*. London, Chatto & Windus. (First edition 1930)
1955. *Collected Poems*. London, Chatto & Windus. (repr. 1984. London, Hogarth Press)
1965. *Milton's God*. 2nd edn. London, Chatto & Windus. (First edition 1961)
1981. *Milton's God*. Pbk edn. New York, Greenwood
1984. *Using Biography*. London, Chatto & Windus
1986. *Essays on Shakespeare*. Ed. David B. Pirie. Cambridge, Cambridge University Press
1987a. *Argufying: Essays on Literature and Culture*. Ed. John Haffenden. London, Chatto & Windus
1987b. *Faustus and the Censor: the English Faust-book and Marlowe's 'Doctor Faustus'*. Ed. John Henry Jones. Oxford, Basil Blackwell
1988. *The Royal Beasts and Other Works*. Ed. John Haffenden. London, Chatto & Windus
Empson, William and David Pirie (eds.). 1972. *Coleridge's Verse: a Selection*. London, Faber & Faber
Felman, Shoshana. 1989. 'Paul de Man's Silence', *Critical Inquiry* 15
Ferguson, Margaret W., Maureen Quilligan, and Nancy J. Vickers (eds.). 1986. *Rewriting the Renaissance: the Discourses of Sexual Difference in Early Modern Europe*. Chicago, Chicago University Press
Fish, Stanley. 1967. *Surprised by Sin: the Reader in Paradise Lost*. Berkeley, University of California Press
1980. *Is There a Text in This Class? The Authority of Interpretive Communities*. Cambridge, Mass., Harvard University Press

1989. *Doing What Comes Naturally: Change, Rhetoric, and the Practice of Theory in Literary and Legal Studies*. New York and London, Oxford University Press

Fry, Paul. 1991. *William Empson: Prophet against Sacrifice*. London, Routledge

Gascht, André. 1953. 'Le danseur du sacré', *Le Thyrse*, Bruxelles

Gazdar, Gerald. 1979. *Pragmatics: Implicature, Presupposition and Logical Form*. New York and London, Academic Press

Gill, Roma (ed.). 1974. *William Empson: the Man and His Work*. London, Routledge & Kegan Paul

Graves, Robert and Joshua Podro. 1953. *The Nazarene Gospel Restored*. London, Cassell

Greenblatt, Stephen. 1980. *Renaissance Self-Fashioning from More to Shakespeare*. Chicago, Chicago University Press

(ed.). 1988a. *Representing the English Renaissance*. Berkeley and Los Angeles, University of California Press

1988b. *Shakespearean Negotiations: the Circulation of Social Energy in Renaissance England*. Berkeley and Los Angeles, University of California Press

1990. *Learning to Curse: Essays in Early Modern Culture*. New York and London, Routledge

Greene, Judith. 1986. *Language Understanding: a Cognitive Approach*. Milton Keynes, Open University Press

Greene, Thomas M. 1963. *The Descent from Heaven: a Study in Epic Continuity*. New Haven, Yale University Press

Greimas, A. J. 1970. *Du Sens*. Paris, Seuil

Hacker, P. M. S. 1986. *Insight and Illusion*. Oxford, Clarendon Press

Hamacher, Werner, Neil Hertz, and Thomas Keenan (eds.). 1989. *Responses: on Paul de Man's Wartime Journalism*. Lincoln and London, University of Nebraska Press

Harding, Sandra and Merill B. Hintikka (eds.). 1983. *Feminist Perspectives in Epistemology, Metaphysics, Methodology, and Philosophy of Science*, Dordrecht, D. Reidel

Harpham, Geoffrey Galt. 1987. 'Language, History, Ethics', *Raritan* 7:2

Hart, Kevin. 1989. *The Trespass of the Sign*. Cambridge, Cambridge University Press

Hartman, Geoffrey. 1970. *Beyond Formalism: Literary Essays 1958–1970*. New Haven, Yale University Press

Hawkes, Terence. 1993. *Meaning by Shakespeare*. London, Routledge

Heidegger, Martin. 1958. *The Question of Being*. Trans. W. Kluback and J. T. Wilde. New York, Twayne

1971. *Poetry, Language, Thought*. Trans. Albert Hofstadter. New York, Harper & Row

Heller, Thomas C., Morton Sosna, and David E. Wellbury (eds.). 1986. *Reconstructing Individualism: Autonomy, Individuality, and the Self in Western Thought*. Stanford, Stanford University Press

Hertz, Neil. 1985. *The End of the Line: Essays on Psychoanalysis and the Sublime*. New York, Columbia University Press

Hill, Christopher. 1977. *Milton and the English Revolution*. London, Faber & Faber

Hirsch, E. D. 1967. *Validity in Interpretation*. New Haven, Yale University Press

Hough, Graham. 1956a. *An Essay on Criticism*. London, Duckworth

1956b. *The Dark Sun: a Study of D. H. Lawrence*. London, Duckworth

Howard, Jean E. and Marion F. O'Connor (eds.). 1987. *Shakespeare Reproduced: the Text in History and Ideology*. New York and London, Methuen

Hunter, G. K. 1978. *Dramatic Identities and Cultural Tradition: Studies in Shakespeare and his Contemporaries*. Liverpool, Liverpool University Press

Hurford, James and Brendan Heasley. 1983. *Semantics: a Coursebook*. Cambridge, Cambridge University Press

Husserl, Edmund. 1960. *Cartesian Meditations*. Trans. Dorion Cairns. The Hague, Nijhoff

1978. *Formal and Transcendental Logic*. Trans. Dorion Cairns. The Hague, Nijhoff

Jacobs, Carol. 1978. *The Dissimulating Harmony: the Image of Interpretation in Nietzsche, Rilke, Artaud, and Benjamin*. Baltimore, Johns Hopkins University Press

Jameson, Fredric. 1979. *Fables of Aggression: Wyndham Lewis, the Modernist as Fascist*. Berkeley, University of California Press

1981. *The Political Unconscious: Narrative as a Socially Symbolic Act*. London, Methuen

Johnson, Samuel. 1968. *Selected Writings*. Ed. Patrick Cruttwell. Harmondsworth, Penguin

Jonson, Ben. 1947. *The Collected Works of Ben Jonson*. Ed. C. H. Herford Percy and Evelyn Simpson. Oxford, Clarendon Press

Kenner, Hugh. 1958. 'Alice in Empsonland', *Gnomon*. New York, McDowell, Obolensky

Kermode, Frank. 1979. *The Genesis of Secrecy*. Cambridge, Mass., Harvard University Press

1983. *Essays on Fiction 1971–82*. London, Routledge & Kegan Paul

1989. *An Appetite for Poetry*. Cambridge, Mass., Harvard University Press

Kunitz, Stanley J. (ed.). 1955. *Twentieth-Century Authors: A Bibliographical Dictionary of Modern Literature. First Supplement*. New York, H. W. Wilson

Lardreau, G. 1988. *Fictions philosophiques et science-fiction*. Arles, Actes Sud

Leavis, F. R. 1932. *New Bearings in English Poetry*. London, Chatto & Windus

1933. *For Continuity*. Cambridge, Minority Press

1936. *Revaluation: Tradition and Development in English Verse*. London, Chatto & Windus

1952. *The Common Pursuit*. London, Chatto & Windus

1972. *Nor Shall my Sword: Discourses on Pluralism, Compassion and Social Hope*. London, Chatto & Windus

1974. *Letters in Criticism*. Ed. John Tasker. London, Chatto & Windus

Lecercle, Jean-Jacques. 1990. *The Violence of Language*. London, Routledge

Levinson, Stephen. 1983. *Pragmatics*. Cambridge, Cambridge University Press

Lévi-Strauss, Claude. 1958. *Anthropologie structurale*. Paris, Plon

Lewis, C. S. 1942. *A Preface to Paradise Lost*. London, Oxford University Press

1960. *Studies in Words*. Cambridge, Cambridge University Press

Lewis, Wyndham. 1927. *The Lion and the Fox: the Role of the Hero in the Plays of Shakespeare*. London, G. Richards Ltd

Loraux, Nicole. 1984. 'Le corps étranglé', *Actes de la table ronde: 'Du châtiment dans la cité. Supplices corporels et peines de mort dans le monde antique'*. Rome, Ecole Française de Rome

1985. *Façons tragiques de tuer une femme*. Paris, Hachette

Lowes, J. Livingston. 1927. *The Road to Xanadu*. London, Constable

Lyons, John. 1977. *Semantics*. 2 vols. Cambridge, Cambridge University Press

Macherey, Pierre. 1978. *A Theory of Literary Production*. Trans. Geoffrey Wall. London, Routledge & Kegan Paul

Miller, J. Hillis. 1987. *The Ethics of Reading: Kant, de Man, Eliot, Trollope, James, and Benjamin*. New York, Columbia University Press

Milton, John. 1957. *Complete Poems and Major Prose*. Ed. Merritt Y. Hughes. New York, Odyssey Press

Mitchell, W. J. T. (ed.). 1987. *Against Theory: Literary Theory and the New Pragmatism*. Chicago, University of Chicago Press

Mizener, Arthur. 1938. *Partisan Review* 5

Mizumura, Minae. 1985. 'Renunciation', *Yale French Studies* 69

Murray, J. A. H., H. Bradley, W. A. Craigie, and C. T. Onions (eds.). 1884–1928. *A New English Dictionary on Historical Principles*. Oxford, Oxford University Press

Murray, K. M. Elisabeth. 1977. *Caught in the Web of Words: James A. H. Murray and the Oxford English Dictionary*. New Haven and London, Yale University Press

Negt, Oskar and Alexander Kluge. 1972. *Offentlichkeit und Erfahrung: zur Organisationsanalyse von bürgerlicher und proletärischer Offentlichkeit*. Frankfurt a. M., Suhrkamp

Nelson, Cary and Lawrence Grossberg (eds.). 1988. *Marxism and the Interpretation of Culture*. Urbana and Chicago, University of Illinois Press

Norris, Christopher. 1978. *William Empson and the Philosophy of Literary Criticism*. London, The Athlone Press

1985a. *The Contest of Faculties: Philosophy and Theory after Deconstruction*. London, Methuen

1985b. 'Reason, Rhetoric, Theory: Empson and de Man', *Raritan* 5:1

1988. *Paul de Man: Deconstruction and the Critique of Aesthetic Ideology*. New York and London, Routledge

1990. *What's Wrong with Postmodernism: Critical Theory and the Ends of Philosophy*. London, Harvester Wheatsheaf

1991. *Spinoza and the Origins of Modern Critical Theory*. Oxford, Basil Blackwell

Oakeshott, Michael. 1959. *The Voice of Poetry in the Conversation of Mankind. An Essay*. London, Bowes & Bowes

Patterson, Lee. 1987. *Negotiating the Past: the Historical Understanding of Medieval Literature*. Madison, University of Wisconsin Press

Pavel, Thomas. 1987. *Fictional Worlds*. Cambridge, Mass., Harvard University Press

Pecheux, Michel. 1982. *Language, Semantics and Ideology: Stating the Obvious*. Trans. Harbans Nagpal. London, Macmillan

Press, J. 1969. *A Map of English Verse*. Oxford, Oxford University Press

Pritchard, R. E. 1987. 'Milton's Satan and Empson's Old Lady', *Notes and Queries* 232

Propp, Vladimir. 1968. *Morphology of the Folktale*. Trans. L. Scott. Austin, University of Texas Press

Putnam, Hilary. 1981. *Reason, Truth and History*. Cambridge, Cambridge University Press

1983. *Realism and Reason*. Cambridge, Cambridge University Press

Ransom, John Crowe. 1938/9. 'Mr. Empson's Muddles', *Southern Review* 4

Richards, I. A. 1926a. *Principles of Literary Criticism*. London, Kegan Paul, Trench, Trubner & Co

1926b. *Science and Poetry*. New York, W. W. Norton

Robins, R. H. 1967. *A Short History of Linguistics*. London, Longman

Rorty, Richard. 1982. *Consequences of Pragmatism*. Minneapolis, University of Minnesota Press

Rosset, C. 1967. *Schopenhauer, philosophe de l'absurde*. Paris, PUF

1977. *Le réel, traité de l'idiotie*. Paris, Minuit

1988. *Le principe de cruauté*. Paris, Minuit

Russell, Bertrand. 1957. *'Why I Am Not a Christian' and Other Essays on Religion and Related Topics*. London, Unwin

Sperber, Dan and Deirdre Wilson. 1986. *Relevance: Communication and Cognition*. Oxford, Basil Blackwell

Spivack, Bernard. 1958. *Shakespeare and the Allegory of Evil. The History of a Metaphor in Relation to his Major Villains*. New York, Columbia University Press

Stein, Arnold. 1977. *The Art of Presence: the Poet and Paradise Lost*. Berkeley, University of California Press

Taylor, Mark C. 1984. *Erring: a Postmodern A/Theology*. Chicago, University of Chicago Press

Traversi, Derek. 1954. *Shakespeare: the Last Phase*. London, Hollis and Carter

Tuve, Rosemond. 1950. 'On Herbert's "The Sacrifice"', *Kenyon Review* 12:1
1952. *A Reading of George Herbert*. London, Faber & Faber

Veeser, H. Aram (ed.). 1989. *The New Historicism*. New York and London, Routledge

Waters, Lindsay and Wlad Godzich (eds.). 1989. *Reading de Man Reading*. Minneapolis, University of Minnesota Press

White, Hayden. 1973. *Metahistory: the Historical Imagination in Nineteenth-Century Europe*. Baltimore, Johns Hopkins University Press
1978. *Tropics of Discourse: Essays in Cultural Criticism*. Baltimore, Johns Hopkins University Press

Williams, Raymond. 1973. *The Country and the City*. London, Oxford University Press
1983. *Keywords: a Vocabulary of Culture and Society*. London, Fontana. (First edition 1976)

Wimsatt, W. K. 1954. *The Verbal Icon: Studies in the Meaning of Poetry*. Lexington, University of Kentucky Press
1976. *The Day of the Leopards: Essays in Defence of Poems*. New Haven, Yale University Press

Winters, Yvor. 1947. *In Defense of Reason*. Denver, University of Denver Press

Wittgenstein, Ludwig. 1961. *Tractatus Logico-Philosophicus*. Trans. D. F. Pears and B. McGuinness. London, Routledge & Kegan Paul

Worton, Michael and Judith Still (eds.). 1990. *Intertextuality: Theories and Practices*. Manchester, Manchester University Press

Index of names

Since most of these entries could be duplicated with items under the heading 'Empson on ...', the editors have not thought it necessary to supplement the index with page references for the various works of Empson discussed in the text. Readers should have no difficulty in locating the relevant sources by cross-referring between the chapter in question, the index of names and consolidated list of references. See also the numbered footnotes for works by other authors not included in the reference section.